T0366449

Contemporary China

CONTEMPORARY CHINA

1949 to the Present

Gilles Guiheux

Translated by Andrew Brown

polity

Originally published in French as *La République populaire de Chine. Histoire générale de la Chine (de 1949 à nos jours)* © Société d'édition Les Belles Lettres, Paris, 2018

This English edition © Polity Press, 2023

The translation of this book was made possible with support from the Institut universitaire de France (IUF); the Faculté Sociétés et Humanités, Université Paris Cité; and the Fédération sciences sociales suds (F3S).

Polity Press
65 Bridge Street
Cambridge CB2 1UR, UK

Polity Press
111 River Street
Hoboken, NJ 07030, USA

ISBN-13: 978-1-5095-5249-8

A catalogue record for this book is available from the British Library.

Library of Congress Control Number: 2022945382

Typeset in 11.5 on 14 Adobe Garamond
by Fakenham Prepress Solutions, Fakenham, Norfolk NR21 8NL

Printed and bound in the UK by CPI Group (UK) Ltd, Croydon

The publisher has used its best endeavours to ensure that the URLs for external websites referred to in this book are correct and active at the time of going to press. However, the publisher has no responsibility for the websites and can make no guarantee that a site will remain live or that the content is or will remain appropriate.

Every effort has been made to trace all copyright holders, but if any have been overlooked the publisher will be pleased to include any necessary credits in any subsequent reprint or edition.

For further information on Polity, visit our website:
politybooks.com

Contents

Acknowledgements

The body of social sciences research on contemporary China is extensive. In France, there is a tradition that dates back to the founding in 1959 of the Centre de recherche et de documentation sur la Chine contemporaine (Centre for Research and Documentation on Contemporary China); this later became the Centre Chine de l'École des hautes études en sciences sociales (China Centre of the School of Advanced Studies in the Social Sciences). Several generations of researchers have been trained since those days. I here express my gratitude to those who taught me and to all my colleagues who are keeping this tradition alive: historians, political scientists, anthropologists, geographers, sociologists and economists. This work, which draws widely on the research of others, is also the result of more than twenty years of teaching. I owe a great deal to conversations with my students, in particular at the Université Paris Cité since 2006. I would also like to thank Damien Chaussende, the editor of the collection, Caroline Noirot of the Éditions des Belles Lettres, and Elise Heslinga of Polity, for their confidence, their patience and their attentive and generous comments.

Introduction

On 1 October 2019, the People's Republic of China celebrated its seventieth anniversary. Thirty years of Maoist totalitarianism had been followed by forty years of reform and opening-up. There were huge transformations in this country which, originally poor, went through four glorious decades of continuous growth. Industrialization and urbanization took place at a rate never before experienced by any human society. For a closed country, it is surprisingly open despite the persistence of an authoritarian political system, and it has become one of the engines of the world economy. Its economic and cultural elites, its students and its middle classes travel in their hundreds of thousands around the world. Though a member of the socialist camp, China has converted to capitalism. Having learned from its Soviet Big Brother, it is now seen as a role model for many leaders in the Global South and actively defends its interests on the international stage. China was once distant; now it has probably never seemed so close to us.

The conditions in which we learn about China have changed. My first stay in Beijing dates back to 1983, and I never had the experience of travelling in a goldfish bowl, as Lucien Bianco had mockingly noted of tourism in his own day – limited to visits to schools, businesses, and model people's communes, all showcases for the regime's achievements.[1] It has become much easier to work on contemporary China. Travel restrictions linked to the nature of the political system have been partly lifted.

In China itself, at the end of the 1970s, history as a discipline, along with the other human and social sciences, reappeared. Of course, it is still difficult to write the political history of the contemporary period. The Communist Party continues to exercise a monopoly on the practice of power, but also on the interpretation of history, especially for such painful times as the Great Leap Forward, the Cultural Revolution and the tragic events of 1989. But historical publications are becoming

1

more numerous, as publishing opens up to market forces. They include volumes of memoirs, testimonies and biographies, as memory becomes part of a context of privatization and 'familialization'.[2] These stories come from personalities who played a leading role, or from their families, but also from the ordinary victims of Communism who have collected photographs, eye-witness accounts and materials. These all provide new sources for history seen from both above and below, and they help us to reconstruct local scenes.[3] As for contemporary political life, still largely opaque, the era of China-watching does not seem to be completely over. Since the reforms, society has been much easier to access, but the institutions at the heart of power continue to be reluctant to open their doors to researchers. Outside China, however, the opening of archives and the publication of compilations of materials have shed new light on various turning points in contemporary history.

It is possible to conduct fieldwork. Statistical information, however imperfect, is available on almost all economic and social subjects. Collaborations are forming between Chinese researchers and foreign colleagues. Even if we do not always have data equivalent to those which exist on other countries, data that would allow us to practise sociology, anthropology or economics in the same way, the difficulty for the researcher is no longer the scarcity of sources, but rather their abundance.[4] The present work, which is resolutely multidisciplinary, thus draws on recent studies of China from 1949 to the present day.[5] Without being exhaustive, it focuses on politics, the economy, society and culture, emphasizing, as much as possible, a history of the Chinese people in all its diversity.

While China has become closer to us, our knowledge of it still remains incomplete and sometimes faulty. In this regard, my book sets itself three ambitions. The first is to run counter to perspectives that overstate the novelty of the Communist regime: I emphasize instead the multiplicity of inheritances, including the continuity between the Chinese Communist Party's programme of action and that of the reformers and revolutionaries of the early twentieth century and the Republican interwar period. In many ways, the promises made in 1949 were not new. China also adopted goals and ways of exercising power from the Stalinist Soviet Union. The radical new directions taken, whether in 1949 or 1979, were therefore less clear-cut than is too often believed, and varied with the different fields of social activity.

My second ambition is to put into perspective the ability of the Chinese totalitarian regime to transform the country. Along with other authors, I argue that the reforms have modernized the economy and society more than did Mao's utopian vision. If the latter's transformative capacities have been overestimated, this is because the political sphere has long been the only observable reality – an obstacle that concealed the real country in which economic and social forces were quite capable of resisting injunctions from above. Of course, the regime has inflicted shocks, but the most violent changed the course of society less than did the longer-term dynamics initiated by the social actors themselves. Against the primacy of political history, I would like to reconstruct a history of human beings that is far removed from official discourse. Social breaks, if they exist, do not necessarily correspond to key moments in political life.

My third goal is to drag China out of the epistemological isolation that has created the impression that the Chinese experience is unique. Industrialization, urbanization, bureaucratization and globalization are phenomena that have accompanied the entry of all human societies into modernity. This is not to argue that China is converging towards Western-style modernity. The current configuration, which may be sustainable, combines integration into the capitalist world economy with authoritarian political practice; it suggests that the path taken is specific to China. I aim to 'de-exoticize' China and analyse its transformations in the light of other human societies, using the same tools taken from the social sciences.

This volume is organized into chronological and thematic chapters. The first chapters distinguish four periods: the establishment of a new regime (1949–57), the excesses of Maoism (1958–76), the priority placed on economic modernization (1976–92), and the construction of a new model (since 1992). In making these divisions, I decided to emphasize the overall trend, even though these periods were of variable lengths. Six chapters follow, on the political system, the economy, society, and education and culture. This arrangement should allow a variety of possible readings.

ONE

Establishment of a New Regime
(1949–1957)

In 1949, as the Chinese Communist Party (CCP) seized power, China faced immense problems. The economy had been devastated by war; public order needed to be restored, and everyday life throughout the country was difficult. By 1957, the achievements of the new regime were considerable. After decades of division, a centralized state with authority over the entire national territory had been re-established. The country was on the road to industrialization; economic growth was rapid. The living conditions of the population had been considerably improved. China, an ally of the Soviet Union, had become militarily involved in Korea, and was now a power to be reckoned with. In September 1956, a meeting of the Eighth Congress of the Communist Party, the first since the seizure of power, celebrated the progress made.

However, the first years of the Chinese Communist regime were not strictly speaking revolutionary. It was not until the end of the 1950s that the contours of a socialist China took shape. What happened between 1949 and 1953 is better described as a transition or an evolution. During this initial period, the CCP brought together all social groups in a broad coalition, while institutions remained semi-democratic, with a mixed economy. The CCP's agenda thus echoed that of many previous Chinese governments. For instance, the construction of an effective central state was the fulfilment of a wish formulated in 1911 by the revolutionaries who overthrew the imperial system. The continuities between the Communist regime and the nationalist regime that immediately preceded it were partly due to the speed of the military victory, much more sudden than expected. In the spring of 1948, a time when, in northern China, the fortunes of war seemed to be favouring the Communist forces, Mao Zedong foresaw another three years of combat. Moreover, even though the CCP had experience in controlling vast rural territories, the cities were foreign to it; the Party therefore needed to fall back on institutions, individuals and social forms of the preceding period. While its

4

ambitions were comparable – to build a strong state, to weaken certain social groups – its methods were partly new. During this initial period, the Party extended to all Chinese society techniques of conversion that had already been tried and tested in the territories it previously controlled. Political campaigns, sometimes very violent (as during the agrarian reform), subjected all populations to the Party's slogans. Far from being the golden age of Chinese Communism, as official history has often described it, this period was marked by the regime's hesitation over which new path to follow. Conditions for the construction of new institutions, for taking over society and forging a connection to the socialist bloc, all bore witness to this.

Building a new state

In 1949, the project of building a strong Chinese state capable of leading the country's modernization and ridding society of the traces of feudalism (*fengjian* 封建) was not new; this had been the ambition of all successive political powers since the fall of the Empire in 1911. The first imperative was that of territorial unity; this was still not completed by 1 October 1949, when the People's Republic of China was established in Beijing. It was to be one of the priority tasks of the new regime. Brought to power by force of arms, the Party relied on the People's Liberation Army (PLA) to establish and consolidate its authority. This too had been a characteristic feature of politics in China for nearly a century: ever since the raising of provincial armies to fight the Taiping rebellion (1850–64), the army had been at the heart of the exercise of power. Once unity was achieved, with the notable exception of the island of Taiwan where Chiang Kai-shek and the Guomindang had taken refuge, the Communist Party set out to establish new institutions.

Achieving unity

The conquest of power by the CCP was primarily military and victory was relatively sudden. Beijing fell after negotiations in January 1949. The PLA crossed the Yangtze and captured Shanghai in April, and Wuhan (Hubei) in May. It no longer met with any decisive resistance. Canton was taken in October shortly after the proclamation of the new regime, and the city of Chengdu was reached in December. At the end of 1949, Xinjiang, Tibet and Taiwan still remained to be conquered.

With regard to ethnic minorities and the peripheral territories they inhabited, the Party hesitated between several projects. The building of a Chinese federation was briefly considered. The peoples of Muslim Xinjiang, Inner and Outer Mongolia, and Tibet were to be granted complete autonomy, and, in accordance with the principle of self-determination of nations, could decide whether or not to join the Chinese federation and the Han people. In 1949, this plan was dropped and the goal was now that of a unified socialist China bringing together Xinjiang, Inner Mongolia and Tibet. All the peoples living in the territories of China were deemed to be Chinese. The new republic needed to achieve the unity of the five nationalities (*wuzu gonghe* 五族共和) – Hans, Manchus, Mongols, Huis and Tibetans – and thus pursued the same ambition that had driven the nationalist regime of Nanjing and, before that, the Qing Empire.

Tibet was of particular importance to the regime for several reasons.[1] Mao and the other leaders were mainly aware of the strategic interest of the territory. They also believed that the international situation was favourable to them; Tibet, de facto independent since 1912, had never been recognized by the international community. They also felt that the situation was militarily favourable to them. Above all, as well as taking over Tibet, the legitimacy and credibility of the new power vis-à-vis both the Chinese people and the rest of the world were at stake. In Tibet, as on the Taiwan question, the Party's mission was to finally achieve the unity of the country after decades of fragmentation.

For all these reasons – strategic, military, diplomatic and political – the Chinese leadership wanted the Tibetan question to be quickly resolved. While the PLA did indeed plan to invade Tibet – a military campaign launched from Sichuan was envisaged from mid-April to October 1950 – the effective takeover of Tibet was ultimately not just a military operation. Political efforts were made in particular to win over the 12-year-old Panchen Lama, who was living in Qinghai. Military operations finally began on 6 October 1950. The Lhasa government requested help from the United Nations, which opted not to respond. On 23 May 1951, a seventeen-point agreement on the 'peaceful liberation of Tibet' was signed in Beijing between the representatives of the

6

Fourteenth Dalai Lama and those of the People's Republic. In addition to recognizing Chinese sovereignty, Tibetans were obliged to help the PLA to occupy Tibet peacefully. They yielded control of foreign affairs, border defence and trade, and agreed for the Tibetan army to be gradually incorporated into the PLA. They also agreed to the creation of a new administrative entity, the Military Administrative Committee, separate from Tibetan local government and subject to the Central People's Government. The agreement recognized the right to regional autonomy and maintenance of the political system and the status of the Dalai Lama, as well as religious freedom and a continued income for the Buddhist clergy. This was a significant victory for Beijing, but it was not a fair arrangement: while Tibet was recognized as a permanent and irreversible part of the People's Republic of China, Beijing's commitment to respecting the Tibetan political and social system was itself conditional and provisional. Eight years later, in March 1959, the Tibetan question resurfaced during the popular uprising and the exile of the Dalai Lama to India, from where he denounced the seventeen-point agreement. In the aftermath of the events, Beijing dissolved the Tibetan government. Only in September 1965 was the Tibet Autonomous Region finally created. As for the reunification of the island of Taiwan with the Chinese mainland, it remains to this day a piece of wishful thinking and one of the watchwords of the People's Republic.

Achieving national unity after decades of divisions has been, to this day, one of the foundations of the new regime's legitimacy. Because this ambition was in the process of being realized, Mao Zedong could proudly declare on 21 September 1949, during the first session of the Consultative Political Conference which served as a legislative assembly: 'The Chinese people, who comprise a quarter of humanity, have now stood up ... [We will] never again be a nation subjected to insults and humiliations. We are now standing up (*women yijing zhanqilaile* 我们已经站起来了).'

Administration of the territories

Once the territories had been militarily conquered, the new government needed to take effective control of administrations, revive the economy and establish a foothold in society, both in the cities and in the

7

countryside. This effective takeover of territories and society came about in ways that varied across Chinese territory.

Three types of zones could be distinguished. The north, northeast and northwest areas of the country, where a quarter of the Chinese population lived, came under the control of the Communist Party in 1947 or earlier. It was able to win the support of the inhabitants, in particular the poorest peasants. Here, it mobilized most of those who entered the ranks of the PLA. It was in these areas that the revolution was won. The land had already been redistributed and the Party's aim was now to develop the first forms of agricultural cooperatives. In the 1950s, a third of the rural households in these regions participated in mutual aid teams, the first step towards collectivization. The east, the northwest, the area south of the Yangtze and the centre of the country were the most recently conquered areas. The Party had no resources here in terms of organization or popular support. Unlike in the previous zone, the PLA here took control first of the towns and then of the countryside. The new power was confronted by the presence of anti-Communist forces. Finally, large urban centres constituted a third kind of territory where the Party's presence was very limited until 1949; it could count essentially on underground forces alone, fewer in the south than in the north. These forces had played an auxiliary role in the seizure of power. The CCP was sorely lacking in the necessary skills for the establishment of a new administration.

Faced with such a variety of situations, to consolidate its authority the Party relied on the PLA to take effective control of the conquered territories. On 1 October 1949, China, excluding the separately administered Inner Mongolia and Tibet, was divided into six major military regions. Four of them – the central south, east, northwest and southwest – were run by administrative and military committees. The two regions of the north and northeast, where military power was older, were administered by people's governments. These divisions into large regions remained in place until the promulgation of the new political institutions in 1954.

The strategy of New Democracy (1949–53)

The period 1949–53 was a transitional term in which the Communist Party sought to maximize support and minimize fears among the population.

It capitalized on its ability to restore the country's unity but also on the discredit into which the Guomindang (GMD; the Chinese Nationalist Party) had fallen, in particular among the urban middle classes, who were the main victims of the economic turmoil and rocketing inflation. As a result, the Communists were given a favourable reception, including by representatives of the Chinese bourgeoisie. Robert Guillain, correspondent for *Le Monde*, called his report on the entry of the Communist armies into the country's economic capital 'The Martians take Shanghai'. The conquerors were an army of teenagers who marched solemnly through the streets of the city, wearing straw sandals. Their entry was not accompanied by a requisitioning of food, looting or rape. The passage from one power to another took place without violence; at the tops of buildings or on the façades of department stores, the red flag was hung, where a few days earlier the nationalist flag had still been flying. This first good impression created by the Communist forces contrasted with the deplorable image left by the Guomindang troops.

The programme known as New Democracy (*xin minzhu* 新民主), the title of a text written by Mao in January 1940, aimed to unite all patriots behind the Party banner to rebuild the country. In the cities, only companies under foreign control or establishments most compromised with the Guomindang were nationalized; elsewhere, the Party helped entrepreneurs to restart production. Emissaries were even sent to Hong Kong to try and persuade the capitalists who had fled the country to come back and participate in the construction of the new China; some did return and were given administrative and economic responsibilities.[2] In the countryside, only landowners who did not work their own land (between 3 and 5 per cent of the population) were viewed as 'feudal' forces and evicted; rich peasants were not seen as enemies of the regime.

This so-called strategy of the United Front (*tongzhan* 统战) was also the result of circumstances. The Party lacked sufficient cadres to take effective control of the conquered cities or administer and rebuild the country. Admittedly, new recruits were joining its ranks en masse; between 1948 and the end of 1950, its members increased from 2.8 million to 5.8 million. For the most part, these were peasants without any ideological training in Marxism, who were often even illiterate. The Party also sought to recruit among students and college-educated urban youth. In many cases, the solution adopted was to ask the men already in post to continue to exercise their responsibilities. Many institutions remained in place. In 1950, private organizations, often religious, continued to control almost half of higher education institutions. Most civil servants remained in post; only a small number, those most closely linked to the Guomindang, were dismissed and detained. In the case of the police, for example, nationwide, almost 60 per cent of the forces were maintained following an 'educational clean-up' programme.[3] In Shanghai, in many police stations, lessons on the principles of the New Democracy were given in the morning between 7 and 8 a.m. in order to transform the existing civil servants into perfect police officers in the service of the people.

This programme was also translated into institutional terms. From 21 to 30 September 1949, in Beijing, the CCP convened the Chinese People's Political Consultative Conference (*Zhongguo renmin zhengzhi xieshang huiyi* 中国人民政治协商会议), heir to the Political Consultative Conference convened by the Guomindang in early 1946. As a constituent assembly, it prepared the 1954 Constitution; as a legislative assembly, it voted on legal texts. It had 588 members representing the political parties – the CCP and the small so-called democratic parties – the various regions, professional organizations, the PLA, national minorities and invited guests. Although the CCP officially had only sixteen representatives, it was in fact in the majority thanks to delegates from regional administrations, the PLA and the social organizations it controlled. This assembly adopted a common programme which defined the People's Republic as the 'state of a new democracy', based on the alliance of workers, peasants, the petty bourgeoisie and the national bourgeoisie, under the leadership of the CCP. This therefore excluded the Guomindang and the groups deemed to be 'reactionary'. The supreme state body was the Central People's Government, a commission presided over by Mao that exercised power between sessions of the Political Consultative Conference. The State Council, headed by Zhou Enlai, which assumed the functions of government, was governed by this commission.

New institutions (1954)

These provisional institutions were in force until the promulgation of the Constitution of September 1954. The National People's Congress (*guomin dahui* 国民大会), elected for four years, became the legislative body and the supreme organ of the state. It appointed the Chairman of the Republic, in this case Mao Zedong. At each local level, the executive power of administrations was based on a system of elected assemblies. The government, still under the authority of Zhou Enlai, was renamed the State Council (*guowu yuan* 国务院). The originality of this arrangement lay in the maintenance of the Chinese People's Political Consultative Conference, an assembly without any real power. Endowed with an advisory role, it remained the symbol of the strategy of the United Front.

This Constitution was very close to that drawn up by Stalin in the Soviet Union in 1936, but was distinguished by two notable exceptions. On the one hand, the post of Chairman of the People's Republic, occupied by Mao, was created, while, in the USSR, it was the Chairman of the Supreme Soviet who played the role of head of state. On the other hand, the People's Republic defined itself as a 'unified multinational state' (*tongyi de duominzu de guojia* 统一的多民族国家). The regions of national minorities – 6 per cent of the population but 60 per cent of the national territory – were 'autonomous', but could not secede.

The administrative division into six regions was abolished and the country was now made up of 22 provinces (*sheng* 省), 191 municipalities (*shi* 市), 110 prefectures (*diqu* 地区 or *zhou* 州), 1,673 counties (*xian* 县) and 91,590 townships (*xiang* 乡); the administrative hierarchy was very close to that of the previous regimes. The provinces populated by national minorities were administered within the framework of five autonomous regions (Inner Mongolia, created in 1947; Xinjiang in 1955; Guangxi and Ningxia in 1958; and Tibet in 1965) and prefectures and autonomous districts. Three municipalities came directly under the central government: Beijing, Tianjin and Shanghai. Chongqing was added to these in 1997. At each of these levels, the Party apparatus, the real seat of power, doubled the state apparatus, which was essentially a democratic façade. At the top, it was not the Premier or the government that took the decisions, but the Politburo of the Central Committee, and even more its secretariat composed of five members: Mao Zedong, Liu Shaoqi, Zhou Enlai, Zhu De and Chen Yun. At all administrative levels, Party committees were more influential than government bodies.

Society is brought into line

Building a new state was only the first of the tools used for furthering the regime's goals; the second was the takeover of society. In accordance with Leninist tradition, mass organizations spread the Party among the population; by 1953, the Youth League had 9 million members, the Federation of Trade Unions 12 million and the Federation of Women 76 million. It was, above all, mass campaigns (*qunzhong yundong* 群众运动) that constituted the privileged means by which the Party mobilized the population and imposed its decisions. The first of these campaigns, named 'Resist America, help Korea' (*kangmei yuanchao* 抗美援朝), accompanied the entry of China into the Korean War in the autumn of 1950. In December, there followed another campaign intended to suppress cultural, educational and social institutions 'managed by foreigners or with foreign capital', which aimed to bring all Western-controlled institutions – especially missionary institutions – under the authority of mass organizations. These episodes marked the gradual end of the Communist Party's strategy of opening-up towards all social groups; in both the countryside and the cities, it now intended to transform society. These campaigns were an opportunity to mobilize sometimes the bureaucracy, sometimes the population or a fraction of it, to get them behind the regime's slogans and eradicate dissenting opinions. They made it possible to eliminate those considered to be 'enemies' of the regime.

These mass movements constituted a major element of the political system of the People's Republic. Long considered an original feature of Chinese Communism, they were not, however, strictly speaking an invention of the CCP and bore the mark of a triple heritage.[4] The first element of this was the experience acquired by the CCP in the rural and urban areas it controlled in the 1930s and 1940s, during which it repeatedly eliminated its opponents. There was also the Soviet model and the Stakhanovist movement, in which counter-revolutionaries, landowners and corrupt bureaucrats were singled out as enemies. Finally, there was the model for an episode of mobilization led by the nationalist Party, the New Life Movement, launched in February 1934. The CCP now used the same type of tool but with more force and efficiency. Unlike the Guomindang, the CCP effectively controlled the entire national territory, had a clear ideology – class struggle – and believed in its ability to win the masses over to its political initiatives. The originality of the CCP lay not in the way it named the regime's enemies, as happened in the USSR, nor in its desire to morally transform individuals, as the GMD had the same ambition, but in its conviction of the possibility of gaining the support of the majority. In so doing, the Party took control of Chinese society by violence.

The marriage law (May 1950)

Promulgated on 1 May 1950, the marriage law (*hunyin fa* 婚姻法) was the first piece of legislation whose application was accompanied by a mass movement. The idea was to extend to the entire population – in effect, mainly to the peasant world – the developments that had begun in the 1930s among the urban elites. The law comprised twenty-seven articles and was distinguished by its simplicity. The so-called 'feudal' matrimonial system gave way to the freedom to contractual marriage, to the equal rights of men and women, and to the protection of the legal interests of women and children (Article 1). Cohabitation, polygamy and the betrothal of children were prohibited, as was any demand for money or gifts to contract a marriage, while widows were now allowed to remarry (Article 2). Article 3 stipulated that marriage must be entered into by both partners in complete freedom; marriage through or under pressure from parents was prohibited. Article 15 put legitimate and natural children on an equal footing. Article 17 established a new divorce law which recognized the right of both partners to divorce and to alimony.

The Party strove to enforce the law by organizing various political movements between 1950 and 1953. In public courts, 'feudal' marriages were dissolved and 'despotic' spouses denounced. In fact, the law did not establish equality between the sexes, nor did it remove patriarchal structures. Family structures were not fundamentally altered, and so it was a relative failure with regard to female emancipation. Rather, there was a shift from a 'feudal' patriarchy to a socialist patriarchy. Admittedly, the power of the head of the family declined, to be replaced by the power of the Party, which intervened more and more in the regulation of personal and family affairs; the Party introduced political and class criteria for the selection of spouses, and imposed its mediation in the event of marital discord.

Divorce.
Source: Marc Riboud / Fonds Marc Riboud au MNAAG / Magnum Photos

Agrarian reform

A month later, on 28 June 1950, the agrarian reform law (*tudi gaige* 土地改革) was promulgated. Its application was initially moderate, but became more drastic after China had entered the Korean War. At the end of the year, the emphasis was on class struggle and mass mobilization, even at the cost of social unrest. In the countryside, in order to denounce class exploitation, the Party and its representatives identified the different categories of landowners, rich peasants, moderately wealthy peasants and poor peasants. First applied to northern China, these categories corresponded quite closely to reality, but this was much less the case in the lower Yangtze valley or in southern China, where the majority of the rural population performed non-agricultural tasks as a secondary activity, many landowners were non-residents, and even the less wealthy peasants rented out some of their land. Ultimately, 40 per cent of the cultivated area was redistributed. If the peasants benefited at all, it was the moderately wealthy peasants who were the main beneficiaries.

The reform was accompanied by the recruitment of many new cadres integrated into the lower echelons of the state apparatus, in particular from peasant families labelled as poor and middling. Above all, it was an opportunity to instil in the rural population the idea of class struggle and the new revolutionary norms. To implement reform, the CCP used both conviction and force. The propaganda denounced the perversions of the old society and set out the advantages of the new one. Force employed against landowners was decisive in convincing the population of the new government's intentions. Committees set up by the administration mobilized entire villages against landowners in popular meetings or tribunals. Landowners were humiliated, sometimes executed – between 1 and 2 million are said to have died. While the effect of land redistribution on productivity remains unclear, the main outcome of the reform was political. The old elite was swept away, and the old social order was brought down. A new elite – the village cadres – emerged from the ranks of the poor and middling peasantry.

Campaign for the repression of counter-revolutionaries (February 1951)

In February 1951, a movement 'for the suppression of counter-revolutionaries' was launched in the towns, which lasted until 1953. Officially, it was a question of eliminating the partisans of the old regime, the former members of the Guomindang, the spies in its pay and other resistance agents. In fact, the definition of the term 'counter-revolutionary' was very broad, and anyone could be denounced, convicted and executed. This was an opportunity for the regime to get rid of criminals and bandits. The movement is believed to have killed between 700,000 and 2 million people, depending on the sources, to which can be added all those sent to the labour camps.

Agrarian reform in the countryside and the movement against counter-revolutionaries in the cities had similar objectives: to denounce the enemies of the new regime, to destroy the social status of opponents – or of those denounced as such – and to win over the population to the new policies, increasing the power of the state over society. Whereas, during the conquest of power, the Party had tried to reconcile the greater part of the rural and urban populations, it now resorted to violence.

Tribunals were organized at which the regime's alleged opponents were subjected to popular revenge. The accused did not have any opportunity to defend themselves.

Unlike the Stalinist regime, where the political police exercised violence, here the population as a whole was associated with the hunt for the enemies of the regime. This is the way in which China was different from its Soviet or Republican heritage: it resorted to the public space and to popular participation.[5] Campaigns took the form of accusing enemies in front of a large audience. These sessions of public accusation (*kongsu hui* 控诉会) were organized as a performance, following a script written in advance, with moments of high dramatic intensity and final sessions of applause, unlike the bureaucratic and formalized procedures of the violence in the Soviet Union. The government drew on the shared emotions of the public in order both to arouse hatred against class enemies and to make the masses adhere to the regime. Sometimes, real theatrical stages were constructed. The fate of the convicts was decided before the sessions of accusation and only those guilty of the most heinous crimes were brought before the public. Those who spoke out to denounce their exploiter and recount his crimes at those 'meetings where the sufferings endured are related' (*suku hui* 诉苦会) were carefully selected for their ability to arouse emotion; they were preferably chosen from among the oldest or youngest accusers, or from the women among them; and they were told in advance what to say and when. The flow of what looked like a performance was tightly controlled, although it could appear spontaneous. After hearing the victims, the perpetrators confessed their faults and were then sentenced. Thus, all the witnesses present were collectively complicit in state violence.[6]

It was through this efficient and inexpensive procedure that the population rallied to the new norms defined by the Party. These two campaigns also resulted in the recruitment of new cadres, which strengthened the state's capacity to coerce society. In cities and in the countryside, the number of agents of the state increased, as did its capacity for direct intrusion into daily workplaces. The violence of these two campaigns was also rooted in the regional context, that is, China's involvement in Korea and in the Cold War. The regime would never again embark on equivalent campaigns aimed at the extermination of social groups. In subsequent campaigns the victims were criticized by the masses, they lost their jobs, were sent to jail or sentenced to internal exile, but they were rarely executed. The violence of these two campaigns was also a reflection of the high degree of self-confidence of the political leadership, which truly believed in its moral duty to condemn its 'enemies'.

The Three-anti Campaign (December 1951) and the Five-anti Campaign (April 1952)

In the cities, in late 1951 and early 1952, two successive movements emerged that were mainly aimed against the bourgeoisie. The Three-anti Campaign (*san fan* 三反), launched in 1951, mostly targeted 'corruption, waste and bureaucracy' – urban cadres corrupted by too great a proximity to the bourgeoisie. This was actually a matter of eliminating those executives whose recent rallying to the regime had been too opportunistic. The campaign then shifted to attack the capitalists themselves, accused of provoking and encouraging the misconduct of officials. Launched in April 1952, the Five-anti Campaign (*wu fan* 五反) was officially aimed at five evils: bribes, tax evasion, embezzlement of state property, fraud in contracts with the state, and illegal obtaining of economic information from the state. This campaign against the bourgeoisie was waged on the basis of quotas that corresponded to different degrees of sanctions, ranging from a simple warning to execution, via imprisonment and re-education through labour. In fact, it was non-Communist values that had hitherto been tolerated that were now under attack. This was a way for the Party to break up traditional social relations in industrial and commercial enterprises – in other words, the paternalistic relations between the bosses of companies both large and small and their employees. These two campaigns apparently resulted in 500 executions, 4,000 long-term prison sentences, and 30,000 sentences of less than ten years.

The impact was mostly political. Campaigns revealed new cadres loyal to the regime and contributed to the emergence of a new urban elite. Above all, they gave rise to the creation of Party committees in many private companies, which collected useful information on their functioning; they were de facto laying the ground for the nationalization of industrial and commercial enterprises that took place at the end of

1955. The bourgeoisie would then be incapable of putting up even the slightest resistance.

Bringing intellectuals to heel

Intellectuals, understood in the Chinese sense of the term (*zhishi fenzi* 知识分子), in other words all those who had graduated from secondary or higher education, constituted the last fraction of Chinese society that the Party attempted to bring to heel in the first years of the regime. In 1956, when the country had 600 million inhabitants, there were only 100,000 graduates of higher education, and nearly 4 million people who had graduated from high schools and technical colleges. Rallying the intellectuals to the new regime was far more the result of an objective necessity – in order to build the new China, their collaboration was essential – than of a properly political option.

The conversion of intellectuals to the revolution initially took the form of a reform of the higher education system. In 1949, the latter was instructed to learn from the Soviet model. It thus favoured the training of scientific personnel specializing in practical and technical disciplines instead of the liberal arts. Practical training aimed at producing technicians and specialists of all kinds was favoured. The focus on science and technology was based on political concerns – to assert the primacy of the proletariat over other classes, to develop it numerically and qualitatively since the Party claimed to be its vanguard and its justification. In particular, it accorded with the needs of economic development.

Ideological re-education was carried out by means of literary affairs that artificially assumed an exemplary character and a national dimension. One early campaign, called 'Criticism of Hu Shi', took place in 1951; it was named after one of the great intellectuals who had played a role in the 1919 May Fourth Movement. A pragmatist philosopher in the American sense, and a liberal in politics, Hu Shi was attacked on the personal level as a scientist. His role in the anti-Confucian movement and his use of the vernacular in literature were criticized; he was accused of careerism and of being a lackey of American imperialism. In early 1952, a movement to 'overhaul' intellectuals linked to the Three-anti Campaign invited thousands of intellectuals, Communists included, to carry out their own re-education through a programme of appropriate readings, by examining their lives and their ideas, by self-criticism and public confession. The most violent of these campaigns was the one launched in the spring of 1955 against Hu Feng, a renowned writer, Marxist and disciple of Lu Xun. Hu had dared to publicly criticize the Party's cultural policy. He was accused of treasonably working for the Guomindang and the imperialist powers; he was arrested, and disappeared.

The most traumatic episode was the Hundred Flowers Campaign (*baihua qifang* 百花齐放) and the anti-rightist crackdown that followed. This campaign began as a movement of rectification (*zhengfeng* 整风) inside the Party, analogous to the campaign in Yan'an in 1942–44; it was then a matter of eliminating 'dangerous political tendencies' so as to wage war more effectively on the Japanese and the Guomindang. On 2 May 1956, in a speech, Mao uttered the famous slogan: 'Let a hundred flowers bloom, let a hundred schools of thought contend.' But this text was not published and it was a commentary by Lu Dingyi, head of the Party's Propaganda Department, on 26 May, that launched the campaign. Lu called for the development of a new golden age of intellectual production. He mentioned the need to encourage 'independent thinking' and 'free discussion' in order to stimulate university life. He invited intellectuals to use their freedom to express their opinions on the arts, literature and the sciences. The other dimension of the campaign was political, as intellectuals were allowed to criticize the cadres in order to improve the functioning of the bureaucracy. The objective then was to reform the Party so that it was more in line with the objective of economic construction. The evils denounced were the 'subjectivism' of Party members (applying unsuitable concepts and methods to current problems), 'bureaucratism' (cutting themselves off from the masses and from social reality in order to constitute a new privileged elite at the expense of the interests of the people) and 'sectarianism' (feeling superior to the rest of society). In mid-1956, a study programme was launched within the Party. However, at the Eighth Congress held in the autumn, the question of rectification remained a minor point. Only in the following year did the movement pick up speed.

A few months later, in February 1957, Mao relaunched the movement and reaffirmed the need for a rectification, in particular in his famous speech 'On the Correct Handling of Contradictions Among the People', which would not be made public until June. He announced that intellectuals must play a major role in the movement to criticize the Party, a position that met with considerable resistance, in particular within the propaganda organizations, as they were aware of the dangers of allowing criticisms to be expressed. On 12 March 1957, in a speech to the Propaganda Department, Mao repeated this call to speak out freely and to criticize. However, these texts were not immediately published in the *People's Daily*, a sign that not all the bureaucracy agreed. Initially, the response of intellectuals to this invitation to speak out was timid – understandably so in view of the various movements of ideological renovation to which they had been subjected since the campaign for the reform of thought in 1951–52. Then, in May 1957, the movement gained momentum. In the press and on university campuses, some questioned the Party's ability to lead China during the period of construction of socialism, emphasizing the flaws in the way the cadres conducted their day-to-day management. Above all, the political system and the Party's monopoly on political space were criticized. For example, one student from Beijing put it this way: 'We are favourable towards the Party leadership, but we are resolutely opposed to a party making decisions on its own.' The concrete ways in which the Party exercised power were denounced.

In the face of such widespread criticism, and after having been the architect of the new opening-up, Mao now ordered the repression that began in June 1957. The anti-rightist movement first affected leading members of the democratic parties, accused of wanting to overthrow the regime. The press attacked them violently. Meetings were organized to bring them into line. They were forced to confess their mistakes. However, they were mostly back in their old positions by 1958–59. This was not the case with many intellectuals labelled rightist, driven to suicide or sent to the labour reform camps that were now being organized for the first time on a large scale. Among the victims of the repression were the female novelist Ding Ling, a former Vice President of the Writers' Union, and younger writers such as Wang Meng. It seems that more than 500,000 people were ousted from their responsibilities and replaced, in educational and cultural institutions in particular. One of the consequences of the crackdown was increased Party control over these institutions. The Hundred Flowers Campaign therefore ended in a failure that permanently compromised the relationship between the

Party and the intellectuals. The most likely explanation is undoubtedly Mao's mistaken feeling that intellectuals could contribute positively to a matter as delicate as the rectification of the Party, and his failure to imagine that they might not share the same interests as the latter. Mao believed that he could trust the intellectuals to participate in this rectification, but he did not perceive their mistrust – the result of the pressures they had recently endured in those early years.

In the end, after a brief period of conciliation, violence, marginalization and the elimination of resistance were the means whereby the Party took control of Chinese society. Mass campaigns were the preferred tool for bringing society into line. Some of these campaigns aimed to mobilize the bureaucracy, or a fraction of it, in support of a specific political initiative – reform of the police force or nationalization of the private sector. Others aimed to modify the behaviour of certain social or professional groups, such as the campaigns against prostitution or against the consumption of opium, and the campaign for the reform of thought in 1953. Still others mobilized both the bureaucracy and the rest of society to transform behaviour – especially in public health. The most important campaigns were those that mobilized very large sections of the rural or urban populations and generated a high degree of popular participation.[7]

Forging links with the socialist camp

The violence that characterized Chinese politics in the early years of the People's Republic was also due to the regional and international context, China's involvement in the Korean conflict and the onset of the Cold War. The People's Republic, proclaimed on 1 October 1949, was immediately recognized by the USSR, the latter's European satellites, and a few Asian countries including India. Beijing's main objective in diplomatic relations was, therefore, to build up good relations with its socialist Big Brother. In December 1949, Mao, on his first trip abroad, led a delegation to Moscow to pave the way for a treaty of friendship, alliance and mutual assistance that was signed on 14 February 1950. The outbreak of the Korean War definitively anchored China in the socialist camp. With the assistance of its ally, China also embarked on an orthodox programme of economic development based on the socialization of the means of production. Nevertheless, China actually obtained far less than it wanted from its partner, and the alliance between Moscow and Beijing, the result of difficult negotiations, was fragile from the outset.

The Sino–Soviet alliance

The alliance with Moscow was not the only option considered by the Chinese Communists. In March 1949, with victory in sight, Mao again adopted a conciliatory attitude towards the United States. He even considered establishing diplomatic relations with Washington; in June, he declared that the new Communist regime was ready to establish diplomatic relations with anyone who broke with the nationalist regime of Chiang Kai-shek. However, a few weeks later, in July 1949, Mao explained in an editorial in the *People's Daily* that China had chosen its side: that of socialism over that of imperialism. This turnaround was due to several factors.[8] First, China needed economic aid, and only the USSR could provide that. Also, Mao's main concern was to restore the unity and integrity of the country under his rule. However, following the Treaty of Yalta and the agreement signed by Moscow with the nationalist government in August 1945 at the end of the war, the USSR recovered rights that had formerly belonged to Tsarist Russia: control over the Manchurian railways, the city of Dalian and the use of Port-Arthur (Lüshun) as a base for its navy. Any conflict with Stalin would entail the risk that these territories might remain under Soviet rule for a long time.

The importance given by the Chinese leadership to its relations with the USSR explains Mao's decision to leave for Moscow in December 1949. Relations with Stalin were difficult from the outset, as the latter feared seeing a new Tito emerge in China – all the more likely an eventuality given that non-Communists were present in the organs of government of the People's Republic. The treaty of friendship, alliance and mutual assistance was signed in the presence of Mao by the Premier Zhou Enlai and the Soviet Minister of Foreign Affairs Andrei Vishinsky on 14 February, when Mao finally left Moscow.

The treaty was first and foremost a military pact intended to demonstrate the unity of Moscow and Beijing in the face of any resurgence of Japanese militarism supported by its American protector. In this regard, it provided a theoretical justification for the San Francisco peace treaty between Japan and its Western allies, and the Japanese–American security treaty signed soon after. China managed to obtain some concessions from Moscow, which agreed to renounce some of its gains from the treaty signed with the nationalist government in 1945. The Soviets undertook to transfer the Manchurian railway to China before 1952 and to withdraw their troops from Port Arthur. In return, Mao, as Chiang Kai-shek had done, recognized the independence of Outer Mongolia; he also accepted the creation of joint Sino–Soviet companies to exploit the mineral resources of Xinjiang – modelled on the USSR's exploitation of the natural resources of the satellite countries of Eastern Europe. In terms of economic aid, Mao obtained 300 million dollars in loan pledges over the next five years. This was less than the 450 million dollars obtained by Poland a year earlier, and the devaluation of the rouble announced in February 1950 reduced this sum by a quarter; moreover, the Chinese had just ten years to repay these credits. The tensions arising from these agreements did not subside until the outbreak of the Korean War.

The Korean War

Hostilities on the Korean Peninsula began on 25 June 1950, when North Korean troops moved south of the 38th parallel, which until then had acted as the border. Did Mao take part in paving the way for the conflict? This began only five days after the promulgation in China of the agrarian reform; the importance of this law suggests either that Beijing did not intend to enter the conflict, or that it believed that the conflict would end in an early victory for the North Korean leader Kim Il-sung. Beijing's immediate concern was not so much the war in Korea as US President Truman's decision on 27 June to place the US 7th Fleet in the Taiwan Strait. Zhou Enlai denounced an 'act of aggression' against the integrity of Chinese territory, and the Chinese press showed more interest in the Taiwanese question than in the Korean conflict itself. On 15 September, the American counter-offensive, under the auspices of the United Nations, began. On 1 October, South Korean forces in turn crossed the 38th parallel. It was on this day that Mao, ignoring a majority of his generals who were hostile to the participation of Chinese forces, decided to bring 'volunteer' troops into the conflict, under the leadership of Peng Dehuai. The country was therefore again at war. In July 1951, peace talks began, which led two years later, on 27 July 1953, to a ceasefire along the 38th parallel.

The fighting in Korea cost China dearly in terms of men. Of course, the 'Resist America and Help Korea' mobilization campaign strengthened patriotism and helped consolidate the new regime. But the negative consequences of Chinese engagement were significant. China, described as an 'aggressor' by the United Nations, was now isolated on the international stage. It was excluded for twenty years from the United Nations. The goal of reunification with Taiwan was postponed due to the interposition of the US 7th Fleet; the Republic of China was now protected by American power. In terms of financial cost, Beijing would later reveal that half of the debt contracted in the early 1950s with the USSR had been used to finance the war. Even though no one in Beijing spoke up against Moscow at the time, criticism would be heard in the 1960s and 1970s.

An orthodox economic policy

China's anchoring in the socialist bloc also took the form of the adoption of the Soviet model of organization of the economy based on the planning and nationalization of the means of production. This applied not just to Beijing's foreign policy or a concern for ideological orthodoxy, but also to pragmatic considerations. If it were to realize the old dream of making China 'rich and powerful' (*fuqiang* 富强), the Party was aware it had to overcome its inexperience in development policy. Mao himself would admit this in the early 1960s: in the early years, the Party had lacked the experience necessary to administer the economy of the entire country and this is why, during the first Five-Year Plan, it had no choice but to imitate Soviet methods. While the CCP had experience in rural policy, in many areas it had no clear path to follow. Under these conditions, the decision to follow the Soviet Union was inevitable: it was the only country to offer economic aid, and the only example of a socialist country that had achieved rapid economic development on the basis of an initially backward economy.

Within the framework of socialism, development planning was coupled with the nationalization of the means of production in the countryside as well as in the cities. Even before 1949, in the liberated areas of northern

China, the socialization of agriculture had been initiated by the creation of the first forms of cooperatives, namely mutual aid teams: farmers retained individual ownership of the land and means of production, but labour power was pooled. In 1952, 40 per cent of farming families were members of mutual aid teams. In 1952–53, the first so-called lower-level cooperatives appeared: landownership was now collective, but individual farmers received remuneration for their contribution in soil, tools and animals. Collectivization was gradual, accelerating and then slowing down several times between 1952 and 1955. Cooperatives were created and then dismantled. The vacillation reflected both the concrete organizational difficulties on the ground and the debates within the Party itself on the pace to follow. Mao's intervention in May 1955 and his speech in July 1955 were decisive in speeding up the process. A broad consensus then emerged for at least two reasons: on the one hand, because the maintenance of private property risked triggering the development of rural capitalism and endangered the consolidation of socialism, and, on the other, because the success of the first Five-Year Plan and industrialization largely depended on progress in terms of agricultural production. During the winter of 1955–56 most of the higher-level cooperatives were created: land was collectively owned and farmers were paid in proportion to their work. By the end of 1956, collectivization was completed.

The process of collectivization was less violent in China than it had been in the USSR.[9] Admittedly, peasants resisted in comparable ways – by withdrawing from cooperatives, reducing investment and activity, slaughtering herds – but, overall, resistance was much lower. The smooth transition was due first of all to the effectiveness of the Party apparatus in the countryside; the Party was represented in every village through committees, and a new rural elite had emerged under the first agrarian reform, which gave land to peasants. It was also due to the government's agrarian policy, which provided the majority of farmers with benefits, and which left them little choice but to cooperate; agricultural input, credit and the sale of crops were now in the hands of cooperatives. Staying aloof from collective structures was not a viable option. Furthermore, unlike the Soviet policy towards the kulaks, the Chinese authorities did not envisage the physical elimination – or deportation – of rich peasants: stripped of their lands, humiliated at public meetings, they could still partake in cooperatives. Finally, the propaganda insisted on the objective of improving peasants' standard of living. Government policy could therefore attract the support of the greatest number.

In the cities, the nationalization of commercial and industrial activities, prepared by the Five-anti Campaign, was completed by the end of 1956. The state now directly or indirectly controlled almost all production. Two categories of enterprise coexisted: public enterprises, which were largely dominant and on the state's payroll, and collective enterprises, which were under the supervision of local authorities – such businesses were generally smaller in scope. At the same time, instruments for centralized planning were being put into place. A significant economic administration was set up; the state statistics office was established in 1952, as was the state planning commission responsible for managing the national plan, and the state economic commission in charge of short-term plans was set up in 1956. The sectoral ministries, several dozens of them, were responsible for implementation.

An interpretation of Chinese economic policy in terms of the importance of the Soviet model must be qualified by emphasizing the weight of the heritage of the People's Republic. There was already a history of economic and industrial planning in China prior to 1949.[10] As early as 1922, Sun Yat-sen, then leader of the Nationalist Party, insisted on the role of state planning in his text published in English under the title *The International Development of China*. During the Nanjing decade, several development plans were drawn up by the Reconstruction Commission (1928) and the Ministry of Industry (1931, 1932). Few resources were brought into play: these were mainly lists of objectives. After the Manchurian incident and the Japanese encroachments on Chinese territory, a veritable modern economic bureaucracy emerged under the leadership of the Ministries of Railways and Communications and the National Reconstruction Commission, which became the National Resources Commission (NRC). In keeping with the times, building a scientifically-led economy through central planning appeared to be the appropriate response in times of crisis; to protect threatened national interests, the central state needed to take over from private economic interests, and from provincial and foreign initiatives. After 1937 in particular, the state industrial sector developed a technocratic culture through the almost exclusive recruitment of engineers. In 1937, the NRC controlled 23 industrial establishments and employed 2,000 people.

Seven years later, in 1944, it controlled 103 industrial establishments with 160,000 workers, and employed more than 12,000 people. Planning no longer aimed merely to support the war economy but to prepare for reconstruction in peacetime. Resisting American pressures demanding the privatization of industry, the NRC increased its control over the national economy; in 1947, with 33,000 employees, it controlled 67 per cent of industrial capital and 230,000 workers. In terms of planning, there were several kinds of continuity between the Nanjing regime and the People's Republic. First of all, there were the companies; the establishments controlled by the NRC became state-controlled businesses under the authority of the central government. Then there were the industrial projects being carried out in particular in the north-east of the country. There was the general approach to industrial development based on large investments, with the mobilization of large amounts of capital, notably in the service of national defence; the planning priorities were, until 1959, in part similar to those of nationalist planning. Finally, there was a continuity of staff; some of the NRC's employees, in particular in managerial positions, continued their tasks within the state planning commission. While some fell victim to the anti-rightist campaign of 1957, it was mainly the Cultural Revolution that would marginalize them. When it came to implementing Soviet-style planning, the principles, personnel and structures were therefore already in place.

No sooner had it been set up than this model of economic organization underwent various adjustments. Aware that the USSR had started from a more advanced industrial base, and that China, to catch up, could not be satisfied with the growth rate experienced by the USSR, Chinese leaders called for a review of the model, which Mao theorized in his speech of April 1956 on 'The Ten Major Relationships'. One crucial question was that of the investment ratio between heavy industry on the one hand and light industry and agriculture on the other; Mao criticized the overemphasis on heavy industry and called for increased effort in agriculture and light industry. When it came to central government power, Mao criticized excessive centralization and called for more responsibility at local levels. Another area where the Soviet model was called into question was that of the modernization of the People's Liberation Army. Though there was no wish to revert to a guerrilla army, there was criticism of the specialization and the excessive importance placed on hierarchy. It was not a question of abandoning the goal of modernization, but of modernizing while keeping intact the traditions of the PLA and its popular character.

The Eighth Party Congress (1956)

The Eighth Party Congress, held in September 1956, brought this initial period in the history of the People's Republic to a close. This was the first Congress since the seizure of power and was held eleven years after the previous one, which had met in 1945. In the meantime, the Party had seen its membership rise from 4.5 million in 1949 to 10.7 million. This was an opportunity for the Party to congratulate itself on the scale of its achievements – the victory of 1949 and the first transformations towards a socialist society of 1955–56 – and to appraise their outcome, since many problems remained to be resolved.

This 1956 Congress marked less of a personal success for Mao than the previous one. Reference to Mao's thought (*Mao Zedong sixiang* 毛泽东思想), written into the Party's statutes in 1945, disappeared. The importance of the collective character of political leadership was affirmed. Measures were taken to prepare for Mao's possible retirement to a second, less operational front and to prepare for his succession. As a result, the post of honorary Chairman of the Party was created, which would be given to him in the event of retirement. The position of Liu Shaoqi as heir apparent was reinforced by the fact that he presented the political report, a task assumed by Mao in 1945. Liu Shaoqi did indeed succeed him as Chairman of the Republic in April 1959.

The Party leadership remained stable. Almost all the members of the Central Committee were re-elected. The new Politburo Standing Committee consisted of the same five members who had previously formed the secretariat of the Central Committee that it succeeded: Mao Zedong, Liu Shaoqi, Zhou Enlai, Zhu De, and Chen Yun, as well as Deng Xiaoping, who was promoted. The staff of the Politburo was doubled to accommodate the PLA marshals who were not yet members, as well as the Deputy Premiers. At the top, power was now in the hands of civilians: the Politburo had twice as many civilians – members of the Party or government – as it did soldiers; the Central Committee had three times as many.

This stability was due to the unity of the political leadership, which explains why Mao could declare at the Congress: 'Our Party is more united than at any time in its history.' It contrasted with the conflicts that had very quickly characterized the Communist Party of the Soviet Union, or the CCP in the 1920s and 1930s. Only one significant purge took place during this period: the ousting in 1954–55 of Gao Gang of the State Planning Commission and Rao Shushi of the CCP Organization Department. They were presumably ousted as part of a power struggle for the main positions of responsibility that the 1954 Constitution and the next Congress would assign.[11] But this episode had little impact on the Party's internal cohesion.

During this period, Mao, who had brought the Party to power, remained the undisputed leader. His position was also strengthened by three major initiatives he embarked on without garnering the approval of other members of the leadership: entry into the Korean War, the acceleration of collectivization and the launch of the Hundred Flowers Campaign. While the human cost of engagement on Korean soil was very high (180,000 dead), China benefited in terms of national security and prestige within the socialist camp. During 1955, Mao decided to accelerate agricultural collectivization after having slowed down the movement a few months earlier; the results at the end of 1956 beat even the most optimistic forecasts. As for the Hundred Flowers Campaign launched in 1956–57, although it weakened Mao for a few weeks, the turnaround in his position in mid-1957 allowed him to recover. Throughout this period, Mao's action was limited to the areas with which he was most familiar: revolution – the strategies that allowed the Party to strengthen its power and deepen social transformations – rural questions, foreign policy and relations with intellectuals. In areas with which he was unfamiliar, particularly in economic construction, Mao was content to arbitrate in a direction that remained orthodox. In order to build a socialist society, priority was given to the transformation of property structures and to rapid industrialization. Compared to later periods of the People's Republic, Mao's personal initiatives remained circumscribed and his political impact was relatively limited.[12]

Conclusion

Even though in 1957 the regime faced many problems, its achievements were significant: social order had been re-established, economic development initiated, national pride restored, the living conditions of the people improved, and institutional and social transformations made it possible to envisage the march towards socialism. These successes can be attributed to several factors. First, the Party's effectiveness in winning popular support. Initially, the United Front's policy, effective against the Japanese and the Guomindang, made it possible to maximize support. Then, the techniques of mass mobilization, tested in rural bases during the war, ensured the implementation of agrarian reform, and then collectivization. Force and violence convinced everyone that resistance was useless. Another positive element was Party unity. The importance of Soviet aid was another. During this initial period in the new regime's existence, the strategies implemented met the objectives in an efficient way. Collectivization was an acceptable solution to the problem of increasing agricultural production. The socialization of the urban private sector eliminated capitalism and facilitated the establishment of a planned economy. Mass movements made social transformations possible, while the establishment of strong institutions allowed for the planning of economic development. In later periods, the Party was divided, the population resisted and the strategies implemented were in contradiction to the objectives pursued.

Different regions and social groups did not live through these early years at the same pace or under the same conditions. Military campaigns continued after the autumn of 1949. Certain fractions of the national territory would not be totally 'liberated' – that is to say, invaded and conquered – until the end of 1951 or, in the case of Tibet, in 1952. Certain sections of society – intellectuals, the bourgeoisie – were subjected to more coercion than others; this was sometimes exercised in a public and violent manner, sometimes it was private and more subtle. This period also saw the establishment of the coercive apparatus that would constitute a cornerstone of the political apparatus. Propaganda institutions provided control over the media, education and, more broadly, people's minds. The public security system, prison institutions and labour camps were other tools for bringing society into line. In addition to noting the diversity of experiences, I have emphasized the pragmatic dimension of the decisions taken. The shortness of the period of New Democracy was not foreseen, let alone planned. The most recent studies have revealed the complexity, the disorder and even the erratic nature of government action in those early years.

Finally, I have insisted on the plurality of heritages on which the People's Republic was built. They included the practices of the Party in the liberated areas, the lessons of the Soviet experience, and also the legacy of the Nationalist Party. What was achieved in this first period was not only the extension of what the CCP had already put in place before 1949 – class struggle, the mass line – but also the continuation of measures initiated by the Guomindang; I have mentioned the launch of the New Life Movement, the militarization of the political and the establishment of growing state control over the economy. Among the first achievements of the regime, the reunification of the territory, the definitive expulsion of foreign imperialists, the reconstruction of a government with authority over the whole country and the return to peace all fulfilled aspirations dating from the mid-nineteenth century. They were not, properly speaking, part of a 'Communist' revolution.[13] In the framework of the People's Republic, the originality lay not so much in the objective (building a powerful unitary state to ensure economic and social development) or the means of achieving this (mobilizing society) as in the absolutism involved. Political power had never been so powerful and it combined with the ambition to gain popular support. Mass campaigns were thus the main mechanism for consolidating the regime and establishing socialism. Other political campaigns would follow: the Great Leap Forward, the Cultural Revolution, the fruit of a series of norms and practices that were developed during the period of the Civil War and these initial years. The results would be tragic because they would no longer allow the targeted objectives to be achieved. Successes would be followed by failures.

TWO

Maoism and Its Excesses (1958–1976)

The period 1958–76 was marked by two major and lastingly traumatic events for Chinese society as a whole: the Great Leap Forward (1958–60) and the Cultural Revolution (1966–69). These two episodes were extra-ordinary in more ways than one: the first because it caused the biggest famine in China in the twentieth century; the second because it was an operation to destroy the political apparatuses launched by the very same man who had contributed to their construction. The years 1960–65 and 1969–79 were intermediate periods in which few major decisions were taken and the latent conflicts between leaders did not lead to the victory of any one of them. These two decades ended with the death of Mao in September 1976.

The choice to present these various episodes together is due to the major political role played by supreme leader Mao Zedong against a backdrop of tensions and disagreements within the ruling elite. Unlike the previous period, which was characterized by a united political leadership, shifting coalitions of actors now clashed from one period to the next, over several issues. Simultaneously, throughout these two decades, the Party, accepted by the great majority while the regime was being established, lost its legitimacy among different sections of the population; relations between government and society were loosening.

The Great Leap Forward (1958–60)

The Great Leap Forward (*dayuejin* 大跃进) was an attempt to adapt the Soviet economic model to the specific circumstances of China in order to accelerate development. Until then, the strategy followed had been of Stalinist inspiration: priority was given to heavy industry, and in particular to metallurgy, while light industry and agriculture were neglected even though most of the population worked in these sectors. Costly in terms of investment, this strategy neglected the country's main asset: its large workforce. Mao amended the Soviet programme to take full advantage of this head start. The priority of heavy industry was maintained, but now agriculture was also to be taken into account. The economy must 'be able to walk on two legs' (*liang tiao tui zoulu* 两条腿走路). Although capital and technology were scarce, it was necessary to mobilize the only resource that China had in quantity, namely its workforce – especially in the agricultural sector, where growth would make it possible to provide the production necessary for the development of industry. In all sectors, innovation was stimulated and ambitious goals were set. In industry, increasing production meant using both modern and traditional methods; steel would be produced both in modern steel complexes and in the courtyards of houses. Technical norms, and those who formulated them, were despised: the point was to produce more, and faster. By redoubling efforts, the goal was to 'catch up with Great Britain in fifteen years' (*shiwunian ganshang yingguo* 十五年赶上英国).

Origins of the Great Leap Forward

Economic considerations were the main drivers of this shift in the development programme. The Soviet-style strategy of the planning system ensured a transfer of resources from agriculture to heavy industry. In the Soviet Union, agriculture generated export surpluses that helped to finance imports of machinery and technology, and to produce enough food for the growing urban workforce. In China, the agricultural surplus was much smaller. The dilemma facing the Chinese authorities was therefore the following: how could they convince farmworkers to increase their production and the volumes marketed – handed over to the state – while investment was concentrated in heavy industry? For Mao, the answer lay in political mobilization.

Societal considerations were also at the origin of the turnaround. The strategy defended by Chen Yun, a member of the Politburo and the main architect of the economic policy, was based on effective centralized planning capable of simultaneously developing agriculture, light industry and heavy industry. However, the central planning bodies had been an indirect victim of anti-rightist repression. This had ruled out any resorting to experts or the urban intelligentsia, and any development strategy based on their collaboration. Many competent personnel had been sent to the camps. Resources of human capital to carry out such a strategy had become scarce. Similarly, in the countryside, the anti-rightist movement was directed against those who had protested against collectivization, a policy that emphasized the organization of people's work as a factor likely to increase production. In town and country alike, the repression had therefore strengthened those who believed that the key to development lay in popular mobilization under the aegis of the Party, and not in calling on 'bourgeois experts' in the bureaucracy.

The launching of the Great Leap Forward was also due to the evolution of relations between the Party and the masses. The attempt at political liberalization in 1956–57, instead of restoring confidence, led to the deterioration of the social climate. The regime felt under threat, and hardened its line, radically reaffirming its project. According to Jean-Luc Domenach, the Great Leap Forward can be seen as 'the brutal reaction of a young political organization that had just suffered its first serious wound and suddenly, as if to ensure its existence, turned on what, in its view, had founded it'.[1]

Finally, the Great Leap Forward had strictly political causes. Mao's position in the political arena was affected by the type of economic development strategy being followed. The Party Chairman derived his authority from his positions on foreign policy, rural policy and social transformations, and was not at all familiar with planning, financial techniques or anything related to the urban economy. The complexity of the issues relating to economic development limited his role. Other factors were the history of the Party itself, and the nostalgia that was already taking hold for the Yan'an period, when the mobilization of the masses, the attacks on bureaucratism and the disdain for material obstacles had saved the Chinese revolution. Above all, differences within the ruling elite played an important role. Those at the top of the Communist Party were de facto divided on what to do. Liu Shaoqi, second in importance after Mao, and Deng Xiaoping, head of the Central Committee secretariat, had much to gain from the Great Leap Forward, which strengthened the role of the Party; they supported the strategy as early as 1958. Deng, who supported the anti-rightist campaign, played a key role in guiding the Great Leap Forward. Liu was more independent, but Mao, who was ready to cede his place as head of state, suggested that he stand 'in the second line'. Liu's support for Mao was undoubtedly linked to the former's need to obtain the favours of the latter. Indeed, Liu succeeded Mao as Chairman of the People's Republic in April 1959.

In 1958, the only two declared opponents were Premier Zhou Enlai and Chen Yun. Zhou Enlai saw the prerogatives of his administration being weakened as part of the Great Leap Forward. Chen Yun's opposition stemmed from a strategic disagreement. He believed that only material incentives (farmworkers should see their produce being bought at a good price and they should be able obtain consumer goods) could increase agricultural production, and that political exhortations would not suffice. Just as Stalin swept away Bukharin's opposition, so Mao ignored Chen Yun's advice. It was therefore a convergence of factors that contributed to the formal adoption of the policy of the Great Leap Forward in May 1958, on the occasion of the second session of the Eighth Party Congress. The creation of people's communes (*renmin gongshe* 人民公社) was adopted in August 1958.

Successive stages of the Great Leap Forward

At the beginning of 1958, confidence in and enthusiasm for the new policy were very real both within the Party and among the population. Excellent weather, which counterbalanced the confusion created by the people's communes, ensured good harvests. In industry, projects launched under the first Five-Year Plan were starting to bear fruit. In the autumn, field trips showed that the situation was deteriorating. In some areas, the excellent harvest was not being gathered because the peasants had been mobilized by local industry or had gone to town to work for state-owned enterprises; the population lacked food. At the end of 1958, Mao realized that adjustments had to be made. A second phase of rest and moderation began and lasted until the summer of 1959.

In July 1959, the plenary session of the Central Committee meeting in Lushan highlighted the divisions at the top of the Communist hierarchy. Peng Dehuai, Minister of Defence and one of the ten marshals of the People's Liberation Army (he came, moreover, from the same province as Mao Zedong), denounced the misdeeds of the Great Leap Forward. He is said to have become aware of the difficulties during a trip to his hometown of Xiangtan in Hunan. He is also said to have received numerous letters denouncing the famine and revealing to him the extent of the statistical falsifications.[2] Another event may have prompted his criticism: the visit he made to Eastern Europe in May 1959. He noted that the main cause of the Hungarian Uprising of 1956 was in fact the leftist excesses of the economy. He concluded that the Great Leap Forward carried within itself the seeds of a possible future uprising. On his trip, Peng met Khrushchev, who may also have expressed his dissatisfaction with the new Chinese strategy and its consequences in terms of military cooperation. Be that as it may, almost immediately after Peng's return to Beijing on 12 June 1959, the USSR suspended nuclear aid and, for the first time, voiced public criticism of Chinese strategy. When Mao launched his attack on Peng, he accused him of collaborating with Khrushchev.

On 14 July, unable to meet Mao, Peng wrote him a letter in which he summarized his criticisms. He questioned his excessive personal power, and expressed his belief that the damage induced by the Great Leap Forward was greater than the benefits. Mao then made this letter public, distributing it to all the participants in the plenary session. On 23 July, Mao drew a clear line between permitted criticism and Peng's 'rightist opportunism'. He declared that the latter was seeking not so much to give him advice, but to attack him personally. Peng and his clique needed to go through a process of rectification. All participants were surprised by the violence of Mao's response.

This violence was due not only to what Peng had stated, but also to the dispute between the two leaders. Thanks to the Great Leap Forward, Marshal Lin Biao, whose relationship with Peng Dehuai (his superior in the hierarchy) was prickly, returned to the forefront of the political scene and joined the Politburo Standing Committee in May 1958. Mao was undoubtedly seeking to get rid of Peng and he seized this opportunity. In addition, Liu Shaoqi succeeded Mao as Chairman of the Republic and appeared to be his successor. Perhaps Mao saw Peng's criticisms as an attempt to weaken him, including his right to appoint his own successor.

The plenary session marked a break in the history of the Party, which had until then tolerated quite heated internal debates, as long as all the leaders aligned themselves with the final decision adopted. In Lushan, Mao called internal criticism 'factional activity' and asked everyone to choose between him and his adversary. This marked the beginning of a fierce crackdown. At a meeting of the Central Military Commission in September 1959, Peng was formally removed from his post as Defence Minister and invited to engage in study for several years. Three other senior Party cadres, seen as of the same mind as Peng and described as a 'military clique', were also ousted. Mao's staunch supporter Lin Biao was promoted to Defence Minister, giving Mao more control than ever over the PLA. The crackdown affected the PLA more broadly, as well as any political leaders who were more or less reluctant to initiate the Great Leap Forward. In 1959 and 1960, 3.6 million Party members were purged.

As a second consequence of the Lushan plenary session, at the end of August 1959, the Great Leap Forward entered a final phase, combining a revival of radicalism with anti-rightist politics and lasting until September 1960. Attempts to consolidate matters were suspended and a second Great Leap Forward began, with disastrous consequences. Brief attempts to organize the urban communes took place, and urban cadres were sent out into the countryside. This strategy ended in failure. Statistics not published until 1981 revealed that agricultural production in 1960 represented only 75 per cent of that of 1958 and that it continued to decline in 1961. In heavy industry, production fell by 46 per cent in 1961 compared to 1960, then again by 22 per cent between 1961 and 1962. In light industry, production fell by 10 per cent in 1960, by 20 per cent in 1961 and by a further 8 per cent in 1962. Shortages of goods were combined with food shortages. This new Great Leap Forward resulted in the biggest famine of the twentieth century in China.

The Great Famine (1959–61)

The 'three years of great famine' (*sannian dajihuang* 三年大饥荒) were, until recently, not recognized in modern Chinese history. As a direct consequence of the Great Leap Forward, these years were not discussed. In addition, the Communist Party blocked all access to information about this episode. Since then, the gradual opening of the various Chinese archives has made it possible to better understand the contours of the Great Famine, thus corroborating what sociologists and historians could only speculate until they had access to different primary sources: the Chinese government bore the greater part of the responsibility for this tragedy, which involved scenes of horror (sickness, summary executions, cannibalism). Since 2008, historiography has taken a decisive step, focusing in particular on the local effects of famine, the behaviour of cadres and the attempts of the starving to survive.[3]

The number of victims is controversial. Mortality rates (per 1,000 inhabitants) rose from eleven in 1957 to fourteen in 1959, jumping to twenty-eight in 1960, then dropping to fourteen in 1961. The impact was greatest in 1960. Based on statistics published in the early 1980s, opinions differ. Xizhe Peng has stated that there were 23 million dead in fourteen provinces.[4] According to Basil Ashton, there were 30 million deaths and an equivalent shortfall in births.[5] Jasper Becker, drawing on documents internal to the Chinese government, estimates the number of victims to have been between 43 and 46 million.[6] Yang Jisheng estimates that 36 million people lost their lives abnormally and that the deficit in births approached 40 million. Thus, the Great Famine would have cost China nearly 76 million people.

The famine hit provinces and regions very unevenly. The cities were relatively safe and the phenomenon was mainly rural. At the end of 1960, when the food crisis hit certain regions, the central government decided to import grain from Australia and Canada. The northernmost provinces, from Heilongjiang to Inner Mongolia, Shanxi and Shaanxi, suffered less than most; while Anhui, Henan, Sichuan, Gansu and Guizhou were among those most affected. All kinds of factors explain these differences: the number of collective canteens, the predominance of agriculture, the level of poverty in the province and the radicalism of provincial leaders. The two neighbouring provinces of Jiangxi and Anhui experienced contrasting situations: a surplus of 180,000 deaths in the first (1.06 per cent of its population) and 6,330,000 in the second (18.37 per cent of its population). The gap stems from the difference in natural conditions (much more favourable in the less densely populated Jiangxi), the difference in tax levies (lower in the former revolutionary bases of Jiangxi) and, finally, the unequal zeal shown by provincial leaders in carrying out food requisitions and running the infrastructure: the majority of zealous provincial leaders were acting less out of conviction than out of careerism.[7]

In order to survive, peasants adopted all kinds of strategies. Sometimes the local authorities themselves promoted and praised plant and animal food substitutes: bark, stems, leaves, roots, insects, rats and field mice.

Some people sold their children. Others chose to run away. Young women prostituted themselves. Cannibalism was the most extreme survival technique. In the province of Anhui (where 15 per cent of the population died – between 5 and 6 million people), in the district of Hao, due to recurrent cases of cannibalism, there was even a trade in human flesh. It was sold by some at market stalls, while others traded as itinerant vendors, moving from one township to another.[8]

Natural causes

The first official speech on the disaster took place during the so-called Seven Thousand Cadres conference which met in January 1962. In a speech, Liu Shaoqi blamed the famine on 'leftist errors', on the lack of experience in the construction of socialism, and on the weather. Leftist mistakes were the result of over-enthusiasm on the part of cadres. Thus, the tragedy was the result of good intentions.[9] Decisions that had resulted in millions of deaths become mere 'mistakes'. Liu Shaoqi quoted a farmer in Hunan province for whom the disaster was caused 70 per cent by human action and 30 per cent by nature. The role of natural disasters was debated at the top of the Communist hierarchy. In the end, the official position used opposite proportions, so as to clear the Communist Party: the official thesis remains that the disaster was caused 70 per cent by natural disasters, and 30 per cent by human error. In the text adopted by the Central Committee in 1981, entitled *Resolution on the History of the Party since the Founding of the People's Republic*, the catastrophe was blamed both on leftist errors (the struggle 'against rightist deviationism'), the weather, and the withdrawal of Soviet experts – a point that Liu did not mention in his speech in 1962. In 1981, external forces – the weather and relations with the Soviet Union – therefore occupied a greater place in the official explanation of the disaster.

The argument that natural disasters were to blame is not convincing. Although 1959, 1960 and 1961 were all years of floods (rainfall 80 per cent higher than the annual average), they were distinctly lower than those of 1954 or 1973. In addition, the floods were of normal volume in those years, whereas the floods of 1954 were extremely severe, causing drownings, but not large-scale famine. In general, if we compare the weather in the years of the Great Famine with the years before and after, from 1951 to 1990, precipitation in the years of the Great Famine was not exceptional.[10]

Human errors

The main reason for this famine came from the excessive demands of the Great Leap Forward. Since the country had set very high production targets and estimates, peasants were forced to sell much more to the state, including by digging into their own rations of cereals, fodder and seeds. During the Great Leap Forward, Mao set up a never-ending race to reach numerical objectives. All administrative levels (provinces, cities, districts, municipalities, factories) were involved in reaching objectives whose figures were falsified. This race for numbers had disastrous effects. Indeed, the inflated figures served as the basis for the various production quotas levied, in particular for export. As a result, the proportion of crops seized was much greater than it should have been, which de facto worsened the famine.

The construction of collective canteens – as peasants were requested not to take their meals at home – is also considered to be one of the main causes of the famine.[11] The day after the Lushan plenary session, the campaign against rightists gave new impetus to the canteens: by the end of 1959, they were feeding 400 million people, more than seven out of ten members of the people's communes (98 per cent in Henan, one of the provinces where the famine was the most devastating). According to Yang Jisheng, if this practice had not been implemented, the death toll could have been reduced by a third and even in some areas by half.

Political responsibilities

With the notable exception of Chen Yun, one of the few leaders who expressed reservations, most members of the regime were silent, or even stated their approval of what they actually disapproved of. The most controversial aspect is Mao's personal responsibility.[12] At the end of the autumn of 1958, he condemned certain current practices, such as peasants being forced to work without being fed or given necessary rest, all of which was resulting in epidemics, famine and deaths. During the pause phase from September 1958 to July 1959, Mao was informed that production was being carried out to the detriment of the living conditions of the population, and was warned of cases of epidemics – typhoid fever, dysentery, polio – associated with the population being inadequately fed. In the spring of 1959, Mao even denounced the leftist excesses that had been committed. But in July 1959, after the confrontation with Peng Dehuai, he revived the radical policies he had previously condemned. According to Thomas Bernstein, Mao deliberately chose to ignore the lessons learned from the first phase of the Great Leap Forward in order to be able to achieve the ideological and development goals he had set for himself. Forgetting the lessons of the end of 1958, Mao's acts betrayed a wilfulness and stubbornness that make him responsible for the catastrophe.[13]

According to Frank Dikötter,[14] Mao was informed in real time of the dire situation; he received numerous reports about it, as well as personal letters from courageous individuals warning him of the disaster. However, he ignored them for at least two reasons. On the one hand, he saw the Great Leap Forward as a military campaign in which any casualties were a necessary evil. On the other hand, in general, for all those leaders of the Party who had lived through the campaigns of encirclement of the Guomindang, the Long March and the Civil War, these losses seemed minor compared to the Communist paradise that was being built. In addition, several official reports sent to Mao, such as those by Communist economists Li Xiannian, Li Fuchun and Bo Yibo, insisted that the food problems did not stem from a drop in production, but from inadequate routing between the productive countryside and the towns.

In October 1960, the leaders became aware of the catastrophe and put an end to radical collectivist policies; in the countryside, this meant a return to families working the land. Politically, the Great Leap Forward and the famine put an end to the consensus within the country's leadership for a long time; they were now divided on a whole series of issues. While Mao recognized that political mobilization alone could not produce accelerated economic growth, he remained convinced that it could play a role, though others believed otherwise. While he was optimistic about the pace of a return to normal, others were less so. His prestige was severely affected. In the ranks of the Party, demoralization spread. The paradox is that after such a failure and such a catastrophe, the

Communist Party and its leader contrived to remain in power, a paradox that can be explained in part by the way in which the government managed the memory of the event.[15]

Pragmatism and political divisions (1960–65)

At the end of 1960, the policy of the Great Leap Forward was therefore abandoned. Mao, forced to defend himself against various attacks, stepped back and let Liu Shaoqi and Deng Xiaoping restore in tandem a more pragmatic economic policy, in collaboration with Zhou Enlai, Chen Yun and economic officials. Opposition grew between Mao and the Party's ruling hierarchy. However, at the end of 1962, Mao again took the initiative and succeeded in getting the Party to approve a direction that was ever more radical and divergent from that of the USSR. The army started to play a leading role in the mass campaigns that heralded the Cultural Revolution.

Mao's adjustment programme and political withdrawal

In July 1960, the Soviet Union put an end to all scientific and technical cooperation with Beijing, which needed to deal with the deterioration in the agricultural situation. At a conference held in Beidaihe in July and August, the Second Great Leap was officially ended and the policy was now 'agriculture at the base, industry as the dominant factor'. Agriculture now took precedence over heavy industry and the watchwords were 'consolidation and readjustment'. Liu Shaoqi, Chairman of the Republic, and Deng Xiaoping, Deputy Premier and Secretary General of the Central Committee, carried out investigative work in the form of inquiries that served as the basis for a series of programmatic texts.

The 'Sixty Articles on People's Communes' (1960) saw the production team as the basic accounting unit and authorized private plots of land. This charter essentially governed Chinese agriculture until 1978. The increase in the number of people's communes was accompanied by a reduction in their size. The 'Seventy Articles on Industry' (1961) rehabilitated experts and the use of material incentives. Material incentives and the remuneration of piecework were re-established in factories.

The 'Eight Articles on Literature and the Arts' (1962) promised the reintroduction of traditional art forms and allowed artists to tackle new subjects. The 'Sixty Articles on Higher Education' (1962) stressed the need for quality education. All these policies marked a departure from the priorities of the Great Leap Forward. Experts and expertise were again at the forefront. Central bureaucracy was again privileged over local initiatives. The masses were appealed to not through ideological mobilization, but on the basis of private material interest.

In January–February 1962, during the aforementioned conference of 7,000 cadres, the leaders gave their explanations for the Great Leap Forward. This was an opportunity for the open manifestation of differences. Liu Shaoqi gave the main speech. Regarding the method of leadership, he called for more democratic centralism and less personal leadership. He criticized the violence of the campaign against 'rightist opportunists', and called for the rehabilitation of Peng Dehuai. Deng Xiaoping reaffirmed the interest of 'Mao Zedong thought', but at the same time supported Liu by calling for the rehabilitation of the rightists. Peng Zhen, Mayor of Beijing and Party leader for the capital, delivered the speech most critical of Mao. He questioned the role of the Party: the central power approved false information, issued contradictory directives and ignored economic reality. In this context of trenchant criticism, Mao conducted his own self-criticism and admitted his incompetence in the economic field. In the months that followed, Mao withdrew from the daily routines of political life. He increasingly delegated the conduct of internal affairs to the Party secretariat and to the government. He no longer sat at the meetings of the Politburo. The decision-making process became more and more informal.

Within the ruling elite, there was a clash between two different views of the situation. For Mao, supported by some, including Lin Biao in the army, the country was on the road to recovery and so it was again becoming possible to accelerate the transition to socialism. Mao also opposed any further decollectivization in agriculture. For Liu Shaoqi, Deng Xiaoping and Chen Yun, the situation had not recovered. In the countryside, decollectivization needed to be pursued. In the cities, former capitalists and the intelligentsia needed to be encouraged to restore the economy. This was the context in which Deng, defending individual farming, uttered an aphorism that would make him famous:

'It doesn't matter if a cat is white or black, as long as it catches mice.' The clash between these two approaches took place in Beidaihe in August 1962. In an atmosphere of political tension, Mao stressed the need to continue the class struggle. He criticized campaigning for a system of individual responsibility and called for a campaign of 'socialist education' to rectify the Party apparatus in rural areas. He warned of the danger of capitalist or feudal restoration.

Socialist Education Movement (1962–65)

Mao may have been in the background, but he remained dominant in two areas: the conduct of diplomacy, on the one hand, and military matters on the other. The conflict that developed in the Party was in fact closely linked to the ideological dispute between Beijing and Moscow. In view of the improvement in the economic situation, Mao relaunched the collectivist and egalitarian themes developed in 1958. Mistrustful of cadres and intellectuals, he believed that only mobilization of the masses and external control of the Party could prevent a revisionist degeneration of China, analogous to that experienced by the Soviet Union. Lin Biao, loyal to Mao, and Defence Minister since September 1959, endeavoured to consolidate his position in the army. Lin thus took a series of initiatives to strengthen the role of the army within the Party.

Lin made appointments in order to better ensure his control over the Defence Ministry. He re-established the pre-eminent position of the Party's Central Military Commission (CMC), whose role was diminished due to disagreements between Peng Dehuai and Mao. By re-establishing the role of the CMC, Lin brought Mao, the only civilian member of the Commission, closer to the military. Lin also increased the number of Party members in the military. The first provincial secretaries became political commissioners of the army, which placed them under the authority of the general policy department of the PLA. Leaders of military districts became secretaries of regional Party offices. In this way, double affiliations to the Party and the army increased, with the effect of strengthening the political role of the PLA.

Lin encouraged the study of 'Mao Zedong Thought' in the military. In September 1960, he launched a movement for the study of politics in order to restore the morale of troops severely affected by famine in the

44

countryside. In order to give access to Mao's texts to mostly illiterate soldiers, a collection of simplified texts was produced, *The Thoughts of Chairman Mao* or, more literally, *Quotations from Chairman Mao* (*Mao zhuxi yulu* 毛主席语录), often known as the *Little Red Book*. From 1962, the PLA also increased its control over the civilian population, setting up a civilian militia under military control.

A few months after being criticized, in September 1962 Mao launched a new rectification campaign called the Socialist Education Movement (*shehuizhuyi jiaoyu yundong* 社会主义教育运动). Initially confined to rural cadres, it then spread to culture as a whole. At the tenth plenary session, which met from 24 to 27 September, conflicts between leaders were expressed openly. Mao reaffirmed the need to continue the class struggle. He opposed decollectivization and demanded that communes remain intact or be re-established where they had been dissolved. The first act of the movement was the dismissal of Deng Zihui, head of the Rural Labour Department of the Party, who had opposed Mao's agrarian policies since 1955, and who had been replaced during the Great Leap Forward by Tan Zhenlin. Certain economic freedoms and the system of contracts conceded a few months previously were also repealed. A gigantic field survey was launched, requiring the dispatch of numerous teams to check on local cadres. The results of this investigation were used as a basis for the drafting of the programme published in February 1963 under the name of the 'Ten Point Circular'; Mao played a personal role in the drafting of this document. This text relaunched the class struggle in the countryside. He denounced former landowners, rich peasants and the new bourgeoisie who were profiting from the commercial activities that had been newly authorized. He denounced false accounting, fraud in collective granaries, the misappropriation of state property and the incorrect allocation of work points. Yet, at this point in the movement, the cadres should be subject to only moderate criticism, as '95 per cent of cadres are good or relatively good'. It was the local associations of poor peasants, who had spearheaded the accelerated collectivization, who were to exercise control.

This first text was followed by two other documents that revealed the struggles between leaders to control the movement. A second circular, drafted by Peng Zhen and Deng Xiaoping, was published in September 1963. It prescribed corrective measures adapted to the evils observed, and organized the reform of the Party. It would be vigorously denounced as revisionist by the Cultural Revolution. It nevertheless deepened the movement – but by hierarchical and punctilious methods, rather than by an appeal to the masses.

In September 1964, a new Ten Point Circular, this time written by Liu Shaoqi, was published. Rural cadres were excluded from the survey process and replaced by thousands of urban cadres sent into the field. Between 5 and 10 per cent of the rural cadres (between 1.5 and 2.5 million people) were purged. The model of self-sufficiency promoted by the Dazhai brigade in Shanxi province, dear to Mao, was questioned, a sign of Mao's difficulty in winning acceptance for his ideas on agricultural policy. In another area, that of cultural policy, Jiang Qing, Mao's wife, was also struggling to make her ideas triumph. In June 1964, the Party secretariat created a group to coordinate reform efforts with Peng Zhen as its head. But this group continued to adopt the preferences of the Beijing establishment, represented in the group by Lu Dingyi, head of the Party's Propaganda Department. The only area where Mao's views won the day was the army.

Maoization of the PLA and preparation for war

Throughout this period, Lin Biao took a series of initiatives which led to the Maoization of the military institution. In 1963, the People's Liberation Army established several figures as models of political righteousness, including Private Lei Feng, who had died in a traffic accident but won praise for his devotion to his comrades and his selflessness. In December, Mao called on the people to 'learn from the PLA'. The release of *The Thoughts of Chairman Mao* began in May 1964. In 1965, military ranks were removed, at least nominally, as were the distinguishing signs related to them, and the spirit of Yan'an was glorified. This initiative made the army appear as the most politically advanced body, since it was putting into practice the egalitarian ideals of the revolution. In 1965, the PLA took control of the public security forces, which would be of great service to Mao and Lin during the Cultural Revolution.

Simultaneously, and throughout this period, the PLA was almost continuously on a war footing. A first conflict, linked to the vagueness of the borders in the province of Tibet, pitted China against India on the borders of the Himalayas. The Tibetan crisis of 1959 – the uprising of the population against the gradual takeover of Tibet by Beijing and the flight of the Dalai Lama to India – led to military clashes in the autumn of 1962, in which the PLA emerged victorious, though this brought no substantial solution to the problem of the delimitation of the borders. The PLA also intervened in Burma between November 1960 and February 1961, when it was called on by the Burmese government to attack the Guomindang groups who had taken refuge in its territory since the end of the Civil War. In June 1962, the PLA was also preparing for an invasive operation conducted from Taiwan.

The economy had been largely at the service of the defence industries for several years. Already during the Great Leap Forward, the whole of society was told to follow the example of the PLA: everyone should learn to become a soldier. New plans for arms production were launched. Many civilian industrial establishments were transformed into defence industries. After 1963, approximately 3,000 factories would be

1965, soldiers participating in earthworks, Nanning area.
Source: Marc Riboud / Fonds Marc Riboud au MNAAG / Magnum Photos

transformed. The defence industries were put into a state of maximum mobilization during the 1960s.

In the mid-1960s, the so-called 'Third Front' strategy was implemented, which consisted of moving industrial establishments deemed too vulnerable to attack either from the Soviets in the northeast or from the United States (which was increasingly active in Vietnam) in the south. This was particularly the case of industrial establishments engaged in nuclear power. At the end of 1965, China was de facto a highly militarized society preparing for war. The best graduates went to work in defence industries or industries related to defence. Priority was given to the defence industry and to the development of new weapons, in particular nuclear weapons and missiles. These were Mao's decisions and they met with very little resistance among the political leadership.

The most common view of the period 1960–65 focuses on political conflicts within the elite, conflicts that are seen as the premise of the Cultural Revolution. Liu Shaoqi, Deng Xiaoping, Zhou Enlai and Chen Yun were in the spotlight, while Mao, who wished to relaunch the 'class struggle', was in the background. However, other trajectories would have been possible. Without the Cultural Revolution, militarization of society and the economy could have been the main story of China in the 1960s.[16] Besides the power struggles within the apparatuses and the conduct of class struggle, other state-building processes were at work. These included the growing role of law in the regulation of conflicts (divorce thus became an almost standard process) and in the regulation of crime (which was on the decline). These processes of institutionalizing the regime were halted by the Cultural Revolution and would not resume until after 1976.

The Cultural Revolution (1966–69)

According to official history, the Great Proletarian Cultural Revolution (*wuchan jieji wenhua dageming* 无产阶级文化大革命) describes the ten-year period that began with the return of Mao to the political scene in 1966 and ended with the arrest of the Gang of Four (*siren bang* 四人帮), whose main leaders were Jiang Qing, Zhang Chunqiao, Yao Wenyuan and Wang Hongwen. The new political leadership then officially proclaimed the end of the episode. Strictly speaking, the term

'Cultural Revolution' refers solely to the three years of anarchy and hysteria that Mao provoked by launching young high school and college students, the Red Guards (*hongweibing* 红卫兵), against the Party apparatuses. Criticizing the very real bureaucratization of the regime, Mao was launching a new revolution so that the regime would become again what it no longer was: revolutionary.

This was not a circumstantial episode but a major break in the history of the People's Republic and of twentieth-century China. Its consequences have lasted right up to the present day.[17] The failure of the Cultural Revolution, indeed, led China, under the leadership of Deng Xiaoping, to embrace the Western model of economic development. From this point of view, it was to prove the source of a far greater upheaval in mentalities than even Mao had imagined. What is unique about this period is that the political crisis was deliberately initiated by the supreme leader of the regime. Mao himself questioned the legitimacy of the Party. He mobilized social forces that would weaken his own government. He provided activists with the political and ideological rhetoric to drive the protests. The man who had brought down the Guomindang regime was launching a revolt against the regime and the men he himself had appointed. But, unlike 1949, this second revolution was not guided by a vision or a project. It simply overthrew the old regime, leaving behind chaos and disorder.

The Cultural Revolution was, first and foremost, the result of the conflicts that divided the political elites. It was a power struggle at the top conducted via a mass movement that degenerated into a spontaneous movement that was harshly suppressed.[18] The political dimension was therefore much more important than the properly cultural dimension. The Cultural Revolution can even be seen as Mao's last great revolutionary project.[19] It involved responding in advance to any risk of a shift in Chinese Communism on the revisionist model set up in the USSR on the coming to power of Khrushchev. It also entailed an analysis of the internal situation and Mao's desire to silence the criticisms formulated within the Party itself following the Great Leap Forward. This political struggle at the top left its mark on individuals and families, mainly in the cities, who experienced suffering and trauma. Thus, the Cultural Revolution marks a break not only in the political history of modern China, but also in that of individuals and families whose lives were lastingly marked: a whole generation of young Chinese men and women would not go to college.

Between 1966 and 1969, there were four successive periods. The beginnings of the Cultural Revolution lasted from autumn 1965 until the spring of 1966. Mao developed a political base, bringing him into conflict with the leaders of the CCP whom he considered to be 'revisionist.' At the eleventh plenary session in August 1966, he obtained the support of the Central Committee for a critique of revisionism on a much larger scale. He then launched the Red Guards on Party institutions. At the end of 1966, political institutions in many Chinese cities were breaking down. Between January and August 1967, attempts to seize power by the Red Guards and revolutionary rebels were accompanied by the increasing prominence of the proletariat and the People's Army; the country sank into civil war. During the summer of 1967, the repression of the Red Guards by the armed forces began; the Cultural Revolution strictly speaking ended with the holding of the Tenth Party Congress in April 1969.

The beginnings (October 1965–July 1966)

The Cultural Revolution began with the critique of a play. In October 1965, the Shanghai newspaper *Wenhui Bao* (文汇报) published an article attacking *Hai Rui Dismissed From Office*, a play written by Wu Han, one of Beijing's deputy mayors. The play is about a mandarin sacked by a Ming Emperor whom he has criticized. The newspaper article was signed by Yao Wenyuan, a propagandist close to Jiang Qing. In the eyes of the Maoists, this play indirectly advocated the rehabilitation of Peng Dehuai, and thus entailed a questioning of the Great Leap Forward. As well as the author, it was in fact Peng Zhen, Mayor of Beijing (and, more importantly, the man in charge of the group formed in June 1964 to reform cultural policy), who was being targeted. A few months later, in May 1966, the same newspaper published another article by Yao Wenyuan which this time attacked *The Three Family Village*, a series of already old chronicles by three authors, Teng To, Wu Han and Liao Mosha. The article was then reproduced throughout the national press. Yao Wenyuan questioned the way these chronicles praised upright mandarins and thus, in his view, fostered nostalgia.

The supporters of a new cultural policy won their first victory in May 1966. The 'Cultural Revolution group' in charge of drafting a charter for the Cultural Revolution and comprising five leaders, including Peng Zhen, Lu Dingyi – Minister of Culture and head of the Propaganda Department of the Central Committee – and Kang Sheng, was dismissed. Peng Zhen was accused of seeking to impose a rightist direction on the revolution and resisting Mao's thought. As of 16 May 1966, a new 'Cultural Revolution group' was formed, which now brought together Jiang Qing, Kang Sheng, Chen Boda, Yao Wenyuan and Zhang Chunqiao. The same day, a circular from the Central Committee, known as the 'May 16 Circular' (or the 'May 16 Notification'), justified the nascent revolutionary movement. The Great Proletarian Cultural Revolution was launched. Henceforth, and until the plenary session of August 1966, the Party was led by two competing groups: one comprised Mao and his circle, called on the students to rebel and developed an unprecedented personality cult around the Party Chairman; the other was led by Liu Shaoqi, Chairman of the Republic since 1959, and Party administration officials who endeavoured to channel the struggle against 'revisionism' into the conventional framework of a rectification movement.

A few days later, the movement was launched on the campus of Peking University (*Beijing daxue* 北京大学). On 25 May, Nie Yuanzi, then Party Secretary of the philosophy department of the University, and six other comrades wrote the first 'Marxist-Leninist *dazibao*' calling on students to rebel against their professors and to defend Chairman Mao. This *dazibao* (大字报 big character poster) singled out the Rector of the University, Lu Bing, as a target for the students and became another founding text of the Cultural Revolution. Yuanzi's attack was actually orchestrated by Kang Sheng. In fact, none of the original signatories of this document was actually a student; all were members of cadres or teachers of Marxism-Leninism, and all (except one) were veteran members of the Party.

On 1 June, Mao ordered that Nie's text be published throughout the country; he called it 'a declaration even more beautiful than that of the Paris Commune'. Immediately, schools and universities became polemical battlegrounds; this was the beginning of a significant movement of criticism of intellectuals and teachers led by the students themselves. *The People's Daily* announced that the 'imperialists' must be purged. In June 1966, working groups were sent by the Politburo of the Central Committee to Peking University, and to institutes and secondary schools in Beijing and the provinces, to calm things down. At Peking University, however, Nie's group won a total victory. The University's senior administrators and teachers were attacked; the aim was to eliminate all those who had the wrong class origins or connections with people abroad. Public sessions of accusation were held; there were similar sessions throughout the country. The accused wore high paper hats, with slogans around their necks or on their bodies, and they were subjected to physical violence: their arms were tied behind their backs, their hair was pulled and sometimes they were severely beaten. On 17 June 1966 alone, on the Peking University campus, 178 cadres, teachers and students were dragged onto stands, accused in front of a screaming crowd, and beaten violently.

On 24 July, the working groups were dissolved, a sign of the victory of the hardliners in the Cultural Revolution. On 26 July, the Party decided to close universities and secondary schools for six months, as an excuse to take time to reform education systems and curricula; they would remain closed for several years. On 28 July, the Red Guards wrote a letter to Mao justifying the purges; Mao responded with his support in an article entitled 'Fire on the headquarters' (*paoda silingbu* 炮打司令部).

In August, the eleventh plenary session of the Central Committee put an end to the diarchy of power. Because only half the members took part and a certain number of Red Guards from the city of Beijing were present, the decisions taken amounted to a real coup d'état. Under the control of the army, which was now run by revolutionaries, the plenary session reorganized the top of the Party hierarchy: Peng Zhen was expelled from the Politburo, Liu Shaoqi was relegated from second to eighth place in the hierarchy, Lin Biao replaced him as number two in the regime and Mao's presumed successor, while Kang Sheng and Chen Boda, leaders of the new Cultural Revolution group, entered the Politburo. On 8 August, the plenary session adopted a 'Sixteen Point Declaration'. The Cultural Revolution now pursued a new objective: 'to destroy everything in the superstructure that does not correspond with the socialist economic base' and 'to overthrow those in the Party who hold authority and have taken the capitalist path'. This plenary session transformed what was still a student movement into a nationwide mass campaign, calling on not only students but also workers, peasants, soldiers and all revolutionaries to 'transform the superstructure'.

This text also opened up spaces of freedom by authorizing 'the four great freedoms' (*sida ziyou* 四大自由) of the 'great democracy' (*da minzhu* 大民主): the rights 'to speak freely, to express one's opinion, to write large print posters and to organize debates'. Even if these freedoms were part of a constrained ideological climate, for many young activists they signified the end of classes and the chance to travel without limits across the country to propagate the thought of Mao Zedong. Many young people enthusiastically joined the Red Guard movement.

Mobilization of the Red Guards (August 1966–January 1967)

The Cultural Revolution was like a huge rectification movement in which the accusers, as in the Hundred Flowers Campaign, came from outside the Party. This time, it was the younger generation that played the main role in the attempt to purify the Party from its 'bourgeois' and 'revisionist' elements and embark on the struggle to 'put down the four old things' (*po sijiu* 破四旧): old ideas, culture, customs and habits. Starting from the spontaneous organizations that emerged in universities and schools, the Red Guards gradually included many employees of administrations and businesses.

The Red Guards played their part in the most exalted moments of the Cultural Revolution; on 18 August 1966 and the days that followed, they paraded in their millions in Beijing. Holding up the *Little Red Book*, they sang 'The East is Red' (*dongfang hong* 东方红), which had become the de facto national anthem. This song compared the supreme ruler to the sun: 'The East is red / The sun is rising / In China, Mao Zedong has appeared.' It was broadcast throughout the day over loudspeakers in every town and village. The Red Guard parade in Beijing followed another major episode in the ruler's personality cult, when the press revealed that on 16 July Mao had swum for an hour and five minutes in the Yangtze River in Wuhan. While rumours circulated about his state of health, 5,000 people had apparently swum at the same time as him. Rafts, bearing his image and covered with slogans and multi-coloured banners, floated on the river.

The Red Guard organizations recruited their members according to contradictory criteria: they were either children of the 'red' categories or, on the contrary, of the classes that the Party had persecuted since 1949. These different factions clashed, often violently, and the situation sometimes got out of control. In Beijing, on the Beida campus, by mid-October 1966, 3,000 students had formed a total of ninety-two separate organizations, of which only three were of significant size. Half of the teachers' residences and 80 per cent of middle and senior cadres were checked out. The Red Guards conducted a total of 536 apartment inspections and countless interrogations and struggle sessions (*pidou dahui* 批斗大会).[20]

Some authors have argued that the rival factions of the Red Guard organized themselves on a social basis. 'Conservative' factions tended to bring together individuals in a favourable social position – students from intellectual families in universities or well-paid skilled workers in factories, for example; as supporters of the existing system, they felt that the institutions and traditions of the Party must be preserved. 'Radical' factions included members from much less favourable social positions who therefore had every interest in overthrowing the existing system: students from working-class families with poor university results or workers of rural origin leading precarious lives in the cities.

An analysis of the clashes between the two main rival factions on the Beida campus suggests that this assessment needs to be qualified.[21] The two clashing factions were doctrinally and programmatically very similar, and the struggles were more about personalities. The factual conflicts were the result of competition and rivalry between groups from the same movement hostile to the old Party leadership, a movement that had its origin within the very same Party apparatus.

Another initiative taken by Mao at the eleventh plenary session consisted of setting up new places of power by creating revolutionary committees (*geming weiyuanhui* 革命委员会) elected from within each working or teaching unit. These committees had to remain under the leadership of the Party. Mao's intention, therefore, was not to dismantle the Party or make it lose its leadership role, but to replace a large proportion of the central and local officials. Mao shifted centres of power in the apparatus rather than destroying it. At the top of the apparatus, the Central Committee and the Politburo lost all power. This was exercised by Mao on whom directly depended four separate bodies with varying responsibilities. Between 1966 and 1968, the Cultural Revolution group – Chen Boda, Jiang Qing, Kang Sheng, Zhang Chunqiao, Yao Wenyuan and three Red Guard chiefs – was the country's main decision-making body. The army, controlled by Lin Biao, constituted a second place of power and, from January 1967, played a role both in protecting the country's vital services and in supporting the radical left. The security services, both official (the Ministry of Public Security) and unofficial (led by Kang Sheng), constituted a third pole. Finally, the State Council, headed by Zhou Enlai, was one institution that remained relatively untouched during the years 1966–68. Zhou continued to exert a real influence on the conduct of state affairs. In the provinces, the Party apparatus struggled to resist attacks from Red Guard organizations, but collapsed in late 1966/early 1967 in the places where the latter were powerful.

Militarization in the face of revolutionary seizures of power (January–August 1967)

At the end of 1966, the situation in Shanghai became more and more unstable. Aligning themselves with the excesses of the student organizations of the Red Guard, factory workers and office workers eagerly turned on the Party committees of their work units, and in turn formed rebel groups. At the beginning of November, Wang Hongwen, a 33-year-old textile worker, established the Headquarters of the Revolutionary Revolt of Shanghai Workers, which the city authorities refused to recognize. Zhang Chunqiao, sent by Beijing as a conciliator, endorsed the demands of the headquarters and ordered Shanghai's First Secretary, Cao Diqiu, to make a public self-criticism. Two days later, Mao approved of Zhang Chunqiao's action and further proclaimed that in all commercial, industrial and government establishments, workers had the legitimate right to form mass organizations. Like the student Red Guards, workers' groups were divided into rival factions: anarchist 'revolutionary rebels' against the organizations in power, and 'proletarian revolutionaries' keen to preserve the Party's leadership. On 30 December 1966, tens of thousands of workers waged street battles. Strikes broke out. The port was paralysed. The workers sent to the countryside during the famine following the

Great Leap Forward demanded the right to return. On 3 January 1967, Wang Hongwen, at the head of his rebel group, took control of the city's major newspapers. On 9 January, supported by Zhang Chunqiao and Yao Wenyuan, the Red Guards overthrew the municipal government of Shanghai. Mao then instructed Zhang Chunqiao to set up a new government, the People's Commune of Shanghai (*Shanghai renmin gongshe* 上海人民公社) proclaimed on 5 February, supposedly on the model of the Paris Commune. In terms of elections, the commune was established with the help of the army, which Zhang Chunqiao used to get the city back on track in the face of the radical Red Guards. The immediate effect of the seizure of power in Shanghai was to give a powerful impetus to revolutionary violence.

At the beginning of 1967, the first revolutionary committees were formed in Shanghai, Heilongjiang, Guizhou and Shandong, but in most provinces the process was far from smooth. More often than not, conflicts erupted between the incumbent civil power, the military forces and the mass organizations, which were themselves divided. During the first six months of 1967, only six out of the twenty-nine provinces succeeded in establishing their revolutionary committees. The increasingly violent clashes were sometimes armed. In some provinces, radical groups seized weapons at PLA premises, while the latter provided conservative organizations with weapons.

In February 1967, certain important members of the Politburo began to denounce the very process of the Cultural Revolution. Chen Yi, the historic head of the Red Army who had become foreign minister in 1958, and Field Marshal Ye Jianying openly expressed their criticisms – which Mao saw as a questioning of his legitimacy and his pre-eminence. These attacks had the effect of reviving the movement, just as Peng Dehuai's attacks on the Great Leap Forward in Lushan had revived the latter. More and more leaders were targeted by the Red Guards. Liu Shaoqi and Deng Xiaoping were attacked in the Press and then arrested in the summer of 1967. The former, expelled from the Party by the twelfth plenary session of the Central Committee in October 1968, was sent to prison, where he died in 1969; the second went into internal exile in Canton. Chen Yi was himself violently taken to task and removed from power despite the protection of Zhou Enlai. He nevertheless retained his titles, but no longer had any responsibilities.

The events that unfolded in Wuhan in July 1967 revealed the tensions arising from the interventions of the PLA, which had been requested to facilitate the establishment of new structures of power. As in many large cities, the capital of Hubei was the scene of relentless fighting between competing factions of the Red Guards. On 14 July, Mao visited the city, which was increasingly paralysed by clashes between the Workers' General Headquarters, the revolutionary faction entrenched on a University campus, and the Million Heroes, a conservative faction that recruited from among steelworkers and included many Party members. While Mao decided to support the revolutionary faction, the local garrison refused to comply and gave its support to the Million Heroes. Mao was forced to leave the city secretly; on 19 July, the two envoys from Beijing were kidnapped. Troops directly controlled by the government of Beijing and the intervention of Zhou Enlai quickly put an end to this incipient civil war.

The return to order (1967–69): bringing the Red Guards to heel and the Ninth Congress

One of the consequences of the events in Wuhan was a resurgence of radicalism. Among the victims of this new impetus were foreign diplomats and the Ministry of Foreign Affairs. Diplomats stationed in Beijing were attacked and the British embassy was burnt down. In August 1967, for a week, the Ministry of Foreign Affairs was occupied by revolutionary rebels and the People's Republic was de facto deprived of diplomacy. But the crisis also accelerated the reconstruction of the Party. Mao called on the army to restore order and disarm the Red Guards. With the support of Lin Biao and Zhou Enlai, he weakened the Cultural Revolution group by removing its more radical members. Jiang Qing was forced to make a virtual act of self-criticism and Chen Boda joined Lin Biao. On 5 September, a joint decision taken between the Central Committee, the Central Military Commission, the State Council and the Cultural Revolution Group authorized the PLA to use force against the Red Guard organizations resisting the restoration of order. It was no longer a question of destroying the old political order, but of rebuilding a new political order. The Red Guard organizations were dismantled; nearly 4.7 million young people were sent to the countryside between 1968 and the end of 1970.[22] Party cadres were sent to 'May Seventh Cadre Schools', in reference to a speech by Mao on 7 May 1966 in which he called on all sectors of the country to turn into 'schools of revolution'; participation in agricultural work was meant to ensure their re-education. This marked the end of the Cultural Revolution.

The re-establishment of order increased the influence of the army over the revolutionary committees, the formation of which was accelerated from August 1967 and completed in September 1968. At the provincial level, soldiers occupied half of the seats (54 per cent): the PLA chaired twenty-one of the twenty-nine provincial committees, while civilian cadres took 25 per cent, and the rebels 21 per cent. The new political order was distinct from the previous one not so much in its structure as in its composition; never since the early 1950s had the army occupied such a prominent political position.

At the Ninth Party Congress held in April 1969, the military reaped the political benefits of the role they had just played. The Congress brought together 1,512 delegates appointed by the revolutionary committees, and not elected by the Party as in the past. The PLA dominated this Congress; two-thirds of the members of the Congress, more than 50 per cent of the members of the Central Committee, and twelve of the twenty-five members of the Politburo came from its ranks. This Congress also saw an increased representation of the provinces: provincial delegates occupied two-thirds of the seats of the Central Committee, whereas they had occupied only 38 per cent in the Eighth Central Committee.

Mao made a remarkable comeback onto the political scene. In the new Party statutes, the reference to Mao Zedong thought was reinstated, after being abolished in 1956 following criticism from Deng Xiaoping and Liu Shaoqi. The latter were excluded from the Central Committee, as were the majority of its former members, including several educated in the Soviet Union with which relations were strained. Lin Biao's political influence was now stronger. As Minister of Defence, Deputy Party Secretary and key player in the Cultural Revolution, he read the report to Congress on 1 April. The Party's new statutes described him as 'a close comrade in arms and successor to Comrade Mao Zedong'.

And yet, behind the façade of unanimity and the glorification of Mao, the issues that had divided the political leadership were far from resolved. Admittedly, the Maoist left was now well represented in the

Politburo – Chen Boda, Jiang Qing, Zhang Chunqiao and Yao Wenyuan were all members – but it was in competition with the representatives of the People's Army. Representatives of the civil administration, led by Zhou Enlai, and the security services led by Kang Sheng also viewed with concern the strengthening of the military institution, now called upon to play an administrative and supervisory role that had traditionally devolved to the Party and its representatives. Within the army itself, Lin Biao could not count on full support.

Responsibilities and consequences

Mao played a decisive role in the launching and then the unfolding of the Cultural Revolution. This tragic period was triggered by his identifying a series of ills affecting Chinese society. Local Party organizations, especially in the countryside, had become increasingly corrupt and ineffective. The upper echelons of the administration and the Party had too many cadres who were underqualified and engaged in routine bureaucratic practices. If Mao's diagnosis was correct, his interpretation of it was wrong. According to him, bureaucratism and inequalities were a sign that China was on the 'revisionist' path, and he identified the cause as the presence of 'capitalists' or 'bourgeois elements' at the top of the Party. The remedy he proposed was the revival of the class struggle within the Party itself. This interpretation was linked to his analysis of the evolution of the Soviet Union. Mao denounced the 'revisionism' of both Soviet foreign and national policy and decided that the cause lay in the degeneration of the Soviet Communist Party. Once he had made this diagnosis of the Soviet situation, he could pass a comparable judgement on the Chinese situation.

Mao feared that in China, as in the USSR, the revolution would be killed off by the bureaucracy, which had been set up as a new exploitative class. He was worried that his closest lieutenants, Liu Shaoqi, Deng Xiaoping, Zhou Enlai and Chen Yun, would again, as they had attempted in 1961–62, try to decollectivize the land and follow a 'revisionist' path by 'forgetting the class struggle'. The Cultural Revolution was, therefore, not only a struggle on the part of Mao to win back the fullness of his power, but also a struggle to impose the totalitarian utopia of an egalitarian socialism.

In order to realize his plan, Mao mobilized young people from universities and high schools, calling on them to criticize capitalist tendencies on campuses and also at the highest level of the Party bureaucracy. If the main responsibility for the Cultural Revolution rests with Mao, his followers must also shoulder some of the blame. The younger generation was involved for a variety of reasons – some out of sincere enthusiasm, others out of strategic interest, still others out of conformism. Some participated out of devotion to the man who had liberated China from imperialism and warlords, others because a space had opened up in which they could express their grievances against a particular individual. Over time this popular support waned, but Mao was easily able to mobilize a sufficiently large number of followers to endanger the Party.

The Cultural Revolution was therefore not just the expression of an internal Party conflict; it unleashed a veritable civil war. This stemmed first of all from Mao's own conviction that it was up to the masses to bring about the emergence of revolutionary forces. What was at stake between the summer of 1966 and the autumn of 1967 was the authorization given to young people to emancipate themselves from their elders by means of violence – a generational one-upmanship.[23] The Cultural Revolution gave an opportunity to young people born after 1949 to relive the revolutionary fever of the heroic age of Yan'an that it had never personally experienced. It was an urban movement that concerned everyone, as schools, universities, administrations, factories and businesses were all affected; but rural China, with the exception of the areas on the outskirts of cities, was not affected.

If Mao, and the many young people who followed him, is overwhelmingly responsible, the attitude of the other leaders also needs to be understood. His supporters were, on the one hand, the radical group, particularly well established in Shanghai, and, on the other, various leaders of the PLA, starting with Lin Biao. But we can also criticize those who did not resist Mao's orders. Zhou Enlai and Deng Xiaoping, for example, participated in the criticism of Peng Zhen in April 1966. More generally, all members of the Politburo approved the purges of the Propaganda Department in May 1966 and the adoption of the Sixteen Point Declaration at the eleventh plenary session of the Central Committee in August.

The economic impact of the Cultural Revolution was moderate. In agriculture as in industry, the level of production fell in 1966 and 1967 before rising again in 1969. This was much less than the effects of the Great Leap Forward. The consequences, however, were highly significant in the fields of culture and education. The offer of cultural products was drastically reduced, since only films or plays deemed revolutionary were authorized for production and distribution. So that university and high school students could participate in the movement, universities were closed over the summer of 1966 and high schools in the autumn. They would not reopen for four years. Libraries and museums were destroyed. Historic sites and religious buildings were damaged or razed. The most serious consequences affected people such as academics, writers and intellectuals. During the trial of the Gang of Four, it was officially stated that 2,600 people in the arts and literature, 142,000 cadres and teachers from the Ministry of Education, 53,000 scientists and technicians from research institutions, 500 professors from universities of medicine under the Ministry of Health had been 'falsely accused and persecuted'; an unspecified number of them had died.

One of the first and most famous victims was writer Lao She, then President of the Chinese Artists' Association. On 23 August 1966, along with thirty other personalities from the cultural world, he was taken to the Temple of Confucius in Beijing, where Red Guards were burning costumes from the Beijing Opera. While he considered himself to be a spokesperson for the poorest sectors of society, he was denounced as a petty-bourgeois intellectual in front of thousands of people. Red Guards shaved half of his head, poured black ink on his face and hung a sign around his neck saying 'monsters and demons'; he was severely beaten. He returned home that same evening, but disappeared the next day. He allegedly threw himself into Lake Taiping in despair. This official version has been disputed but is plausible insofar as, in China, suicide is a strong political act.

Within the Party, the purges were massive. 70 per cent to 80 per cent of the regional or provincial leaders were changed, and four of the six Party Secretaries General. At the regional level, twenty-three of the twenty-nine secretaries at the provincial level were ousted. In central bodies, the eviction rate was around 70 per cent. Only nine out of twenty-three members of the Politburo, four members out of thirteen of the secretariat, and fifty-four members out of 167 of the Central Committee still held their posts after the Cultural Revolution. Half of the fifteen premiers and forty-eight ministers were still members of the State Council as of 1969. Three million people were sent to May Seventh Cadre Schools. Others were beaten and tortured. Some were killed in prison or committed suicide. Liu Shaoqi, arrested in 1967 and beaten by Red Guards at the end of the year, died in prison in 1969. This was also the fate of Peng Dehuai and Tao Zhu, former members of the Politburo, of the Mayor of Shanghai Cao Diqiu, and of the Vice Minister of Public Security Xu Zuzhong. Children of leaders were also among the victims: Deng Xiaoping's daughter was sent into exile with her parents; his defenestrated son remained handicapped; Zhou Enlai's adopted daughter was tortured by the Red Guards. Ultimately, if the Cultural Revolution failed, it was because once the established order had been destroyed under the onslaught of the Red Guards, Mao had no other political model to offer. He had managed to win back power from the Party leadership, but he had no other political institutions to propose. The army, the only institution still standing, reaped the fruits of chaos.

The end of Maoism and the crises of succession (1969–76)

In the aftermath of the Ninth Congress, Mao's personality cult ceased, economic activity resumed and local Party organs were gradually re-established and took control of the revolutionary committees. This marked the return to a certain institutional normality and moderation in economic policy. Mao's victory had been consecrated by the Ninth Party Congress held in April 1969, which endorsed the choice of Lin Biao, Minister of Defence, as Mao's new successor. But that did not ease tensions between rival factions that clashed openly in political meetings. The period that began in 1969 and ended in 1978 was in fact dominated by conflicts at the top of the apparatus. Between 1969 and 1971, the political system was dominated by the army and the person of Lin Biao. Mao lost all confidence in the latter, and he mysteriously disappeared in September 1971. After his physical elimination, political life was again dominated by the question of succession.

The Lin Biao era (1969–71)

The Ninth Congress should have marked a return to normality. It represented victory for Mao and his allies, members of the former Cultural Revolution group, who made up more than a third of the Politburo's workforce (nine out of twenty-five). But the struggles at the top of the political apparatus continued between three groups: the military around Lin Biao; the cadres of the civil apparatus around Zhou Enlai, who sought to exclude the leaders of the Cultural Revolution and return to the economic policy of readjustment of the early 1960s; and the left wing of the Cultural Revolution, who attempted to save most of its programme. The issues around which the struggles were organized were the reconstruction of the Party and the state apparatus, and international relations. Since the People's Liberation Army dominated the revolutionary committees, it was overrepresented in the Party bodies emerging from the Ninth Congress; Lin Biao resisted calls for a rebuilt Party that would win back control of the army and the nation.

As regards the reconstruction of the state apparatus, there was a debate over the draft of a new Constitution. In March 1970, the Politburo proposed to abolish the post of head of state, a position held by Mao from 1945 to 1959, then by Liu Shaoqi from 1959 to 1968, and since left vacant. But Lin Biao was in favour of the post being re-established and occupied by Mao himself. Lin Biao led manoeuvres, including mobilizing his wife Ye Qun, to advance his views. Several contradictory hypotheses can be advanced as to why Lin took the risk of displaying his disagreement with Mao: a feeling of insecurity or illegitimacy, or an overconfidence in the support he felt he could draw on.[24]

The conflict over the post of head of state broke out during the second plenary session of the Ninth Central Committee, held in Lushan (Anhui) from 23 August to 6 September 1970. Without notifying Mao, Lin Biao expressed in his opening speech his conviction of the need to enshrine in the new Constitution Mao's major role as leader, head of state and supreme commander, and also the role of Mao's thought as national ideology. Lin emphasized 'Mao's genius' in order to show his own dedication and pursue his own goals, a strategy with which it seems Mao had disagreed from the start of the Cultural Revolution. During the plenary session, Lin's supporters took the same position and stated that anyone who opposed the creation of the post of head of state would be accused of obstructing the theory of Mao's genius. Mao would later explain that he was aware of Lin Biao's tactics: to demand the post of head of state for Mao and, if the latter refused, to give him the post anyway. Mao counter-manoeuvred so that the proposal was ultimately not adopted, a sign of his continued ability to manipulate the Party elite. The only victim at the time was Chen Boda, who was deposed and fell out of favour. The conflicts that broke out during this plenary session lasted until the summer of 1971. The official explanation emphasizes the existence and the attribution of the post of Chairman of the Republic; however, Lin actually opposed Mao on other essential points, criticizing his economic policy and the rapprochement with the United States and denouncing the subordination of the revolutionary committees to the Party committees resuscitated by the Ninth Congress.

In terms of economic policy, there were two conflicting agendas. Lin Biao and his supporters, agreeing on this point with the left of the Cultural Revolution, defended the return to the Maoist project of the Great Leap Forward, with its mobilization and egalitarianism, while the representatives of the state apparatus and the Party, around Zhou Enlai, sought to consolidate the readjustment policy implemented in the early 1960s. In terms of foreign policy, Lin Biao would be accused, after his death, of 'isolationism' and 'chauvinism', which suggests that he was opposed to a rapprochement with the United States. However, throughout 1970, as Lin campaigned for the post of head of state, Chinese–American contacts increased. Mao and Zhou Enlai thought it was increasingly dangerous to simultaneously oppose both the superpowers with the same vigour, and believed that a tactical rapprochement with the United States, which was making overtures in Beijing, was becoming possible and even necessary. While Lin Biao's position has never been clarified, it is clear that in an isolated and militarily threatened China, the PLA had an important political role to play.

In the aftermath of the plenary session, attacks were launched not directly against Lin but against his supporters, forced to officially disavow the views they expressed. Lin Biao's allies were driven from the positions of strength they occupied. In particular, in December 1970, Lin's group lost control of the Beijing military region. The garrison of the capital was now headed by Li Zihou, a supporter of Zhou Enlai. Lin's position was not that strong. Admittedly, in August 1971, twenty-two of the twenty-nine provinces were ruled by the military, but Lin's supporters did not hold a dominant position. They controlled only five provincial directorates. Fourteen provinces, including Beijing, were led by coalitions with no particular connection to the leader of the PLA.

Elimination of Lin Biao in September 1971

It was in this context of an open conflict between Mao and Lin Biao that the latter disappeared on 13 September 1971. The events are very obscure and the official version was not to be formulated until 1973 by Zhou Enlai in his report to the Tenth Party Congress: Lin and his accomplices – his wife Ye Qun and his son Lin Liguo – apparently sought to flee to the USSR on board a military plane which crashed in Mongolia after the failure of an attempted 'counter-revolutionary coup'.

Preparations for this coup were said to have started in February 1971 under the code name 'Operation 571', a homophone of the expression *wuzhuang qiyi* (武装起义) which means 'armed uprising'. It allegedly involved young officers led by Lin Biao's son Lin Liguo, deputy director of the General Bureau of the air force, and around twenty other conspirators. The plan was to assassinate Mao on his special train. Zhou Enlai was informed of this plot through Lin Biao's daughter, Lin Liheng. Lin Biao, his plot discovered, took a flight on the night of 12–13 September. At 3 a.m. on 13 September, Zhou Enlai convened the Politburo – Mao was not present – and announced that Lin had fled. On the afternoon of 14 September, Zhou learned from the Soviet embassy in Ulaanbaatar that Lin Biao's Trident had crashed at around 2:30 a.m. on 13 September in Mongolia. The nine passengers were all dead. Many questions remain to this day unanswered; above all, these unlikely events reveal the atmosphere that reigned in the upper echelons of power: the rival leaders no longer communicated with each other and Politburo meetings were no more than a stage for ritualized confrontations.

In the short term, the death of Lin Biao allowed Mao and Zhou to purge the Politburo and the leadership of the People's Army of all Lin's supporters; around sixty military leaders followed Lin Biao in his fall. However, this did not put an end to the domination of the PLA over civil political apparatuses – three generals with provincial responsibilities, for example, remained members of the Politburo. Thus, the fall of Lin Biao did not result in the withdrawal of the army from the political arena. Nevertheless, his ousting coincided with a comeback of the leaders of the old apparatus, whom the Cultural Revolution had criticized and persecuted. In April 1973, Deng, rehabilitated, became Vice Premier again; he became Vice Chairman of the Party in 1975.

But Lin's death did not resolve the crisis at the top of the Party. Supporters of development through mass mobilization continued to clash with supporters of a moderate agenda. Above all, the crisis revealed the way the system worked. Amidst the backdrop of division, leaders spied on one another. An atmosphere of conspiracy reigned, reminiscent of the intrigues that divided the imperial palace in Beijing at the end of the imperial era, or the Soviet leadership in the Stalinist era.

The end of Maoism (1972–76)

While the military's influence receded after the fall of Lin Biao, it continued to play a decisive role in the political arena. It is the army that helped to maintain the balance between the radicals and the moderates, and then ultimately secured the victory of the latter over the former after Mao's death.

One immediate question was the reconstruction of the leadership, and the appointment of a new successor to Mao. Three groups emerged within the Politburo. First were the radicals who, along with Mao, had launched the Cultural Revolution. This coalition included Kang Sheng (whose role was declining due to health problems), Jiang Qing, Zhang Chunqiao, Yao Wenyuan and Xie Fuzhi (who joined the group during the Cultural Revolution as Minister of Public Security, and died in 1972). A second group included the surviving leaders of the Cultural Revolution who collaborated with Mao even though they were opposed to it: the Premier Zhou Enlai, the Vice Premier Li Xiannian, the Vice Chairman of the Republic since 1959 Dong Biwu, and three old marshals, Zhu De, Liu Bocheng and Ye Jianying. Mao drew closer to this group by rehabilitating a number of leaders ousted by Lin Biao, including Deng Xiaoping who returned from Jiangxi to Beijing in March 1973. A third group included those who were promoted as a result of the Cultural

Revolution. These were mainly military officials: Xu Shiyu, Chen Xilian, Li Desheng and Wang Dongxing.

Zhou Enlai was arguably the highest ranking ruler after Mao, but Mao never wished to name him as his successor. Moreover, his doctors diagnosed cancer in May 1972. That same year, he worked to restore the production system in the factories, and to restart the education and research system.

In the absence of a successor capable of preserving the achievements of the Cultural Revolution and of being accepted by a majority, Mao made the surprising decision to bring Wang Hongwen into the Politburo in May 1973, along with two other beneficiaries of the Cultural Revolution: Hua Guofeng, First Secretary of Hunan province, and Wu De, First Secretary for the city of Beijing. Wang Hongwen embodied the young and the workers, two social groups that played a major role during the Cultural Revolution. In August 1973, at the Tenth Party Congress, Wang was appointed Vice Chairman and member of the Politburo Standing Committee. He became the third most important figure in the Party after Mao and Zhou.

The Tenth Congress, meeting in secret in Beijing from 24 to 28 August 1973, demonstrated a precarious balance between radicals and moderates. Admittedly, Zhou Enlai managed to ensure a first wave of rehabilitations and to launch an economic development programme. However, the radicals, until the demise of Mao, retained a formidable hold over the propaganda organs and therefore over several essential levers of power. The new Politburo Standing Committee headed by Mao had nine members instead of five in 1969. It was divided into two groups: on the one hand, four radicals or figures in radical circles (Wang Hongwen, Kang Sheng, Zhang Chunqiao and General Li Desheng); on the other, four moderates: Zhou Enlai, Marshal Ye Jianying, and two Party veterans, Marshal Zhu De and Dong Biwu. Also entering the Politburo as ordinary members were Hua Guofeng, Wu De and Chen Yonggui, whose careers had been made by the Cultural Revolution. The political guidelines set up by Congress were contradictory. Zhou Enlai produced a report criticizing Lin Biao and pleaded for increased attention to economic issues. Wang Hongwen, whose rise in prominence had been recent and dramatic, called for new revolutions.

67

The day after the Congress, the radicals launched a movement that targeted the Premier. The campaign attacked the traditional values of Confucian idealism and humanism, which were accused of providing a basis for elitism, as well as contempt for work and the manual worker. Its starting point was an article by Yang Rongguo, professor of philosophy in Canton, published in the *People's Daily* on 7 September 1973. Indirectly, by drawing on a historical analogy, the aim was to denounce Zhou Enlai, who was reproached for his aristocratic origins, his policy of rehabilitating the cadres, and his programme of restoration in the administration, the economy and the educational system. The radicals denounced their adversaries as being 'in the pay of the exploiting classes, like Confucius'.

What made this campaign so complex was Zhou's ability to reorient it and come up with an interpretation radically opposed to that of its promoters. On 18 January 1974, with Mao's consent, the Party published a document prepared under the leadership of Jiang Qing entitled 'The Doctrines of Lin Biao, Confucius and Mencius'. This text marked the start of the campaign 'Criticize Lin Biao, Criticize Confucius' (*pi Lin pi Kong* 批林批孔). Those who rehabilitated old families, those who looked to the past and sought to restore a bygone order, were denounced. With an editorial in the *People's Daily* on 1 July 1974, the campaign changed direction and became an instrument in the hands of the moderates, a movement against the radical ideology 'in favour of a production oriented towards economic goals'. The emphasis was now on the need for science, new technologies and economic development; the Confucians were criticized for wanting to restore the old order or for despising economic problems. Despite the weakness of Zhou Enlai, who had been hospitalized since 1 June 1974, the campaign ended at the end of the year with the victory of his policies being endorsed by the National People's Congress (NPC).

At the fourth NPC in Beijing, from 13 to 17 January 1975, Zhou Enlai set out the programme of the four modernizations (*si da xiandaihua* 四大现代化), in agriculture, industry, national defence, and science and technology, which would become the Party's official policy from 1976; this plan was the updated version of a proposal already made at the previous NPC in 1964. This same Congress approved a new constitutional text presented by Wang Hongweng and marked by its brevity (a mere thirty articles), its Maoism and its dictatorial character.

The fourth NPC also marked the return of Deng Xiaoping, reinstated in his post as Deputy Premier. Deng had disappeared from the Chinese political scene in the autumn of 1966, and returned to the Politburo and the Party's Central Military Commission in December 1973. On 4 October 1974, Mao proposed that Deng be appointed first Deputy Premier and thus the designated successor of Zhou Enlai. At a meeting of the Politburo in January 1975, held in the presence of Zhou Enlai, it was decided that Deng should also be a member of the Politburo Standing Committee and Vice Chairman of the Party, as well as Vice Chairman of the Central Military Commission. In compensation, Zhang Chunqiao was appointed second Deputy Premier, and director of the Political Department in the PLA.

It appears that Mao then moved away from Jiang Qing and his Shanghai allies. One possible explanation is growing marital disagreement. Indeed, in 1975, Jiang Qing moved out of Zhongnanhai and settled in the Diaoyutai residential complex.[25] Throughout this busy year, Mao's attitude towards Deng was ambiguous. He supported his policy and defended it against radical attacks, but, at the same time, he allowed Zhang Chunqiao and Yao Wenyuan to continue to defend their positions. This ambivalence on Mao's part can be blamed on his indecision or his growing inability to exercise his responsibilities; he was suffering from Parkinson's disease and was less able to express himself orally.

The conflict between radicals and moderates dragged on in the months that followed. The left launched attacks against bourgeois elements and the revisionism of the Party. Mao himself launched a campaign for the study of the dictatorship of the proletariat, which demanded a levelling of the wages of industrial workers, the restoration of the role of the people's communes and the abolition of all forms of private property.

The death of Zhou Enlai on 8 January 1976 caused a new political crisis. Two candidates were best placed to succeed the Premier: Deng Xiaoping among the moderates and Zhang Chunqiao among the radicals. For Mao, appointing Deng would mean the risk of the latter succeeding him. Appointing Zhang Chunqiao would upset the political balance. To everyone's surprise, Hua Guofeng, the sixth Deputy Premier, was appointed interim Premier on 3 February 1976. He was also put in charge of the day-to-day work of the Party. Born in 1921, Hua Guofeng had started his career in Hunan province. He rose to Beijing thanks to the elimination of Lin Biao: he was elected a member of the Politburo at the Tenth Congress in August 1973, and promoted to Deputy Premier and Minister of Security in January 1975. As an apparatchik, Hua was not an ideologue but a compromise candidate acceptable to all, moderate enough to be accepted by the military and radical enough – inasmuch as he owed his career to the Cultural Revolution – to be accepted by Jiang Qing's group.

The radical left, however, expressed its dissatisfaction, in particular Zhang Chunqiao, who coveted the post. The radicals then made a major mistake: instead of collaborating with potential allies, which would undoubtedly have allowed them to retain power after Mao's death, they quarrelled with everyone. Thus, when Zhou died, they used the newspapers they controlled to attack his memory, notably through the Shanghai *Wenhuibao*. On 25 March, Zhou was accused of being 'on the capitalist road'.

But they had not reckoned on possible demonstrations of popular support. On 30 March 1976, Beijing residents spontaneously started paying homage to Zhou by laying wreaths in Tiananmen Square. Thousands of people marched. On 4 April, Tomb-sweeping Day (when the dead are remembered), 2 million people entered the square. Texts were displayed attacking the radicals, defending the memory of Zhou and demanding that Deng be put in charge. On the evening of 4 April, the Politburo met in the absence of several members including Zhu De, Ye Jianying, Li Xiannian and Deng Xiaoping. Hua Guofeng allied with the radicals and denounced the provocateurs of Tiananmen Square. Between 4 and 5 a.m., the square was cleared; those present were arrested. Word spread and thousands of people flocked there. By the morning, 10,000 people had gathered there again. In the evening, the Politburo denounced the 'Tiananmen incident' (*Tiananmen shijian* 天安门事件) as a 'counter-revolutionary revolt'. A brutal crackdown began. Deng was relieved of his duties but allowed to retain his status as a member of the Party; he took refuge in Canton where his allies controlled the military forces. On 7 April, Mao ordered Hua to become full Premier and first Vice Chairman of the Party. On the evening of 30 April, at the end of an interview with Hua, Mao is said to have uttered the sentence on which he would rely to legitimize his power: 'With you in power, I don't need to worry' (*ni banshi, wo fangxin* 你办事, 我放心).

The political developments from January to April 1976 apparently ensured a temporary victory for the left. In fact, the quarrels continued between the moderates, supported by the civil and military cadres of the Party's provincial leadership, and the left of the Cultural Revolution that was better established at the central level, in particular within the mass organizations and the secret police. As for the model that China should follow – class struggle and development based on the mobilization of the workforce, or a stable political organization and development focused on technical modernization – there was still no clear answer.

Amid this feverish atmosphere in the upper echelons of the regime, bad news arrived in waves. On 6 July 1976, Marshal Zhu De, aged 89, died. On 28 July, at 3:52 a.m., there was an earthquake in Tangshan (Hebei), east of Beijing. According to official figures, the death toll was 242,419 – some sources say three times more – with 164,000 injured. Protests with different agendas took place across the country. Some, manipulated by the radicals, attacked Deng Xiaoping. Others, more spontaneous, supported him. Tensions ran so high that the radicals feared action against their interests; the Shanghai militia, formed in 1967, was placed on high alert in August.

When Mao died on 9 September 1976, a few minutes after midnight, the leadership was divided and the country bruised. The army decided to support Hua Guofeng; confirmed in his post of Premier, he was appointed Party Chairman and Chairman of the Central Military Commission. Hua thus succeeded both Zhou Enlai and Mao Zedong. At first hesitant, then under pressure from the country's main military leaders, he put an end to the attempts to seize power by those close to Mao by eliminating the revolutionary left. On 6 October, the Gang of Four, Jiang Qing, Wang Hongwen, Zhang Chunqiao and Yao Wenyuan, and their main supporters, were arrested. Had they been intending to seize power? To this day, nobody knows. Their strategic mistake lay in not having forged an alliance with the beneficiaries of the Cultural Revolution, first and foremost Hua Guofeng, and having stayed on in Beijing after Mao's death when they had a stronghold in Shanghai, protected by a militia of 100,000 men.

Thus, the alliance between the representatives of the administration on the one hand, and the army and the secret services on the other, made it possible to eliminate the main political heirs of the Cultural

Revolution. However, Hua and his allies from the ranks of the secret police and the mass organizations derived their legitimacy directly from Mao, and would seek to preserve the Maoist heritage as much as possible. The arrest of the Gang of Four marked the end of the revolutionary left, but this did not yet mean that Maoism was a spent force.

Conclusion

With the exception of the years of hiatus at the start of the 1960s, the period 1958–76 was marked by a very personal exercise of power concentrated in the hands of Mao and those he favoured. In 1959, the Lushan plenary session inaugurated a long list of clashes, sometimes violent, between rival factions. These factions, organized at the beginning of the period on the basis of ideological differences, were gradually consolidated in accordance with personal affinities and positions. Mao took advantage of these divisions by playing one against the other, in a game reminiscent of the coteries that had clashed at the imperial palace before the fall of the empire in 1911. The political system had been organized around Mao's person, so that his death was bound to bring about profound changes. Once the father of the Chinese revolution had gone, the question of normalizing the functioning of the Party and the state apparatus demanded an urgent response.

On the economic and social levels, the results of eighteen years of Maoism present a mixed picture, to say the least. China's attempt to catch up with the developed countries had failed. While progress had been made in industry and agriculture, it had not been enough. While the Western world enjoyed decades of continued prosperity, and the vast majority of its middle classes entered the era of mass consumption, the Chinese population as a whole remained poor. Above all, while Mao rightly denounced the gap between rural and urban China, this gap widened. As Lucien Bianco writes, Mao preferred 'revolutionary fervour to improving the condition of the masses';[26] by remaining revolutionary, Mao's China lagged ever more behind. This Maoist choice of permanent revolution was finally and definitively undermined at the third plenary session of the Eleventh Central Committee in December 1978.

THREE

Giving Priority to Economic Modernization (1976–1992)

With the death of Mao Zedong, a new era dawned. However, the break with the previous period was gradual and the real turning point did not take place until December 1978, two years after the death of the father of the Chinese revolution. Deng Xiaoping decided to abandon the revolutionary project; the reformist leaders set the country on a path of economic modernization that would rapidly improve the material conditions of the population. A quarter of a century after the seizure of power, the Communist Party finally achieved one of the objectives it had set itself when it seized power and which had been constantly postponed by Mao's utopian project: to modernize the country and enable it to catch up. This was first and foremost a political decision that aimed to revive the legitimacy of the regime among an exhausted and demoralized population. The change of direction was therefore made not so much out of any ideological conviction of the benefits of another model, but rather out of political opportunism. The first economic reforms – the decollectivization of agriculture and opening up to foreign investors – were, moreover, conceived as an amendment to the planning system in place; they aimed to make it more efficient and in no way to bring it down. They did not mark a break, strictly speaking. The turning point of 1978 did not aim to build another economic and social model.

Moreover, in 1978, Deng Xiaoping, loyal to the idea of reform, was already 74 years old. He had been associated with the adventure of Chinese Communism ever since the 1930s. For a long time, he was close to Mao Zedong, but he moved away from him in the early 1960s. A familiar political figure, already elderly, he nevertheless managed to embody renewal. But the economic reforms caused tensions. Ten years after their launch in 1989, against the backdrop of an economic and social malaise affecting the entire population, both urban and rural, the regime was experiencing a historic crisis. Never since its founding had it been so challenged by ordinary people. Deng Xiaoping sided with the

73

conservative forces to reinstall the dictatorship of the Communist Party that some had believed they could change. Thus, the hopes of all those in China and abroad who believed that economic reform inevitably heralded political reform were dashed.

The Hua Guofeng transition (September 1976–December 1978)

Hua Guofeng combined the functions occupied by Zhou Enlai and Mao Zedong, as both Premier and Party Chairman as well as chair of the Central Military Commission; he led the country from September 1976 until December 1978. During these two years, he tried to preserve the Maoist heritage he represented, while other competing political forces strove to marginalize it. These forces finally succeeded, at the third plenary session of the Eleventh Central Committee in December 1978. Restored to office, Deng Xiaoping, a pragmatist leader, was the main political figure opposing Hua and his neo-Maoist programme. This era of transition was marked by two important political episodes: the Eleventh Party Congress in August 1977 and, in March 1978, promulgation by the Fifth National People's Congress of a third Constitution, after the 1954 Soviet-inspired Constitution and the one of 1975 created by the left wing of the Cultural Revolution. In December 1978, a number of the differences that had set neo-Maoists and pragmatists at loggerheads during these two years were finally settled.

Hua Guofeng had been designated by Mao himself as his successor, and his extensive power was beyond dispute. However, he faced conflicting demands for continuity and change. He could not totally disown the Cultural Revolution to which he owed his rapid rise, but he was also confronted by the ambitions of Deng Xiaoping and his supporters. At a Party working conference in March 1977, some veterans, including Chen Yun and Wang Zhen, demanded the return of Deng to the responsibilities he had held before his second ousting in April 1976. Under pressure, Hua Guofeng resigned himself to accepting Deng's rehabilitation in July 1977 at the third plenary session of the Tenth Central Committee. Deng Xiaoping then returned to all the functions he had previously held: Vice Chairman of the Party and of the Central Military Commission, member of the Politburo Standing Committee, Chief of the General Staff and Deputy Premier.

The conflict between the newly promoted and the veterans

The Eleventh Congress (August 1977) marked a return to normal Party functioning. The 'victorious end of the Cultural Revolution' was proclaimed, and its results were not questioned. A few weeks earlier, in July, members of the Gang of Four (Jiang Qing, Zhang Chunqiao, Yao Wenyuan and Wang Hongwen) were banned from the Party for life. In November 1980, they were put on trial, along with six other people – five senior officers close to Lin Biao who had helped him in his rise to power in 1971, and Chen Boda, Mao's former personal secretary. During the trial, broadcast on television, and viewed by everyone as a piece of political theatre, they were accused of being directly responsible for the persecution of 729,511 people and the deaths of 34,800 of them.[1] Zhang Chunqiao remained silent, while Jiang Qing railed against a court she deemed illegitimate. Both would be sentenced to death; the sentence was suspended for two years, giving them a chance to repent. The other defendants were sentenced to prison terms. Jiang Qing would commit suicide in prison in 1991.

During the Congress, the two opposing political tendencies gave rise to contradictory positions. The new political leadership was the result of a compromise. One-third of the members of the Central Committee elected at the Tenth Congress, its most left-wing elements, were not re-elected. The appointments to the Politburo tended to favour the survivors and beneficiaries of the Cultural Revolution. Among the five members of the new Politburo Standing Committee, Deng Xiaoping was the only figure to oppose Hua Guofeng.

In the economic field, the modernization plan launched by Zhou Enlai before his death was approved. At the same time, Hua proposed a ten-year development plan (1976–85), which drew on the Maoist models of Dazhai in agriculture and Daqing in industry; the production team in the poverty-stricken Shanxi Province and the Heilongjiang oilfields had become benchmarks in 1964 for their self-sufficiency, their ability to tackle natural obstacles, and the zeal of the workers. In the official PRC narrative of economic policy during the late 1970s, Hua Guofeng is depicted as advocating a leftist approach to growth with outdated Maoist concepts, while Deng Xiaoping is credited with setting China on its new course of reform. As Sun and Teiwes have shown,[2] this is largely a myth.

After the arrest of the Gang of Four, all leaders agreed on the priority of promoting production. At a December 1976 conference, Hua defined revolution as the liberation of productive forces, cited the population's desire to make up the enormous economic losses caused by the Gang as soon as possible, and pointed to the rapid development of the national economy as a priority. Hua initiated an important shift of focus from the ideological preoccupations of the previous decade to the prosaic tasks of nation-building.

The following spring, in March 1978, the Fifth National People's Congress approved this ambitious and unrealistic economic development plan, for which Hua Guofeng managed to obtain the support of former Zhou Enlai collaborators including Ye Jianying, Li Xiannian and Yu Qiuli. Most importantly, Congress adopted a new Constitution, following that of 1975 proposed by Zhang Chunqiao, which had comprised only thirty articles. This text, despite Mao Zedong's successors' mistrust and even hatred for the Soviet Union, incorporated many Soviet-style constitutional structures.[3] Much of the structure of the 1954 Constitution was restored and some of the more drastic provisions removed. The 1978 Constitution was not, however, a complete return to that of 1954; much of it was given over to radical ideology. Thus, the first two articles were identical to the 1975 text:

> Article 1. The People's Republic of China is a socialist state of the dictatorship of the proletariat led by the working class and based on the alliance of workers and peasants.
> Article 2. The Communist Party of China is the core of leadership of the whole Chinese people. The working class exercises leadership over the state through its vanguard, the Communist Party of China. The guiding ideology of the People's Republic of China is Marxism-Leninism-Mao Tsetung Thought.[4]

The Party's leading role over the state and society was thus mentioned in the body of the text and not only in the preamble, as had been the case in 1954. The revolutionary committees, institutions created during the Cultural Revolution, were preserved, but reduced to simple administrative bodies. The presidency of the Republic, suspended by the de facto disappearance of Lin Biao in 1969, was not re-established, but a new Chairman of the Standing Committee of the National People's Congress was elected in the person of Ye Jianying, who exercised the functions of head of state, based on the model operative in the Soviet Union.

The struggle between the newly appointed leaders, led by Hua, and the veterans of the CCP, led by Deng, intensified after the convening of the National Congress. Deng gradually managed to place his men in the civil and military apparatuses and strengthened his positions, while Hua found himself more and more isolated. Deng obtained the rehabilitation of hundreds of victims of the Cultural Revolution, including the economists Sun Yefang and Xue Muqiao, and the Marxist philosopher Hu Qiaomu, who became the first President of the Chinese Academy of Social Sciences, recently created in 1977. Hua Guofeng's economic programme was criticized as a 'new Great Leap Forward', and a re-qualification of the events of April 1976, considered in October 1978 to be 'revolutionary', was requested.

This political offensive at the top took place in an atmosphere of debate and social unrest. A pro-democracy movement began in November 1978 in Beijing. Posters with large characters (*dazibao* 大字报) were hung at the Xidan crossroads in the centre of the capital. By the end of the year, all the major cities in the country were affected. The majority of these texts, couched as formal complaints, protested against court decisions or personal political persecution, and demanded a review. Others criticized Mao Zedong and called for the rehabilitation of leaders who had been sentenced during the Cultural Revolution. Yet others were calls for democracy, the establishment of a socialist legal system and respect for human rights.[5] The most famous text was signed by Wei Jingsheng and called for the realization of a 'fifth modernization', in reference to the programme of four modernizations formulated by Zhou Enlai and further developed by Deng Xiaoping. According to Wei, this programme could be achieved only if a modernization of the political system, marked by the full exercise of civil liberties, was initiated.[6] At the end of 1978, the main means of expression used by these newly organized movements were 'underground newspapers' (*dixia kanwu* 地下刊物) published in a few hundreds or thousands of copies, similar to the clandestine (*samizdat*) Russian magazines that appeared in the 1960s and 1970s.

The activists involved in this movement were young people aged between 20 and 40.[7] The oldest of them had served as Red Guards during the Cultural Revolution – as was the case with Wei Jingsheng.

The younger had participated in the Tiananmen Square events of April 1976, after which some of them were arrested. They worked in factories, government or schools. Some were the sons or daughters of high-ranking cadres – Wei Jingsheng's father, for example, worked for the state planning commission. Confirmed intellectuals – academics, researchers, writers – did not play a part in this campaign, although they had already been victims of two tragic episodes, the Hundred Flowers Campaign and the Cultural Revolution. In political terms, the participants fell into two main groups.[8] Reformers favoured democracy within the existing political and economic system; they didn't question socialism, or the dictatorship of the proletariat, or the leading role of the Party; they called for the true realization of Marxism in China. Other more daring activists opposed the dictatorship of the proletariat exercised by a single Party with a monopoly of ideology. They advocated a multiparty system. The main document produced by this group was Wei Jingsheng's text calling for the 'fifth modernization', democracy. They did not really propose institutional reforms; rather, they saw democracy as a remedy against the risk of a new Cultural Revolution. The point was to prevent the reappearance of the absolute and arbitrary rule of one man, or any cult of personality. What they demanded was not participation in the choice of leaders or in political decision-making, but respect for citizens' rights, the rule of law, and control of power.

Simultaneously, during these debates in the streets and the parks, and via the underground press, there was a twofold social movement sweeping through the big cities. On the one hand, there were protests by peasants coming to formulate grievances or complaints, in particular to the central authorities in Beijing. They spoke out against local cadres that had left them without work for years, or subjected them to arbitrary treatment. On the other hand, there was the illegal return to the cities of educated young people who had been sent to the countryside after the Cultural Revolution. They constituted a population of marginalized people who, not being properly registered, had no access to housing or work and therefore resorted to illegal means to survive. There was thus a great risk that the democratic movement would rely on social unrest to gain momentum.

The third plenary session of the Eleventh Central Committee met in December 1978 in this context of social and political mobilization in the country's big cities. By the time it ended, the decisions it had reached represented a major turning point in the history of the People's Republic. The most important was a reform of agricultural policy. The degree of collectivization was lowered and the way was paved for a gradual dismantling of people's communes and a return to family working of the land. In the countryside, the existence of private plots of land was now guaranteed and free markets were allowed. The system of responsibility (*zeren zhi* 责任制), already introduced by Wan Li in the province of Anhui and by Zhao Ziyang in Sichuan, was gradually extended across the country; this too meant a return to family farming. The provinces gained many economic prerogatives, particularly in fiscal matters and foreign economic relations. In industry, egalitarianism and Maoist management methods were challenged.

In political matters, appointments foreshadowed the gradual marginalization of the heir chosen by Mao Zedong on his deathbed. Hua Guofeng retained the chairmanship of the Party but found himself in a minority within the Politburo, into which four leaders now made their entry: Chen Yun, a member of the Politburo Standing Committee who became Vice Chairman of the Party; Madame Deng Yichao, the widow of Zhou Enlai; Hu Yaobang, in charge of the Communist Youth before the Cultural Revolution, now also appointed head of the Propaganda Department; and General Wang Zhen, a strong supporter of Deng's return. In February 1980, Hua Guofeng handed over the post of Premier to Zhao Ziyang. In the months that followed, he was gradually ousted from the other positions he held: in June 1981, at the sixth plenary session of the Eleventh Central Committee, he handed over the chairmanship of the Party to Hu Yaobang and that of the Central Military Commission to Deng Xiaoping; in September 1982, he was forced to leave the Politburo.

In addition to these appointments, several decisions signalled the desire for a return to normal functioning of the country's institutions. A Central Commission for Discipline Inspection was created and chaired by Chen Yun. The rehabilitation movement accelerated and was extended posthumously to important victims of Maoism, such as Bo Yibo, Yang Shangkun and Peng Dehuai, who had died in prison in 1974. Between 1977 and the middle of 1980, about 2.8 million people were rehabilitated.[9] The Party was committed to separating the functions of the Party apparatus from those of the state apparatus, to restoring 'socialist legality' and 'democratizing' representative institutions. This plenary session therefore marked the final defeat of the newly appointed leaders and the triumph of the veterans.

A veteran to embody renewal

The paradox was that it took a 74-year-old man, associated with both the revolutionary conquests of the 1930s and the leadership of affairs since the proclamation of the Republic, to open a new era for Chinese Communism. Born in 1904 into a family of landowners in Sichuan province, Deng Xiaoping was exposed to a foreign environment very early on. He was a college student in Chongqing in 1918 and two years later, in 1920, like Zhou Enlai and Li Lisan, he went to France as part of the Work and Studies movement. Initially employed in several industrial establishments, Deng took part from 1924 in the activities of the Chinese Communist Youth League. In January 1926, pursued by the French police, he left Paris for Moscow. Studying at the Communist University of the Workers of the East, and then at the Sun Yat-sen University where revolutionary cadres were trained, he became a professional revolutionary. He became a member of the Chinese Communist Party in the capital of the Soviet Union in 1926. Unlike Mao Zedong, who had no international experience before 1949, Deng Xiaoping spent six years in Europe. In 1927, on his return to China, he exercised several responsibilities successively in the service of the Communist Party. He was sent first to the northeast, and was later active in the Party's underground organization in Shanghai, and then in military operations in the southern provinces of Guangdong and Guangxi. It was during the Long March, at the Zunyi conference in January 1935, that he joined the Party's ruling elite and began working with Mao. After the proclamation of the People's Republic, Deng was put in charge of directing military operations in the south of the country, which had not yet been fully liberated. He participated in the operations to conquer Chonqging and Chengdu in Sichuan, then Tibet in 1950. In 1952, he settled in Beijing. Appointed Deputy Premier in December 1952, he was a member of the State Planning Commission, and Minister of the Economy from September 1953 to June 1954. In 1954, he abandoned all his duties, with the exception of that of Deputy Premier, to become Secretary General of the Party's Central Committee, director of the Organization Department and Vice Chairman of the National Defence Commission. He entered the Politburo in 1955, and became Secretary General of the Central Committee in 1956, a post he held until the Cultural Revolution. He supported Mao during the anti-rightist campaign of 1957 and then during the launch of the Great Leap Forward. After the failure of the latter, he turned away from Mao and became, with Zhou Enlai, one of the main architects of the economic readjustment of 1960–62. From 1966 to 1973, he disappeared from the national political scene and was exiled to Jiangxi province. He reappeared in 1973 after the dismissal of Lin Biao, thanks to the support of Zhou Enlai. The riots of April 1976 were followed by yet another disgrace; he was again dismissed from his post before being reinstated in his post as Vice Chairman of the Central Committee at the Eleventh Congress in July 1977.

As a professional revolutionary, Deng Xiaoping undoubtedly espoused the revolutionary cause more out of strategic interest than out of ideological conviction. He believed in Communism to the extent that it seemed to him best able to defend both his own interests and those of the Chinese people. His career as a soldier and politician, marked by reversals and also by an interest in economic issues, reveals the traits of a pragmatic Communist.[10] Deng adopted out of pragmatism the slogan of the four modernizations – industry, agriculture, national defence, science and technology – first formulated by Zhou Enlai in 1964. While he committed the country to the path of reform and opening-up (*gaige yu kaifang* 改革与开放), two terms that in everyday Chinese marked the new direction taken in 1978, it was because he saw this as the best way to accelerate the pace of development and finally improve the living conditions of the population. Deng was especially able to carry out this project since, on two occasions, he had been ousted from the political scene: in 1966 during the Cultural Revolution, and again ten years later during the events of April 1976 in Tiananmen Square. Like many other citizens of the People's Republic who in the late 1970s called for a review of unjust judgements, Deng Xiaoping was a victim of the mistakes of the Maoist regime. Despite his long political career, including as Mao's close civilian and military collaborator, this dual persecution meant that he could embody renewal. By initiating a rupture similar to that experienced by the Communist Party of the Soviet Union in February 1956,

Deng Xiaoping set out to restore the legitimacy of a political regime that had lost its credibility.

The first reforms (1979–86)

In 1979, the goal of Deng and his supporters was to accelerate the development of the economy; they believed that they would achieve this by amending the planned system. There was, therefore, no question of transforming society or the political system. The need, at each stage, to create a consensus explains why the reform process was a gradual, frequently interrupted process. It was the subject of ongoing negotiations and haggling within the ruling elite between reformers and conservatives. Reforms were initiated in the countryside because they were politically less costly there. After a policy of relative liberalization (1979–80), the following two years were marked by a harder approach. After 1984, Deng had enough support to extend the reforms to urban China. By the mid-1980s, the movement was far enough advanced for voices to be raised, including within the Party, to promote political reform.

Deng Xiaoping comes to power

In December 1978, Deng Xiaoping's views prevailed against the backdrop of political and social tensions in the big cities. By the beginning of 1979, debates in the streets, in parks and in underground publications were gaining more and more attention. On 25 March, Wei Jingsheng, the most radical activist, published a scathing text entitled 'Democracy or a New Dictatorship' which referred to the 'metamorphosis of Deng Xiaoping into a new dictator'. In the days that followed, there was a crackdown on the movement. On 29 March, Wei was arrested; hundreds more arrests followed. At the end of his trial on 16 October, Wei was found guilty of seeking to 'overthrow the government'. His participation in the movement and then his trial marked the start of a long career as a dissident first in China, then outside China after 1997.[11]

During the struggle he waged against the newly appointed, Deng clearly used the movement for his own benefit. Once he had achieved his ends, he put a stop to it. More broadly, the 'spring of democracy', alluding to the Prague Spring, was possible only because it was permitted or even favoured by the ruling elites. Deng and his supporters, veterans of the regime or victims of Mao's arbitrary rule, supported a pro-democracy rhetoric that eroded the legitimacy of their opponent. The newly appointed behind Hua Guofeng were at the same time anxious to mark their differences with the policies followed during the preceding period; they tolerated and encouraged this kind of language in order to gain popular support and consolidate their position. The situation at the top of the political apparatus had temporarily opened up a space of freedom beyond the control of the Party. Once Deng had won, this space was closed. At the same time as the arrests took place, in March 1979, Deng Xiaoping defined the four fundamental principles (*si xiang jiben yuanze* 四项基本原则) that would henceforth be regularly invoked to mark the limits of any liberalization. The socialist path, the democratic dictatorship of the people, the leading role of the Party, and Marxism-Leninism and Mao Zedong thought therefore constituted four elements on which the Chinese leadership could not compromise; in 1982, these principles would even be incorporated into the preamble of the Constitution.

At the top of the apparatus, the newly appointed in Hua's circle were gradually marginalized. During the fifth plenary session of the Eleventh Central Committee, in February 1980, the 'Little Gang of Four' (Wang Dongxing, Ji Dengkui, Wu De and Chen Xilian) was ousted from the Politburo, while Hu Yaobang and Zhao Ziyang entered the Politburo Standing Committee. The secretariat of the Central Committee resumed its functions; Hu Yaobang, having been merely the head of the secretariat, regained the title that had been Deng Xiaoping's until 1966: Secretary General of the Central Committee. In September 1980, a new State Council was formed; Hua Guofeng handed over as Premier to Zhao Ziyang, and several veterans – Deng Xiaoping, Li Xiannian and Chen Yun – also left the government. At the end of 1980, Deng relieved Hua Guofeng of the last and most strategic post he held, chairmanship of the Party's Central Military Commission, a post he officially took over in June 1981. At the same time, Deng had to cede ground to the more conservative or moderate elements of the anti-Maoist coalition that had enabled him to take control of the Party in December 1978.

A sign of the lack of consensus among those who joined forces against Hua Guofeng was that the years 1981–83 were marked by a slowdown in reforms. Premier Zhao Ziyang could not pursue the de-planning movement. Administrative devolution was halted, and central controls were strengthened in key areas of the economy. Politically, the new government line became evident during the reassessment of the Cultural Revolution and through various campaigns and movements. Nevertheless, Deng managed to introduce a number of reforms that further institutionalized the regime.

The sixth plenary session of the Eleventh Central Committee, meeting in June 1981, adopted a text that to this day constitutes the official historical interpretation of the Cultural Revolution; it is titled *Resolution on Certain Questions in the History of Our Party since the Founding of the People's Republic of China*. This text followed a document adopted in 1945 called *Resolution on Certain Questions in the History of Our Party*, which had institutionalized and legitimized the cult of Mao Zedong within the Party and established the general model for the treatment of history by the Party.[12] The adoption of this text illustrates the concessions that the reformers were forced to make to the leaders who favoured a more orthodox path to the Maoist goal. Admittedly, this text gave a critical assessment of the Cultural Revolution, defined as the period 1966–76. It denounced the crimes of Lin Biao and the Gang of Four – who had just been found guilty at their trial in the winter of 1980–81. However, the text largely spared Mao, and took pains to minimize his responsibilities. 'Some decisions' made during the Great Leap Forward and the Cultural Revolution were referred to as 'Mao's mistakes'. But his historical role was described as positive overall; Mao Zedong remained a 'great proletarian revolutionary'.

Rehabilitation of the victims of the Cultural Revolution, and more broadly of the arbitrariness of Maoist policy, was part of the same desire to open a new page in the history of the People's Republic, while the population was exhausted and the government largely delegitimized. Elite members were rehabilitated, such as Liu Shaoqi and Peng Dehuai, both of whom had died in prison in 1969 and 1974 respectively. Hundreds of thousands of other verdicts were also revised. Victims of unjust political sanctions were rehabilitated and class labels that dated from the anti-rightist campaign of 1957 were removed, for the first time since 1949.[13]

The Twelfth Congress (September 1982) formalized the political changes that had taken place since December 1978 and attempted to institutionalize the way the Party operated. The political line adopted emphasized economic development, and the class struggle was relegated to the background. In his report, Hu Yaobang endorsed a new managerial policy that promoted the promotion of younger and more competent managers, while a pension system was also introduced.

Several organizational changes now normalized Party life. The position of Chairman, a Chinese exception inherited from the Maoist era, was abolished and, as in all Communist parties around the world, it was now the Secretary General of the Central Committee who became the main leader. He was endowed with broad powers, in particular that of convening the meetings of the Politburo and of its Standing Committee, and of directing the activities of the secretariat. The Standing Committee was transformed into a collective leadership under which the Secretary General, one of the members of the governing nucleus, officiated. The Party's usual norms for recruitment and discipline were restored.

Forty-six per cent of the members of the Central Committee were newcomers, while, at the provincial level, the leadership teams largely stayed the same. But the personnel changes also revealed the need for Deng Xiaoping to come to terms with his allies. Although Hua Guofeng left the Politburo, reformists and Deng supporters within it continued to share power with Chen Yun's friends, Zhou Enlai's former collaborators and the military. Some officials were hostile to Hu Yaobang (Deng Liqun, Yu Qiuli and Yao Yilin). Many leaders from the Deng generation were unwilling to hand over power. Ye Jianying, Li Xiannian and Chen Yun continued to sit with Deng, Hu and Zhao Ziyang on the Politburo Standing Committee.

The campaigns of criticism and repression of the first half of the 1980s were another illustration of the bargaining that reformists were obliged to engage in. These movements aimed to remedy the consequences of the relaxation of controls on the population and the spread of new ways of life and types of thought from abroad. In 1982, a major campaign against corruption was launched with the support of the Party's Discipline Control Commission, chaired by Chen Yun; it set about stigmatizing the harmful effects of economic opening-up, which continued in 1983 with a movement of rectification within the Party. In 1983, at the instigation of Peng Zhen, a campaign against crime was launched. The courts were encouraged, often in defiance of the new criminal procedures, to sentence to death tens of thousands of delinquents, arrested more according to quotas set by the Party than according to the gravity of their crimes or offences – a sign of the still very political functioning of justice. In the same year, a campaign 'against spiritual pollution' was launched by Deng Liqun, director of the Party's Propaganda Department, with the support of Deng Xiaoping; it targeted all those who were influenced by Western ways of life or thought. Many young people and intellectuals were harassed or even condemned to terms of re-education through labour and sometimes imprisonment. But this movement did not last.

Rehabilitation of the law

The desire for stabilization and institutionalization at the heart of the reformist and modernizing project was illustrated by the promulgation of a fourth Constitution, still in force today. It reveals the rehabilitation of law sought by the new regime. With 138 articles, it was the longest of the constitutions of the People's Republic (the previous ones contained 106 in 1954, 30 in 1975, and 60 in 1978); it was part of the rehabilitation of law that had begun in 1978, and was another step in the reconstruction of the state. The ideological dimension (class struggle) and the institutional dimension of the Cultural Revolution (people's communes and revolutionary committees) disappeared, while some aspects that had been abolished (the presidency of the Republic) were restored. The preamble confirmed the four fundamental principles and emphasized the need for modernization.

While, in 1978, article 2 had defined the role of the Party as 'the core of leadership of the whole Chinese people', in 1982, the Party was no longer mentioned in the constitutional text except in the preamble, which recalled the leading role of the Party at the historical level and its successes, as in 1954. Article 5 further states: 'No organization or individual may enjoy the privilege of being above the Constitution and the law.'[14] The concept of the dictatorship of the proletariat was abandoned in favour of the more ambiguous notion of 'the people's democratic dictatorship'. The rights and duties of citizens are described in chapter II, just after the general principles, as in the Nationalist Constitution of 1947, whereas they previously appeared at the end. The description of the competences of the various central state bodies, the National People's Congress, the

State Council and local and judicial institutions occupies most of chapter III. The presidency of the Republic, suspended since 1969, was reintroduced; Li Xiannian, close to Deng, was elected to this post in April 1983.

One of the innovative points of this Constitution, one representative of the new political line, is the mention of a 'socialist legal system'. Previous constitutions had demanded that workers in state agencies obey the law. In the 1975 Constitution, references to the law were minimized in favour of ideological references. In 1982, the law returned to centre stage. Indeed, the law occupied a place in the reform project that it had never before enjoyed in China, not even in the mid-1950s. There was now an explicit desire to 'govern in accordance with the law' (*yifa weizhi* 以法为治) and thus mark a break with the arbitrariness of the Maoist period. This was because everyone recognized that the disasters China had experienced were not only manmade but the consequence of a system, and it was therefore this system that must be reformed. Thus, the communiqué of the third plenary session of the Central Committee of December 1978 specified: 'In order to safeguard [the] people's democracy, it is imperative to strengthen the socialist legal system so that democracy is systematized and written into law in such a way as to ensure the stability, continuity and full authority of this democratic system and these laws.'[15]

The main architect of this process of building a socialist legal system was Peng Zhen, the mayor of Beijing, Vice Chairman of the National People's Congress and Chairman of its Law Committee since June 1979. Another example is the adoption of a Penal Code and a Code of Criminal Procedure in July 1979: these constituted real progress compared to the state of lawlessness of the previous period, despite a still highly politicized exercise of justice. This effort was also in accordance with the imperatives of opening-up; the publication in July 1979 of a law on mixed Chinese–foreign business was the sine qua non for the participation of foreign businesses in the modernization of the Chinese production apparatus.

The main problem raised by this new Constitution, like the new legislation, was that of its application, even though article 5 stated: 'The People's Republic of China exercises power in accordance with the law and establishes a socialist country under the rule of law. The state upholds the uniformity and dignity of the socialist legal system.'[16] In the immediate term, this effort was part of the institutionalization of the regime and a strategy to win back its legitimacy.

The acceleration of reforms (1984–86)

The mid-1980s saw further progress in the reform movement. In 1980, four cities had been opened to foreign investors as part of the creation of Special Economic Zones (SEZs): Shenzhen, Zhuhai and Shantou in Guangdong province, and Xiamen in Fujian. In February 1984, Deng Xiaoping proposed opening up fourteen coastal towns. In October, the Party approved a major reform plan that extended the introduction of market mechanisms to industry and promoted a resumption of administrative devolution. The heart of the economic system was now concerned with reforms. In 1985, Deng, at the height of his power, succeeded in imposing on the army an extensive restructuring, in the form of a reduction in manpower of one million, and Hu Yaobang speeded up the renewal of leadership teams both at the centre and in the provinces. In 1986, the delicate question of reforming political structures was considered and debated at the highest level. Some, in China and abroad, believed that the country was embarking on the path of democratization.

The question of the transition of industry and services to a market economy was now raised for the first time, albeit in cautious terms. In October 1984, at the third plenary session of the Twelfth Central Committee, a programme of 'reform of economic structures' was adopted; it aimed, on the one hand, at extending the autonomy of state-owned enterprises and freedom of prices, and, on the other, at encouraging the development of private industrial activities or activities in cooperation with foreign partners. This continued de-planning process deepened the divisions within the Party. In 1985, conservatives (Li Xiannian) and moderates (Chen Yun) relied on the problems caused by the reforms (overheating, inflation, corruption) to voice ever more criticisms. Supported by Deng Xiaoping, the reformists, at the cost of tactical concessions – such as the re-establishment of central controls – pursued their strategy.

In September 1985, at a national conference of Party representatives, new political leaders were promoted to central and provincial bodies. Ninety-one new officials joined the Central Committee. The number of military personnel fell from forty-one to thirty-one. About ten veterans left the Politburo, including Marshal Ye Jianying, Madame Deng Yichao and Wang Zhen. Among the new entrants were Li Peng, who cut a conservative figure, and also people from the circles of Hu Yaobang and Zhao Ziyang such as Hu Qili, placed in charge of ideology. At the provincial level, fifteen first secretaries and thirteen governors out of twenty-nine were replaced. At the central level, as in the provinces, the new leaders were younger, in their fifties for the most part, and better qualified.

In the spring of 1986, there was a lively debate on political reform among both political leaders and intellectuals. The reformers, including Hu Yaobang, Wang Zhaoguo, Zhu Houze, the new director of the Propaganda Department, and Wan Li, advocated a devolution of powers, a better distribution of tasks between the Party and the state, the establishment of a professionalized public service, an improvement in the legal system and institutions for controlling the administration and a 'democratization' of popular assemblies. For them, political reform, like the economic reform that it was to accompany, was not intended to challenge the socialist system, but to modernize it and make it more effective in the service of growth.

Some reformist intellectuals went further and tried to introduce ideas of democracy, the rule of law and pluralism. Among them were Yan Jiaqi, director of the Institute of Political Science at the Academy of Social Sciences of China, and Fang Lizhi, Vice Rector of the Scientific and Technical University of China (Hefei, Anhui); they questioned the legitimacy of the Party dictatorship. Yan called not for a better division of labour, but for a clear separation between the Party and the state. Drawing on the writings of Locke and Montesquieu, he favoured the establishment of a system of checks and balances like that set up by those who had drafted the American Constitution. Without openly calling for the separation of the executive, legislative and judicial powers, he advocated the establishment of democratic elections both within the Party and in government bodies; and above all, he sought the gradual abandonment of the pre-eminence of the Party.

In September 1986, the Chinese leadership was divided into two camps that advocated apparently irreconcilable development and reform strategies. On the one hand, the reformists, led by the Party Secretary

General Hu Yaobang and Premier Zhao Ziyang, sought to continue the transition to a market economy and instil a certain dose of modernity and flexibility, even of freedom and democracy, within the political system. For them, political reform was essential to remove obstacles to economic reform.

On the other hand, the conservatives were in favour of maintaining a largely planned economy and a regime tightly controlled by the Party. At their head were Party veterans such as Chen Yun, who was a retired former economic policymaker, Li Xiannian, head of state until March 1988, and Peng Zhen, President of the National People's Congress until March 1988. They feared that a relaxation of Party control would foster ideological and social disorder. In September 1986, the sixth plenary session of the Central Committee adopted a 'Resolution with Regard to the Guiding Principles of the Construction of a Socialist Spiritual Civilization', a concession made by Deng Xiaoping to the conservatives.

The struggle between rival factions intensified with student protests in Beijing and other cities in December 1986, as students demanded more freedom and democracy. The conservatives sought the opportunity to orchestrate an attack on the Secretary General, whom they accused of weakness in his fight against the degradation of ideology. Deng was forced to distance himself from Hu Yaobang, his presumed successor. Zhao Ziyang succeeded him and Li Peng became Premier.

The failure of Zhao Ziyang and regime crisis (1986–89)

Despite this concession to the conservatives, Deng Xiaoping ordered Zhao not to let the campaign against liberalization hinder political and economic reform. For Deng, political reform was limited to 'the separation of Party and government'. This meant changing administrative procedures in order to limit the intervention of the organs of the Communist Party in the affairs of the government, and to allow the latter to function in a more autonomous and expert way, especially in the management of the economy. This project was presented by Zhao Ziyang at the Thirteenth Party Congress. In order to prepare ideologically for the acceleration of economic reform, the Congress also announced that China was at the 'preliminary stage of socialism', that is to say at a stage where it was acceptable to use certain capitalist methods such as the market and profit-based management to facilitate economic growth. However, in the spring of 1988, plans for political reform were abandoned, as was a plan to abolish the state price control system for major components and industrial products, since this plan had triggered panic buying. In this climate of social discontent in the face of the deteriorating economic situation, the spring 1989 democracy movement made its appearance; this was the most important episode of protest against the Communist Party that the People's Republic had ever known, and its most serious political crisis.

Aborted political reform

At the Thirteenth Congress held in October–November 1987, Zhao Ziyang succeeded in having the Central Committee adopt the most ambitious political reform plan of the Deng Xiaoping era. The aim of this plan was to improve a socialist system that the Party admitted to be still in its 'primitive phase'. Zhao proposed a set of cautious political reforms that helped to reverse the Party's grip on the state and society. He proposed a clear separation of the organization and the mission of the Party from the state. The Party should continue to exercise political leadership over the country and recommend candidates for leadership positions in the state apparatus, but Zhao called for the gradual abolition of Party groups in administrations, businesses and social organizations. He supported greater decentralization, in particular in favour of villages and street committees, as well as a clarification of relations between the centre and the provinces. He promised further administrative simplification and the establishment of an administrative law that had hitherto been completely nonexistent. He decided on the creation of a real civil service limited to administrative officials (4 million out of a total of 27 million), divided into two categories: on the one hand, political officials recommended by the Party and formally elected by the competent people's assemblies, and, on the other hand, professional civil servants recruited by competitive examination, trained in a national administrative institute to be created, and obeying career rules similar to those of Western civil services. He envisaged the establishment of a system of consultation and dialogue between government and society that did not exclude the organization of referendums on specific issues. He called for an expansion of the prerogatives of people's assemblies, greater autonomy for unions and the enactment of laws establishing important public freedoms. Finally, he discussed the establishment of a legal system, in particular court independence and a better application of the laws.

This programme gave priority to the redesign of the administration and did not call into question the leading role of the Party; in this respect it did not modify the bases of the political system. It was approved by the Party leaders, essentially the same leaders as before. Zhao Ziyang was elected Vice Chairman of the Party's Central Military Commission, behind Deng Xiaoping, becoming his presumed new successor, and ahead of Yang Shangkun, the real head of the army. The Politburo was now made up of an equal number of reformists and conservatives. The Politburo Standing Committee was made up of five people: two reformists (Zhao Ziyang and Hu Qili, responsible for ideology), two conservatives (Li Peng, made Premier the day after the Congress, and Yao Yilin, Deputy Premier in charge of the economy), and a centrist (Qiao Shi, in charge of the Party Organization department).

Until the summer of 1988, Zhao Ziyang continued to be in charge of the economy and, on Deng's instructions, he introduced the measures approved at the Thirteenth Congress. He succeeded in replacing Peng Zhen with a reformist, Wan Li, as head of the National People's Congress and in preserving several allies in the new State Council. But he was obliged to resign himself to seeing Yang Shangkun succeed Li Xiannian as President of the Republic, and ultra-conservative Wang Zhen being appointed Vice President of the Republic. In the summer of 1988, faced with the deterioration of the economic situation, marked in particular by accelerating inflation, Deng did a volte-face and instructed veterans Chen Yun and Bo Yibo to take the lead in economic reform. This change was formalized by the third plenary session of the Thirteenth Central Committee meeting in September 1988. At the same time, Zhao endeavoured to implement his political reform. He dismantled the Party groups at the provincial and central levels, and encouraged the people's assemblies to exercise a right of scrutiny over the choice of political officials recommended by the Party. He favoured the promotion of non-Communists to the administration. He persuaded the National People's Congress to approve a law on administrative procedure which, for the first time, allowed citizens to seek judicial recourse against the administration. He protected many intellectuals and allowed them to publish certain liberal newspapers. Yet, when the events of May 1989 broke out, Zhao Ziyang had already lost much of his hold over the state apparatus that was by then in the hands of Li Peng.

The reimposition of dictatorship

The first demand made by the protesters in the spring of 1989 was the rehabilitation of Hu Yaobang, the purged Secretary General of the Party. They then demanded an acceleration of reforms, and a more effective fight against corruption in the leadership; these wishes then turned into demands for democratic change, even if several of the protesters had a fairly simplistic view of human rights and political pluralism. The movement was led by idealistic and quite naive students, most of whom had not experienced the harshness of Maoist repression. But the Tiananmen Square hunger strikers gained the support of tens of millions of other citizens, workers and employees, who for weeks took to the streets in many cities to demand a response from the government. The latter first tried to procrastinate, hoping that the movement would fade away, and then engaged in limited dialogue with the protestors before finally giving the order to clear Tiananmen Square by force. In the process that led to this decision, the upper echelons of the Party experienced their worst divisions since the Cultural Revolution.

The student movement began with a tribute to the memory of the reformer Hu Yaobang, who had been forced to resign from his term as Secretary General in January 1987, and died on 15 April.[17] Two days later, Beijing students demanding his posthumous rehabilitation demonstrated in his memory, away from the university campuses. On 19 April, they found themselves in front of the Party headquarters from where they were violently dispersed by the police. They then moved to Tiananmen Square, which they occupied. This was not yet a radical protest movement; most of them recognized the Party leadership and presented themselves as respectful, though disappointed, supporters of the long-term reform project. The students marched more in mourning than in protest. Their message centred on the need to accelerate political reform and expose corruption. Only a minority raised more delicate issues such as democracy or freedom of the press and shouted hostile slogans against the Party and certain leaders. On 20 and 21 April, the first autonomous student associations appeared; they were illegal, and had no precedent except during the Cultural Revolution. On 22 April, at the funeral of Hu Yaobang, a very large peaceful demonstration took place in Tiananmen Square in front of the People's Palace, seat of the Congress.

Leaders were divided over their assessment of the movement. Zhao Ziyang, whose job it was to manage the situation as the Party's Secretary General, convinced the Politburo and Deng Xiaoping to adopt a moderate line, believing that the movement would run out of steam. He felt confident enough to go on an official trip to North Korea for a week. In his absence, Premier Li Peng called a new meeting of the Politburo on 24 April, to hear reports on the expansion of the student movement in Beijing and the rest of the country. On 25 April, an informal meeting brought together members of the Politburo and Deng Xiaoping at his home. The former persuaded Deng that hostile forces had joined the movement and that the students were becoming more and more radical. Deng then described the movement as 'unrest' (*dongluan* 动乱) – a term used to refer to the chaos caused by the Cultural Revolution. His words were repeated in the *People's Daily* editorial the next day. Far from setting limits not to be crossed, this text radicalized the students.

The demonstrations resumed, and demanded a review of this description. New groups of students arrived in the square. Whole train-loads of people arrived from the provinces. On 4 May, more than 300,000 of them marched in Beijing and other major cities. Demonstrations spread in the provinces. On 10 May, the Politburo met again and failed to agree on the line defended by Zhao Ziyang. The student movement was itself divided. Some returned to college, others joined the strike. New leaders emerged, new questions were asked, and new participants, including intellectuals working in universities and research centres in Beijing, showed their support for the students.

On 13 May, the students announced that they were starting a hunger strike to demand that the viewpoint stated in the 26 April editorial be revised. Zhao Ziyang was ready to give in to the demand, but Li Peng opposed it, fearing it would set a dangerous precedent. On 15 May, the demonstrators took advantage of the arrival of Mikhail Gorbachev and foreign televisions to make themselves heard. Three days later, a million of them were gathered in Tiananmen Square demanding the retirement of the elderly Deng Xiaoping and the resignation of Premier Li Peng. The two sides, both the demonstrators and the government, were becoming radicalized. On the one hand, the leadership felt under siege and blamed Zhao for the situation. On the other, the protesters swore to die rather than withdraw.

On 16 May, the Politburo Standing Committee was convened, but Zhao Ziyang failed to convince his colleagues that the only way to end the hunger strike was to accept the students' demands for changing the opinion of the 26 April editorial. The next day, Deng's opinion was again sought. This time, after consulting the elders,[18] he sided with Li Peng; he was now in favour of repression and the proclamation of martial law. A new meeting of the Standing Committee was called on the 17 May, and the vote on martial law was split, with two votes for (Li Peng and Yao Yilin) and two votes against (Zhao Ziyang and Hu Qili), with Qiao Shi abstaining. On 18 May, the eight elders met with the Politburo Standing Committee, in Zhao's absence, as well as Hong Xuezhi, Liu Huaqing and Qin Jiwei, members of the Central Military Commission; they formally decided to proclaim martial law.

On the morning of 20 May, Li Peng signed the decree instituting martial law. Two weeks elapsed between this decision and the entry of tanks into Tiananmen Square; during this time, some Party officials (Zhao Ziyang, Hu Qili, Yan Mingfu, Rui Xingwen) and army veterans (Marshals Xu Xiangqian and Nie Rongzhen, and General Zhang Aiping) openly opposed the use of force. The immediate effect was that Beijing residents crowded at the gates of the city to prevent the entry of PLA troops. Millions of demonstrators demanded freedom of expression, trade union independence, the right to vet their leaders and an end to corruption in the leadership. On 25 May, the army threw in its lot with the conservatives. On 27 May, the eight elders met at Deng Xiaoping's home and chose Jiang Zemin, Mayor of Shanghai, as Zhao Ziyang's successor as Party Secretary General; his candidacy was supported by Chen Yun and Li Xiannian. On 29 May, the students erected the famous goddess of democracy (*minzhu nüshen* 民主女神), a plaster statue modelled on the Statue of Liberty, in the centre of Tiananmen Square. On 2 June, a new meeting of the elders with the three remaining members of the Politburo Standing Committee, Li Peng, Qiao Shi and Yao Yilin, confirmed the decision to evacuate the square by force. At 2 a.m. on 4 June, the 27th

Corps of the People's Army entered the square with tanks. According to an internal Party report, the military intervention caused the death of 241 people. International organizations cite 1,000 deaths. To this day, the association of Tiananmen Mothers, which calls on the government to shed light on the events, has still not been given any satisfactory answers.

In the short term, these events were followed by brutal repression. In the medium term, they committed the regime to a conservative reaction. Several tens of thousands of people were arrested. Heavy sentences were passed. At the trials that took place in Beijing in January and February 1991, the most prominent dissident intellectuals (Chen Ziming, Wang Juntao) were sentenced to very heavy sentences (thirteen years in prison), while student leaders were treated with a calculated leniency – four years in prison for Wang Dan.

Some student leaders managed to escape through the police net and fled abroad. Beijing lived under martial law for eight months. University campuses were brought back under control. The research institutions that had opened up in the 1980s were all closed. The Academy of Social Sciences expelled its most cutting-edge researchers. To this day, the repression of what was officially a 'counter-revolutionary riot' is a taboo subject; the term *liusi* (六四, 64, for June 4 – i.e., June Fourth Massacre), by which the movement is commonly known, is banned from all publications and the Internet.

At the end of June, the governing bodies of the Party confirmed the new positions of those leaders who had been involved in the events. On 23 and 24 June, at the fourth plenary session of the Thirteenth Central Committee, Jiang Zemin was elected Secretary General of the Party; along with Song Ping and Li Ruihuan, he joined the Politburo Standing Committee. Zhao Ziyang, Hu Qili, Rui Xingwen and Yan Mingfu lost their positions in the Party. In November, at the fifth plenary session of the Thirteenth Central Committee, Deng Xiaoping abandoned the last official post he still held, resigning from the chairmanship of the Central Military Commission; Jiang Zemin succeeded him. While Jiang now combined the two highest offices in the Party, observers wondered about the real extent of his power. In 1989, his power base was narrow and he was viewed as a transitional ruler. Jiang, supported by Chen Yun and Li Xiannian, was a conservative whose beliefs clashed with Deng's steadfast will to uphold the goal of modernization and the policy of reform and opening-up. Within the Central Military Commission, Deng continued to have important contacts through Yang Shangkun, his half-brother Yang Baibing and Admiral Liu Huaqing.

One immediate effect was that the political position of Deng Xiaoping was weakened. He had less influence than when Hu Yaobang and Zhao Ziyang, the two successors he had chosen for himself, had been active. Economic policy was in the hands of Li Peng. An engineer by training, Li did not have an ideological approach to economic problems, but he allied with the conservatives. They made an attempt to reimpose strict controls on the economy, with macroeconomic imbalances attributed to a loss of control of the economy. This programme, which represented a step backwards in the reform movement, quickly failed.

Macroeconomic policies associated with austerity were combined with efforts to recentralize. Quotas were set on investments and credit growth; this led to a deceleration in the growth of banking credit. Rural businesses were to be the main victims of the credit crunch. Price controls were re-established and reinforced on certain consumer products and inter-mediate goods. There was also a return to sectoral policies as opposed to the regional policies put in place by Zhao Ziyang who had favoured coastal areas. Investments were channelled into the state industrial sector. The proportion of investment in heavy industry reached its highest level since 1978. The number of products subject to planning was rising. More generally, the aim was to increase the proportion of the economy corresponding to the plan.

The results were not what had been anticipated. The decline in demand did indeed reduce bottlenecks, but also caused a recession. The growth rate of production fell from 11 per cent in 1988 to 4.21 per cent in 1989 and 3.92 per cent in 1990. The official urban unemployment rate reached 2.6 per cent in 1989, its highest level since 1982. The consequences were even more brutal in rural areas, with a drop in non-agricultural rural employment, which fell from 95 million in 1988 to 92 million by the end of 1989.

The situation for state-owned enterprises, far from improving, deteriorated. The government asked them to cushion the consequences of the recession. Priority was given to political and social objectives relative to short-term profitability imperatives. In order to ensure employees' wages, they were to be kept busy, even if they were not actually needed.

They were asked to maintain their production, financed on credit, even if their products were not sold. The result was a decline in the profitability of state-owned enterprises. After 1989, losses in the state industrial sector became significant for the first time since the start of the reforms. While some sectors whose products were highly controlled (oil and coal) were traditionally in deficit, new sectors were now also making a loss, such as the textile industry. After 1990, state-owned enterprises stopped contributing positively to the state budget. Thus, the programme of the conservatives, who had originally aimed to defend state-owned enterprises, ended up weakening them.

Changes in the balance of political power also lay behind the conservatives' failure. Representatives of local governments – Zhu Rongji for Shanghai and Ye Xuanping for Guangdong in particular – opposed measures to strengthen taxation to benefit the centre. Provincial and local governments emphasized their spending obligations and the reduction of their incomes, a consequence of the austerity policy. Local governments prevented rural industries from being seriously affected by the discriminatory policies of the centre, especially in coastal provinces like Zhejiang, Jiangsu or Shandong, where rural businesses generated a large share of tax resources. At the end of 1990, as a result of slower growth – and not thanks to better planning or a better coordination of economic decisions – the markets were again in equilibrium; inflation was under control. The conditions were now in place for reform to be relaunched.

Conclusion

The achievements of the first cycle of reforms that ended in 1989 were significant. Growth in production had been rapid and had finally allowed the standard of living of the population to take off. In the countryside as in the cities, life became easier. A private economic sphere had emerged and society enjoyed more and more areas of freedom. The state apparatus had undergone a major shift in the direction of decentralization. Thanks to economic reforms, provincial capitals became political forces with which the centre had to reckon; the central state constantly needed to negotiate with the provincial bureaucracies. Faced with the rise of centrifugal forces, some people were reminded of the feudalization of Chinese institutions.

What the events of 1989 showed was that economic reforms were not accompanied by democratization of the regime. Any direct challenge to the power exercised by the Communist Party was met with severe repression. After the tragic failure of the 1989 movement, most citizens turned away from politics. Since the demand for reform addressed directly to the regime had failed, some turned to society, hoping to stimulate the birth of a civil society. Since reform was not going to come from above, they would strive to ensure that it came from changes in society itself.

The period ended with the failure of the conservative project, which was definitively abandoned. There was therefore no alternative to establishing a market economy, and no coherent way of making the plan and the market coexist. In October 1992, the Fourteenth Party Congress recognized that China had changed the system of organization of its economy. The objective of the reform would be to dismantle the plan in order to create a true market economy. This change became possible only in the wake of Deng Xiaoping's last major political act. The 88-year-old Deng went on a 'tour of the South' (*nanxun* 南巡). He travelled to Hubei, Jiangxi, Guangdong, Fujian and Shanghai to revive the reform process that he himself had initiated fourteen years earlier.

FOUR

Building a New Model (after 1992)

The three most recent decades of the history of the People's Republic began with the last political act of 88-year-old Deng Xiaoping. While he no longer occupied any leading position within the Party or state apparatuses, and had not appeared in public for a year, between 18 January and 12 February 1992 he went successively to Wuhan, Shenzhen, Zhuhai and Shanghai. This historic trip was celebrated as the 'trip to the South' (*nanxun* 南巡), recycling an old expression used to designate the Emperor's inspection tours in the provinces. In his speeches, Deng confirmed the validity of the reforms of which, since 1978, he had been the great architect. Reaffirming his project of abandoning the revolution in favour of economic growth, he declared that 'the function of the revolution is to liberate the productive forces'.[1] Between the old and the new ways of allocating resources, he saw no contradiction, provided that wealth was created: 'Whether there is a little more planning or a little more market does not constitute any essential difference between socialism and capitalism ... The plan and the market are both economic means. The nature of socialism is to liberate the productive forces, to develop them, to eliminate exploitation and the polarization between rich and poor in order so as ultimately to access a common wealth.' He criticized the political line practised since 1989: 'Reforms require more boldness, as well as the courage to experiment', just as he denounced 'left-wing' errors: 'One hears for example that the reforms are opening up the door to capitalism and allowing it to develop, or even that the main risk of peaceful development comes from the economy; we can recognize the "left-wing" discourse.' He praised the SEZs where investors and companies enjoyed unusually favourable conditions: 'Special Economic Zones belong to the socialist family, not to the capitalist family, as we see in Shenzhen.' Deng also responded to those who were alarmed by the differences in wealth between provinces: 'Overall, that is to say at the national level, it is certain that we have the means to gradually and smoothly resolve the question posed by the differences in wealth between the coast and the interior of the country.'

At the end of this trip, and hearing his plea for the revival of reforms, the ruling elite agreed with Deng Xiaoping, who now definitively defeated the conservative clan led by Chen Yun. The market economy enjoyed a new legitimacy. This turning point encouraged many households to go into business, and it is from this time that dates the expression 'plunge into the sea' (*xiahai* 下海), to designate those who take the leap into the unknown – into the private economy. So the man who had started the country on the path of reforms and opened up the economy fourteen years earlier now relaunched the process that had been halted in 1989. This kind of language was repeated throughout 1992 by the organs of propaganda and endorsed by the Fourteenth Party Congress in October. The quarrels between the proponents of planning and the supporters of the market were then finally over; the goal recognized by all was now to build a 'socialist market economy'. The leaders recognized that the incremental changes initiated since 1978 inevitably led to a change of model. Initiatives continued over two decades to build this market economy; a major milestone was reached when the People's Republic joined the World Trade Organization in 2001.

This new model was not only economic; it was also social and political. Rapid growth, often in double digits, was accompanied by a radical transformation of the largely reconstructed and extended cities, which now welcomed a huge influx of migrants from the countryside. Society became more complex, and new social groups with contradictory interests appeared. If growth had benefited everyone in the previous period, it was now becoming more and more unequal. Portions of the population, in cities and in the countryside, were made up of those who had been left behind. These rapid and dramatic social transformations were not accompanied by a political revolution. The Communist Party managed to stay in power and remained the architect of change. This was partly because the Party knew how to adapt to new economic and social realities, and partly thanks to the unity of its leaders; while they sometimes had differing opinions, they were no longer divided as they had been in the 1980s.

Two men, each for a decade, held supreme responsibility as Secretary General of the Party: Jiang Zemin (1989–2002) then Hu Jintao (2002–12).

They combined this post with the Presidency of the Republic, the former from 1993 to 2003 and the latter from 2003 to 2013. The office of the Premier was, during these two decades, occupied by three figures: Li Peng (1988–98), Zhu Rongji (1998–2003) and Wen Jiabao (2003–13). Xi Jinping and Li Keqiang have been in office since 2013. The political system is therefore surprisingly stable compared to previous periods in the People's Republic; however, we can identify shifts in the political choices of successive teams. The absolute priority given to growth under Jiang Zemin was followed by a more sustained attention to social issues under Hu Jintao. Xi Jinping, on the other hand, under the guise of a 'Chinese dream', appealed to nationalism and promised prosperity for all. After a quarter of a century of reforms, China has become the second largest economy in the world after the United States, and the model of economic, social and political organization that it has built over three decades of reform is powerfully alluring for all nations that aspire to escape from poverty and build a better future. The first Olympics held on Chinese soil in 2008 and the World Expo in Shanghai in 2010 were unique opportunities to celebrate China's successful development in front of the whole world. More recently, the effectiveness of the measures taken by Beijing to contain the coronavirus pandemic has reinforced China's position as a world power.

The Jiang Zemin decade: authoritarian, conservative and pragmatic leadership (1989–2002)

An engineer in power

The Fourteenth Party Congress, meeting in Beijing from 12 to 18 October 1992, endorsed the proposals made by Deng Xiaoping at the beginning of the year and proceeded to re-elect the leadership. The report presented by Jiang Zemin thoroughly accepted the imperatives of a sustained rate of growth and the establishment of a 'socialist market economy', a concept that emphasized the failure of the classic socialist economic model and legitimized the revival of reforms on the ideological level. The reform of prices and companies was again a priority. Decentralization and individual initiative were honoured. There was talk of a 'primary stage of socialism', an expression used by Zhao Ziyang at the previous Congress in 1987, in order to bring the reforms and opening-up introduced since 1979 into the canons of Marxism-Leninism. This confirmed the failure of Chen Yun and the supporters of an essentially planned economy where the market would be merely a supplement. China was now firmly committed to the generalization of market mechanisms.

Jiang Zemin and Li Peng retained their positions and remained on the Politburo Standing Committee, which was increased from five to seven members. Two of Chen Yun's circle, Yao Yilin, head of economic affairs, and Song Ping, head of organization, both aged 75, retired. Three younger reformist leaders came onto the scene: Zhu Rongji, Deputy Premier and number two in the government; Liu Huaqing, Jiang Zemin's Vice Chairman in the Central Military Commission; and Hu Jintao, Party Secretary in Tibet. The latter, aged 49, was the youngest member of the new Standing Committee; while he had the reputation of being an economic reformist, he was politically conservative – he led a policy of brutal repression in Tibet. The most important appointment to the Politburo Standing Committee was Zhu Rongji, former Mayor of Shanghai, who effectively suppressed protests in his city and prevented a general strike during the events of 1989. Apart from Li Peng, and to a lesser extent Qiao Shi, head of police and justice, none of the Party's leading core members was directly associated with the 4 June crackdown. Two veterans of the Party supposedly hostile to Jiang Zemin were ousted from the military leadership: Yang Shangkun left the Politburo and the Central Military Commission; his half-brother Yang Baibing was dismissed from his posts as Secretary General of the Central Military Commission and director of the army's General Political Department. The Yang brothers had allegedly attempted to create a faction within the army. This Congress created a sense of unity and stability. However, several questions remain unanswered: the succession of Deng Xiaoping, the fate of Zhao Ziyang and the verdict on the events of June 1989, and the contradiction between economic reform and political conservatism.[2]

The Eighth National People's Congress, meeting in March 1993, transformed the political orientations adopted by the Party in the autumn into laws. The Constitution was reformed to incorporate the phrase 'primary stage of socialism'. In the Basic Law, the term 'socialist market economy' now replaced 'planned economy', and the expressions 'state-owned economy' (*guoyou* 国有) and 'state-owned enterprises' replaced 'state-managed economy' (*guoying* 国营). The provisions relating to state planning were removed and replaced by others that required the state to strengthen economic legislation and macroeconomic control. The Congress also made a series of appointments. Jiang Zemin succeeded Yang Shangkun as President of the Republic, thereby strengthening his power over the state apparatus. Qiao Shi succeeded Wan Li as Chairman of the National People's Congress. Li Ruihan was appointed Chairman of the Chinese People's Political Consultative Conference, a post left vacant by Li Xiannian's death. Rong Yiren, descendant of a famous family of Shanghai entrepreneurs from the Republican period, and not a member of the Communist Party, was appointed Vice President, replacing conservative Wang Zhen, who had died on the eve of the Congress meeting.

The new government, charged with supporting the transition to a market economy, was formally led by Li Peng, aged 65, who was appointed Premier for a second five-year term. But he suffered from heart problems, and it was Vice Premier Zhu Rongji, also President of the People's Bank of China, who had de facto control over economic policy. He adopted centralizing measures in the face of economic overheating and the indiscipline of the provinces. For example, he was the architect of a tax reform adopted in November 1993 intended to replenish the coffers of central government. In a political atmosphere that evoked the end of a reign, as the public appearances of Deng Xiaoping were increasingly rare, Zhu Rongji was the main rival of Jiang Zemin and Li Peng.

Born in 1926, Jiang Zemin was originally from Yangzhou, in the province of Jiangsu. His trajectory was representative of that of an entire generation. Having grown up under the Japanese occupation, he studied successively at the National Central University of Nanjing and then at the National Chiao Tung University in Shanghai, from which he graduated in electrical engineering in 1947. He continued his training in Moscow in an automobile production plant, and was then appointed to Changchun, capital of Jilin province in Manchuria. He then spent his entire career in the Ministry of Electronics, which he took over in 1983. Two years later, in 1985, he was appointed Mayor of Shanghai and then the city's Party Secretary. In 1987, he became a member of the Politburo. In 1989, after the dismissal of Zhao Ziyang, he was elected to the post of Secretary General and made Chairman of the Central

Military Commission, but he was then seen as a compromise candidate, with little in the way of Party support and no real power. Chosen by Deng Xiaoping, who described him as the 'core' (*hexin* 核心) of the third generation of leaders of the Communist Party, Jiang appeared to have no charisma and no solid power base within the army or the Party, doomed to remain in the shadow of his protector. While awaiting the political struggle that would ensue following the death of Deng Xiaoping, he was considered a transitional leader.

Jiang, however, would stay in power for a long time. The two brothers Yang Shangkun, President of the Republic since 1988, and Yang Baibing, general and member of the Central Military Commission, both veterans of the Long March, were supposedly hostile to him; they left the commission during the Fourteenth Congress. In March 1993, Jiang Zemin succeeded Yang Shangkun as President of the Republic; from that date on, he was therefore at the head of the apparatuses of the Party, the army and the state.

Jiang scored another victory with the elimination of Chen Xitong, Mayor of Beijing and ally of Li Peng, long regarded as a political rival. Chen was ousted from power in the first major corruption scandal involving senior leaders. In April 1993, accused of receiving bribes related to real estate, the Vice Mayor of Beijing, Wang Baosen, committed suicide. A few days later, Chen Xitong was removed from his post. In July, he was arrested. Chen had been mayor of the capital since 1987 and had played an important role during the events of June 1989, placing the city's services at the full disposal of the army; he was thus acting as a liaison between the military and public security. The autonomy that Beijing enjoyed, such as town planning projects that were not subject to central government oversight, its proximity to officials engaged in real-estate speculation, and its lavish spending had undoubtedly made Chen an ideal scapegoat. He was finally expelled from the Party in September 1997, during the Fifteenth Congress, then sentenced by the courts in 1998 to sixteen years in prison. This was the first trial of a former member of the Politburo since the conviction in January 1981 of the Gang of Four. Months before his death in June 2013, Chen confided in his memoirs that he was in fact the victim of a political purge and that the alleged corruption was only a pretext. His fall stemmed, he said, from a conflict between the group from Shanghai, which included Jiang Zemin, Zhu

Rongji, Wu Bangguo and Huang Ju, all members of the Politburo, and the group from Beijing.

In the months that followed, Jiang's authority was bolstered by the peaceful demise of two of the People's Republic's top leaders. On 10 April 1995, Chen Yun, representative of the conservative camp, and considered to be the advocate of planning versus the market economy even though he had not been involved in government for a long time, died at the age of 90; this had no effect on government policies. And on 19 February 1997, Deng Xiaoping died, at the age of 93. His death, too, had no major impact. The period of mourning came to an end soon after his funeral on 25 February. After this death, Jiang's political authority would no longer be questioned. Confirmed in his functions, his political choices would mark his time. Preparations were being made for two important events: the return of the territory of Hong Kong to Chinese sovereignty on 1 July and the holding of the Seventeenth Party Congress in the autumn.

The rise of nationalism

The celebrations held on 1 July 1997 for the British Crown's handover of the territory of Hong Kong to the People's Republic were one of the most blatant manifestations of the rise of nationalism in China. Throughout the 1990s, the national dimension was the most assertive element in state building. This was nothing new, as Chinese Communism had always had a strong national dimension; Mao's ambition, as early as 1949, had been to restore China to the international stage after decades of humiliation. For some, the exaltation of the nation took the place of a Maoist ideology emptied of its substance, as if nationalism could now take over from an orthodoxy in which no one believed anymore. For others, the Maoist revolution remained a determining element, and was now being put at the service of the nation – whereas it had previously been the nation that was at the service of the revolution. 'The new Chinese state was no longer the state of the revolution; it had become the state of the Chinese nation', as Yves Chevrier writes.[3]

It was not just political leaders who lauded the nation, but also intellectuals. The best known of the many nationalist works that appeared in the second half of the 1990s was *China Can Say No* (*Zhongguo keyi shuo bu* 中国可以说不), published in 1996. This pamphlet, which sold more than 800,000 copies, was written by young intellectuals, and was based on the model of a Japanese book signed by a far-right deputy. The authors denounced a plot by the West, and in particular the United States, aimed at preventing China from developing and growing strong; and they displayed their desire to raise China to the rank of the world's leading power and thus end American hegemony.

This nationalism, in its popular dimension, was fostered by the objective of reunification – enshrined in the Constitution of the People's Republic[4] – and in particular by the difficult dialogue with Taiwan. In 1995–96, relations were particularly strained between the governments of the People's Republic and the Republic of China. There were several missile rounds fired in Taiwanese territorial waters. The first, carried out in the middle of 1995, was intended to send a signal to the government of Lee Teng-hui after it had made statements contrary to the goal of 'One China' during a trip to the United States – the two governments of Beijing and Taipei had so far shared the view that there was just one single Chinese nation. The second round of missiles was fired in early 1996, and intended to intimidate the Taiwanese electorate ahead of the presidential election in March. This crisis in the Taiwan Strait contributed to the rise of popular nationalism, as Chinese society unanimously supported the goal of reunification.

On 1 July 1997, in Hong Kong, a process that had begun in the early 1980s and had been marked by the joint declaration of December 1984, signed by the governments of the People's Republic and the United Kingdom, finally ended. This international treaty provided for the return to Beijing of full sovereignty over the entire territory of Hong Kong on 1 July 1997 and the establishment of the principle of 'one country, two systems' (*yiguo liangzhi* 一国两制) which allowed Hong Kong to keep its capitalist system for a period of fifty years, a legal formula originally invented in anticipation of Taiwan's return to Chinese rule. On the evening of the handover, Tung Chee-hwa, an industrialist from Shanghai, became the first head of the executive, replacing the last British governor, Chris Patten. The People's Republic was now in charge of ensuring the security of the territory, and 10,000 soldiers of the People's Army were deployed. The first months of this new regime were grounds for optimism. A year and a half later, in December 1999, it was Macao's turn to be handed over by Portugal to the Beijing government.

Jiang Zemin's consolidation of power

A few weeks later, the Fifteenth Party Congress met in Beijing, from 12 to 18 September 1997. This was the first Congress where the 'third generation' of leaders, the generation of Jiang Zemin and the first that had not played any role in the revolutionary epic, was not overshadowed by the presence of any veterans. Deng Xiaoping was dead, and this Congress might well be seen as the true beginning of the Jiang Zemin era. Indeed, the latter's authority was strengthened. He claimed that he was following the line of the man who had chosen him, and the central theme of the report that he presented to the Congress concerned the deepening of the reforms. 'Deng Xiaoping theory' (*Deng Xiaoping lilun* 邓小平理论) was enshrined in the Party charter, along with Marxism-Leninism and Mao Zedong thought; it required that one 'seek the truth in the facts'. Jiang Zemin also referred to the theory of the early stages of socialism.

With the departure of Deng Xiaoping and the other veterans, the Chinese political scene entered a new era. The technocrats were now in control. Thus, the seven members of the Politburo Standing Committee that emerged from the Congress were all technocrats; they had received a technical education and gained professional experience before entering politics and assuming ever increasing responsibilities.[5] Engineers turned politicians now governed China. Eighteen of the twenty-four members of the Politburo were engineers by training. Technocrats also constituted the majority of the 344 members of the Central Committee. The legitimacy to govern no longer depended on having followed a revolutionary career, but on the possession of skills acquired in another field.

In previous years, Jiang had won two significant political victories: the ousting of the Yang brothers, then that of Chen Xitong; in September 1997, he succeeded in getting rid of Qiao Shi, Chairman of the National People's Congress and the Party's number three, by virtue of his age (he was 70). Qiao, who had championed political and legal reform, and was considered a rival, left his post as Chairman of the Congress in March 1998. Jiang Zemin, born in 1926, then became the oldest of the country's senior leaders.

Jiang surrounded himself with leaders who were technocrats like him, or who had held responsibilities in Shanghai. Wu Bangguo and Huang Ju now joined the Politburo; they were both engineers who had graduated from Tsinghua University and held positions in Shanghai. Wang Daohan, the former mayor of Shanghai, who had preceded Jiang Zemin in this post, was in charge of negotiations with Taiwan. Zeng Qinghong, an engineer by training, had graduated from Beijing Institute of Technology; he made a career in the defence industries and then in the oil sector before joining Jiang Zemin in 1984 as mayor of Shanghai. While still Jiang's assistant, he made his debut as a deputy member of the Politburo at the Congress. As this third generation consolidated its power, it also prepared to prolong it. Leaders under the age of 60, members of the 'fourth generation' with provincial and national responsibilities, now also entered the Politburo, where the average age of members was 63.

At the meeting of the National People's Congress in March 1998, those in power were re-elected in accordance with the decisions taken during the Congress. The most important appointment was that of Zhu Rongji, born in 1928; he became Premier, succeeding Li Peng, while the latter succeeded Qiao Shi as Chairman of the Congress. Zhu Rongji was also an engineer. A graduate of Tsinghua University in electrical engineering, he worked successively for the Department of Industries of Northeast China, and then, from 1952 to 1958, for the State Planning Commission. Having criticized the policy of the Great Leap Forward, Zhu was labelled a 'rightist' in 1958 and sent to teach at a cadre school. Rehabilitated in 1962, he again joined the state planning commission, until 1969. During the Cultural Revolution, Zhu was ousted once more, and from 1970 to 1975 he was transferred to a May Seventh Cadre School to be re-educated. From 1975 to 1979, he was an engineer for a company controlled by the Petroleum Ministry, then director of an Institute of Industrial Economics under the aegis of the Chinese Academy of Social Sciences. From 1979, recruited by Deng Xiaoping, he held various economic management positions with the central government. In 1987, he was appointed Mayor of Shanghai while Jiang Zemin became Party Secretary. He supervised the development of Pudong, a huge territory the size of Singapore that was not very urbanized; it is located east of the historic centre of Shanghai, between the Huangpu river and the sea. As Mayor for five years, he was the main architect of the revival of the economic capital of China. In 1991, Zhu was summoned to Beijing as Deputy Premier. He was simultaneously governor of the Chinese Central Bank. So it was a specialist in steering the economy and a staunch supporter of reforms who held the post of Premier for five years, from 1998 to 2003. Another important decision taken during this session of the Congress was a programme for restructuring the central administration; ministries and commissions were reduced from forty to twenty-nine thanks, in particular, to the abolition of sectoral ministries in industry.

The other important appointment of the spring of 1998 was that of Hu Jintao, born in 1942, who was made Vice President of the People's Republic, which gave him greater international exposure and designated him as a possible successor of Jiang Zemin at the head of the Party. This appointment confirmed the coming to power of representatives of the fourth generation. In 1999, Hu was appointed Vice Chairman of the Central Military Commission, a further step on the path to supreme power.

Two other members of the Politburo under the age of 60 were in charge of economic questions alongside Zhu Rongji: Vice Premiers Wu Bangguo and Wen Jiabao. Another member of this generation was Zeng Qinghong, born in 1939, who was head of the Organization Department of the Chinese Communist Party. This was also the case with provincial leaders: Li Changchun, aged 55, was Party Secretary of Guandong province; Li Keqiang, aged 44, was governor of Henan; Xi Jinping, aged 46, was appointed governor of Fujian. Unlike the generation that preceded it, this one included fewer engineers and more specialists in finance and economics.[6]

The year 1999 should have been one of several celebrations: the eightieth anniversary of the 1919 May Fourth movement, the fiftieth anniversary of the founding of the People's Republic, and the tenth anniversary of the Tiananmen Square tragedy. None of these events was really celebrated. Indeed, the authorities were faced with a serious crisis: a protest movement unprecedented in the history of the People's Republic, with thousands of people closely supervised by an organization demanding its autonomy. On 25 April 1999, more than 10,000 people gathered in front of Zhongnanhai, the seat of political power in Beijing, and silently protested against the attacks on the Falungong (Wheel of Law) movement, demanding that their right to practise publicly the exercises they promoted be guaranteed.

The Falungong (法轮功) was established in 1992 and boasts tens of millions of followers. It is based on the ancient discipline of *qigong*

(气功) transmitted by Master Li Hongzhi;[7] it is distinguished by the way it simultaneously seeks physical and spiritual development. Initially, its spread was recognized and supported by the authorities. But faced with the success of this practice, they attempted to win back control of an organization that sought to be independent. During the summer of 1999, after several weeks of procrastination, the authorities questioned thousands of members of the movement across the country. On 22 July, the Falungong was declared an illegal organization and a press campaign was launched accusing the movement of being directly responsible for about 500 deaths, due both to the movement's opposition to traditional medical care and to the extreme and suicidal behaviour that it encouraged. On 28 July, China issued an international arrest warrant for US resident Li Hongzhi, and a wide campaign of repression began. Trials took place in November, resulting in prison sentences for a few members while several hundred others were sent to be re-educated in labour camps. In December, leaders of the group, all of them members of the Communist Party and holding office in the Party or the state apparatus, were sentenced, some of them to more than ten years in jail. In the months that followed, further protests took place and led to confrontations with the police. In the eyes of the Chinese government, the Falungong was now a sectarian organization. What this episode reveals is the thirst for meaning and spirituality among sections of the Chinese population. The primary reason for the success of Falungong was the spiritual vacuum that the cult of the nation or the worship of money cannot fill – or, as David Palmer writes, 'fertile social ground'.[8] While Communist ideals were widely betrayed, Li Hongzhi was taking a stand against the cynicism of post-Maoist society, which saw material enrichment as the only real human motivation.

Jiang Zemin's initiatives

The year 2000 was marked by two major initiatives: one economic, namely the launch of a policy of rebalancing growth at the national level; the other ideological, namely the formulation by Jiang Zemin of a new theory. The policy of developing the west of the country (*xibu da kaifa* 西部大开发) was formulated at the March 2000 session of the National People's Congress. While the reforms had since 1979 focused on the coastal fringe of the country, it was announced that economic construction would now have to focus on the western regions. Nine provinces and autonomous regions were concerned: Shaanxi, Qinghai, Gansu, Sichuan, Yunnan, Guizhou, Ningxia, Xinjiang and Tibet, as well as the city of Chongqing, directly under the authority of the central government since 1997. The first step was to address development inequalities. This entire region represents 57 per cent of the country's surface area and 23 per cent of the total population, but in 2000, the GNP of the western regions represented only 60 per cent of the national average; 90 per cent of the population in absolute poverty lived in these regions. Another reason for increasing public investment in western China was the high concentration of ethnic minorities, likely to feel discriminated against and therefore to protest. To begin with, this plan for a more balanced development of the country foresaw the construction of new railway lines, airports and dams. This policy was in fact a continuation of the priority given by Deng to coastal regions because he had always believed that, once these had reached a certain level of development, the interior provinces should be developed.

Another initiative was Jiang Zemin's formulation of the 'three representations' theory (*san ge daibiao* 三个代表). On a visit to Guandong Province in February 2000, Jiang Zemin explained that the Communist Party continued to be the key to the success of the reforms provided that it represented not only 'the advanced forces of production', but also 'advanced culture' and 'the interests of the whole people'. The political reasoning behind this new doctrine was clear: by embodying the 'advanced' forces, the Party could maintain its control of society, including its legitimacy and its usefulness. In the following weeks, the mainstream Chinese media quoted his words extensively. On 1 July 2001, on the occasion of the eightieth anniversary of the Chinese Communist Party, Jiang used this formula to announce that the Party must henceforth recruit beyond its usual bases and involve all the talented people. This initiative by Jiang, which was not unanimously approved within the Party, effectively ended the ban on bringing private entrepreneurs into the Party promulgated in 1989. This was a sign that the Party recognized the diversity of the social groups that had emerged as a result of the reforms; it now needed to include representatives of the new emerging social groups within its own ranks.

At the end of the following year, on 11 December 2001, the People's Republic became the 143rd member of the World Trade Organization (WTO). This accession was celebrated in China by the organs of propaganda and the media as a historic turning point, comparable to the launch of the reform and opening-up policy of 1979. Thanks to the WTO, the central government promised, China would move faster along the path of modernization and would be able to accelerate opening-up and reforms aimed at establishing a socialist market economy; it would be able to develop its exports and attract more direct foreign investment. This was the official discourse, which advocated a necessary and beneficial globalization. It was actually the result of a long process. Beijing had submitted a request for integration into what was then still called the General Agreement on Tariffs and Trade (GATT) in July 1986; the WTO was created in January 1995. Thus, at the end of six years of negotiations, China signed thirty-seven bilateral agreements and a 900-page protocol of accession. More than a turning point, this episode constituted a new stage in opening up to the world, as a guarantee of economic development and social and political stability. China's development strategy had been based since 1979 on internationalization, that is to say on direct foreign investment – which financed the modernization of the production apparatus – and trade. While it was not possible for any critical discourse to be expressed in what passed as public space, dissenting voices could be heard in academia and government, in specialized and more low-key arenas. Some denounced the stranglehold of capitalism on China and spoke of widespread privatization and growing social injustices. The WTO was denounced as an instrument in the hands of Western powers whose mission was to homogenize the world and to enslave China. China's participation in the WTO actually reinforced the goals of opening up to the world economy. In this sense, it would act as a constraint on future economic policy choices. Accession to the WTO would be a catalyst and provide an impetus for carrying out significant, if painful, reforms.

In fact, many initiatives were taken in the 2000s to rationalize business law and economic law. Existing regulations were revised and new ones published. Hundreds of laws and regulations relating to international business activities were amended or repealed to bring China into line with its commitments. This marked an acceleration of the immense legislative work undertaken since the mid-1980s. For example, the rules applicable to businesses with foreign capital were almost entirely the same as those for purely Chinese businesses. Labour law now applied to everyone, such as tax law or contract law. Company law was more or less the same for Chinese and foreign firms, with the exception of laws applicable to mixed Chinese–foreign companies. Other projects were pursued: the reform of state-owned enterprises and of financial institutions.

In terms of economic performance, China's accession to the WTO ensured a very rapid growth in foreign trade. Between 1990 and 2011, the share of exports of goods and services rose from 16 per cent to 31 per cent of GDP, while the share of imports of goods and services rose from 13 per cent to 27 per cent. Between 2000 and 2011, China's share in world trade grew rapidly: it rose from 5.2 per cent to 13.2 per cent for exports, and from 4.4 per cent to 12 per cent for imports. China's share in world trade in goods more than doubled between 2000 and 2011 and the country was now second in world trade, behind the United States.

During his tenure, Jiang Zemin had neither the authority nor the charisma of Mao Zedong or Deng Xiaoping, nor even of other major historical figures such as Chen Yun or Yang Shangkun. The policy he implemented was not as innovative as that of Hu Yaobang or Zhao Ziyang. Like Hua Guofeng, to whom he was compared in the early 1990s, he came to power amid intense factional struggles; without a military background or a clear vision for the future, he was seen as a weak leader, whose mission was bound to be short. And yet he held onto power for over a decade. His vision was that of a man concerned with order; an engineer trained in the Soviet Union, he was pragmatic and cautious. Lacking an original programme, Jiang was able to develop the proposals of others, especially those of the person who had chosen him, Deng Xiaoping. This method was not only the result of his own weaknesses, but also the consequence of transformations in the nature of Chinese politics.[9] Faced with increasingly complex problems, leaders sought specific concrete solutions, developed collectively. In this context, Jiang had the political sense that allowed him to manoeuvre. Although he relied mainly on his Shanghai allies, he was able to synthesize multiple contradictions. He was flexible, and could adapt to changing circumstances.

The Hu Jintao/Wen Jiabao era (2002–12): a lost decade?

At the end of thirteen years in power, Jiang Zemin left the post of Secretary General of the Party during the Sixteenth Party Congress held on 8 November 2002. It was the first time since 1949 that the succession of the supreme leader had passed off in an orderly and peaceful manner. His successor, Hu Jintao, aged 59, had been a permanent member of the Politburo since 1992. With the exception of Hu, all the permanent members of the Politburo, including Li Peng and Zhu Rongji, retired and were replaced by younger members.

Hu Jintao was the last ruler after Jiang Zemin to be chosen by Deng Xiaoping to hold the highest office, but in 2002, there were several signs that his power was insecure. Jiang Zemin retained the chairmanship of the Central Military Commission, although he had left the Politburo and the Central Committee, which meant he could retain control over military matters and foreign policy – both Jiang and Deng had held this position from the outset. At the Congress, Jiang Zemin also enshrined his theory of the three representations in the Party charter. Like Deng in his early days, Hu Jintao did not enjoy a majority of supporters in the Politburo Standing Committee, whose number increased from seven to nine; this was interpreted as Jiang's attempt to bring in his associates so they could continue to exert his influence. At least five of the nine members of the Politburo were followers of Jiang, members of the 'Shanghai clique': Jia Qinglin, promoted despite his mixed reputation for having led provinces devastated by corruption (he would be elected Chairman of the National Committee of the People's Political Consultative Conference in March 2003), Huang Ju, Zeng Qinghong, Wu Bangguo and Li Changchun. According to many observers, Jiang exercised a role comparable to that played by Deng Xiaoping after his withdrawal from all the positions he occupied in 1987 at the Thirteenth Congress, with the exception of the chairmanship of the Central Military Commission that he kept until March 1990. In his turn, Hu Jintao was compared to the leader of the transition, Hua Guofeng. So, in the autumn of 2002, Hu still had to prove that he could be an autonomous ruler. In fact, Hu Jintao would manage to consolidate his power much faster than expected – especially in comparison with Deng Xiaoping, who had to compromise between 1977 and 1984 before finally gaining control of the Politburo.

Populist leaders

Hu Jintao was born in 1942, in Jiangyan in Jiangsu province, to a relatively poor family. A brilliant student, he entered Tsinghua University in Beijing, graduating in hydraulic engineering in 1964. That same year, he joined the Communist Party. His professional career began in the poor province of Gansu where he worked on hydroelectric installations and then in the Construction Bureau. In 1981, he spent time at the Central Party School in Beijing, where he was introduced to Hu Yaobang. In 1982, he was appointed Secretary of the Youth League for Gansu province and then transferred to Beijing to the national secretariat of the League. In 1984, he took over the Youth League. In this capacity, he accompanied Hu Yaobang across the country; Hu himself was a former League member. In 1985, Hu was appointed Party Secretary in the southern province of Guizhou. In 1988, he held the same post for the Tibet Autonomous Region, where in 1989 he ruthlessly suppressed political unrest. In 1992, at the Fourteenth Congress, Hu Jintao was chosen by Deng Xiaoping to become, at the age of 50, the youngest member of the Politburo Standing Committee. In 1993, he was put in charge of the secretariat of the Central Committee and of the Central Party School. He was now considered Jiang Zemin's designated successor. In 1998, he became Vice President of the Republic, which allowed him to gain experience in foreign policy. Like his predecessor, Hu Jintao was an engineer who practised his profession before making a career in the Party bureaucracy; this career took place mainly within the Communist Youth League and it was from among its leaders that he would recruit many of his collaborators. Unlike Jiang Zemin and his associates whose careers had often been in Shanghai, Hu Jintao was a leader who came from the poor inner regions of China.

Along with Hu, the entire senior leadership in the state and the Party kept their positions. In March 2003, at the annual session of the National People's Congress, Hu Jintao succeeded Jiang as President of the Republic. Wu Bangguo was appointed Chairman of the National People's Congress, succeeding Li Peng. Wen Jiabao succeeded Zhu Rongji as Premier. Wen, born in 1942 (the same year as Hu Jintao), also came from China's inner provinces. A native of Tianjin, he graduated from the Beijing Institute of Geology and then worked for a long time in Gansu province; he was initially put in charge of a prospecting team from 1968 to 1979, then occupied managerial positions at the province's Geological Bureau from 1979 to 1982. In 1983, he was appointed to the Ministry of Geology and Mining Resources in Beijing, then to the leadership of the Central Committee. During the events of 1989, Wen accompanied Zhao Ziyang when the latter went to meet the protesters in Tiananmen Square. In 1998, he was promoted to the post of Deputy Premier and became a member of the Politburo Standing Committee.

Hu Jintao and his Premier Wen Jiabao were both 60 years old and embodied the 'fourth generation' of Chinese leaders since the founding of the People's Republic. This generation had grown to maturity at the start of the Cultural Revolution and experienced disillusionment with Mao and Communist ideology. Like the third generation, they were technocrats, but there were more lawyers and economists among them.[10] The move from one generation to the next raised hopes for a political revival that some called a Chinese New Deal. In 2002, both inside and outside the country, hopes were high that the new team would not only continue the policy of reform pursued for more than twenty years, but would also have the audacity to introduce innovative changes.

Hu Jintao would soon impose his own agenda. He asserted as early as 2002 that the 'people' (*renmin* 人民) were the focus of his policies – an implicit criticism of Jiang Zemin's exclusive attention to economic growth. In the following years, his policy would be encapsulated in several formulas: 'scientific development' (*kexue fazhan* 科学发展) in 2003, the 'harmonious society' (*hexie shehui* 和谐社会) in 2004, and 'new socialist campaigns' (*shehuizhuyi xin nongcun* 社会主义新农村) in 2005. His initiatives were less personal than those of his predecessor, with the political leadership becoming more collective and Hu Jintao being seen as first among equals in the Politburo Standing Committee. These slogans, indeed, were not credited to Hu himself, but attributed to the 'collective wisdom' of the leaders of the Sixteenth and Seventeenth Central Committees. Similarly, efforts were made to ensure that the various different institutions were represented within the Politburo: the Party apparatus, the state organs and the provinces; this was done in particular to limit the representatives of the security apparatus, starting with the PLA. The aim was to create a better balance between the different interest groups, to strengthen the collective dimension and to ensure that a single sector could not prevail over the others, and that a single leader – the Secretary General – could not use one sector as a power base against the others.[11]

The duo of Hu Jintao and Wen Jiabao gave a new direction to Chinese politics. The slogan that marked their decade in power was 'harmonious society'. The expression was first formulated in 2002, at the Sixteenth Congress, but it was the 2004 plenary session that resolutely called for the 'building of a harmonious society' (*goujian hexie shehui* 构建和谐社会). This was understood in a broad sense and included reducing the wealth gap, increasing employment, improving equity and justice, suppressing corruption, preserving public order and protecting the environment. While reforms had hitherto favoured efficiency, the issue of equality was now under discussion. The concern expressed for a better sharing of wealth constituted a major amendment to the Deng Xiaoping programme. Hu's goal was to achieve a 'moderately prosperous society'. The return of this expression, already used by Deng Xiaoping in 1979 as the ultimate goal of modernization, reflected the Party's concern to improve the material living conditions of 'ordinary people' (the *laobaixing* 老百姓). More broadly, Hu Jintao and Wen Jiabao paid what was, among Chinese leaders, unusual attention towards the poorest and especially those who had not benefited from the twenty years of reforms, and who had even been their victims. In January 2003, one of Hu's first political gestures was to visit poor farmers in Inner Mongolia and Shanxi. Wen Jiabao, meanwhile, spent the 2003 Chinese New Year in the northeast, celebrating it with miners at the bottom of a pit. These visits, widely publicized by the propaganda organs, helped to build an image of the Chinese leadership that was more human and closer to the people than usual.

The health crisis caused by Severe Acute Respiratory Syndrome (SARS) was the first test to which the new leadership was exposed. SARS was detected in late November 2002 in Foshan, Guangdong Province, but it took more than six months for Beijing to recognize the scale of the event and take appropriate action. The government then managed the crisis efficiently. In the winter of 2002, the sick were hidden away in hospitals and the media were banned from disseminating information; only rumours circulated among the townspeople of Canton and Beijing. The spread of the epidemic outside China via Hong Kong forced the authorities to change their strategy. A sick person from Canton accidentally caused significant contagion in a hotel in Hong Kong on 21 February and the virus then began to spread in Vietnam, Canada and Singapore. The Chinese Ministry of Health sent its first reports to the World Health Organization (WHO) in the middle of February 2003, which launched an international alert on 12 March. On 2 April, the WHO recommended not visiting Hong Kong or Guangdong province; a few weeks later, Beijing, followed by other northern regions, was placed on the list of destinations to avoid. On 20 April, the Minister of Health Zhang Wenkang and the Mayor of Beijing Meng Xuenong were dismissed for having concealed the number of patients affected. At a Press conference, Deputy Health Minister Gao Qiang sharply revised the toll of SARS cases upwards, with more than 300 in the city of Beijing alone. Vice Premier Wu Yi assumed control of the Ministry of Health. Beijing finally opted for a more transparent policy. The Chinese media were at last allowed to disseminate accurate information and the authorities began cooperating with the WHO. Containment measures for infected people proved to be effective. In cities such as Shanghai, public places were closed and populations quarantined. In the countryside, villages were cordoned off. These mass measures, applied systematically, and generally well accepted, ensured that hospitals remained the main hotbeds of infection. By the end of May, the epidemic subsided in Hong Kong and Guangdong, then throughout China, and Beijing was finally removed from the list of destinations not recommended by the WHO on 24 June 2003.

The initial lack of transparency on the part of the Chinese authorities in the management of the crisis caused great suspicion in the international community and it took the dismissal of the Minister of Health and the Mayor of Beijing to see a semblance of confidence restored. Admittedly, only under external pressure from the international press, and in particular from Hong Kong and the WHO, and thanks to the courage of a certain number of Chinese doctors, did Beijing change its strategy after six months of lies and concealment; but in the end the new leadership team, by relying on transparency and collaboration with the WHO, gained credibility in this crisis. Hu Jintao and Premier Wen Jiabao appeared on television every day, congratulating the medical profession.

In spring 2004, the second session of the Tenth National People's Congress proceeded to a new revision of the Constitution.[12] One of the changes decided was both ideological and political in scope. It involved including in the preamble of the constitutional text Jiang Zemin's theory of the three representations; this theory was added to the four fundamental principles and to Deng Xiaoping's theory as an important doctrine guiding the action of the nation. This was the logical culmination of its inclusion in the Party's charter in 2002, and was a recognition that Jiang Zemin had played a major political role in building Chinese socialism in the wake of Mao and Deng. Just as the inclusion of Deng Xiaoping's theory ended the period in which Deng was in charge, so the inclusion of the three representations signalled the end of Jiang's mission.

A second important decision taken by the National People's Congress was the strengthening of the constitutional protection of private property, confirming the further development of a market economy. Article 11 of the 1982 Constitution stated that the individual economy of urban and rural workers was a complement to the socialist public sector, and that the state protected its rights and legitimate interests. The individual economy of urban and rural workers referred at the time to individual industrial and commercial households (*geti gongshang hu* 个体工商户) as well as rural households under contract. In 1988, article 11 was amended to state: 'Non-public economic sectors that are within the scope prescribed by law, such as individually owned and private businesses, are an important component of the socialist market economy.' Furthermore: 'The state shall protect the lawful rights and interests of non-public economic sectors such as individually owned and private businesses.'[13] In 2004, article 13 of the Constitution was revised and now specified that 'the legal private property of citizens is inviolable', a formulation echoing article 12, which refers to the 'sacred and inviolable' character of public property. If, unlike the latter, private property was not considered sacred, it was nevertheless now recognized as inviolable. In addition, in the event of expropriation or requisition of private property by the state, the revised Constitution now provided for compensation by the state.[14] At the end of several years of debates and struggles for influence between jurists, as well as between representatives of the state sector and private companies, an almost equal protection was henceforth ensured to public and private property. This was an important step in the construction of the socialist market economy.

In February 2005, in a long address to the Central Party School, Hu Jintao detailed the motives and modalities of building a 'harmonious socialist society'. Recalling that 'China has produced throughout its history a great number of thoughts on social harmony', he placed his project in a historical tradition that gave his speech cultural legitimacy. He mentioned thinkers such as Confucius, Mozi and Mencius, and utopian projects such as the kingdom of the Taiping, or the ideal society of the 'great unity' described by Confucius in the *Book of Rites* (Li Jing 礼经). In October 2005, on the occasion of the fifth plenary session of the Sixteenth Central Committee, the Party announced a series of political initiatives within the framework of the eleventh Five-Year Plan (2006–10) which gave substance to the project of a harmonious society and a more balanced and sustainable development, more oriented towards ordinary people and 'weak groups' (*ruoshi qunti* 弱势群体). The main initiative was the plan to build 'new socialist countrysides'. The main objective of this new policy, aimed at the countryside where 750 million Chinese still lived, was to resolve the various ills that had afflicted much of the rural world for the previous fifteen years.

Indeed, after having been privileged during the first reforms, the Chinese countryside and peasants were relegated to the background, behind industry and the cities. The 1990s were characterized by total abandonment of the countryside.[15] As a percentage of average urban income, average rural income increased from 39 per cent in 1978 to 54 per cent in 1985, before collapsing to 36 per cent in 2000 and 30 per cent in 2005.[16] The growth of rural income had been much slower than that of urban income. And it was not just a problem of income: in many other fields, such as education, pensions, access to health and control of land, peasants' rights were in decline, which explains the rise of protests. To increase income, the law enacted in autumn 2005 provided for the abolition of all duties and other agricultural and para-agricultural levies as of January 2006. The objective was also to increase production and make China a major agro-food exporting power. The conditions for acquiring rural land, which were the source of many conflicts, were to be revised. In terms of education, the authorities planned to introduce free education for all peasants in 2007. In terms of access to healthcare, the state was ready to dedicate, over the next five years, 20 billion yuan to the renovation of buildings and the upgrading of equipment in rural health centres and certain district hospitals. A public health insurance scheme aimed to cover 80 per cent of rural regions by the end of 2008. In addition to these promises, there was a desire to relaunch infrastructure work outside the big cities. In March 2006, the National People's Congress officially approved the policy of building new socialist countrysides, which clearly reflected the will of the Hu Jintao and Wen Jiabao tandem to fight against inequalities of all kinds and build a harmonious socialist society.

The Seventeenth Party Congress met in Beijing from 15 to 21 October 2007.[17] As was customary, it made a number of appointments to the leadership team, although there was less change than at the previous Congress. Hu Jintao was re-elected for a second term at the head of the Party. The new Politburo Standing Committee had four new members: Xi Jinping (aged 54) and Li Keqiang (52), who were now the youngest, and He Guoqiang (aged 64) and Zhou Yongkang (65), who had both previously been members of the ordinary Politburo. The ordinary Politburo had seven newcomers: Wang Qishan (aged 59), Liu Yandong (62), Li Yuanchao (57), Wang Yang (52), Zhang Gaoli (62), Xu Caihou (64) and Bo Xilai (58). The average age of the members of the new Politburo was 62, compared to 63 in 1997 and 72 in 1982. Twenty-three of its twenty-five members had a university education, compared to none in 1982. For the first time, the number of technocrats, engineers and graduates in the hard sciences decreased. In 1997, sixteen out of seventeen were graduates, including fourteen engineers. In 2002, there were seventeen engineers. In 2007, of the twenty-three university graduates, there were only eleven engineers, and two hard science graduates. Ten members had a degree in humanities and social sciences. Its composition also shows a balance between the representatives from the coastal fringe provinces (ten members) and those from the interior (fifteen members from the central provinces and none from the western provinces). The Politburo was composed, as was now the custom, primarily of civilian leaders. Twenty-two members had no military experience, either in the PLA or in the military bureaucracy. Twelve of the twenty-five members had joined the Party during the Cultural Revolution and three after 1976. The others joined in the early 1960s, on the eve of its outbreak. This Politburo was in line with the developments underway within the ruling elite; it was better educated, less technocratic and essentially civilian.

These appointments aimed to pave the way for the succession of Hu Jintao at the next Congress, five years later. Xi Jinping's entry into the Standing Committee without having previously been an ordinary member of the Politburo signalled that he would be Hu's probable successor in 2012. It was in the same way that Jiang Zemin's succession had been prepared: Hu Jintao had been appointed a member of the Standing Committee without previously being an ordinary member of the Politburo and had been appointed to positions of responsibility – Executive Secretary of the secretariat and Director of the Central Party School, followed by Vice President of the Republic in 1998 to give him international visibility, and Vice Chairman of the Central Military Commission in 1999. Likewise, in December 2005 Xi Jinping was appointed Executive Secretary of the secretariat and President of the Central Party School. Affiliated with neither Hu nor Jiang Zemin, Xi Jinping had previously been in charge of two of the country's wealthiest provinces, Zhejiang and Fujian.

Halfway through his ten-year tenure, Hu's authority emerged stronger for several reasons. First, the 'Shanghai clique' had been weakened, notably by Zeng Qinghong's departure from the Politburo Standing Committee. The dismissal of Chen Liangyu from the Party leadership in Shanghai a few months earlier had also contributed to this. Chen Liangyu, a protégé of Jiang, was ousted from his post as Secretary of the Shanghai Party on 25 September 2006 in a scandal over the city's pension funds. A member of the Politburo, Chen was the highest political figure accused of corruption since the arrest of Beijing Party Secretary Chen Xitong in 1995. Hu also promoted Li Keqiang to the Standing Committee; Li was clearly one of his protégés, and the foreign press reported that Hu considered him to be his successor. Other allies were also promoted: Li Yuanchao to the Organization Department – which gave him control over appointments – Wang Yang to the head of Guangdong province, and Liu Yandong, who, like Hu Jintao, had come from the Youth League, to the Politburo. Hu Jintao's political report focused on the notion of 'scientific development' (*kexue fazhan* 科学发展). Hu explained that the economy needed to be developed in a more balanced way, and less attention paid to the growth of GNP per se, with more focus on the ecological costs. He said that the notion was 'people-centred' and stressed the need to move towards sustainable development, from extensive to intensive growth. Without giving a specific example of how to achieve this goal, he referred to better use of natural resources. In doing so, Hu was responding to a growing concern among the Chinese population. Above all, at this Congress, Hu managed to include his 'theory of scientific development' in the charter of the Communist Party. This was a personal success because Deng Xiaoping and Jiang Zemin both had to wait until the end of their respective terms in office to include in the same text the thesis of 'the construction of socialism with Chinese characteristics' for the former (in 1992) and the theory of the 'three representations' for the latter (in 2002).

Crises in Tibet and Sichuan in 2008

In the spring of 2008, the government faced two major events: deadly protests in Tibet in March and a violent earthquake in Sichuan in May. It managed to effectively curb these two crises so that China could celebrate in August with great pomp, together with the whole world, the first Olympics ever organized on its soil. The crisis in Tibet began on 10 March 2008 with peaceful protests by monks in Lhasa on the anniversary of the Dalai Lama's flight on 10 March 1959.[18] On 14 March, the protests degenerated into violent riots directed against non-Tibetan inhabitants and their property. The security forces withdrew in the face of the onslaught of rioters, who included monks, and only gradually won back control of the city the next day, making numerous arrests. Protest movements were taking place throughout the territory of the Autonomous Region, but also in areas with a strong Tibetan presence in the four neighbouring provinces. In Lhasa, according to the authorities, the human and material toll was heavy: nineteen people were killed by rioters and 1,000 shops and public buildings destroyed. The episode resulted in hundreds of arrests and several months of paramilitary presence in the streets of Lhasa and in the Tibetan neighbourhoods of Chinese cities such as Chengdu. Protest movements had been taking place regularly in Tibet; what was new this time was the high level of violence: attacks resulting in the deaths of Han civilians, the sacking of government buildings and Han and Hui businesses. The Beijing government explained the revolt as a plot hatched from abroad by the Dalai Lama and the Western anti-Chinese forces backing him. In fact, the causes were to be found in the failure of the economic development policy and the restrictions on culture and religion. Thanks to massive investments from the central government, Tibet was indeed experiencing very rapid economic growth; the autonomous region's GDP more than quadrupled between 1997 and 2007 while that of China tripled. The railway linking Tibet to Qinghai, opened in July 2006, brought many tourists. But this development was very much for the benefit of Han and Hui migrants, and to the detriment of the environment, traditional beliefs and lifestyles of Tibetans; it resulted in a Sinicization of the autonomous region. At the same time, control over religious life tightened. It was forbidden to venerate or display photographs of the Dalai Lama, and Buddhist religious practice was prohibited for government employees and students; on the other hand, monks and nuns were required to submit to patriotic education sessions. The events in Tibet were a sign of the failure of a policy aimed at compensating for coercive measures by providing economic development.

A few weeks later, on 12 May 2008, an earthquake measuring 7.9 on the Richter scale hit a mountainous region in western Sichuan province, with the city of Wenchuan at its epicentre. This was the deadliest earthquake in China after the Tangshan earthquake in 1976 that had killed nearly 240,000 people. The damage was considerable. There were nearly 70,000 dead, 368,000 injured and 15 million displaced people. The government mobilized very quickly: 130,000 soldiers from the People's Army as well as paramilitary forces were sent to the region to deliver food to the victims. The Youth League and the Chinese Red Cross also sent relief materials and teams. What caught the attention of observers was the reaction of society, as tens of thousands of people volunteered; associations, businesses and the media mobilized to relieve those who were suffering and to participate in the reconstruction effort. A week after the earthquake, the Sichuan provincial branch of the Youth League mobilized nearly 200,000 volunteers, half of whom were students. In two weeks, public donations amounted to more than 30 billion yuan.[19] Hundreds of nongovernmental organizations (NGOs) were involved, both national and international. As a condition for being able to intervene in the field, these organizations were associated with local governments or mass organizations such as the Women's Federation or the Youth League. The intervention of NGOs in the crisis clearly showed that they could play a positive and constructive role in building a harmonious society. The Sichuan tragedy led to an acceleration of discussions to facilitate their development – which required new procedures of registration and control. Although praised for its initial response to the earthquake, the Chinese government had nonetheless sought to quell a major scandal: the construction of schools with no respect for earthquake standards. Large numbers of these collapsed and buried many young children, hence their nickname 'tofu schools'. The tragedy was felt all the more cruelly by families given the single-child policy, as each child carried all the hopes of its parents. The repressive apparatus endeavoured to prevent those concerned from being heard, and organizations or individuals – such as artist Ai Weiwei – from mobilizing to help them assert their rights.

Two 'campaigns of mass distraction'

The Twenty-First Olympic Games were held as planned in Beijing from 8 to 24 August 2008. They were preceded abroad by controversies over respect for human rights – because of the recent events in Tibet – and environmental protection: these led to the carrying of the Olympic torch being punctuated by incidents, notably in London and in Paris. They crowned fifteen years of efforts: Beijing had applied for the first time in 1993 to host the 2000 Games, but its candidacy was rejected because of the crushing of the democratic movement of 1989. The 2008 Games were an opportunity to reshape the northern districts of Beijing, and, above all, for the regime to strengthen its legitimacy in the eyes of the public, both Chinese and international. It was therefore a formidable propaganda operation, described by Anne-Marie Brady as a 'campaign of mass distraction'.[20] The successful staging of the Beijing Games was the culmination of years of work under the leadership of Xi Jinping to demonstrate China's rejuvenation to the world and celebrate it as a newly determined, united, powerful and rich country.

The opening ceremony crystallized the image that China intended to convey to the Chinese public and to the rest of the world.[21] This was the first time that China had presented such a spectacle to so vast an international public. Designed by filmmaker Zhang Yimou, in collaboration with the People's Liberation Army, it traced the history of China. After a brightly illuminated countdown on the lawn, a fireworks display was set off; then 2,008 people, all moving together, pounded traditional Chinese drums, chanting a proverb from Confucius. The first part of this opening show, which preceded the parade of athletes, was titled 'A Brilliant Civilization' and commented on the inventions attributed to China in the premodern era. It referenced the invention of the compass, gunpowder, paper and printing, the silk trade and the building of the Great Wall. The second part was titled 'A Glorious Era' and described contemporary China and its hopes for the future. While the great Tang and Ming dynasties were honoured, neither that of the Qing, which marked a weakening of China in relation to Europe, nor the events of the twentieth century were mentioned. So the nineteenth century post-1840, Republican China and China from the 1950s to the 1990s were all ignored. A highly selective view of history was traced; its authors had eliminated moments of radicalism, struggle and also of democratic aspiration.

A few months later, in the spring of 2010, the Shanghai World Expo was a second campaign of mass distraction. It was placed under the harmless slogan 'Better City, Better Life' (in Chinese *chengshi, rang shenghuo geng meihao* 城市,让生活更美好, a more accurate translation of which would be 'the city makes life even better'), which echoed the concept of the harmonious society formulated by Hu Jintao. Each exhibiting country was invited to reflect on the city of the future from a perspective of nature conservation and energy self-sufficiency. This was an opportunity to celebrate urban life when there had been a massive exodus from the countryside for three decades, and half of the Chinese population still resided in the countryside. As the Olympics helped reshape the city of Beijing, Expo 2010 accelerated the reconstruction of the lower Yangtze metropolis, especially Pudong where the main buildings were located, including the Chinese pavilion. It was also a celebration of the rebirth of the city undertaken under the impetus of Deng Xiaoping, then of Jiang Zemin and Zhu Rongji. Shanghai, which had lost its lustre under Mao, thus regained its status as a global megalopolis. Expo 2010 set this daughter city, China's economic capital, at the centre of the world. The organizers also hoped to hold the largest universal exhibition of all time.

And indeed, between 1 May and 31 October 2010, the Expo welcomed 73 million visitors, many of them from rural areas who came, as if on pilgrimage, to admire with pride the achievements of the reforms. Two years after the Olympics, the country had once again demonstrated its ability to organize a global event. Expo 2010 was an important milestone in the affirmation of Chinese soft power.

As another symbol of its regained power, in December 2013 China became the third nation to achieve a moon landing after the United States (in 1969) and the USSR (in 1976). In doing so, the country showed that it had managed to catch up with the first space powers. In Chinese public opinion, this technological achievement strengthened national pride. Hosting the Olympics, Expo 2010 and the achievements of the space programme all provided opportunities for propaganda campaigns that built confidence in the existing system and shifted attention away from thornier issues.

Indeed, on the eve of the Eighteenth Party Congress, which appointed a new leadership team, the Hu/Wen tandem had produced a mixed bag of results. Some even spoke of a lost decade. When he came to power, Hu took a number of initiatives that marked a turning point from the previous period. While growth was still necessary, it needed to be sustainable and able to remedy social and regional inequalities in order to build a more harmonious society. Making less room for ideology, it adopted an attitude closer to the people. Inside and outside China, many people had pinned their hopes on the new leadership. Ten years later, they were disappointed. To be sure, growth had continued and China had become a global economic giant; the Olympics, the World's Fair and the successful moon mission had brought the regime's achievements and ambitions to the eyes of the world. Admittedly, a number of initiatives were completely in line with the announced programme: the elimination of taxes on agricultural production, public investments in the interior provinces to help them catch up, and social housing programmes in cities for the poorest households. But that had not stopped inequalities from growing or corruption from reaching new heights. In addition, no progress had been made on political reforms. The situation of dissidents had not improved, nor that of NGOs. The rising middle class had reason to be dissatisfied: media and Internet censorship was still fierce, students were increasingly struggling to find jobs after they graduated from college. The political system itself had still not stabilized, as evidenced by the conditions of succession.

The fifth generation of leaders in power (after 2012)

Change of political personnel

The Eighteenth Party Congress met in Beijing from 8 to 14 November 2012. As expected, by the end of Hu Jintao's ten-year term in office, the composition of the Party's governing bodies had been largely renewed. Of the 376 members of the Central Committee there had been a 64 per cent changeover, while 60 per cent of the twenty-five members of the Politburo, 71 per cent of the seven members of the Standing Committee and 64 per cent of the eleven members of the Central Military Commission had changed. Following the Congress, in line with the trend of the previous two decades, the Politburo team was younger and better educated. Fourteen members retired on the principle that all members aged 68 or over at the time of a Congress had to leave the Politburo. The average age of new members was just over 61, down from 62 in 2007. In terms of local origin, fourteen members were from the coastal provinces and eleven from the central provinces – none was native to the western provinces. The vast majority were civilians: twenty-one of the twenty-five members had no military experience. In terms of education level, nineteen of the twenty-five members of the Politburo held a university degree and another five had graduated from the Central Party School – in 1982, none of the members of the Politburo had had a university degree. The proportion of technocrats decreased in favour of those who had studied the humanities and social sciences. In 1997, sixteen of the seventeen graduates had been technocrats, including fourteen engineers. In 2002, the Politburo included seventeen engineers and one geologist; in 2007, it had only eleven engineers, four economists, one political scientist and three graduates in human sciences. In 2012, of the eighteen politicians who graduated from the university, only four were engineers, six had studied economics, two international relations, two literature, one history and one political science. Thus, within the Politburo Standing Committee, Xi Jinping and Li Yuanchao had a doctorate in law, Li Keqiang a doctorate in economics, Wang Qishan had a history degree, Bo Xilai had a degree in journalism and Wang Yang a degree in management. The predominance of engineers, characteristic of the 1990s – due to the fact that the engineering sciences were a politically safer choice than the humanities and social sciences in the 1950s and 1960s – was declining. Although they continued to represent a part of the ruling elite, their monopoly on the exercise of power at the top was crumbling. While the generation that preceded them had focused their efforts on growth and technological development, some speculated that the leaders of the fifth generation, with an increasing number trained in political science and law, would be more sensitive to legal and political reforms. The diversity of skills assembled at the top of the Party apparatus, and the increasing level of education, also reflected the complexity and the increasing technicality of the problems needing to be solved.

A new generation of leaders, described in China itself as the fifth generation, was now taking the reins of power. Born in the 1950s and early 1960s, they had suffered under the Cultural Revolution. Unlike the previous generation who had already graduated when the fifth generation was just starting out, most of the latter were still in elementary, middle or high school, and so for ten years they had lost the opportunity to study. As *zhiqing* 知青 (educated youth), they had been sent for several years to inland towns or to the countryside; this was the experience of five members of the Politburo Standing Committee: Xi Jinping, Li Keqiang, Zhang Dejiang, Liu Yunshan and Wang Qishan. They resumed their university studies when the higher education system started functioning again after 1978. They joined the national leadership at the Seventeenth Party Congress and the Eleventh National People's Congress, held respectively in October 2007 and March 2008. Like the previous generation, these leaders lacked the strong political ties and solidarity characteristic of those who had fought in battle together: the Long March, the anti-Japanese war and the revolutionary conquest.

Seven of the nine former members of the Politburo Standing Committee retired and its size went down from nine to seven members. The decline in membership can be attributed to struggles between rival factions: that of Jiang Zemin's protégés, led by Wu Bangguo, Chairman of the National People's Congress, and Jia Qinglin, Chairman of the Chinese People's Political Consultative Conference, and that of Hu Jintao and Wen Jiabao. Another explanation is the effect of the age of candidates for membership of the Poliutburo Standing Committee. Members of Congress were appointed for five years, a rule scrupulously followed since 1982; and since 2002, members of the Politburo who were 68 years old at the time of Congress had to retire. This explains why the Secretaries General could serve only two terms: Hu, born in 1942, became Secretary General at the age of 60 in 2002; in 2010 he turned 68 and therefore retired in 2012. Xi Jinping, born in 1953, turned 59 in 2012; he was 68 years old in 2021 and should have stepped down in 2022. The fact that the Secretary General has two consecutive terms and is around 60 years old when he takes office may explain the choice of Xi Jinping.

Xi Jinping, a 'prince' in power

Born in 1953, Xi Jinping was the second son of Xi Zhongxun (1913–2002), a historic leader of the Party who had played a part in winning power, was persecuted during the Cultural Revolution, then rehabilitated, and was a former deputy chair of the NPC (1988–93). The new Secretary General was thus one of the current leaders of China who had been born into the aristocracy of the Communist Party and, as such, raised in the reserved district of Beijing, Zhongnanhai. As the son of one of the first revolutionaries, he was one of the 'princes' (*taizi* 太子) of the Communist regime. His entry into adulthood was severely affected by the Cultural Revolution. In 1968, Xi was 15 when his father was sent to work in a factory in Luoyang and then imprisoned. As part of the Down to the Countryside Movement (a campaign sending urban youth out to the countryside), Xi spent seven years in Shaanxi working on a farm and then as Party Secretary in a village in the Yanchuan district of Yan'an. Describing himself as a 'son of the yellow earth', this episode helped him to fabricate his own myth. In 1975, aged 22, he resumed his studies in Beijing at Tsinghua University, where he graduated four years later with a degree in chemical engineering. He later continued his studies and obtained a doctorate in law. Besides his genealogy and his skills, his long experience in the provinces helps to explain why Xi Jinping was chosen to succeed Hu Jintao. He joined the Communist Youth in 1971 and the Party in 1974. His career as a politician took place successively in three provinces, Hebei (1982–85), Fujian (1985–2002) and Zhejiang (2002–07). In 2007, following Chen Liangyu's ousting, he was appointed to lead the Party in Shanghai, a post he held for only six months, after which he was promoted to the Politburo Standing Committee. At the meeting of the Eleventh NPC in March 2008, he was elected Vice President of the People's Republic, which prepared him for the highest office. He was then in charge of sensitive issues such as preparations for the 2008 Olympic Games and the management of the special administrative regions of Hong Kong and Macao. Aged 59 in 2012 – which meant he could serve two five-year terms before the age of 70 – Xi Jinping was one of the brightest 'princes' and belonged neither to the Shanghai clique of Jiang Zemin, nor to that of Hu Jintao. As is customary, the Twelfth NPC in March 2013 ratified the Party's choices and elected Xi Jinping as President of the Republic. It also elected Li Keqiang to the post of Premier.

The conditions of the handover from Hu Jintao to Xi Jinping were much less peaceful than they appeared because the Party Congress was being held after events that testified to particularly heated power struggles at the top of the apparatuses. Bo Xilai, a member of the Seventeenth Politburo and Party Secretary for the city of Chongqing, was dismissed in March 2012 after incredible episodes. Bo, like Xi Jinping, was a 'prince', son of Bo Yibo (1908–2007), one of the main revolutionary leaders, and he had had a distinguished career. He was Minister of Commerce from 2004 to 2007, and was then appointed Communist Party Secretary in the huge municipality of Chongqing. He made himself popular there thanks to his fierce struggle against the local mafia and his openly neo-Maoist policies. He set up social housing programmes for the most disadvantaged and brought back the 'red songs' of the Cultural Revolution. In March 2012, while attending the annual NPC session in Beijing, he was suspended from his duties and then expelled from the Politburo and the Central Committee. In September 2013, a few months after his wife had been sentenced for the murder of a British businessman, Bo Xilai was given a life sentence for corruption, embezzlement and abuse of power. Apart from the financial and criminal affairs in which Bo Xilai and his wife were involved – not unique among senior Chinese leaders – their fall was probably the result of a desire on the part of the members of the Central Committee to get rid of a man whose charisma and populism contrasted with the habits of the regime's cadres and were too reminiscent of the excesses of Maoism.

Internal authoritarianism

After Xi Jinping took office, other leaders were also sacked in a major anti-corruption campaign. In the first years of his tenure, Xu Caihou, Vice Chairman of the Central Military Commission, and Zhou Yongkang, a member of the Politburo Standing Committee and Minister of Public Security, were dismissed. Many regional officials, managers of state-controlled businesses and central administrations were also implicated. Under the guise of fighting corruption, Xi's goal was to eliminate political rivals and consolidate his power. From this point of view, the Chinese political system, which for twenty years had been marked by an increasingly collective practice of the exercise of authority, was marked by a real inward turn: under Xi, this exercise was more personal than ever since the Great Leap Forward and the Cultural Revolution. The campaign against authoritarian corruption was also a way for him to establish his popularity among the poorest parts of the population by creating an image of someone who attacks the privileges of the cadres. In another inward turn, Xi Jinping's first term in office was marked by a significant reduction in freedoms; the death in prison of dissident Liu Xiaobo, the 2010 Nobel Peace Prize winner, and numerous arrests of human rights activists and lawyers all bear witness to this, as well as the tightening of control of the Internet. The strengthening of the powers of the CCP was accompanied by an ideological consolidation and increasingly common allusions to Marxist-Leninist doctrines, the basic bedrock of the Party, as well as a cult of personality to a degree unheard of since the Cultural Revolution. Likewise, a constant ideological war was waged against pernicious 'Western influences'.

Special attention has always been paid to the way minority populations are ruled. For geopolitical reasons, the border province of Xinjiang, on the frontiers of Tibet, Central Asia and Russia, populated by a Muslim minority, the Uighurs, has always been closely watched; in the aftermath of a series of terrorist attacks carried out by separatists in Beijing and Kunming in 2013 and 2014, the repression changed in nature. In Xinjiang, this was based on the implementation of massive surveillance technologies, supported by artificial intelligence, which tracked everyone's movements and words. Since 2017, re-education camps have been built and are said to have accommodated hundreds of thousands, if not one million people – in 2020, the province had 26 million inhabitants, 58 per cent of whom belonged to ethnic minorities. Religious and cultural practices described as 'extremist' are now used to justify detention. The authorities, for whom these centres are places of 'transformation through education' (*jiaoyu zhuanhua* 教育转化), deny that the detentions are arbitrary; they maintain that these measures are essential to combat terrorism and ensure national security. The many testimonies published in the international press, however, attest to a prison system, forced sterilizations and a veritable process of indoctrination to erase the distinctive signs of Uighur culture and the cultures of other Muslim ethnic groups. This extremely repressive policy demonstrates an overt brutality and indicates the impunity enjoyed by the Chinese authorities in the international arena. Despite many protests, China is not criticized as stringently as it should be, given the level of human rights violations it commits. This is also the sign of its influence on the international system, particularly within the assemblies of the UN organizations. However, it is not certain that this strategy will achieve the desired objectives; on the contrary, it could lead to the permanent alienation of the Uighur population and of other Muslim minorities.

It was also in the name of defending the national interest and denouncing the role of foreign powers – chiefly the United States – that Hong Kong society was brought to heel in 2020. While the territory of the Special Administrative Region should have kept an original model of governance summarized by the expression 'one country, two systems' (*yiguo liangzhi* 一国两制) for fifty years, i.e. until 2047 – a model characterized by considerable autonomy – Beijing imposed a National Security Law on 1 July 2020. After fifteen months of an unprecedented protest movement against a bill providing for the extradition of criminals to China, the law passed in Beijing bypassed the local constitution and its bodies. Its purpose was to prohibit subversion, sedition and secession. It was followed by systemic reforms – including that of the electoral system, which now ensured that only 'patriotic' officials, i.e. those loyal to Beijing, could be elected. In this way, all opposition was eliminated. This was followed by the arrest of many members of the opposition, the self-dissolution of the main organs of civil society, and the disappearance of many media channels, in particular Jimmy Lai's highly popular *Apple Daily*. This meant a general erosion of freedoms. Xi Jinping thus seemed ready to sacrifice Hong Kong and the advantages that the territory brought to China, on the pretext of alleged attacks on national security organized by foreign powers. In doing so, he betrayed the international commitments made by Deng Xiaoping when Hong Kong was handed back to China, commitments that provided for the maintenance of the territory's autonomy until 2047. He took the risk of sullying the image of the People's Republic, of ruining its relations with Europe and the United States, and also of burying the dream of reunification with Taiwan for which the model of 'one country, two systems' had been devised.

The surveillance of the entire population by artificial intelligence became widespread during the Covid-19 epidemic. On 22 January 2020, Beijing decided to quarantine Wuhan, where the epidemic began – a measure later extended to the whole of Hubei province and other parts of the country. After several weeks of inaction and procrastination, the ruling elite finally understood the gravity of the situation and were unanimous in taking some extraordinary decisions. Health measures were based on the mobilization of social forces at the level of neighbourhoods and villages, which made it possible to reduce social interactions to a large degree, but also on the mobilization of technological means – tracking applications to follow the movements of individuals, implementation of QR codes to authorize or prohibit access to particular spaces, and so on. Thanks to Covid-19, China was therefore strengthening its lead in the use of artificial intelligence and big data to control its population. All these measures proved to be incredibly effective. On 8 April 2020, the Wuhan quarantine was lifted. Thereafter, the maintenance of draconian measures – including testing the populations of entire cities at the appearance of the slightest case of infection, and the almost total closure of external borders – ensured a very low level of spread of infection. In December 2020, China officially recorded 111,000 cases of infection and fewer than 5,000 deaths since the start of the epidemic, compared with 49 million infections and 788,000 deaths in the United States, and 22 million infections and 615,000 deaths in Brazil. Unexpectedly, and even though the epidemic had begun in Wuhan, it opened up opportunities for the Communist Party to strengthen its legitimacy and promote its authoritarian model of governance. As early as September 2020, Xi Jinping proclaimed China's victory in the battle against the pandemic. On the international scene, the Chinese authoritarian model appeared superior to liberal democracy in preserving the lives of citizens. The Party-State therefore initially emerged triumphant from the crisis.

However, the arrival of the Omicron variant, and then of its derivatives, revealed the limits of this strategy. Chinese vaccines are less effective than messenger RNA vaccines and China's oldest citizens, those most at risk, are also the least well vaccinated. Due to the poor choices made in terms of vaccines, ending the country's policy of closure would expose China to hundreds of thousands of infections and thousands of deaths, while the healthcare system would be unable to cope with the influx of patients. But the cost of pursuing the policy is very high. A single infection leads to neighbourhoods or entire cities being placed under quarantine, and disrupts the daily lives of thousands or hundreds of thousands of people. In the spring of 2022, Beijing and Shanghai were subjected to draconian lockdown measures which were accompanied by loud protests from the urban middle classes against restrictions affecting their freedom of movement. The virtual shutdown of economic activity in a large number of sectors has severely damaged the country's economic and social situation. Growth has slowed down and unemployment is rising. Above all, it seems that the main factor behind the decisions taken is the image of the Party and its leader Xi Jinping, who cannot be criticized at any level. Any experts who raise doubts are silenced.

In programmatic terms, at the start of his first term in office, Xi set out to realize the 'Chinese dream' (*zhongguo meng* 中国梦), an expression that took on the dimension of an official ideology and which was used by propaganda organs to adorn the streets of towns and villages across the country. In many ways, this was an updated formulation of the dream of all Chinese leaders for over a century – to restore the Chinese nation to its greatness and also to make all citizens proud and happy, as a pledge of social and political stability. The aim was also undoubtedly to fulfil his promises before the anniversary of the creation of the People's Republic in 2049. At the beginning of 2021, China celebrated the eradication of extreme poverty and set a new goal of 'common prosperity' (*gongtong fuyu* 共同富裕). This new mantra from the Communist Party, a response to rising inequalities caused largely by soaring property prices and the rising costs of education, was soon translated into dramatic action. Businesses offering additional courses to children were required to transform themselves into nonprofit organizations. New regulatory measures aimed to remedy real-estate speculation. Powerful private tech companies – Tencent, Alibaba, Meituan and JD.com – were also subject to restrictive measures. After promoting their development, the government set out to fight against their increasingly hegemonic power. They were all required to develop their philanthropic activities for the benefit of the weakest members of the population. These decisions, while vigorous, could weigh negatively on growth in the short term – falling stock prices, and the near bankruptcy of the leading real-estate producer both in China and the world – and leave uncertainty as to the real and long-term scale of the redistribution of wealth.

Expansionism abroad

In October 2017, at the end of the Nineteenth Congress of the Communist Party, Xi Jinping's mandate was renewed; his presidential term was also renewed in March 2018. The 'thought of Xi Jinping' (*Xi Jinping sixiang* 习近平思想) was also incorporated into the Party's charter on this occasion. In his speech to Congress, the president described the country in glowing terms as an economic, strategic and ideological giant and welcomed the fact that it was closer than ever to achieving the goal of 'the great national renaissance'. He thus orchestrated the return of China to the place that was naturally its own, and which a century of humiliations caused by its own mistakes, Western colonialism and external aggression had caused it to lose. In addition, he readopted the political proselytism that was characteristic of his predecessors, and set up the Chinese model as an example for other countries in Africa or Asia that sought to accelerate their modernization. At this Congress, Beijing claimed to be the ideological rival of the West.

The Taiwan question is one of the main points of tension between China and the United States. In fact, relations across the strait have regularly known periods of tension, as when, in 1995, the Clinton administration granted President Lee Teng-hui a visa to travel to the United States, or on the occasion of Chinese military exercises aimed at putting pressure on Taiwanese public opinion. Officially, the positions of the various protagonists have not changed. On the one hand, the United States recognizes the principle of 'one China' at the same time as it is committed to giving Taiwan the means to defend itself. On the other hand, Beijing is striving for a peaceful reunification without having renounced the use of force. Nevertheless, in recent years military activity has intensified near the island, accompanied by increasingly belligerent rhetoric. One of the factors of tension was the 2016 election of Democratic Progressive Party candidate Tsai Ing-wen as President of the Republic of China; she was re-elected in 2020. In 2022, Russia's invasion of Ukraine has heightened fears that China too may one day embark on a military adventure to retake territory it claims to be its own in the name of the 'one China' principle. No one knows if Beijing will maintain the political line it has followed up to now: no military intervention as long as Taiwan does not secede. The United States, for its part, reiterates that it opposes any unilateral change to the status quo and does not support Taiwan's independence.

China also used its economic and financial power to serve strategic expansionism, of which its 'New Silk Roads' project, also called the Belt Road Initiative (BRI) (*yidai yilu* 一带一路, which translates as 'one belt, one road'), was the main component. Through a network of investments in infrastructure, the 'roads' were both on land (via Central Asia, Russia, Iran and Turkey to Europe) and on sea (to Australia and Latin America, as well as to South and Southeast Asia, Africa and Europe). This programme, first mentioned by Xi Jinping on trips to Indonesia and Kazakhstan at the end of 2013, was added to the Party's charter at the 2017 Congress. The project was grandiose, and sometimes presented as a Chinese version of the Marshall Plan. More than fifty countries signed agreements. It was not only a question of developing or intensifying economic relations, but also of promoting the geopolitical interests of China, in particular on the African continent – of which it had become the main trading partner in 2009. Presented as a strategic plan coordinated by the upper echelons of the state, it was in reality a multitude of disorderly initiatives on the part of state-owned enterprises (much more than those of the private sector) seeking operations abroad that would be more profitable than on the national market. For some people, the project is essentially economic; it aims to secure supplies of raw materials and open up infrastructure markets to state-owned companies. For others, it signals a great geopolitical ambition aimed at restoring China to its place in the world. The latest avatar of this policy, in 2020, was due to the Covid-19 pandemic, as a result of which Beijing promoted 'sanitary silk roads' where public health issues occupied a central place. Observers noted that, unlike with development projects led by the United States or Europe, Chinese funding comes in the form of loans rather than aid. Thus several partners in the BRI are now trapped in debt and risk having to sell assets to China, in particular infrastructure such as ports, if they are unable to pay interest or to repay loans. Forty-two countries are indebted to China at an amount exceeding 10 per cent of their GDP. In the case of Laos, its exposure is almost 30 per cent of its GDP, the highest rate in the world, followed by Sri Lanka, Kenya and Ethiopia.

China, whose military budget is constantly growing, is no longer just an Asian power but a world power. In March 2018, the project of a 'community of destiny for humanity' (*renlei mingyun gongtonti* 人类命运共同体), an expression that first appeared in 2012, was added to the Chinese Constitution, confirming that it was planning to transform the world.

Conclusion

By the start of the twenty-first century, the Chinese Communist Party had succeeded in building a new model of political, economic and social organization that has no equivalent in the rest of the world. The regime remains authoritarian and the CCP does not tolerate any autonomous social organization; the market has replaced planning but the state sector remains important; society is riven by multiple tensions but does not explode. This model is the pride of Chinese citizens, at least of most urban-dwellers, whose aspirations of wealth and power have finally been satisfied. Outside China, it arouses the admiration of nations that have not yet emerged from poverty. In Asia, it is also a cause of concern to those who fear the rise of an imperialist China. This new model is the result not of an ideological and totalitarian ambition like the Maoist model, which failed to export itself, but of a pragmatic and tentative process of trial and error. It is very largely the belated result of the political will of Deng, who relaunched reform in 1992. As we will see in the following chapters, a quarter of a century of incremental, progressive, hesitant reforms has transformed China more than did two decades of Mao's utopian ambitions.

If all political leaders since 1992 have affirmed the singularity of the Chinese trajectory, the existence of a 'Chinese model' (*zhongguo moshi* 中国模式) has been the subject of debates among intellectuals in China and abroad, in particular at the time of the global financial crisis that broke out in 2008 and during the sixtieth anniversary of the People's Republic in 2009. For some, such as Pan Wei, professor of political science at Peking University, and educated at Berkeley, China must reject the Americanization of its economy and its society; he opposes the ideology of the free market and defends the maintenance of state-owned enterprises and a public banking sector that will allow the construction of infrastructures. In his view, if China has succeeded, it is because it has been able to maintain continuity with its traditional culture. He is among those who seek to promote a new Chinese model based on the Communist heritage and current economic success. For him, democracy is not a prerequisite for progress, and the West does not understand China. He is close to the leaders; he is the herald of a China proud of the power it has regained, which intends to invent and impose on the world a new political system.

Xi Jinping's term in office marks the transition to a new era.[22] For more than three decades, since the late 1970s, China experienced rapid growth, a certain ideological openness and relative political stability made possible by partial institutionalization. Since the early 2020s, growth has decelerated significantly, the workforce has been in decline, the country is ideologically closing in, there is vigorous repression of all dissenting views, and previously adopted political norms are being dismantled. At the same time, China's ability to contain the coronavirus epidemic as early as April 2020, and the lack of US leadership during the crisis, have created a diplomatic opportunity; Beijing presents itself as the new world power. There is now a war between competing models.

FIVE

Forms of Government: From Arbitrary Rule to the Aborted Attempt at Institutionalization

The Chinese Communist Party gained power thanks to the mobilization of peasants who had become soldiers. It was heterodox with regard to the Marxist-Leninist tradition. In the two decades that followed this conquest, the Party strove to erase this heritage and placed the working class at the centre of its social, economic and political project. When it came to state building, it drew inspiration from its Soviet counterpart. In Beijing, as in Moscow, power was concentrated in the hands of a small number of rulers, especially the first, Mao Zedong. However, the Chinese political system had a certain number of specific features. While the Soviet Communist Party, in particular under Stalin, relied on the police and the secret services to maintain its grip on society, in China it was by other means that the Party ensured the assent of society for its project. Mao preferred to mobilize and indoctrinate in order to create a 'new man'. More recently, the paradox that needs to be explained is that of the sustainability of Chinese Communism. While all its counterparts – with the exception of Vietnam, North Korea and Cuba – disappeared, and democratically inspired regimes emerged, the Chinese Communist Party and the political regime of which it is the heart have survived.

Since the 1980s the Chinese economy and society have undergone a radical transformation. Too often, the immobility of the political system is emphasized. But it has not stood still. On the contrary, it is because this system has been able to adapt that it has endured. As Chapter 6 will show, the economic reforms initiated in 1979 had no ambition to bring China out of Communism. Ten years later, the events in Tiananmen Square and the fall of Communism in the Soviet Union and Eastern Europe led the Party to undertake a methodical analysis of the internal and external challenges it faced.[1] Various debates led to transformations of the Party itself, and its relationship to the state, society and the economy. The Party not only reacted to events, it also took the initiative for reforms that strengthened its capacity to govern the country. Therefore, just because China did not embark on the path of building a democratic political system, this does not mean that other reforms of a different nature did not take place. Aware of the challenges it faced, the Party broadened its recruitment base, promoted new generations of leaders, transformed its ideology, fought corruption and consolidated its own institutions. The Chinese Communist Party at the start of the twenty-first century was therefore no longer that of the end of the 1970s. If the institutional framework had hardly changed since 1989, or even since 1949, state institutions had been adapted: civil servants were more competent, procedures for consulting society or for resolving disputes had been put in place, and the system of repression had been modernized. No doubt also because economic and social problems were more and more complex to manage, and the interests of different players more and more diverse and contradictory, China moved from the arbitrary rule of one man to a much more technocratic form of rule. This explains the resilience of the Chinese political system.[2] Because the Communist Party is the actual place where power is exercised and all decisions are made, this chapter begins with an analysis of the functioning of its central and local bodies. Then we will put the strategy defined by the Party into practice on the ground. The chapter ends with an analysis of the relationship between state and society.

The Communist Party: organization, ideology, adaptation

The Communist Party runs the state. It is within it, at all levels of the administrative hierarchy, from the centre to the local level, that the political decisions are taken that the bureaucracy then applies on the ground. The leading role of the Party is also exercised through the *nomenklatura* system – that is, the control of appointments to the highest positions in the state apparatus and state-controlled businesses. The Party also controls the army through the Central Military Commission (*zhongyang junshi weiyuanhui* 中央军事委员会) chaired by the Secretary General of the Central Committee (*zhongyang weiyuanhui zong shuji*

Table 1. Congresses and leaders of the Chinese Communist Party after 1945

Number	Year	Number of Party members	Party leader*	Number of Politburo members	Number of Standing Committee members
Seventh	1945	1,211,000	Mao Zedong	13	5
Eighth	1956	10,730,000	Mao Zedong	17	7
Ninth	1969	22,000,000	Mao Zedong	21	5
Tenth	1973	28,000,000	Mao Zedong	21	9
Eleventh	1977	35,000,000	Hua Guofeng	22	7
Twelfth	1982	39,650,000	Hu Yaobang	25	6
Thirteenth	1987	46,000,000	Zhao Ziyang	17	5
Fourteenth	1992	51,000,000	Jiang Zemin	20	7
Fifteenth	1997	59,900,000	Jiang Zemin	22	7
Sixteenth	2002	66,355,000	Hu Jintao	24	9
Seventeenth	2007	73,360,000	Hu Jintao	25	9
Eighteenth	2012	82,600,000	Xi Jinping	25	7
Nineteenth	2017	89,447,000	Xi Jinping	25	7
Twentieth	2022	96,712,000	Xi Jinping	24	7

* The first leader of the Party was the Chairman from 1945 to 1982, when the post was abolished. Since then, and in accordance with all other Communist parties, the leader has been the Secretary General of the Central Committee.

中央委员会总书记). Finally, it is the Party that mobilizes the whole of society to meet the goals it sets.

Party organization

The Party is organized according to the same principles as those set up in the USSR by Lenin and then Stalin, starting with democratic centralism. This requires decisions to be preceded by broad debate; once taken, they are to be applied unanimously, without any challenge. The reality is quite different, and decisions are generally taken in a way that is, if not always centralized, at least very hierarchical. In fact, the conditions for political debate, more than sixty years after the founding of the People's Republic, remain very opaque. The vicissitudes of individuals' careers are just as opaque; leaders are partly appointed and partly elected, elections being only the last stage of a selection process. The total number of senior cadres (*lingdao ganbu* 领导干部) subject to the *nomenklatura* system – that is, appointed or recommended by the Party – is close to ten million. In this context, each Party committee has a list of leadership positions to be filled within the structures under its jurisdiction – state bodies (local governments, people's assemblies, businesses, etc.), mass organizations, official NGOs. Since the mid-1980s, the system has been decentralized, leaving more responsibilities to lower levels. The number of cadres reporting directly to the Central Committee and the Organization Department is around 5,000.[3] The reforms have also been accompanied by the introduction of a dose of uncertainty in the election of governing bodies. At the election of members of the Central Committee, the number of candidates has grown slightly higher than the number of positions to be filled: 5 per cent higher in 1987, 10 per cent in 1992, 5 per cent in 1997 and 2002, 8 per cent in 2007 and 9 per cent in 2012.[4]

The National Congress of the Chinese Communist Party (*dang quanguo daibiao dahui* 党全国代表大会) is the Party's assembly. It is held every five years – a rule ignored in Mao's time but respected since 1977 (see Table 1) – and brings together around 2,000 delegates who are in principle elected, but in reality selected. These delegates represent forty electoral districts; in 2012, 70 per cent of them represented local authorities, 13 per cent the People's Army, with the rest representing central Party and state organs and businesses. This assembly exercises limited influence over the political decision-making process that takes place in other forums. When Congress opens, everything is already decided. One important task of Congress is the adoption of the report presented by the Secretary General at the opening session. Another major task is the election of governing bodies – this has been a more open process ever since the number of candidates has exceeded the number of vacancies.

Congress elects the Central Committee (*zhongyang weiyuanhui* 中央委员会) for five years; this is the most important body, as the secretariat and central departments depend on it. It brings together the 300 main officials of the country. A third of its members represent the central Party and state apparatuses, 40 per cent the provincial leaderships, 20 per cent the military: the remainder come from state-owned enterprises or the private sector. Unlike in the Maoist era, it is no longer political struggles that explain the turnover of members, but the gradual introduction of rules on retirement age (generally 65 years) and time limits for each position (a five-year term, renewable once). Although many decisions are made in its name, it actually has little more power than Congress. It is a body of ratification rather than a place of decision. It meets in plenary session at least once a year when convened by the Politburo. Since the early 1980s, these sessions have been held in the autumn and endorse decisions or documents prepared by the Party leadership during the summer.

The Politburo (*zhengzhi ju* 政治局) is elected by the Central Committee for five years. It is the supreme body for deliberation and approval of Party decisions. It is made up of twenty to thirty officials controlling the Party, state and army, and representing the main interest groups and factions that run the country. During the Maoist era, the Politburo was dominated by the military and radical ideologues, then at the start of the reforms by old leaders who had survived the Cultural Revolution. The patriarchs of the regime ceased to be members in 1987. Since the early 1990s, the Politburo has included representatives of the main centres of national power; on it there sit two representatives of the army, the Party leaders of the four municipalities of provincial rank, representatives of the other provinces, the directors of the four departments of the Central Committee (general affairs, organizations, propaganda, political and judicial affairs) as well as representatives of state institutions (the President and Vice President of the Republic, of the National People's Congress and of the Chinese People's Political Consultative Conference). The average age has become younger: 72 in 1982, 64 in 1987 and 61 on average since 1992. The level of education has also risen; it was dominated by engineers in the 1990s, but there is now a wider range of skills represented.

The Politburo Standing Committee (*zhengzhiju changwu weiyuanhui* 政治局常务委员会), its small nucleus, is in fact the main decision-making body. It runs the country from day to day; it meets every week. This institution was created in 1956 at the Eighth Party Congress, and was composed of five to nine members (see Table 1); it was continuously chaired by Mao until his death in 1976. In 1956, its seven members were Mao Zedong, Liu Shaoqi, Zhou Enlai, Zhu De, Chen Yun, Deng Xiaoping and Lin Biao. For a long time, there were no rules about its composition, even though the Party Chairman (then the Secretary

General from 1982 onwards) and the Premier were systematically members. Since the reforms, it now includes the leaders of the Party apparatus, the National People's Congress and the Chinese People's Political Consultative Conference. No soldier has been a member since 1997. Since 1979, the principle of collegial leadership has also been reaffirmed on several occasions, but the collective nature of the decisions is questionable. Its members are now in charge of specific files. They head the 'leading groups' (*lingdao xiaozu* 领导小组) of the Central Committee. These have no official existence because they are instances of deliberation and coordination, and not of decision. Some of these groups are temporary, others permanent. They cover areas such as financial and economic matters, ideology and propaganda, rural labour, foreign affairs, national security, and the questions concerning Taiwan, Hong Kong and Macao.

The Chairman of the Party (*dang zhuxi* 党主席), who in 1982 became the General Secretary of the Central Committee (*zhongyang zongshuji* 中央总书记), is the number one in the country. Since 1993 he has also been the President of the Republic and of the Central Military Commission of the Party and the state. This combination of the three functions has significantly strengthened his position, and has also resulted in a limitation of his tenure. The tenure of the head of state can only last for two terms (article 79 of the Constitution), while that of the General Secretary, though it is not limited, is in practice subject to the same restrictions. The two penultimate General Secretaries of the Party thus each served two five-year terms at the head of state institutions: from 1993 to 2003 for Jiang Zemin, from 2003 to 2013 for Hu Jintao. The current Secretary General, Xi Jinping, had the Constitution amended in March 2018 so that he could extend his presidential term as well as that of Secretary General indefinitely. On 23 October 2022, Xi Jinping created history, becoming the first leader of the ruling Communist Party after party founder Mao Zedong to get re-elected for an unprecedented third term in power. Xi's election for the third term in power formally ends the rule of more than three decades followed by his predecessors of retiring after a ten-year tenure.

The Central Military Commission (*zhongyang junshi weiyuanhui* 中央军事委员会) plays an important political role. In 1943, it succeeded the Military Committee of the Communist Party, set up in 1927 and

146

chaired by Mao Zedong since 1935, and commanded the armed forces. The post of Chairman of the Commission is one of the most important positions in the People's Republic, along with those of President of the Republic and Secretary General, as evidenced by the list of its holders: Mao Zedong until 1976, Hua Guofeng from 1976 to 1981, Deng Xiaoping from 1981 to 1989, Jiang Zemin from 1989 to 2004, Hu Jintao from 2004 to 2012 and Xi Jinping since November 2012. In June 1989, Deng Xiaoping played a major role in resolving the crisis when he was no longer at the head of either the Party or the state, but still headed the Central Military Commission. Since 1993, the positions of Chairman of the Central Military Commission, President of the Republic and Secretary General of the Party have been held by the same man: Jiang Zemin, Hu Jintao and now Xi Jinping. The 1982 Constitution created a State Military Commission alongside the Party's Military Commission; their members are identical.

The Party has its own administrations, headed by the secretariat of the Central Committee and present at each administrative level. The most powerful of them is the Organization Department (*zhongyang zuzhibu* 中央组织部) which manages the careers of the 5,000 highest Party and state cadres, as well as those of state-controlled businesses and establishments, but also indirectly 10 million senior cadres in the country; this administration exercises supervision over the personnel ministry within the state apparatus. Another important administration is the Central Propaganda Department (*zhongyang xuanchuanbu* 中央宣传部) whose directive is to disseminate the discourse of the Party and which exercises its authority over all the administrations and enterprises that play a part in this mission (the Ministries of Culture and Education, the General Bureau of Press, Publications, Broadcasting, Cinema and Television, and the organizations in charge of censorship). The Central Department of the United Front (*zhongyang tongyi zhanxian gongzuo bu* 中央统一战线工作部) is responsible for implementing the strategy of alliance between the Party and non-Communist social forces. After playing an important role in the early years of the regime, this department found a new function with the policy of reform and opening-up as the Party tried to win over to its policy new social strata such as private entrepreneurs. It is this department that coordinates the 'eight democratic parties' – their official name – which persisted in China after 1949, within the framework of an alliance with the CCP, and the mass organizations: the Federation of Trade Unions, the Federation of Women and the League of Youth. The Central Political and Judicial Commission (*zhongyang zhengfa weiyuanhui* 中央政法委员会) brings together those responsible for public security, the law courts, the public prosecutor's department, justice and state security; it has authority over public security matters. The Central Commission for Control of Discipline (*zhongyang jilü jiancha weiyuanhui* 中央纪律检查委员会) is the Party administration in charge of investigating the leading central and provincial cadres; it is responsible for fighting corruption. It is therefore at the heart of all cases that result in the ousting and conviction by courts of Party members involved in cases involving money and politics, at both the top and bottom of the hierarchy. It has therefore been a strategic administration ever since the fight for corruption was placed at the top of the Party's agenda in the 2000s. The Central Party School in Beijing and the network of schools at the provincial, municipal, and district levels play a major role in the training of all cadres.

Within provinces (*sheng* 省), municipalities (*shi* 市), prefectures (*diqu* 地区 or *zhou* 州) and urban districts (*qu* 区), and within counties (*xian* 县), townships (*xiang* 乡) and villages (*cun* 村), the Party has local committees whose leaders are largely co-opted through the upper echelons. At the provincial, municipal and district levels, the local Party Congress is elected every five years. As at the central level, it is the standing Committees and local Party secretaries that exercise executive power. The Party secretary of each constituency usually combines their function with that of the head of the administration – governor or mayor. This is a sign that the reality of power is within the Party apparatus and not within the state.

Party members

The vitality of the Communist Party can be seen from the fact that its membership has grown steadily since the seizure of power. The Party had 1.2 million members in 1945, 10 million in 1956, 28 million in 1969, 39 million in 1977, 51 million in 1987, 59 million in 1997, 73 million in 2007, 89 million in 2017, an 96 million in 2022 (see Table 1). This represents a growing percentage of the population: 1.6 per cent in 1956, 4.1 per cent in 1977, 4.6 per cent in 1987, 4.7 per cent in 1997, 5.5 per cent in 2007, 6.4 per cent in 2017 and 6.6 per cent in 2022. The reform policy was thus accompanied by a net increase in this percentage. This does not, however, make the Communist Party a mass party. Compared to its counterparts in the USSR or Eastern Europe, it has a much lower profile in society as a whole; while this ratio is close to that of the Soviet Union before its collapse (7 per cent), it is a long way from that previously displayed by the German Democratic Republic (14 per cent) or North Korea (16 per cent).[5] The CCP, a party of peasants when the People's Republic was founded, is now a party of educated cadres. Whereas peasants were in the majority in 1956 (69 per cent of members), this was no longer the case in 1981, and by 2017 they represented less than a third of the members (30 per cent). Workers saw their share increase (14 per cent of members in 1956, 18 per cent in 1981) and then decrease (8.5 per cent in 2017). It should also be noted that, very often, peasants and workers are village cadres or union officials. In 2017, almost a third of members were either state or Party employees (8.4 per cent), or technical or managerial cadres (23.7 per cent); 40 per cent of members have received a higher education. In 2017, women represented only 24 per cent of the members. Today, therefore, the Party is essentially made up of male cadres. In line with the ongoing transformation of society, it is becoming the party of the urban middle class, although it still has in its ranks members of the categories on which it has historically relied, namely peasants and workers.

Ideology

One can reasonably assume that people join the Party not so much out of ideological conviction as out of opportunism, to defend personal or collective interests – those of a city, a region, a business or a sector of activity. While it may be thought that the phenomenon has accelerated with the reforms, this is nothing new. In the months that follow the seizure of power, the Party is confronted with an influx of new members, and this partly explains the campaigns for the rectification of the cadres launched in 1951–52. If, in Mao Zedong's time, the Party had a revolutionary project, the turning point taken by Deng Xiaoping involved abandoning the revolution to launch the country along the path of economic modernization and bring more material well-being to the population. However, it seems that the Party's theorists felt that its legitimacy could not be based solely on economic and social results.[6] Under the impact of the fall of the Soviet Union in 1989 and the loss of power by the nationalist Party (the Guomindang) in Taiwan in 2000, they deemed it necessary to adapt and innovate in ideological matters so as to legitimize the sustainability of the Party's power. Party ideology therefore changed a great deal with the reforms. Until 1992, the Party's statutes referred only to Marxism-Leninism and Mao Zedong thought as 'guides for action'. In 1997, 'Deng Xiaoping theory' was elevated to the same status; in 2002, it was the turn of Jiang Zemin's 'three representations' to be included. In 2007, at the Seventeenth Congress, Hu Jintao's 'concept of scientific development' was described as a 'guiding principle'. In November 2012, it was elevated to the rank of 'guide to action'. This gradual development, made up of successive additions, reveals the Party's willingness to adapt to new socioeconomic realities, while remaining faithful to its foundations.

In 1945, 'Mao Zedong thought' (*Mao Zedong sixiang* 毛泽东思想) appeared in the Party charter. This was mainly a strategy for seizing

Beijing, 1965.
Source: Marc Riboud / Fonds Marc Riboud au MNAAG / Magnum Photos

power, a revision of the thought of Marx and Lenin to suit the case of China. In the years that followed, it was essentially a form of empiricism, a theory recorded in circumstantial texts, rooted in experience and entirely focused on action. Mao denounced scourges that were very real: inequalities between cities and the countryside, between manual workers and intellectuals, the unchecked power of the bureaucracy and the emergence of a privileged caste. To remedy this, he proposed ideological mobilization and permanent revolution. For him, politics was at the root of social change; it was therefore not necessary to have fully developed productive forces before one could transform out-of-date production relations; the more economically backward a country, the easier its transition to socialism. Ideology was enough to motivate individuals. According to him, the countryside could be reshaped and production increased thanks to a massive organization of the workforce; an inspired population could, merely by pooling its labour forces, be more efficient. These were the principles that guided him as he launched the Great Leap Forward. Mao rejected the idea that the revolutionary crisis itself could not last, that it was just a particular moment in the acceleration of social change. He acted as if he denied the need for restructuring that would allow social innovations to take shape and become consolidated. Instead of long, gradual changes, he preferred violent and abrupt changes. Out of idealism, because he preferred to maintain revolutionary fervour rather than bask in achievement, he launched the Cultural Revolution – a revolution against the degeneration of the Chinese revolution. While he was the chief architect behind the construction of Party and state, he took the risk of destroying the former – a risk that was, however, calculated, since he could rely on the military institution to take things in hand in 1969. Attacking the very real scourges of Chinese society, Mao implemented radical and utopian policies that proved impracticable. At the end of the 1970s, the results of the permanent revolution were unresolved economic and social problems, a weakened bureaucracy and an exhausted population, difficult to mobilize. The goals imposed by Mao in the last twenty years of his life ultimately diverted the revolution from what should have been its primary task: development. As Lucien Bianco writes: 'For Mao's glory, it would have been better if he had died, like Lenin, a few years after the triumph of the revolution. This would have been better for the Chinese revolution, too.'[7] In contemporary China, despite this negative assessment,[8] part of the population, especially rural people, feel nostalgia for a period that dreamed of equality. Some politicians – notably Bo Xilai, ousted in spring 2012 – resorted to the same populist recipes.

'Deng Xiaoping theory' (Deng Xiaoping lilun 邓小平理论) was included in the Party's statutes at the Fifteenth Congress in 1997, after Deng's death. Just as 'Mao Zedong thought' varies according to the periods considered, 'Deng Xiaoping theory' corresponds only to the period when he was in power, after the third session of the Eleventh Central Committee in December 1978. His ideas constitute a rather eclectic whole, made up of a critique of Maoism and economic pragmatism. Deng abandoned violent revolution in favour of reform, inaugurating 'socialism with Chinese characteristics'; this constituted a new stage in the realization of Marxism in China which could last more than a century. The phrase most often referred to by Chinese leaders with regard to this theory is 'seeking truth from facts', taken from a speech given in 1978 titled 'Emancipating our minds, seeking truth from facts, and forming a whole to look to the future'. Inspired by this theory, any political decision should be judged by three criteria: whether it is conducive to promoting the growth of the productive forces, to expanding state power and to raising people's standard of living. Priority is clearly given to the enrichment of citizens and the nation as a whole.

Jiang Zemin's theory of 'three representations' (san ge daibiao 三个代表) was written into the Party's statutes at its Sixteenth Congress in the autumn of 2002. According to Jiang, the Party was now called upon to represent 'the most advanced productive forces', 'the most advanced culture' and 'the fundamental interests of the people'. This formula, later described as a 'major' contribution to the history of Communism, can be understood as the abandonment of the Marxist concept of class struggle; the Chinese Communist Party became the Party of the entire Chinese nation and no longer of the proletariat alone. It was also about bringing into the Party representatives of new social groups that had emerged as a result of the reforms, in particular private entrepreneurs, and, more broadly, broadening its sociological base to the emerging middle class. The Party gave up presenting itself as the party of the working class and aspired to gather around it the elites, whether economic, political or cultural.[9]

'Scientific development' (*kexue fazhan* 科学发展) constituted Hu Jintao's ideological contribution to the history of the building of socialism in China. Unlike his two predecessors, Hu very quickly added his mark to the Party's statutes because it was at the end of his first five-year term, in October 2007, at the Seventeenth Congress, that the Party included this term in its statutes – whereas Deng had already died and Jiang had retired when their contribution to the realization of socialism was enshrined in the regime's fundamental texts. The notion can be understood as a reaction to criticisms of the priority given exclusively to economic growth, to purely quantitative objectives; henceforth, emphasis would be placed on the social and ecological dimensions of development. This was also a way of complying with the international language relating to sustainable development. The formula indicated the Party's willingness to develop a strategy that could address social and environmental imbalances. The notion of 'harmonious socialist society' (*shehuizhuyi hexie shehui* 社会主义和谐社会), enshrined simultaneously in the Party statutes, presented two remarkable innovations from the point of view of Party ideology. It was, on the one hand, a way of recognizing the existence of serious social contradictions and of seeing that they were the consequence of economic and social transition. In a February 2005 speech, Hu Jintao mentioned the existence of 'increasingly complex interests emanating from distinct social sectors' and the emergence of 'all kinds of thoughts and cultures'; this marked his recognition of an increasingly complex pluralistic society and the existence of competing interests. The notion was, on the other hand, a means of mobilizing an imagined Confucian tradition – a taste for order, stability, strong rule – to enrich and renew Marxism. The term 'harmony' evoked traditional values based on self-control, derived from the Confucian morality of a self-disciplined individual, and his contribution to social order and stability. It was also a concept that assigned a key role to the Party in the process of social engineering and nation-building.

In November 2012, a few months after his assumption of the post of Secretary General, Xi Jinping declared that 'the greatest Chinese dream (*zhongguo meng* 中国梦) is the great rebirth of the Chinese nation'. After that, the apparatuses of propaganda were intensely mobilized around this expression, which was displayed through the towns and countryside. The outlines of this dream were imprecise. On the one hand, it took up an old idea, first mentioned by Liang Qichao (1873–1929), a reformer of the late Qing; this idea was contemporary with the aspiration to make China a 'rich and powerful country' (*fuqiang* 富强). On the other hand, the notion was inspired by the American Dream, largely adopted by the new Chinese middle classes, with their aspirations to comfort and material well-being. The aim was apparently to make that dream come true in China. The new president Xi thus placed the aspirations of society at the heart of his political programme. In October 2017, at the Nineteenth Congress, 'Xi Jinping thought' was included in the charter of the CCP. A few months later, in March 2018, 'Xi Jiping's thought of socialism with Chinese characteristics for a new era' was added to the constitutional text. Unlike the collegial forms of leadership that had developed during the terms of his predecessors, Xi centralized the exercise of power. His 'thought' was studied in dedicated study centres in universities and administrations alike, and his image saturated the public space; it was a return, unprecedented since Mao, to a personality cult of the supreme leader.

As the last dimension of the Party's ideology, nationalism had always played a legitimizing role since 1949. It was born in China from the confrontation with the Western world in the second half of the nineteenth century. Ever since the Opium Wars, intellectuals and politicians had been obsessed with the need to restore China to its place on the international stage. The reformers of the end of the Qing dynasty, the nationalists of the Guomindang, the intellectuals of the 1919 May Fourth movement: they were all fighting to make China a 'rich and powerful' country. It was an important dimension of the revolution of 1949. When Deng declared in 1979 'let's build a socialism with Chinese characteristics!', he was placing nationalism back at the centre of official ideology. Since the 1990s, nationalism had been partly a substitute ideology, all the more necessary after the repression of the pro-democracy movement in 1989. The return of nationalism accompanied the rise of China and the redefinition of its role both regionally and globally. One of the supreme goals of the government was the reunification of all of China under the authority of Beijing; as such, the return of Hong Kong to the mother country on 1 July 1997 was presented as preparing for the more problematic return of Taiwan to the bosom of Beijing. At the end of the decade, the choice of Beijing for the 2008 Olympics and of Shanghai for the 2010 World Expo was celebrated by the propaganda apparatus as a victory for the Chinese nation, now regaining its rank as a world power.

Five generations of leaders

Observers of Chinese political life, as of the Communist Party itself, distinguish five generations of leaders who have been in power since 1949: veterans of the Long March (1934–35) – Mao Zedong, Zhou Enlai, Liu Shaoqi and Lin Biao; officers of the anti-Japanese war (1937–45) – Deng Xiaoping, Hu Yaobang, Zhao Ziyang, Yao Yilin and Qiao Shi; cadres of the socialist transformation (1949–58) who studied in the USSR or in Eastern Europe in the 1950s – Jiang Zeming, Li Peng, Zhu Rongji, Li Lanqing and Li Ruihuan; the generation of the Cultural Revolution (1966–76), which had its first political experiences during the Cultural Revolution and then returned to their studies – Wen Jiabao, Zeng Qinghong, Wu Bangguo and Li Changchun; and finally, the elites of economic reform (since 1978) – Xi Jinping and Li Keqiang, now currently in power. This classification has been used in China even since Jiang Zemin was officially referred to as the 'heart' of the third generation by Deng Xiaoping, a term he himself used to further establish his position as the heir. This division into generations therefore has a legitimizing political function. Yet the boundaries between each generation are difficult to draw. Deng Xiaoping, born in 1904, presented himself as a leader of the second generation, whereas he belonged de facto to the same generation as Mao, born in 1893. Hu Yaobang, born in 1915, was identified as a member of the second generation even though he took part in the Long March.

This categorization highlighted the way the recruitment of political elites developed. The first two generations were largely homogeneous, sociologically and professionally. They came from the countryside, were more often the sons of literate landowners than simple peasants, and were militarily committed to the revolution. The third and fourth generations were made up of engineers turned technocrats. The fifth was the most diverse generation in terms of social background, university education and careers. This sequencing also signals the development of the sources of the leaders' legitimacy: the first generations derived it from their participation in revolutionary conquest at the sides of Mao, while the latter derived it from their acquired skills, both through their university training and their years of experience in local and central Party apparatuses. Power of the charismatic type, to use Max Weber's words, was succeeded by legal-rational power. Power wielded by one man, Mao Zedong then Deng Xiaoping, yielded to a more collective exercise of power, a transition initiated with Jiang Zemin and institutionalized under Hu Jintao. The experiences acquired before men could exercise managerial functions also explain the nature of the policies they conducted. According to Li Cheng, the top priority given to economic growth under Jiang Zemin can, in part, be attributed to the proportion of technocrats in the ruling apparatus, if by that we mean individuals who received a university education in engineering (or the sciences) and who practised the profession of engineering (or were engaged in scientific research) before entering a political career. In the mid-1980s, there were hardly any technocrats in the posts of provincial officials (Party secretaries or governors); in 2000, they represented between half and three-quarters of leaders, depending on the population we look at (members of the Central Committee, provincial officials, etc.).[10] Their position was hegemonic at the end of the 1990s and during the 2000s: they represented 65 per cent of the members of the Politburo in 1992, 75 per cent in 1997, 72 per cent in 2002, 40 per cent in 2007 and 16 per cent in 2012; 86 per cent of the members of the Politburo Standing Committee in 1992, 100 per cent in 1997 and 2002, 78 per cent in 2007 and 14 per cent in 2012. Their decline came with a diversification of the education received by the more recent generations, more likely to be trained in the human and social sciences, especially law and economics. What consequences this development might have remains an open question. The fact that more and more of them are graduating in law could, for example, promote the development of the legal system.[11]

Though it exercises a monopoly on political activity, the Chinese Communist Party is by no means monolithic. It is divided, and one of the features of the Chinese political system is its factionalism. Under Mao, the debates were sometimes very lively, and could even be a matter of life and death for the participants. In July 1959, at the plenary session in Lushan, Peng Dehuai was dismissed from his post as Defence Minister for having criticized Mao; he was then persecuted during the Cultural Revolution. Political debates were a pretext for struggles between factions and, very often, it was not the content of the policies that was at stake. These struggles became particularly violent at the end of the Maoist era: Lin Biao, though designated as Mao's successor, died in unclear circumstances in September 1971; Deng Xiaoping, dismissed during the Cultural Revolution, was dismissed again after the events of April 1976 in Tiananmen Square. After 1978, the level of tension within the elites dropped significantly, and those who were defeated no longer necessarily faced harsh condemnation. This development continued under Jiang Zemin. In particular, all leaders now shared a concern for stability and strove to retain power; debates no longer degenerated into violent and destructive confrontations.[12] Jiang and then Hu were able to maintain the consensus. Relations between the main leaders were calmer and more peaceful than ever in the history of the Republic. The structure of factions changed. There was a shift from factions organized on the basis of personal connections to factions organized on the basis of geographic interests – the 'Shanghai clique' (*Shanghaibang* 上海帮) around Jiang Zemin – or relationships forged by experience – the 'Communist Youth League faction' (*tuanpai* 团派) around Hu Jintao. The importance of the leaders' geographical origin – or their background in such and such a province – was due to the differences in development between the provinces and the importance of experience gained in the increasingly complex management of local realities. There were also significant affinities between the sons and daughters of leaders of revolutionary veterans, nicknamed princes (*taizi* 太子), provincial affinities (*tongxiang* 同乡) and educational affinities (*tongxue* 同学).

Today, two main coalitions are competing within the Party leadership to exercise and control power. On the one hand, there is the so-called elitist coalition, led originally by Jiang Zeming and currently by Xi Jinping; it mainly brings together leaders from families of revolutionary veterans or senior leaders. On the other hand, there is the so-called populist coalition, led originally by Hu Jintao and currently by his protégé Li Keqiang; most of the members of this coalition started their careers in the Youth League, like Hu and Li themselves. Many observers predicted a balanced distribution of posts between the two factions in the 2012 Politburo Standing Committee. In the end, Jiang's camp won out: six of the seven seats went to him, and only Li Keqiang represented the second faction. Nevertheless, Hu's protégés were well represented in other institutions; the Politburo was thus divided equally between the two camps with nine members each, which suggests a concern for balance. In 2017, at the end of the Nineteenth Congress, the composition of the new Politburo Standing Committee suggested that Xi Jinping had once again reached a compromise between the two competing factions: Li Keqiang and Wang Yang were former protégés of Hu Jintao, while Han Zheng and Wang Huning, who had made their careers partly in Shanghai, were close to his predecessor Jiang Zemin.

The reforms paved the way for real efforts to institutionalize the way the Party works. On the one hand, the conditions for selecting members of the Politburo and the Standing Committee are still unknown, the most likely assumption being that they are chosen by the departing members or by powerful leaders already in retirement. On the other, competition for power is now limited by a number of established norms that prevent it from escalating into the violent struggle characteristic of previous periods of the People's Republic. This is evidenced by the development of the conditions under which the supreme leaders are appointed. Mao Zedong himself overthrew two of his presumed heirs – Liu Shaoqi in 1969 and Lin Biao in 1971 – and personally appointed Hua Guofeng in crisis conditions, after the events of 5 April 1976 in Tiananmen Square. When Mao died in September, the appointment of Hua Guofeng as Party Chairman was justified by an undated declaration from the Grand Helmsman, who was said to have confided to Hua: 'With you in power, I don't need to worry.' This legitimacy was not in fact sufficient: in 1978, Hua lost the reality of power and finally lost his post as Party Chairman in June 1981. At an informal meeting of the Politburo, he was replaced by Hu Yaobang. He was then confirmed as Secretary General, in accordance with the Party's charter, by the Twelfth Congress in 1982. But Hu did not finish his term in office, since he was dismissed in January 1987 even though there had been no formal meeting of the Central Committee to ratify the decision of Deng Xiaoping. Zhao Ziyang was then appointed interim Secretary General, and confirmed by the Thirteenth Congress in August of the same year. After having ousted Hu, Deng eliminated the second Secretary General that he himself had chosen, Zhao Ziyang, during the events of spring 1989. Jiang Zemin was then appointed to his post by decision of a group of old timers who derived their legitimacy from their participation in the Long March, sarcastically nicknamed the 'eight immortals' in reference to Daoist deities.[13] They had no formal position in the apparatus, in defiance of the Party charter which stipulates that the Secretary General is appointed by the Central Committee. Thus, four decades after the founding of the People's Republic, the succession proceeds without respecting the rules that the Party had itself set. Twenty years after the return to power of Deng Xiaoping, the re-establishment of operating norms, which had been at the top of his agenda, had still not been achieved. Since then, the handover of power to Hu Jintao in 2002 and Xi Jinping in 2012 was carried out in accordance with the rules.

However, the conditions of the beginning of Xi Jinping's tenure cast something of a shadow over this optimistic view. Several important leaders were eliminated in the name of the fight against corruption, a nagging issue that had been ongoing for twenty years. I will mention three of the most famous cases of leaders being excluded on grounds of corruption and violation of Party discipline. In 1994, the Vice Mayor of Beijing, Wang Baosen, fell under suspicion of 'economic crimes': he committed suicide on 4 April. On 27 April, Chen Xitong, Mayor of the capital, resigned. On 28 September 1995, Chen was dismissed from his post in the Politburo and Central Committee, accused of living a 'dissolute' and 'extravagant' life and of making 'serious mistakes'. On 27 August 1997, on the eve of the Fifteenth Party Congress, he was expelled from the Party before finally being sentenced in July 1998 to sixteen years in prison for 'corruption and a decadent lifestyle'. Ten years later, the fall of the Party Secretary General for the city of Shanghai, Chen Liangyu, also began with accusations of corruption being brought against his subordinates; an investigation was opened in August 2006 concerning embezzlement within the city's Labour and Social Security Office. At the end of September, it was announced that Chen Liangyu was involved in 'disciplinary violations'. On 24 September, he was suspended from the Politburo. On 26 July 2007, Chen was expelled from the Party. In April 2008, he was sentenced to eighteen years in prison and all his personal property was confiscated. The case of Bo Xilai, eliminated from the political scene in March 2012, six months before the Eighteenth Congress, was all the more spectacular, as it involved a leader who was himself the son of a veteran of the revolution. On 15 March 2012, Bo Xilai was suspended from his duties as Party Secretary of Chongqing City; a month later he was suspended from the Politburo. In addition to charges of corruption and illegal enrichment, there was the murder of an English businessman, for which his wife, Gu Kailai, was convicted. In all three cases, these leaders were excluded on charges of corruption and on the grounds of violation of Party discipline. They were the subject of criminal investigations and sentenced to heavy prison terms. Procedurally, they were excluded by legal and judicial process, unlike what happened during the Maoist era when politically deposed leaders were the subject of an ideological smear campaign in the Press. From the political point of view, each of these eliminations removed an obstacle to important moments of transition. The elimination of Chen Xitong in 1995 was interpreted as a sign of consolidation of Jiang Zemin's power, as Beijing was a stronghold of resistance to his authority. In 2006, Chen Liangyu was eliminated: he was an open critic of Wen Jiabao who was trying to re-centralize economic policy. His ousting was then seen as a sign of the weakening of the Shanghai clique associated with Jiang Zemin and of the consolidation of Hu Jintao's power in the run-up to the Seventeenth Congress. The elimination of Bo Xilai was just as much part of a factional struggle in the upper echelons of the political apparatus. On the eve of the Eighteenth Congress, and even though Bo did not appear to be a likely candidate for membership of the Politburo Standing Committee, his personality, and his ability to use the national media and the foreign press to organize his own promotion made him someone who would not adapt well to the collective mode of decision-making that emerged during the successive terms of Jiang Zemin and Hu Jintao. Thus, while the mix of political life and business affected the Party at all levels, from top to bottom, the fight against corruption appears mainly to be a tool in the political struggle between the highest leaders. Despite all the commitments made over the previous twenty years, the conditions for an honest exercise of political power in the service of the general interest had yet to be built.

The state apparatus: a democratic façade

Like its Soviet model, the Chinese political system masks the Party's dictatorship behind a façade of seemingly democratic state institutions. At all administrative levels, these are broken down into executive power – local governments and central government – and a system of assemblies.

The supreme body is the National People's Congress (*quanguo renmin daibiao dahui* 全国人民代表大会), elected by the provincial assemblies, themselves elected by the district and township assemblies. In reality, the National Congress has no power and merely endorses the decisions of the Party. Like the constitution of the Soviet Union, the Chinese Constitution guarantees public freedoms, but this too is a matter of pure formalism. In 1954, the first Constitution defined the Chinese state as a 'people's democratic dictatorship', the dictatorship being exercised by the proletariat and, de facto, by its vanguard, the Communist Party.

Unlike the USSR, which was a federation of nations, China is a unitary state, a 'unified multiethnic state' according to the Constitution, which grants no political autonomy. However, article 4 of the 1982 Constitution – the fourth after those of 1954, 1975 and 1978 – provides for economic, cultural and administrative autonomy for the regions of national minorities, which represent less than 8 per cent of the population but occupy 60 per cent of the national territory; they are autonomous but cannot secede. The People's Republic of China recognizes fifty-six ethnic groups on its territory. The Han ethnic group constitutes the majority (92 per cent of the population) and the other fifty-five are characterized as minorities – the identification of the latter being the result of political haggling and not of scientific analysis. The constitution guarantees ethnic minorities the right to administer their own affairs themselves, to draw up autonomous and circumstantial regulations and to use and develop their own language and script. Officially, the state respects and protects the religious freedom of ethnic minorities. In addition, belonging to an ethnic minority allows individuals to benefit from affirmative action policies – laxer regulations on birth control, bonus points for entering college, etc. Autonomous regions or cities (i.e., those inhabited by a minority) have quotas of civil servants of their ethnic group sitting in local government.

The Chinese state is not only inspired by its Soviet big brother, it also carries the legacy of the regimes that came before it. Thus, the administrative division of the People's Republic is hardly different from that of Republican or Imperial China; the country is divided into provinces, prefectures and municipalities, districts and townships. It is undoubtedly at this last level that the changes are most important. The administration of the rural townships was very largely delegated by the imperial state to the heads of the most powerful families or clans; the populations are now supervised, educated and mobilized by the Party. The administrative map defined in the 1950s remains unchanged to this day, except for the creation of Hainan province, an island detached from Guangdong province in 1988, and the creation of the municipality under direct administration of the central government of Chongqing in 1997. At the beginning of the twenty-first century, China had thirty-one provincial districts: twenty-three provinces – including seventeen from imperial China and that of Taiwan over which the government had no authority – five autonomous regions, namely Inner Mongolia (created in 1947), Xinjiang (1955), Ningxia (1958), Guangxi (1958) and Tibet (1965) – four municipalities under direct administration (Beijing, Tianjin, Shanghai and Chongqing) and two special administrative regions – Hong Kong (since July 1997) and Macao (since December 1999).

Executive power

At the top of the executive apparatus, the central government, or State Council (*guowuyuan* 国务院), submits bills to the NPC, establishes the budget, and exercises its authority over ministries and administrations. Its authority is real in all areas where state administration is not duplicated by Party administration: the economy, finance, social services, science and education, and family planning; since the 1990s the number of ministries has fallen dramatically, dropping to twenty-five by 2013. At each level of the administrative hierarchy, state administration is under the control of the Party. At the central level, the head of government – the Premier (zongli 总理) – is the number two in the Party. He is assisted by Deputy Premiers, all members of the Politburo (four in 2018) and State Councillors (five in 2018). Deputy Premiers and State Councillors, who are divided into different sectors, form a small cabinet. They are the main government officials who run the state administration. The Council of Ministers meets rarely – quarterly, in general – and with some irregularity; it has a formal and symbolic character.

At the various levels of administration, local governments constitute executive power. As at the central level, they are accountable both to the people's assemblies at the corresponding level and to state administrative bodies at the higher level. Local state and Party organizations are closely interwoven. In the 1980s, economic reforms were accompanied by a devolution of powers; Beijing delegated broad powers to local authorities, starting with the provinces, especially in terms of economic and social development. Secondly, Beijing worked towards partial and limited recentralization. The 1994 tax reform, implemented by Zhu Rongji, recentralized public finances. The old contractual sharing of tax revenues between the centre and the provinces, which led the former to borrow money from the richest of the latter, was replaced by a new system of revenue sharing which distinguishes three types of taxes: those intended for the centre, those collected by local authorities, and those shared between the centre and the localities. This reform resulted in the dismantling of extra-budgetary funds collected by local governments and an increase in the share of tax revenues collected directly by Beijing – around 50 per cent since then. In 1995, a new system for the evaluation and circulation of political leaders was put in place; it consists in judging senior cadres on the basis of the results of their actions according to a certain number of criteria: growth rate, fiscal capacity, birth control and, more recently, social stability and environmental protection. This system explains the excessive priority given by all leaders to GDP growth rates, to the detriment of other elements. In fact, the territories have a high degree of autonomy. Territorial units, whether they be provinces, cities or townships, are in competition with each other; this has locally led to excessive and redundant investments. For example, the Pearl River Delta has five airports – in Hong Kong, Macao, Canton, Shenzhen and Zhuhai. This autonomy also has advantages and allows for experimentation and pluralism. Thus, reforms were initiated in the four Special Economic Zones, as they were known in 1980 (Shenzhen, Zhuhai, Shantou in Guangdong and Xiamen in Fujian). More recently, Bo Xilai wielded a populist, authoritarian and neo-Maoist form of power in Chongqing, while Wang Yang experimented with a more liberal model, relying on the use of NGOs in Guangdong province.

Elected assemblies

The Constitution grants broad powers to the National People's Congress, but in reality this institution remains marginal. Like the Supreme Soviet in the Soviet Union, its main function is to legitimize the dictatorship of the Communist Party. Its Chairman is the number two in the state apparatus. Elected for five years by the provincial assemblies, the almost 3,000 members (there were 1,226 in 1954) represent thirty-four territorial constituencies – twenty-three provinces, five autonomous regions, four special municipalities, and two special administrative regions – and the People's Army. All MPs are recommended by the Organization Department. Since 1993, around 70 per cent of them have been Party members. They are not professional politicians since they only sit for two to three weeks a year in Beijing in March. Between sessions, parliamentary work is carried out by the Congress's Standing Committee, comprising 160 members, which in fact passes most of the laws. The activities of the Congress were practically suspended during the ten years of the Cultural Revolution (1966–76), and it has regained a more significant role since the 1990s. At its annual spring session, the Congress votes the laws and the budget prepared by the government; it approves the activity reports presented by the various ministers. It has no control over government work and only plays a secondary role in law-making. It is also the Congress that elects ministers, the head of government and head of state. The rule is that there is only one candidate per position; his success is therefore measured by the percentage of votes obtained. Thus, in March 1998, Zhu Rongji was elected Premier with the highest score (2,890 votes) while Jiang Zemin was elected head of state with 2,882 votes (36 votes against and 29 abstentions). In 2003, Zeng Qinghong was elected to the post of Vice President with only 87 per cent of the votes. To date, the NPC has never rejected a law or refused to elect a nominated leader.

Local assemblies play a role similar to the NPC within their administrative constituencies. They were reinstated in 1979 after about fifteen years of dormancy. At the township and district levels, members of local assemblies are elected by direct universal suffrage for a five-year term. While the number of candidates exceeds the number of seats to be filled, the Party nevertheless controls the process. They are often chaired by the Party Secretary of the constituency, and remain chambers for recording decisions made by the Party committee and prepared by the government. Nevertheless, since the mid-1990s, the NPC and local assemblies have gradually increased their influence over the governments they are supposed to elect and control. While they are no more democratically elected than in the past, they have managed to promote representatives of the country's new elites. Thus, the NPC has billionaires among its ranks; likewise, some private business leaders use their own funds to finance election campaigns in order to be elected members of local assemblies. The assemblies therefore nowadays represent the diversity of Chinese elites.

At the end of the 1980s, the establishment in the countryside of village committees (*nongmin weiyuanhui* 农民委员会) and, in towns, of residents' committees (*jumin weiyuanhui* 居民委员会) – an institution of the 1950s that fell into disuse – could lead people to believe in a grassroots democratization of political institutions. The reform began in November 1987 when a law was promulgated on village committees; this was extended to towns in December 1989. These committees, set up gradually during the 1990s, were in fact elected during what were in effect pluralist elections.

In the countryside, the village committees, responsible to the representative assembly of the villagers, serve as a relay for the municipal governments in the implementation of national policies, in particular in matters of birth control, public order, taxation, education and management of financial resources – investment decisions, the running of village-owned businesses, and management of communal land. The committees play a role in mediating minor conflicts, organizing weddings and funerals, and helping underprivileged people, but their powers are restricted both by the village Party cells and by the township authorities as well as their representatives in the villages who continue to have a monopoly on administrative action in the countryside. In towns, the town-dwellers' committees organize public order at the neighbourhood level (they play an important role in control and supervision of society) and social action (particularly for the most vulnerable, the elderly, disabled and unemployed).

It is the collapse of village authorities, following the decollectivization of land, and the growing risk of anarchy in the countryside that led to this reform. From this point of view, the introduction of village elections was not the first step in democratization, but a means of restoring social order in the countryside. When it comes to appointing members of the village committee – which then elects the village head (*cunzhang* 村长) for three years – the procedures and methods of appointment vary from place to place. Even where competitive elections are held, Communist Party members, both among candidates and elected officials, continue to dominate. The Party, both in the countryside and in the cities, controls the supply of candidates. In some villages, a local Party Secretary is elected. Elsewhere, elected villagers are encouraged to join the Party after the election. In the cities, the grip of the Party and the state is even stronger.

This last development has helped to reverse the process of selection and promotion of Communist cadres. Previously, village leaders were chosen from among Party members; today, more of them can join the Party apparatus only after demonstrating their competence. This development reflects an obvious weakening of the Party's organization in the countryside and changes the average profile of these members; these new members are more and more often entrepreneurs or influential people, heads of the main families, who find it to their professional advantage, or the advantage of their clan, to become responsible for the village and therefore the main interlocutors of the municipal government. Conversely, these newly elected officials have the economic or political capital to bargain with local Party and state authorities for benefits and protection for their communities. Thus, a class of local notables has been formed that increasingly resembles the gentry of the imperial or even republican era, or a new rural bourgeoisie in the case of commercial or industrial activities.

The Chinese People's Political Consultative Conference (CPPCC *Zhongguo renmin zhengzhi xieshang huiyi* 中国人民政治协商会议) is another body that helps to make the political system appear democratic. It exists at the national level as well as at the level of provinces and municipalities. Heir to the legislative as well as constituent assembly that sat from 1949 to 1954 and the United Front policy that characterized the early years of the regime, it has, paradoxically, no longer had any function since that date. Its 2,000 members (since 1978), elected for five years, represent the Party, the three main mass organizations (the Youth League, the Federation of Women and the Federation of Trade Unions), the 'eight democratic parties' associated with the CCP since 1949 (and controlled by it), ethnic minorities and certain professions. Their selection is controlled by the CCP. The CPPCC meets in Beijing every spring at the same time as the National Congress. Party members are in the minority in this Congress, whose raison d'être is to provide a platform for non-Communist elites; it is also a reward for a successful career. It includes scientists, stars of cinema and television, sportsmen and private entrepreneurs. This is also where the bosses of the major Hong Kong companies were appointed before reunification. At the national level, the CPPCC was chaired by Mao from 1949 to 1954, then by Zhou Enlai until 1966. Reactivated in 1978, it was chaired by Deng Xiaoping until 1983. The reactivation of the United Front policy, along with the reforms carried out, indicates a continuity between the 1950s and the contemporary period.

A 'state of laws without a rule of law'[14]

The strongest political innovation since 1979 has been the new place given to law.[15] During the Cultural Revolution, Mao Zedong launched the younger generation against the institutions he himself had helped to build; the functioning of the political system was then unpredictable and highly personalized. It was no longer the Politburo and its Standing Committee that ran the country, but the Group of the Cultural Revolution. The constitution was no longer respected: the National People's Congress no longer met; the President of the Republic was not dismissed by the National Congress but by the Party's Central Committee. In 1978, after a decade of violence and anarchy, Deng Xiaoping set himself the goal of rebuilding stable institutions. This project focused on granting a more important place than ever to law, to replacing 'government by men' (*renzhi* 人治) with government by law. The aim was to consolidate institutions, stabilizing the political system so that the errors of the past could not be reproduced, so that never again could a man, or a group of men, seize power without answering for their decisions. At the end of the Cultural Revolution, law therefore also played a legitimizing role.

The first area in which the law was restored is that of economic relations with foreign countries, in response to the imperative to attract foreign investment to Chinese soil. At the beginning of the 1980s, laws on Chinese–foreign companies, on trademarks and on patents were published. The development of the nonstate economy then required the production of a new set of civil and economic laws. Laws on companies, copyright, competition, consumer rights, stocks and bonds, futures markets and insurance were published. The transition from a planned economy to a market economy involved building the necessary legal framework. In the 1990s, administrative law emerged. In 1990, an administrative procedural law for the first time allowed citizens to challenge the administration in court. The judicial and penitentiary system was also modernized, with a law on prisons (1994), on judges and prosecutors (1995), on the people's police (1995) and on administrative sanctions (1996); for the first time, citizens' avenues of appeal were broadened in face of bureaucratic arbitrariness. Criminal law was modernized. The power of prosecutors, judges and lawyers was strengthened. The law on lawyers (1996) no longer designated them as 'state legal workers' but as 'legal professionals'; they could establish private practices. This production of laws entailed the training of professionals. The study of law had disappeared from the universities; it was now re-established. All legal professions saw their numbers grow rapidly: judges, prosecutors, notaries, lawyers.

More laws and more lawyers ensured that conflicts were no longer settled in an expeditious and arbitrary manner by the bureaucracy. The abundant legislation and the professionalization of legal practitioners, both lawyers and magistrates, did not necessarily lead to the rule of law. The diagnosis made in 1996 by Jean-Pierre Cabestan still seems relevant; China remains a 'state of laws without a rule of law'.[16] Admittedly, in the apparently neutral areas of civil and economic law, legislation is close to that of democracies. But in criminal and administrative law, the objectives of Chinese justice remain notably different from those prevailing in democratic countries. Criminal law continues to have a political character. For example, the existence of a 'counter-revolutionary crime' in the penal code violates fundamental freedoms. While the system of re-education through labour, which deprived an individual of liberty for one to four years and which was beyond the jurisdiction of judges, was abolished in December 2013, other forms of arbitrary detention persist. Party committees continue to exercise oversight over justice, and in particular lawyers. In the same way, magistrates are subject to the Party; despite modernization and professionalization, the judicial institutions do not constitute an autonomous space protected from political injunctions. Finally, the justice system is corrupted by money.

While considerable work has been done since 1979 to build legal standards, and even though lawyers in particular continue to struggle – and take risks – to advance the role of law, legality in China remains authoritarian.

The army in the political system

One of the idiosyncratic features of Chinese Communism is the political role of the army. On two occasions, the country has been under military administration: in the wake of the Party's seizure of power from 1949 to 1952 before civilian provincial officials were put in place, and at the end of the Cultural Revolution when the country was on the brink of chaos, between 1967 and 1970. The Ninth Congress in 1969 was dominated by the army, and the latter appointed a soldier, Marshal Lin Biao, as Mao's successor. Twenty years later, in 1989, the People's Liberation Army was again called upon to intervene to resolve the political crisis; it re-established order in Tiananmen Square in Beijing. During these three episodes, the army acted at the request of the Party. It therefore did not intervene in an autonomous way, in the service of its own ambitions, but always at the request of political power. Since 1979, two major developments have taken place. First, in exchange for declining political clout, the military became more professional. The army would now participate only in decisions that concerned it, those relating to defence and security in the broad sense. While the military is still overrepresented in formal institutions – they constitute 9 per cent of the members of the NPC and occupy 20 per cent of the seats on the Central Committee – no soldier is any longer a member of the Politburo Standing Committee.[17] The supreme decision-making body in military matters is the Party's Central Military Commission – since 1993, alongside the state's Central Military Commission, whose members are identical – headed by the Secretary General, who has, since Jiang Zemin, been a civilian. Second, at Jiang's request, the People's Liberation Army has also withdrawn from the industrial and commercial sphere to refocus on the country's defence and security. In return, leaders have worked for its professionalization and modernization.[18] These were made all the more necessary as its performances, when called upon, were mediocre. In 1969, during the incidents on the Ussuri River with the Soviet Union, and especially in 1979 during the border war with Vietnam, the PLA revealed its weaknesses in training, equipment and logistics. Abolished by Lin Biao in 1965, ranks were re-established in 1988. Salaries and careers were reassessed. In this context of modernization, the PLA underwent significant demobilization. Manpower had increased from 2.4 million to 4.8 million between 1965 and 1981, and then fell sharply: to 3 million in 1990, 2.3 million in 2002 and around 2 million today. In return, the PLA's budget has been steadily increasing. It is largely devoted to increasing its projection capabilities, by air and sea, especially with the permanent prospect of a re-conquest of Taiwan.

The Party-State and society: control, participation, resistance

The regime exercises control over society through a variety of means: a large-scale prison system that depends on a judiciary; a discretionary system of deprivation of liberty under the authority of Public Security; control of the media, education and minds through propaganda; work units; residents' committees; and the *hukou* (户口) system for household registration. Only some of these institutions of control are considered in this chapter. However, in the case of Chinese totalitarianism, relations between the regime and society are not limited to repression or surveillance; political power seeks to obtain the consent of the greatest number for its choices, and, even in an authoritarian context, society has the capacity to resist.

A triple system of repression, confinement and surveillance

From the earliest years, the construction of a coercive apparatus has been a cornerstone of the edifice built by Mao and the Party. As a totalitarian state, China has set up a vast prison system, the main element of which is a network of forced labour camps, equivalent to the Soviet gulag: *laogai* 劳改 (short for *laodong gaizao* 劳动改造, reform through labour). The prison population is said to have consistently exceeded 10 million during the Maoist period, and is still over 2 million, spread across more than 1,000 camps. The Chinese system is characterized by the way its function is not only to lock people up and make them work, it is also a system of 'reform of thought' (*sixiang gaizao* 思想改造).[19]

From this point of view, it is more ambitious than its Soviet counterpart. Unlike Stalin, who eliminated or definitively sent entire categories of the Soviet population to the gulag, Mao aspired to turn prisoners into 'new people'. Another difference is that it is a closed system; prisoners are never returned to their families – a practice that contradicts the goal of re-education. The history of this system is not, however, that of a rise to power culminating in the most extreme and utopian phases, the Great Leap Forward and the Cultural Revolution. In fact, when it came to power, the Party already had experience of state control dating back to the early 1930s and during this period, in the guerrilla zones controlled by the Party, the first institutions of repression and confinement took shape. If the Soviet gulag served as a reference point for the *laogai*, it was also affected by the experience of repression practised in the 1930s in the soviets of Jiangxi, then in the guerrilla zones in northern China in the 1940s. One of the ideas put forward by Jean-Luc Domenach is that the regime locked up the greatest number of people while it was still being established. The Great Leap Forward disrupted the system, with famine killing about a third of Chinese prisoners. A few years later, the Cultural Revolution encouraged revolts and escapes. The beginning of the era of Deng Xiaoping was then marked by numerous releases. Since 1979, we have witnessed a veritable 'decomposition'[20] of the Chinese gulag: reform of thought has collapsed, the regime no longer has the ambition or the capacity to transform men. The vast majority of prisoners are now common law detainees.

Laogai is not the only institution of confinement: other 're-education through labour' camps (*laojiao* 劳教, short for *laodong jiaoyang* 劳动教养) are also run by Public Security on a discretionary basis. These are extrajudicial institutions to which a citizen is sent by administrative decision for a maximum period of four years. Under Mao, most prisoners were victims of political purges. As an instrument of political control, it was also used to prevent the appearance of migrants in cities. At the end of the 1950s, China had nearly 100 *laojiao* centres in which almost a million people were held. The system collapsed during the Cultural Revolution – in 1969 there were only 1,000 people undergoing re-education through labour. From the 1980s, it became an instrument of social control; most of the people in prison are petty criminals (drug addicts or prostitutes, for example). But the system is also being used to incarcerate political dissidents and all critics of the government – petitioners, activists of all kinds, members of banned religious organizations and anyone believed to pose a threat to public order. While article 37 of the Constitution specifies that any deprivation or restriction of a citizen's individual freedom must imperatively pass through an approval or a decision of the People's Procuratorate or the People's Court, many jurists have challenged the constitutionality of *laojiao* since the mid-1990s. In the context of a development of the rule of law, this system, which allows citizens to be arbitrarily deprived of their liberty, became the symbol of the non-respect of rights by the police. It was officially ended by a decision of the Standing Committee of the NPC in January 2014.

While China has always, proportionally, locked up fewer people than the USSR, this is mainly because other institutions ensure rigorous control of the social space, the work unit and the residents' committee. Moreover, although the confinement system persists today, it has been crumbling since the start of the reforms. Under Xi Jinping's tenure, the crackdown on dissenting views, both inside and outside the Party, has increased. In Xinjiang, since 2017, 'camps for transformation through education' have been built; these are described as vocational training centres aimed at combating Muslim terrorism and extremism, in which hundreds of thousands of Uighur and Kazakh Muslims have been locked up.

Today, across the country, the digital revolution and artificial intelligence are equipping public security organs with new surveillance tools. Hundreds of millions of cameras have been installed in streets, stations, buses and taxis, and most are capable of facial recognition. With the coronavirus epidemic, this technological arsenal has increased dramatically. Such massive surveillance is part of a more general strategy of population control, a major element of which is the 'social credit system' (*shehui xinyong tixi* 社会信用体系) which rates citizens and businesses according to their degree of virtue. This brings together a disparate set of public and private initiatives aimed at combating incivility, and more generally at maintaining order. These systems are most often seen by the Chinese population as a guarantee of security and progress in a society where interpersonal relations, or relations with public and private institutions, are marked by great mistrust.

Social coalitions supporting the regime

In the early years, the Communist Party built up a fully fledged totalitarian regime in the People's Republic. Not only did the Party have a monopoly on political activity, but it had the tools to rally its entire society to its slogans. However, it would be wrong to conclude that the small elite that ruled the country was able to impose its views on a passive and silent population. If the Communist Party was able to defeat the Nationalist Party, this was because it succeeded in winning the support of a broad social coalition formed in October 1949 of at least five distinct groups: Party cadres; the industrial workforce; intellectuals; students and secondary school pupils; agricultural workers, farmers, small peasants and a large number of middle-ranking peasants.[21] In the months following the seizure of power, the Party did not hesitate to court members of other social groups, such as the Shanghai capitalists who had fled to Hong Kong and were hesitant about their final destination. It sent emissaries to those who were least compromised with the previous regime to try to convince them that the (genuinely nationalist) Communist Party was best able to rebuild the new China that they too were calling for. It managed to win over some of them, who returned to Shanghai.[22]

This initial coalition continued until the mid-1950s. The history of the People's Republic can then be read as the history of the gradual disintegration of this coalition. The first to leave were non-Communist intellectuals and many students, either because they disagreed with the policy of modelling intellectual life and the educational system on the Soviet model, or because they were victims of the re-education campaigns – the campaign against Hu Feng in 1955, or the repression of the Hundred Flowers Campaign in the spring of 1957. The economic costs of collectivization, and the catastrophe of the Great Leap Forward, followed by three years of famine, led to the regime losing much of its credibility amongst rural populations. The cadres, weakened by the failure of the Great Leap Forward, were persecuted during the Cultural Revolution, which then attacked the privileges of workers in state-owned enterprises. If the Cultural Revolution relied mainly on new generations of students, this was because they formed one of the last social groups likely to give blind obeisance to the slogans of the supreme leader. The crackdown on the Red Guards, who were sent down to the countryside, destroyed the Party's authority among these young people. At the end of the 1960s, Mao Zedong's last supporters were workers in insecure employment, workers at the bottom of the wage scale – those who were mobilized against secure employees during the Cultural Revolution – and students who, thanks to their family ties, were not sent to the countryside. In this perspective, the turning point of 1978 appears as an essentially political initiative to broaden a social coalition that had become too narrow. In the 1980s, the rapid enrichment of that part of the peasantry who benefited from collectivization, and the distribution of additional income to working populations when permission was given to companies to conserve part of their resources, were clearly in line with this goal. In both rural and urban China, the Party regained its stock of legitimacy. After the tragedy of 1989, and the disappointed hopes of part of the urban population eager for political reform, a new social contract was proposed: the maintenance of an authoritarian Party on the one hand, and a rapid improvement in incomes and living conditions on the other. New social categories emerged in this context; they were the major beneficiaries of reforms and opening-up that today constitute the regime's main backers. The emerging middle classes, in all their great diversity, now constitute the main support of the Party.

To rally the population to its cause, the regime has used a specific tool that cannot be found in any Communist regime: 'mass campaigns' (*qunzhong yundong* 群众运动). Their function is to mobilize the population – or a part of it – and to win it over to a policy decided on by the Party. These campaigns do not emerge spontaneously from society but are prompted by the Party, without always being perfectly controlled by it. The first agrarian reform, in the spring of 1950, during which part of the land was redistributed to the peasants, gave rise to a great mass campaign. Peasants were invited to come together and collectively denounce landowners or rich peasants – at least those designated as such by the Party – who were evicted from their land. In the same year, the marriage law also gave rise to the holding of people's courts at which marriages described by representatives of the Party as 'feudal' were denounced. In both cases, it was the Party that chose the villains for the people's retribution. In 1958, the Great Leap Forward was a gigantic mass campaign during which an immense effort was demanded both from the peasants engaged in huge collective works and from the urban workers in factories. The regular mobilization of all or part of Chinese society was partly due to the people's wars conducted in the past; this feature of the exercise of power was part of the Party's strategy to seize power: it relied on the large number of peasants to achieve victory, while despising anything to do with modern technology. These campaigns also stemmed from Mao's conviction that the mobilization of people's minds was stronger than anything (stronger than any skill or expertise, in particular) to move China forward. A rise in ideological awareness would accelerate development. These mass campaigns can also be interpreted as a means for the Party to involve the population in the political choices made by the ruling elite. More recently, the mobilization of the Chinese people to fight the SARS epidemic in 2003 was like a mass campaign. In addition to the initiatives taken by the administrations concerned – the construction of dedicated hospitals, the quarantining of buildings, districts and villages – the intense mobilization of the whole apparatus of propaganda called upon the entire Chinese population to change its everyday habits of hygiene.

Despite being totalitarian, the Chinese regime has experienced several protests. The first important campaign was that of the Hundred Flowers in the spring of 1957. When intellectuals were invited to express themselves freely, in a mass campaign orchestrated by the Party, they produced some severe critiques. For a time, the control exercised by the Party over society was loosened. In the face of these criticisms, the episode was abruptly ended in March. Often, it is the divisions within the ruling elites that make the expression of dissent possible. Support on the part of certain senior leaders, albeit indirect and implicit, and in line with their own objectives, makes the expression of protest possible. This was the case with the first pro-democracy movement in the winter of 1978–79, and again in the spring of 1989. At the end of 1978, both Deng Xiaoping and Hua Guofeng had an interest in allowing the expression of grievances in favour of reform, the former because the critiques were consonant with his own proposals, the latter because they allowed him to mark his own difference from the previous period. Once Deng's interests had triumphed in the political arena, he ended the period of opening-up. In 1989, certain leaders sympathized with the pro-democratic demands, without, of course, being able to express this. Zhao Ziyang went to the square with the demonstrators, a gesture that was criticized by his opponents who refused to compromise. Another sign that the movement may have been encouraged inside the Party is that the attacks of the crowd were selective – Li Peng and Deng were booed – while Zhao Ziyang's name was not mentioned. The proclamation of the state of siege on 20 May 1989 led, among other things, to a hostile petition signed by some of the most prestigious names of the PLA, and the manifest passivity of certain army units in charge of applying this state of siege. Between 20 May and the night of 3–4 June, two weeks elapsed during which negotiations took place with military leaders, as several military veterans openly opposed the use of force. Factional rivalries that paralysed the authorities thus played a major role in the events, and in particular explain the way the episode dragged on. Support from those in power had allowed the protest movement to be launched, but in return it limited its independent political potential.

Opponents without opposition

Never again since 1989 has the Chinese leadership allowed the expression of a protest of such magnitude. However, forms of opposition or resistance to power are still expressed. The majority of those who in the late 1980s had hoped for political reform or had joined the democracy movement subsequently lost interest in political issues.[23] For intellectuals, one possible avenue was to retreat into their academic disciplines at a time when the regime was investing heavily in the higher education system; with better incomes and more professional opportunities, especially in terms of contacts with the rest of the world, many university teachers have chosen to become more professional, to make progress in their discipline and to make the most of international networks. The rise of Chinese scientists in international communities was one of the indirect consequences of their realization that the political space was closed to them. Researchers and professors won their autonomy from the Party thanks to their academic competence.

A minority of activists, however, have refused the terms of the new social contract that grants professional and material benefits at the cost of tacit approval of the regime. Some of the spring 1989 movement leaders sentenced to prison terms have not given up on their ambition to create an opposition force outside the Party. Some are living in exile, such as the former student leader Wang Dan and the Cantonese activist Wang Xizhe; others, such as the historian Bao Zunxin and the literary critic Liu Xiaobo, live in China. They occasionally take the initiative of making their voices heard. Thus, in 1998, in Hangzhou, activists grouped around Wang Youcai, one of the leaders of the June 1989 movement, took advantage of President Bill Clinton's visit to Beijing to try and create a legal party of opposition, the Party for Democracy in China (*zhongguo minzhu dang* 中国民主党). They were wagering that the regime would not resort to repression. This party's charter stated that its objective was 'to establish a democratic political system'. Committees started emerging in several provinces and steps were taken to get it legally registered. But the project was very soon cut short; at the end of 1998, all the party leaders were arrested.

The last major dissent initiative was the publication in December 2008 of Charter 08 (*lingba xianzhang* 零八宪章), so called with reference to the Czechoslovak Charter 77. This text was signed by more than 300 intellectuals and human rights activists who sought to promote democracy. In their view, increasing social conflict and discontent were putting the country in danger so that 'democratic political reforms can no longer be delayed!' The Charter called for an independent judiciary, freedom of association and the end of one-party rule. The participants were soon facing a crackdown. On 8 December 2008, Liu Xiaobo, one of the editors, was arrested; other signatories were questioned by the police. One year later, on 25 December 2009, Liu was sentenced to eleven years in prison 'for subversion'. This decision provoked several international reactions, the best known of which was the awarding of the Nobel Peace Prize to him in 2010. Today, most of those in favour of the triumph of democracy in China are not campaigning for revolutionary changes but for a gradual transition based on the current Constitution. Indeed, since the Party has built up institutions that are in theory democratic, this fiction simply needs to be made a reality, for example by ensuring that elections to the national and provincial assemblies are pluralistic and organized by direct universal suffrage. The future of the Chinese political system is thus partly being played out in debates that involve not only dissidents, but also constitutional experts and other specialists.

Public space and civil society

The inability of regime opponents to organize themselves does not mean that there is no space for speaking out or struggling to influence public policies. Promotion of the rule of law by the regime itself, and the adoption of a new legal arsenal and the training of professionals, have been accompanied, since the early 2000s, by increasing demands for more legal measures. These 'movements for the defence of rights' (*weiquan yundong* 维权运动) mobilize both citizens (workers in conflict with their employers, expropriated peasants, residents complaining about pollution, and so on), and many legal professionals (lawyers and academics), as well as activists and journalists who support them. The dynamics of this informal movement were crystallized by the national scandal of March 2003 represented by the death of a young man, Sun Zhigang, beaten to death in a detention centre for migrants by the Canton police because he did not have his identity papers with him. Journalists and lawyers thereupon denounced the unconstitutionality of the detention and repatriation centre (*shourong qiansong suo* 收容遣送所), created by the State Council and not by a law of the People's Congress. Faced with the strength of this protest, the internment system was finally dissolved in June 2003. These legal activists, particularly critical of the judiciary's lack of independence, do not contest the legislative framework but actually rely on it to carry out their activity, which, according to them, is a means of defending and ensuring respect for the Constitution. Among the best-known activists are Chen Guangcheng, blind since childhood, who taught himself law and defended the cause of women forced to be sterilized or to have an abortion, and Hu Jia, an ardent environmental activist and advocate for AIDS patients. Conflicts between government and society exist and find expression in movements that are most often limited in time and space. However, recent history shows that these mobilizations had a capacity to influence policies.

There is one old institution, almost contemporary with the founding of the People's Republic, that allows citizens to express their critical views on public action: the Bureau of Letters and Visits (*laixin laifang bangongshi* 来信来访办公室).[24] This administration, to which any Chinese citizen can write and to which he or she can resort in person, was created in 1951 to collect citizens' opinions; the objective was to gather praise or criticism that would both actually help to strengthen the exercise of power. However, very quickly, witnesses were attacking local cadres, urging political power to act in accordance with its commitments, and describing unacceptable situations. The institution thus became the main and legitimate means of denouncing the injustices and imbalances of the administration, and of seeking redress. In the years preceding the coming to power of Deng Xiaoping, it was resorted to by those appealing against political sanctions deemed unjust and brought against them after the agrarian reform. Today, this institution can address the complaints not just of individual citizens, but also of collectives, and the field of what can be said to state has widened. Although this is a space of direct address to the political and administrative authorities, however, it remains narrowly limited, and does not allow for open debate on the common good. From this point of view, as it remains to some degree secret and invisible, it constitutes the antithesis of a public space. However, because it connects the rulers and the ruled, it is indeed a true political space.

One privileged space of expression today is the Internet. According to the National Internet Information Office, the body in charge of administering the Internet, the number of users reached 731 million in 2017. Most of them were born after 1980, live in urban areas and have access to education, thus representing a certain middle class. As with other mainstream media, the Party exercises strict control over the Internet. Yet it is in this medium in particular that activists regularly experience limits that must not be crossed. This is the case with contemporary artist Ai Weiwei. He is the son of Ai Qing, a famous poet labelled a 'rightist' during the repression of the Hundred Flowers Campaign and sent to Inner Mongolia and then to Xinjiang. As a renowned artist, Ai Weiwei occupies a special position in Chinese public space. In 2005, he was invited by the Sina Internet portal to open a blog, an invitation which, as was necessary, received the approval of the authorities concerned; he thereupon opened accounts on various social networks. He posted numerous comments on the news, for example on the ethnic tensions between Han and Tibetans in March 2008. He signed Charter 08 when Liu Xiaobo was arrested. The earthquake that laid waste to Sichuan province was a turning point in his blogging activity. He dedicated a site to counting the children who had been victims of the 'tofu schools', built at low cost because of corruption. He adopted fully political positions, and denounced the actions of the authorities. These allowed him to express himself freely until 2009, when he was placed under close surveillance. Ai Weiwei was finally arrested on 3 April 2011, officially for tax evasion, and released on bail a few weeks later. Ai's case is emblematic because he left the elitist art world so that he could speak out in the nascent public space of the Internet. In Séverine Arsène's view, even more than the provocative posture of Ai Weiwei and other famous triggers of virtual protest movements, 'the sharing of information, as well as the acquiescence, indignation, individual testimony and countless other small daily actions that Internet users almost incidentally produce online, constitute a mode of participation so fluid that it almost escapes notice', though this participation is 'powerful'.[25] In fact, the Internet now facilitates the circulation of ideas among increasingly large audiences and allows for the formation of certain public opinions and certain forms of collective action. Beyond censorship and self-censorship, there are legitimate ways of speaking out individually and collectively on the Internet that make forms of mobilization possible. The Internet, as a space for public opinion to find a voice, is also a central factor in legitimizing the political regime.

The Communist Party does not tolerate social organizations being autonomous. The crackdown on Falungong, after 15,000 of its followers surrounded the seat of the government in Beijing in April 1999, is a reminder of this. On the other hand, since the beginning of the 1990s, the Party has allowed the development of NGOs that take up social issues: protection of the environment, distribution of educational and medical services in the countryside to vulnerable populations, aid to sick and disabled people, etc. In the early 2000s, the existence of a third sector was even openly encouraged, as these organizations supplement state action in many areas – including the delivery of educational and health services – and also constitute a reservoir of jobs for young people entering the labour market. One of the oldest Chinese NGOs is responsible for promoting environmental protection; the Friends of Nature (*ziran zhi you* 自然之友) was founded in 1993 by Liang Conjie, the grandson of Liang Qichao. Other organizations work in more politically sensitive areas. The Aizhi association (*aizhi* 爱知), founded by Wan Yanhai in 1994, provides assistance to AIDS patients: peasants who have been infected while selling their blood, prostitutes, drug addicts and homosexual populations in the cities. Wan Yanhai was one of the first to expose the tainted blood scandal in Henan province; he was initially arrested. Most of these NGOs in China work in partnership with the government. Specializing in a specific issue, they help provide solutions to social problems that the state cannot solve. In so doing, they can nevertheless exert pressure on public policies and help to define them. But it is impossible for them to oppose the administration head-on. Legally, most Chinese NGOs are affiliated with state administrations or institutions, hence their name: government-organized nongovernmental organizations (GONGO).

To this day, the Communist Party is not prepared to give up its political hegemony, nor to let society, or fractions of society, get involved in political issues. Regarding Chinese civil society, authors prefer to refer to a 'pseudo-civil society'[26] or an 'interstitial' society.[27] Indeed, Chinese society allows autonomy only in particular, limited, intermediate spaces where it is not permitted to tackle properly political questions. Relative autonomy and the conflicts that regularly arise do not, however, create a civil society in the sense that democratic Western societies have become accustomed to.[28] Of course, political participation is growing, but it is either illegal (as in dissent) or indirect and uninstitutionalized (as in activism or sporadic protests). One of the things the leaders fear, as it would represent a major political risk, is the convergence between opposition intellectuals or dissidents and popular movements. This is the reason why academics, journalists and lawyers committed to the defence of particular causes – AIDS patients, illegal expropriations in town or countryside, victims of industrial pollution – particularly arouse the concern of the authorities.

Conclusion

Since the 1990s, the Chinese political regime has undergone much less change than society or the economy. The Communist Party still exercises a monopoly on political activity. Its mode of operation – the modalities of decision-making, or of the appointment of the senior cadres – remains opaque. However, reforms have been carried out, and the Party's permanence in power cannot be explained only by its monopoly of coercion.

In search of a new legitimacy, the Party said 'goodbye to the revolution'[29] in 1978. It has transformed itself into a managerial Party concerned with economic growth capable of creating jobs and wealth – the sole way of improving the material well-being of the population. In this respect, the CCP is no different from many other ruling parties, including in democratic regimes; it has become more ordinary.[30] Its ideology has adapted to the transformations of society. The Chinese state is no longer a revolutionary state; it presents itself as the state of the Chinese nation which it is restoring to wealth and power. The system of popular assemblies has been strengthened. Democracy has developed relatively well at the village and neighbourhood level. Law occupies an unprecedented place in the organization of society and its relationship with power. Society can mobilize, albeit in a limited way, and make its voice heard. The Party no longer has the same power it did at its peak; its capacity for control and transformation is no longer comparable to what it was during the 1950s and 1960s, at the height of Maoism.

How should we describe the current political system, and what is its future? All observers agree that there has been a shift from a totalitarian Maoist regime to an authoritarian post-Maoist regime. The debate therefore centres on the characteristics of Chinese authoritarianism. Fragmented, reactive, competitive, consultative – all these adjectives are used by observers. Michel Bonnin refers to a 'reformed' or 'softened' totalitarianism, to underline the relaxation of the system and the emergence of spaces of autonomy.[31] Jean-Philippe Béja speaks of a 'post-totalitarian' regime to emphasize the fact that the Party no longer tries to convince the population to support its ideology and that it only needs to obtain apparent conformity.[32] Béja also describes the regime in terms of 'post-political authoritarianism'[33] to indicate that the CCP has moved to the stage of governance without going through that of democracy.[34] The authorities are faced with many problems that can be resolved by resorting to experts who contribute to the creation of public policies, but without the people being consulted. The partners in this governance are mainly NGOs. But the problems are never posed in political terms, debated in the public space by the citizens themselves. Jean-Pierre Cabestan has spoken of an 'enlightened but plutocratic authoritarianism'[35] – a mixture of relaxed authoritarianism and selective liberalization that primarily benefits the elites. Yves Chevrier refers to a 'distended' Communism[36] – i.e., a mode of government whose effective unity is made up of heterogeneous, even opposed, elements in tension with one another. The government allows social bodies to act under merely indirect control – without, however, granting them full recognition or full autonomy.

This adaptation has favoured an institutionalization of the political system. Immediately after 1978, this system initially returned to the way it had functioned before the Cultural Revolution. Then an analysis of the disaster suggested that the lack of effective control over an arbitrary authority had contributed to the disaster. Measures were therefore introduced to limit the power and arbitrary rule of individuals. State organs now meet regularly and in accordance with the Constitution. The regularity of Party Congresses and plenary sessions is also one of the most visible manifestations of this institutionalization. Constitutional procedures and the operating rules of Party institutions are formally respected and more often invoked.[37] The retirement of leaders – a rule recently broken by Xi Jinping himself – made it possible to avoid granting jobs for life. However, this institutionalization remains incomplete due to the state's submission to the Party.

What is the future of this system? For some authors, it could be a transition to democracy – this was the view of Andrew Nathan in 1998.[38] For David Shambaugh, the Party was going through two processes simultaneously in the late 2000s.[39] On the one hand, it was withering away, in the sense that it has much less control now than before over society, the economy and intellectual life. The traditional instruments of control, propaganda and coercion have weakened considerably; opening-up and globalization are working to the same goal. On the other hand, the Party has shown its ability to adapt and reform itself. The government's task today is to provide the population with a number of public goods: health, security, education, environmental protection, social services, etc. A Leninist Party such as the CCP is not, in fact, in an unfavourable position to provide these goods to the population, because responding to these demands requires the state to have a strong capacity for action.

Xi Jinping's mandate, which began in 2013, has been marked by an intensification in the repression of dissenting voices and ethnic minorities, a crushing of civil society, the dismantling of previous political norms, an extreme personalization of power, the rise of nationalism and a falling back on Chinese values. Should we therefore conclude that this is a step backwards? This is what comparisons with the figure of Mao or the period of the Cultural Revolution suggest. This would be a mistake, however, because China is not what it was in the 1960s. It is predominantly urban, prosperous and globalized; and the circulation of people, of information and capital, is intense. Society is complex, socially and culturally diverse. The stake for Mao was to haul the country out of backwardness and project it into modernity. For Xi, the challenge is to rally social forces with conflicting interests behind the Party. As long as the regime provides the greatest number of people with increased income and security, the dictatorship will continue.

SIX

The Creation of Wealth: From Planned Economy to the Market

At the start of the fourteenth century, the Chinese economy led the world in terms of income per capita. In terms of technology, intensive use of natural resources, and its ability to administer a vast territorial empire, China surpassed Europe. Until the beginning of the nineteenth century, it was able to feed a population four times as large, while keeping the average income per capita stable.[1] But the birth of modern capitalism in Europe led to China losing its superiority. In 1820, China entered a period of decline and humiliation. In 1949, the Communist Party came to power with the promise to carry out a programme for the rebirth of the Chinese nation that all revolutionaries and reformers had supported since the end of the nineteenth century: to enable China to escape its poverty and catch up.

The economy of the People's Republic went through two periods. During the first, 1949–78, China adopted, while developing, the Soviet model. The priority was industrialization financed by levies on collectivized agriculture. Despite political instability, growth was around 2 per cent per year. During the second period, in 1978, the launch of reforms and the opening-up of the economy finally allowed the latter to take off. GDP grew by 9.5 per cent per year on average during the 1980s and 1990s. In the 2000s, annual growth was 10.5 per cent. China was now becoming a great economic power; overtaking Japan, it had risen to second place in the world economy by 2010.

In so doing, and after abandoning its revolutionary goals, China became normal in another sense. In the early 1950s, the Communist Party had made the heterodox choice to adapt socialism to fit an under-developed and rural country. In 1978, the country showed many atypical features. It was both poor and overindustrialized in terms of its level of development (almost half of its production was from industry) and not very urbanized (only 18 per cent of the population lived in cities). This huge country, isolated from the rest of the world economy, had developed its own model. Two decades later, China had become an emerging country like any other, whose economic institutions seemed to be converging with those shared by all market economies. I will analyse the socialist cycle, then the cycle of reform, and then show how the path towards the construction of a market economy has not yet been completed.

The socialist cycle

The place of inheritance

In 1949, China emerged from more than a decade of turmoil; the war with Japan (1937–45) was followed by the Civil War (1946–49). The destruction of industrial equipment and agricultural infrastructure, especially irrigation, had been compounded by rampant inflation. The growth the country experienced in the 1920s and 1930s was halted. When the Communist Party came to power, the country was poorer than India, and its economy was pre-industrial: 75 per cent of the population lived on agriculture, which represented 65 per cent of production. Only a quarter of the population lived in cities.

Industry not only represented a small part of output, but was concentrated in the open ports, and since 1931 in Manchuria. One of the reasons for this concentration was the very large proportion of foreign companies in the manufacturing sector. These were mainly present in textiles (weaving), but also in extractive activities or electricity production. Chinese capital was involved in spinning, cigarette and match manufacturing, and flour milling. Chinese industry was first and foremost a consumer goods industry. In this regard, Manchuria, which had benefited from the strategy of the Japanese occupiers, was an exception. The Japanese had set up a coherent industrial system: mining, metallurgy, manufacturing industry, public infrastructure. In 1941, Manchuria contained only 9 per cent of the Chinese population but contributed a third of industrial production, a potential significantly reduced by the destruction of the war and the levies carried out by the Soviet armies. In 1949, although China was poor, industrialization had already started. In this regard, the development by the Japanese of heavy industry in Manchuria paved the way for the industrial strategy of the Communist Party.

At the national level, the existence of a modern industrial sector, even one that accounted for a minority of production, had lasting consequences because it would be the basis for the rapid development of the 1950s and 1960s. Two-thirds of the growth in industrial production during the first Five-Year Plan (1953–57) came from the extension of already existing industrial establishments. This was the case in textile production, one of the highest in the world in the 1930s and, after 1949, the second largest export item – after raw materials and agricultural products – and a major source of foreign exchange to pay for imports. It was also the modern sector from before 1949 that provided the qualified personnel, technicians and managers who, with the help of Soviet advisers, trained the new managers and workers of the 1950s. Without this base, the People's Republic would have had to rely more heavily on foreign technicians, and growth would have been slower.

The transition was also facilitated by the establishment of a war economy by the nationalist regime in the 1930s. The first nationalizations of industrial establishments under the aegis of the National Resources Commission (NRC, *guojia ziyuan weiyuanhui* 国家资源委员会) took place as part of the move of the nationalist authorities from the coast to the interior. In 1937, the NRC controlled twenty-three industrial establishments and mines that employed 2,000 people. At the end of the Second World War, it took over the companies controlled by the Japanese and, in 1947, it controlled 67 per cent of the country's industrial capital.[2] In 1949, the personnel of the NRC ensured the transition to the Communist authorities; they would be in charge of planning after 1953. This continuity in the state management of the economy helps to explain the rapid restoration of the production apparatus so that, from 1952, production was brought back to levels prior to those of 1949.

Another legacy, the experience of a century of foreign encroachments since 1839, left the country with a lasting aversion to all outside influence; it turned in on itself. From this point of view, the turning point of 1978 and the decision to appeal to foreign capital can be read as the relaunch of a dynamic interrupted by the actions of Mao Zedong. This is also true of the industrialization of the countryside, which would first occur where there had been a small rural industry before 1949, and of the geographical balance: after 1979, the lower Yangtze valley resumed its historical pre-eminence while the northeast of the country became less significant. Likewise, China would rebuild its traditional ties with its maritime environment after three decades of closure.

The situation was quickly restored. By the end of 1950, inflation was under control. Agricultural and industrial production resumed and in 1952 exceeded the highest level reached before 1949. In the summer of 1953, the signing of the armistice in Korea opened the way for a new phase of development. In the countryside, the Party launched the 'first agrarian reform' (*diyi tudi gaige* 第一土地改革); 42 per cent of arable land was redistributed, mainly in the newly conquered southern provinces. Peasants became owners of the land they worked. The economic results were less significant than the social transformations that were generated. Admittedly, farms became equal in size, but they remained tiny, on average less than 2 hectares. On the other hand, the agrarian reform eliminated traditional rural elites – 5 million people became victims of meetings staging ideological struggles – and placed the representatives of the Party at the heart of rural society; it was the poorest peasants who felt most grateful to the Party.

In the cities, the new government took over many factories: those that were under the control of the Japanese or the Nationalist Party, those that belonged to capitalists who had fled. Within the framework of the 'new democracy' policy, the Party was open to non-Communists. Just as certain bureaucrats employed by the NRC continued to work for the Communist government with the same missions, so also certain industrialists of the previous period collaborated. The government, now able to mobilize the necessary talent, had very soon restored industry. Public investment was mostly concentrated in the northeast, which was already the most developed area for heavy industries, thanks to the Japanese industrialization programme. Industrial establishments left by the Japanese occupiers were rehabilitated with the help of the Soviet Union. The very positive results achieved by the government at the end of 1952 enabled the passage to the next stage, the launching of a socialist programme of industrialization.

The socialist planned economy

The damage resulting from the years of war, followed by the Korean conflict that led to the country being ostracized, pushed China into the arms of the Soviet Union, the only nation to offer help. The USSR became China's model, its primary business partner and technological supplier. Soviet institutions were copied and prevailed for three decades, even though they were amended in 1958. A command economy was set up, without recourse to market mechanisms. In the countryside, land was collective property and management of the agricultural economy was also collective. In the cities, the state owned the factories and controlled the means of transport, communication and distribution. Planners set production targets and allocated resources to companies that had little autonomy: these companies did not set their employment levels, and did not keep their profits.

The priority was industrialization financed by the countryside. Industrial products were expensive and agricultural products cheap; the terms of trade were thus favourable to industrial enterprises controlled by the state and unfavourable to the countryside. Peasants were forced to meet production quotas at low fixed prices, while industrial enterprises, even when inefficient, generated a large surplus that allowed the state to invest. Consumption was sacrificed to investment, whose share in GDP

Factory in the Anshan area, 1957.
Source: Marc Riboud / Fonds Marc Riboud au MNAAG / Magnum Photos

reached 26 per cent in 1954 and more than 40 per cent during the Great Leap Forward; it fell to 15 per cent in 1962 and then remained between 25 and 35 per cent until 1978, a particularly high level for a poor country. The majority of this investment went to industry, and within the latter to heavy industry (80 per cent). The result of this forced industrialization was a very rapid growth in industrial production: 11.5 per cent per year between 1952 and 1978.[3] Over the same period, the proportion of industrial production in GDP rose from 18 per cent to 44 per cent, while that of agriculture fell from 51 per cent to 28 per cent. Entire industrial sectors were created from scratch: cars, chemicals and electrical equipment. This trajectory was accompanied by a change in geography; while the Chinese economy was mainly on the coasts, priority was now given to the interior regions. If a planned economy constituted the general framework, it was interpreted differently in different periods between 1952 and 1979, and with contrasting results. Successes were followed by resounding failures or catastrophes. The cycles of economic activity corresponded to those of political life. The most tragic episode was the Great Leap Forward, followed by the Cultural Revolution.

The years 1953–57 corresponded to the first Five-Year Plan. In fact, this was a time of constant change in economic policy. While Chinese leaders agreed to adopt the Soviet model, disagreements arose over the pace of transformation, the degree of centralization needed, and the opportunities for an incentives policy on wages in urban areas. In addition, the general framework of the Soviet model was not applied uniformly throughout the country.

In agriculture, in the autumn of 1953, the state set up a monopoly on the grain trade, with peasants being obliged to deliver production quotas at prices set administratively well below those of the market. Private trading saw its share drop drastically, while the first cooperatives were granted most of the credits and means of production. Peasants were obliged to hand over their cereal production even as the organization of production remained family-owned, though they were invited to join cooperative farms. In terms of industrial development, 156 projects were launched, all located in interior or northeastern provinces, with the aim of shifting the centre of gravity of the Chinese economy away from the coast. They were based on the import of technologies and the training of personnel by the USSR. Nearly 6,000 Soviet advisers were sent to

China, while 10,000 Chinese students made the reverse trip. In towns and cities too, the organization of production remained mixed; private entrepreneurs continued to operate factories and businesses. Two years later, the reform movement was relaunched.

The collectivization of agriculture was first thought of as gradual and voluntary; farmers were told to join temporary and then permanent self-help groups. At the end of 1954, only 2 per cent of rural households belonged to cooperative forms of production. This pace was considered too slow by Mao and, in the winter of 1955–56, mobilization campaigns were launched to accelerate the movement. By the end of 1955, this rate had risen to 14 per cent; a year later, 98 per cent of them had become cooperatives.[4] In fact, most collectivization took place under coercion, and more than half of the peasantry moved from undertaking individual work on the family farm to the collective agriculture methods of socialist cooperatives. Unlike what happened in the USSR, this did not lead to a fall in agricultural production. The recent land reform had made it possible to recruit into the Party poor farmers who were well trained and available when the next stage, collectivization, came along. Furthermore, there was no equivalent of dekulakization; rich peasants could become members of cooperatives and were not deported. At the beginning of 1956, the same policy of collectivization was launched in the cities; private industrial or commercial enterprises were transformed into cooperatives or joint public–private establishments de facto controlled by the state. In 1956, private ownership of the means of production disappeared and the Chinese economy became socialist. After these brutal changes, at a time when the political climate favoured liberalization, the economic programme adopted at the Eighth Party Congress in September 1956 was marked by moderation.

The Great Leap Forward (1958–60)

The Great Leap Forward was the most tragic episode in the history of the People's Republic. In economic matters, it is often seen as the moment when a properly Maoist vision of socialism took shape, distinct from the Soviet model. It was in fact a period of intensification of the Soviet project, as the principle of the transfer of resources from agriculture to industry was not only maintained but reinforced, and the rate of accumulation remained very high (40 per cent in 1958), with money being devoted as a priority to heavy industry and the import of equipment. It is true that, as he sought a new path, Mao Zedong resorted to pragmatic policies – the promotion of rural industry and recourse to a labour force that had little work during the off-season – but he did not give up the rapid pace of industrialization.

For Lucien Bianco, the Great Leap Forward must be compared to the first Soviet Five-Year Plan (1928–33), because the two episodes were characterized by the same disproportionate effort at industrialization and the same upheaval in the age-old frameworks of rural life. In his view, 'the way in which this original path (imposed by Mao during his last two decades, 1957–1976) claimed to correct the [Soviet] model, was inspired by the same ideals, and radicalized them: it went further in the same direction and, in so doing, worsened the effects of the traumas repeated from the beginning to the end of the 1930s, from frenzied industrialization, collectivization, dekulakization and famine to the Great Terror.'[5]

The most important decision was the establishment of the people's communes (*renmin gongshe* 人民公社) in 1958. As entities with, at the same time, economic, administrative and social functions, each one of the 24,000 people's communes comprised more than 5,000 peasant households. The agricultural workforce was no longer organized on the basis of the village, but on immense territorial units, sometimes larger than the township level. The workers were organized into specialized brigades – 150–200 families – and sent to perform agricultural tasks in areas they did not know; this management of excessively large production units led to a drop in harvests and then to famine. Collective life was taken to an unprecedented degree with the construction of 'large canteens' (*da shitang* 大食堂) where the peasant families now took their meals. Large-scale activities – hydraulic works, reforestation and insect control campaigns – mobilized men to the detriment of properly agricultural tasks. In factories, any material incentive to increase production disappeared. In the countryside, free markets were suppressed. At the same time, economic control was decentralized: production units benefited from greater autonomy; the Party's provincial secretaries became both implementers and inspectors of slogans and their results, which they zealously tried to anticipate or exceed. In terms of technology, it is all about 'walking on two legs' (*liang tiao tui zoulu* 两条腿走路) using both advanced technologies imported from the USSR and the simplest technologies that were more suited to a poor country with an abundant labour force. Steel was produced both in modern steel complexes and in 'small blast furnaces' (*xiao gaolu* 小高炉) set up in the courtyards of houses.

In addition to these strategic choices, in 1958–59 a series of erroneous decisions led the country to disaster. The excellent harvest of the autumn of 1958, due both to good performance and also to reports that were partly inflated, led to two decisions: an increase in government grain purchases, and a reduction in agricultural inputs (earth and men). While agricultural production decreased, paradoxically, the state increased the amount it took. By the end of the year, reports showed that the situation was worsening in some parts of the countryside where food was scarce. In some areas, the excellent harvest was not being gathered because peasants had been mobilized by local industry or major hydraulic infrastructure works, or had gone to the towns to work for state-owned enterprises. Mao realized that adjustments had to be made. At the start of 1959, a return to planning practices began. Some targets, such as steel production,

Province of Gansu, 1957. Wheat harvest.
Source: Marc Riboud / Fonds Marc Riboud au MNAAG / Magnum Photos

were revised downwards. However, the braking of the movement was interrupted by the eruption of factional struggles at the top of the Party. The clashes that broke out in July 1959 in Lushan led to a relaunch of the Great Leap Forward. Harvests dwindled, food stocks were running out. China was experiencing a real crisis in subsistence, the main cause of which was the blindness of its leaders. In 1960, poor weather conditions and Khrushchev's withdrawal of Soviet advisers worsened the crisis without causing it. Famine broke out, mainly affecting the countryside, while towns continued to be fed. The provinces of the interior, in particular Sichuan, Guizhou and Anhui, were the worst hit. By the end of 1961, famine had cost between 25 and 30 million additional deaths, and a birth shortfall of 30 million.

At the beginning of 1961, a new economic policy was put in place. Twenty million workers recently settled in the towns were sent back to the countryside. Investment was slowing down. Mao was temporarily no longer in control and it was Zhou Enlai and Deng Xiaoping who formulated a policy of pragmatic readjustment that would serve as a benchmark after 1979. Agriculture, now considered the basis of the economy, took priority over industry. Policies inspired by Bukharin that had been shelved at the time of collectivization now prevailed over any Stalinist logic. It was hoped that an improvement in the agrarian economy would stimulate peasant demand and industrial development. In 1962, Deng Xiaoping uttered his famous aphorism, 'It doesn't matter if a cat is white or black, as long as it catches mice', which summed up his pragmatism. While agriculture, light industry (especially the sectors that served agriculture: chemical fertilizers and pesticides) and consumption were relaunched, Stalinist priorities were not abandoned. The economic administration was recentralized. In companies, the power of managers was strengthened, payment for piecework and bonuses were restored.

In the countryside, collectivization was organized. The regulations, set out in sixty articles and adopted in March 1961, governed the functioning of the people's communes until the end of the 1970s. They were no longer production units, but simple administrative entities planning management. From now on, the production teams organized work and distributed crops. There were only twenty to thirty families in each, and their territory was usually just one village district. The scale of work collectives once again respected the need to maintain their bond to the land. Free markets were reopened. Pay conditions would fluctuate: egalitarianism was at its strongest during the years 1968–71 and 1974–76. These adjustments came with another break in the dynamics of agricultural growth. Hitherto, this had remained traditional in type, based on an intensification of the use of inputs: the densification of the population, hydraulic improvements and an ever-increasing supply of organic fertilizers. In the mid-1960s, China began its green revolution, with the mechanization of irrigation, the use of chemical fertilizers and the use of scientifically selected seeds. This new model of production ensured unprecedented increases in agricultural yields, mainly of the grains that make up the staple diet. Wheat was the cereal that showed the biggest increase: from 1952 to 1965, output progressed little, from 7 to 10 quintals per hectare; it had doubled by the end of the 1970s.[6]

In 1964, as the country was just recovering, Mao launched a campaign of investments in the interior provinces, aimed at forming a 'third front' (*sanxian* 三线). The idea was to create an industrial base in the centre of the country, free from the strategic threats posed by the USSR in the north and the United States in the south and east. Factories and new railway lines were built, especially in the Sichuan and Guizhou provinces. This momentum was then slowed down by the launch of the Cultural Revolution, which had few economic consequences, then relaunched when the latter ended in 1969. Just as the tension between China and its neighbours was at its height and the country was operating in a state of quasi-autarky, the economy experienced a new Great Leap Forward concentrated on the third front. The priority was investment in military industries and the recruiting of military personnel from among the cadres of civilian industry. A militarization of society and the economy took place. Material incentives and bonuses were abolished in factories. Organization was decentralized, rural industries promoted. In 1971, when the growth of industrial production was too rapid in relation to agricultural production, the pace of investment growth slowed down and the priority for the third front was put on hold. Zhou Enlai and Deng Xiaoping conducted a moderate policy. Growing divisions within the ruling elite paralysed the decision-making process until 1976. Mao's death in September 1976 put an end to the stasis of the system, and Hua Guofeng formulated a ten-year development plan that provided for the launch of 120 major projects in heavy industry. China is said to have bought the necessary technologies through the sale of oil on the international market. But it quickly became apparent that this programme was unworkable.

Assessment of the Maoist period

In the final analysis, economic growth in the Maoist period was perfectly real: 6 per cent per year between 1952 and 1978. Despite the cost of the Great Leap Forward, the Cultural Revolution and diplomatic isolation, the GDP tripled, while income per capita grew by a factor of 1.8 and labour productivity by 1.6. Industrialization was massive, with industry's share of production rising from 15.5 per cent to 54.1 per cent of GDP. But China was still an underdeveloped country, where agriculture employed 85 per cent of the working population. Living conditions remained difficult. From 1953 to 1979, agricultural production experienced an average annual growth rate of 2.5 per cent, while the population growth rate was slightly above 2 per cent. The annual growth rate of cereal production was only slightly ahead of population growth, hence the persistence of rationing. Despite the progress made, the gross amount of grain available per capita had barely changed since the 1950s, amounting to 320 kilograms per year. From 1961, this ration was maintained only by repeated recourse to imports. In the interior of the country, due to inadequate transport systems, pockets of famine remained; 10 per cent of the rural population (80 million people) had a ration of less than 150 kilograms of raw grain per year. Agriculture did not meet the needs of industry, either. Cotton production, for example, was insufficient to supply the spinning mills, and China was forced to import: in 1975, 30 per cent of the raw material used by the spinning mills came from abroad.

The increase in agricultural production resulted solely from a quantitative increase in the factors of production employed – the amount of labour and material inputs after 1965 thanks to the green revolution – and not from increased productivity. This extensive growth was a consequence of the perverse effects of planning and the price system. Maoist policies had imposed cereal self-sufficiency everywhere, to the detriment of local specializations. Above all, the strategy of deliberately low agricultural prices to finance industrialization at a lower cost prevented peasant incomes from rising, and slowed down the development of industry, which had no market. While the system had indeed maximized the extraction of resources from agriculture so as to direct them to industry, agriculture had been unable to provide sufficient surplus, and industry did not create the necessary jobs for an abundant workforce. This explains the repeated concern of leaders, if not to change the system, at least to experiment with other avenues or to revise the initial model. The experiments carried out – the contractualization of agricultural holdings in Anhui in 1962–63 and the decentralization practised in the early 1970s – would serve as reference points in the subsequent period.

The investment in industry had been achieved by sacrificing consumption and services. Growth in household consumption – 2.3 per cent per year – had been very slow. While economic development is usually accompanied by a decrease in agriculture's share of production and an increase in services, this did not happen. The share of services in production fell from 29 per cent in 1952 to 24 per cent in 1978,[7] mainly because of the decline in commercial activity. In 1952, there was one commercial job for every 81 people; in 1978, there as one for every 214.[8] The insufficient number of products for final consumption – irrespective of any improvement in their quality – imposed rationing not only for agricultural products, but manufactured ones as well. Grain and cotton, as well as bicycles, watches and sewing machines, were rationed from 1955 until the 1980s, whereas rationing in the Soviet Union was abolished after the Second World War.

Another major flaw in the model was the insufficient creation of new jobs, as industry primarily consumed capital and services were neglected. Between 1952 and 1978, the labour force increased by 191 million people, but modern industry and services absorbed only 37 per cent.[9] As a result, in 1978 the agricultural labour force grew by 70 per cent compared to 1952, so that there was hardly any growth in cultivated areas and the country as a whole was industrializing. Underemployment was a major problem, especially in the countryside. In industry, the return on investment was slow because industrial establishments were large, complex, and capital-intensive. The result was a slowdown in the growth of industrial production, from 17 per cent per year between 1952 and 1957 to 8 per cent between 1970 and 1979.

While the Soviet model of organization of the economy and its successive adjustments did ensure growth, it was insufficient to allow a rapid rise in the standard of living of the population. At the end of the 1970s, the country's leaders thus faced two challenges. The first was to stimulate agricultural production, which would be achieved through liberalization (that is, dismantling collectivization) and improving the terms of trade. The second imperative was to create jobs at a time when the situation was deteriorating rapidly in cities faced with the coming of age of cohorts born after 1962 and the return of urban-dwellers sent to the countryside in the 1970s. The quickest way, and the least costly in terms of investment, to provide work for this workforce was to promote the development of a manufacturing sector that was intensive in terms of labour and services.

The reform cycle

The launch of a reform movement at the end of 1978 was first and foremost the result of a certain political situation. Deng Xiaoping was in conflict with Hua Guofeng and the neo-Maoists. While he had hitherto supported the priority given to heavy industry, he now seized on agrarian questions to promote a policy different from his opponent's. In so doing, he found himself in a position to embody the new direction and to win back the legitimacy of the Party, eroded by the mistakes of the Cultural Revolution. He was confronted with the inadequacy of agricultural production and the growth of urban unemployment, so the decisions he took had to do with that specific conjuncture: increase agricultural prices, give more autonomy to rural households and foster new industrial and service activities. After the years when ideology had been predominant, pragmatism won out. Among the Chinese leadership, however, there was no consensus as to a coherent vision of how the economy should be reorganized, even if all agreed on the need to improve the existing economic system. So, lacking any overall vision and in the absence of the necessary political support, Deng Xiaoping undertook what were inevitably gradual reforms, marked by temporary advances and setbacks. Until 1984, these mainly concerned the rural world. They were then extended to urban businesses. The objective of the reformers was to improve the existing system by injecting a dose of the market;

the assumption was that economic actors would modify their overall behaviour to cope with market forces. What they had not envisioned was that the share of the economy regulated by the market would grow much faster than that operating according to the plan, so that the planned economy would become proportionately much smaller and give way to the market. Growth was concentrated in the market-driven sector of the economy, or, to use Barry Naughton's phrase, the economy 'grew out of the plan'.[10] The coexistence of the plan and the market, however, entailed imbalances that led to the cessation of the reform process in 1989. It was relaunched in 1992, when the country definitively embarked on the path of building a market economy. After the experiments came the time for systemic reforms.

Decollectivization of the countryside

At the end of 1978, the objective was to stimulate agricultural production by increasing farmworkers' incomes. Recognizing the critical state of agriculture, the third plenary session of the Eleventh Central Committee decided on a 20 per cent increase in the purchase prices of agricultural products handed over to the state, a decrease in the prices of inputs for agriculture and an increase in credits for agriculture. The reorientation of economic strategy was ratified by a Central Committee working conference in April 1979, which reduced investment in heavy industry and increased resources for agriculture and consumption.

The dismantling of people's communes was carried out with the utmost discretion between 1978 and 1983. Initially, it turned out that remuneration in work points distributed by the production team was not much of an incentive, as, more often than not, it rewarded working time and not the actual work carried out. Rather than paying for days of work or tasks that were difficult to measure, the reformers decided to link peasants' remuneration to their final production, which could only be done by individualizing each person's output and dividing the teams. Several 'systems of household responsibility' (*jiating lianchan chengbao zeren zhi* 家庭联产承包责任制) were proposed, involving a more or less extensive division of labour collectives. In the case of 'farming packages for families' (*baogan daohu* 包干到户), families became fully responsible for their profits and losses, selling their crops and paying for their own materials. Families paid the state an agricultural tax, and sold contracted harvest quotas to state agencies; they also had to contribute to the remuneration of village managers and employees (teachers and nurses), participate in chores for the maintenance of the infrastructure and comply with family planning obligations, etc. Once these obligations were fulfilled, financially autonomous family farms were solely responsible for their profits and losses. There was a de facto decollectivization and a shift to contractual relations between the rural administrations and peasant households.

This formula, first tested in the province of Anhui under the leadership of Wan Li in 1978, spread to the whole countryside in 1982. At the end of 1984, more than 95 per cent of peasant families were working under contracts. This marked a return to family farming. When the first farming packages were signed in 1981 and 1982, land was allocated to families for terms of two to three years. From 1984, leases were signed for periods of fifteen years or more. The land was divided equally between families, most often in proportion to the number of people in each household (more rarely in proportion to the available labour). The allocated land could not be sold by the beneficiary family.

The other aspect of agricultural reform was the development of free markets for agricultural products. The share of agricultural products handed over to the state, outside the quotas, increased rapidly. In order to ensure urban supply, the state was also forced to pay much more for its purchases, either at prices 'outside the quotas', or even at 'negotiated' prices aligned with those of free markets. Overall, from 1978 to 1984, the average prices paid to farmers for all types of produce increased by 54 per cent, more than double what planners had expected.

The return to family farms and more profitable prices led to an unprecedented boom in harvests. Between 1978 and 1984, cereal production increased by 33 per cent, or 5 per cent per year on average, with peaks of 9 per cent in 1982 and 1983. The increase was even more spectacular for industrial crops: the production of oilseeds doubled between 1978 and 1984, cotton production tripled, meat production increased by 70 per cent. For the first time in decades, there was a significant take-off. During the 1990s, growth remained notable even if it was slower. In a few years, food consumption patterns were revolutionized. The proportion of grains decreased rapidly as the consumption of meat, fish and fruits and vegetables increased. China experienced a real glut of food.

Business reform

One of the unintended consequences of the reforms in the countryside was the rapid development of a nonstate rural industry in the form of 'township and village enterprises' (*xiangzhen qiye* 乡镇企业). Originally, there were collective enterprises, controlled and managed by municipalities or production brigades whose job was to produce goods for agriculture – tools, for example. In order to increase the resources of collective structures, the restrictions limiting their activities were lifted and these companies could now buy agricultural products for processing. Near towns and cities, urban businesses were encouraged to subcontract part of their activities to them. When collective structures crumbled in 1981–82, these rural enterprises became more and more independent and focused on the search for profit. Their rapid development was due to the conditions in which they operated. In urban areas, companies had easy access to capital (because of low budget constraints) but labour was expensive (because they also needed to provide accommodation and healthcare for their employees). The opposite was true in the countryside: wages were low but access to capital more difficult. Thanks to the support of local governments and the mobilization of household savings, rural businesses developed all the more quickly because they benefited from favourable taxation; while state-owned enterprises had to hand over almost all of their earnings, township and village enterprises were taxed little – and they could respond to a demand for manufactured products in the countryside, reinforced by rising incomes. Initially, these rural enterprises developed in the gaps of the planned economy: either they collaborated with urban state-owned enterprises as subcontractors, or they responded to a demand that the latter were not able to meet. Complementary to the state economy, they nevertheless helped to transform the entire economic environment which, for all companies, of whatever kind, was becoming more competitive.

The reform of state-owned enterprises began in July 1979 with a twofold objective: to increase their autonomy and to combine planning with the market. For political reasons, these initiatives were halted in

1981 and did not resume until 1984. At the end of 1979, more than 6,000 large enterprises, which represented 60 per cent of the production of state-owned enterprises, were authorized to retain a share of their profits, to benefit from a more advantageous system of paying off, and to sell part of their production outside the plan. The company divided the profit it retained into three funds that financed employee services, bonus payments and investments. This system resulted in a rapid growth both in bonuses paid to employees (with a corresponding improvement in urban incomes), and in capital expenditure such as the construction of housing.

The rules binding companies to the state trading system were gradually relaxed in the consumer goods sector. New business establishments, financed by municipal governments, businesses and then individual entrepreneurs, started to emerge. The ban on farmers' markets in cities was lifted and cities encouraged them by reserving spaces for them and constructing buildings to house them. The share of farmers' markets in total urban retail sales rose from 4 per cent in 1978 to 10 per cent in 1982. This marked a diversification of commercial networks, which was also a response to the state's concern to create new jobs. In December 1982, Chen Yun compared the economy to a bird and the plan to a cage in a famous metaphor: 'You can't just keep a bird in your hand, because it will die. We have to let it fly. But it can only fly in a cage because otherwise it would escape. The cage should be the right size, and adjusted regularly. Either way, there has to be a cage.' With these words, Chen Yun reaffirmed the primacy of the plan, with the market remaining on the sidelines.

Lift-off (1984–88)

Unlike in the previous period, the reformers now had an overall vision and approach. The positive results of the first measures allowed Zhao Ziyang to gain acceptance for a compromise in the relationship between the plan and the market. At the heart of the reform strategy was the desire to develop market forces by limiting the space of the plan, getting state-owned enterprises to respond as effectively as possible to market signals. The conservatives, for their part, wanted the plan to be adequate for large companies and all major productions. So there was a shift to a conception that froze the share of the plan in absolute terms, and which therefore ensured that the economy developed gradually towards a situation where the market played the predominant role. The most explicit and complete conversion to economic reforms took place at the Thirteenth Communist Party Congress in October 1987, when Zhao Ziyang, in his report to Congress, spoke of building a 'socialist market economy'. In his view, the authorities must 'gradually reduce the role of compulsory plans and transform the management system into an indirect management system. The new system must be a system in which the state regulates the market, and the market guides businesses.' In saying this, Zhao abandoned compulsory planning and recognized that companies must react to market conditions as a matter of priority. What characterized a socialist economy, he added, was nonetheless the predominance of public ownership.

In 1984, the reform of businesses was relaunched. The objective was to give them enough autonomy to be able to respond to market demands. One major measure involved reforming their management system and increasing the autonomy of the managers. 'Management contract' systems were put in place in 1984 and made general in 1988. The company benefited from increased control over the division of its earnings between profit and wages, and control over the level of the latter. Contractual relations were set up to define the share of the profit handed over to the authorities on which they depended. The role of the Party leader within the company diminished, and was now reduced to ideological questions. The business manager was now solely responsible for deciding on staff recruitment. Managers became powerful figures, which also opened the door to abuse. But it was not enough to do away with the Party's control over the management of the company; effective control of the economic decisions taken within the company had to be handed over to the manager and company directors freed from bureaucracy. In 1984, they were able to freely establish their production plans, on condition that they satisfied the compulsory plan. In 1984, 25 per cent of companies were affected; in 1990, 90 per cent.

The meaning of the plan changed. It increasingly functioned as an indirect means of draining money from businesses, the implicit and fixed levy being equal to the difference between market prices and planned prices, while the company's behaviour was dictated by market conditions. In 1985, it was this type of system that was set up, with the government allowing companies to sell their off-plan production at market prices. The so-called 'two-track' (*shuanggui* 双轨) asset allocation system for goods was recognized. The same product, agricultural or industrial, was subject to a double price, one fixed administratively (lower) and the other fixed by the market (higher). The two coordination mechanisms coexisted for one and the same economic actor: rural households, as well as state-owned enterprises, sold one part of their production at administered prices and another at market prices. Thus, two spheres coexisted: on the one hand, the planned sector with its obligatory deliveries at prices fixed by the state, the size of which had to be maintained in terms of absolute value; on the other hand, the market sector, where prices were free and could grow at the same rate as the economy developed. Nonstate-owned enterprises carried out almost all their transactions at market prices. The innovation stemmed from the fact that state-owned enterprises now also operated in the market, on its margins. The planned volume of production was fixed in advance in absolute terms (and less than the actual volume), which meant that the plan no longer impacted on company decisions; business behaviour was now driven by the market. Production under the plan can be viewed as a fixed charge, a tax levy on the activity of the company. In 1985, 61 per cent of sales were made off-plan in light industry, 33 per cent in industrial intermediate goods and 24 per cent in mining production. The share of the economy regulated by the market gradually became larger than the share regulated by the plan. However, the coexistence of the plan with market experiments favoured corruption and inflation and created social discontent, culminating in the demonstrations in Tiananmen Square in June 1989. The experimental phase of the reforms ended in a social and political crisis.

The end of the reforms (1989–93)

Faced with the crisis, the government brought reforms to a halt. The conservatives tried to backpedal, and put in place a programme to take back control of the economy, marking the return of industrial policy. Regional development policies favouring coastal areas were replaced by sectoral policies. Investments were channelled into the state sector. The share of investment in heavy industry reached its highest level since 1978 – investment in the energy sector increased by 31 per cent between 1988 and 1990. The share of investment in heavy industry reached its highest level since 1978. Another lever was preferential interest rates, now applied so as to favour certain sectors while rural enterprises were the main victims of the credit crunch. The share of the economy corresponding to the plan was also increased. The number of products subject to planning grew. This was to ensure that, as production increased, so did deliveries controlled by the plan. The growth of market prices was capped; the goal was a single price system, subject to the planners' control.

The results were not what had been expected. Declining demand did indeed reduce bottlenecks, but also caused a recession. Households responded to austerity by cutting back their consumption and increasing their savings. The fall in demand for consumer goods and intermediate goods was accompanied by a fall in prices; in December 1989, prices on the open markets were 7 per cent lower than the previous year. This translated into a slowdown in the growth of production – the rate of which fell from 11 per cent in 1988 to 4 per cent in 1989 – and employment. At the end of 1989, urban unemployment reached its highest level since 1982, at 2.6 per cent. The impact was even more severe in rural areas. Rural non-farm employment fell from 95 million in 1988 to 92 million at the end of 1989, while rural areas also had to absorb the influx of temporary city residents who had been made redundant. In Sichuan, 1 million workers returned to the countryside while 0.5 million jobs were lost in rural private enterprises. Political opposition lay behind the failure of the conservatives' plans. Local government officials – Zhu Rongji in Shanghai and Ye Xuanping in Guangdong in particular – opposed raising taxation for the benefit of the centre. Provincial and local governments insisted on their spending obligations – some stemming from central policies – and on the reduction of their revenue as a result of austerity. In provinces where rural industry accounted for a large share of local government revenues – Zhejiang, Jiangsu, Shandong – the latter protected rural enterprises from the policies decided in Beijing. It was no longer possible to discriminate against a sector that had become so important economically. Gradually, policy objectives shifted from controlling inflation to boosting growth. At the start of 1990, Li

Peng affirmed his support for a coastal development strategy and thus distanced himself from the conservatives.

Finally, the failure of the reformers during the period 1989–91 signalled that there was no coherent way of making plan and market coexist. During his trip to the south of the country in January 1992, Deng Xiaoping relaunched the reform movement. In October 1992, the Fourteenth Congress ratified the new orientation and proclaimed the adoption by China of a 'socialist market economy'. If the term 'socialist' had been emptied of its content, the expression 'market' was new; this was the first time that the official objective of the reforms appeared to be transition to a market economy. There was no longer any question of 'growth outside the plan'; the objective of the reforms was now the dismantling of the plan.

The move towards a market economy (1993–2003)

Zhu Rongji was now the main architect of economic policy, first as Deputy Premier from mid-1993, then as Premier from 1998 to 2003. He ended the two-track system at the end of 1993 when all allocation of goods by the plan disappeared, at the same time as prices were liberalized, including the price of coal, which met 70 per cent of the country's energy needs. In towns, grain prices were gradually liberalized. In 1993, only 5 per cent of retail sales and 15 per cent of sales of intermediate products were made at controlled prices.

In January 1994, Zhu Rongji's first major initiative was to adopt a new tax system at a time when budgetary revenues had been sharply eroded, dropping from a third of GDP in 1978 to 10 per cent in 1995. Reforms were implemented to stop this fall and also to broaden the tax base, as well as to create the conditions for a level playing field for all companies, regardless of the form of ownership. The socialist principle of relying solely on state-owned enterprises as a source of income was abandoned in favour of a modern tax system where all businesses were equal. The main source of income was now value added tax (VAT), which applied to almost all products at a rate of 17 per cent. Some basic food products were taxed at 13 per cent. Eleven products were subject to additional taxes: cigarettes, alcohol, petrol and luxury goods. Business income was taxed at a uniform rate of 33 per cent, beyond a certain size and regardless of the form of ownership. Below this, the tax varied from 18 per cent to 27 per cent. The only companies to benefit from special treatment were foreign and part-foreign companies. Similarly, taxes on personal income and landownership were standardized. Tax collection was also recentralized: the central government collected all VAT and 70 per cent of all tax deductions, then remitted money to local governments (previously, the central government had depended on provincial reversions). One of the consequences of the 1994 tax reform was the increase in the share of the state budget in GDP. This had fallen continuously since 1978, dropping from nearly 35 per cent to 11 per cent in 1995; since then it had risen steadily, to over 22 per cent of GDP in 2012. In seventeen years, the share of the state budget in GDP had thus been doubled.

Above all, Zhu Rongji aimed to improve the legal and regulatory environment in which companies operated and to reduce the worst distortions. So he needed to define new rules that would apply equally to all economic players and to regulate competition. The regulatory and administrative reforms affected key sectors: finance, corporate governance and foreign trade. The People's Bank of China, which had been the central bank since 1983, but remained very largely subject to local and central governments, was reorganized by the abolition of provincial levels and the creation of regional offices on the model of the American Federal Reserve. The bank now played a role in the conduct of monetary policy. Access to easy credit for public commercial banks ceased. This meant de facto the establishment of a central banking system. In order to meet the requirements of the World Trade Organization which China sought to join, its government unified the foreign exchange system at the end of 1993 and devalued its currency in January 1994.

One of the major transformations of the 1990s affected the structure of the economy in terms of ownership. During the first fifteen years of reform, from 1978 to 1993, the state sector declined in relative importance, but it continued to grow in terms of both output and employment. At the end of 1993, the adoption of 'company law' (*gongsi fa* 公司法) marked a turning point in the restructuring of the state sector; the latter withdrew, retaining a dominant position in just a limited number of strategic sectors. Smaller enterprises, collective units under the authority of local governments, were privatized. Large state units transformed into limited liability companies with clarified institutions of governance; a number of them – the largest, most modern and most profitable – were listed on the stock exchange, at least as regards part of their capital. This process was interrupted in 1996 by the macroeconomic cooling-down policy and then by the Asian financial crisis; it was relaunched in 1999. Between 1995 and 1999, the number of state-owned enterprises sank from 88,000 to 61,000, following the privatizations, mergers and bankruptcies that mainly affected small businesses. In 1999, the methods of privatization that had applied only to small enterprises were extended to medium-sized enterprises. For local authorities that had full control over the privatization process, from asset valuation to award proce-dures, this was a way to reduce their costs and increase their income. These collective enterprises, mainly rural, were often sold to staff, their managers or local officials.

From the mid-1990s, the number of employees in state-owned enter-prises declined. This was in part due to the change in the legal status of these companies, which remained under public control without any longer being state-owned. But it was also due to massive lay-offs. Employment in state-owned enterprises fell by more than 40 per cent between 1995 and 2005. Between 1993 and 2003, more than 28 million employees of state-owned enterprises were made redundant (this is an underestimated minimum). The most lay-offs occurred in the mid-1990s. A category of *xiagang* workers (下岗, laid-off workers, who had 'stepped down from their jobs') was created, who were not counted as unemployed: affiliated to re-employment centres, they continued, in principle, to receive subsidies – they benefited from social security and received a minimum income. At the end of the twentieth century, the lifelong employment system – the 'iron rice bowl' (*tie fanwan* 铁饭碗), characteristic of urban socialist China, no longer existed. The transition to a market economy came at the cost of the sacrifice of workers in the state sector, once the most privileged class in the regime. At the end of 2004, the national private urban sector employed twice as many people as the traditional state sector, 55 million compared to fewer than 30 million.

During Zhu Rongji's tenure, important and difficult reforms were introduced; their most important achievement was the reduction of the state-owned enterprise sector, sealed by China's entry into the WTO in 2001. The old system had been broken. Accession to the WTO was a continuation of the desire to open up to the world as a condition for economic development, and gave a new, external impetus to reforms as the transition was far from being completed: the banking system was still dominated by state banks, market regulation was insufficient, the governance of state-controlled enterprises remained weak, and, above all, cooperation between economic and political elites made large-scale corruption possible.

China, 1993.
Source: Marc Riboud / Fonds Marc Riboud au MNAAG / Magnum Photos

The Hu Jintao/Wen Jiabao administration: a new activism

When it took over in 2003, the new administration seemed to wish to continue along the reform path of its predecessors. However, the idea quickly emerged that, while the first decade of reforms had benefited everyone, that of the 1990s had left part of the population behind. The programme was therefore amended; the transition needed to be continued, but the government showed greater concern for regions and individuals left behind by growth. The emphasis was no longer on economic reform and building a market economy, but, at least rhetorically, on social policy and redistribution. This was accompanied by renewed interventionism, described by Barry Naughton as a 'new state activism'.[11] In the previous period, the state sector had been seen primarily as a legacy of the past; now the state had to play an important role in a market-dominated economy. This was a real turning point, one that was accentuated with the global crisis of 2008–09. In this context, progress in moving towards a market economy slowed down dramatically.

The first shift in economic policy set social issues back at the centre of the agenda, and in particular the situation of the peasants. Agricultural taxes were reduced and then abolished in order to reduce the tax burden on rural households. Two other major measures were taken: creation of a cooperative health insurance system (in 2003, 96 per cent of rural households had no health insurance) and a budgetary effort to ensure universal elementary education.

Second, if at the local level the state sector continued to shrink, initiatives were taken to consolidate it at the central level. In 2003, the State Assets Supervision and Administration Commission (*guoyou zichan jiandu guanli weiyuanhui* 国有资产监督管理委员会, better known by its acronym SASAC) was created, a ministerial-level administration that took over management of the most important state-owned enterprises (telecommunications, gas, electricity, oil, etc.). The objective was to strengthen their governance by structuring them and creating large profitable companies, occupying a dominant position in their sector. The consequence was a stabilization of the size of the state sector.

A third shift was a more active policy for industry and technological innovation. Sectoral plans were developed to help companies adapt to the new environment, especially after joining the WTO; it was no longer a question of dictating their development trajectory, but of favouring national industries in a context of increasing international competition. This was the case in the car industry and in the integrated circuit industry where planning was inspired by policies implemented in Taiwan decades earlier. In 2005, a medium- and long-term plan for the development of science and technology (2006–20) aimed to make China an innovative country. The weight of research and development expenditure in GDP, which had fallen to 0.7 per cent in 1997, reached 1.3 per cent in 2005 and 2.01 per cent in 2013 (World Bank data). One of the key elements of this new technological policy consisted in an effort to define and impose specific technical standards.

While in the 1990s the focus was on building market institutions and reforming the economy, the agenda in the mid-2000s thus involved the setting up of social policies, and investing in human capital and technology. The onset of the global economic crisis in 2007–08 prompted a swift, forceful response, which observers felt was effective. Major infrastructure construction programmes were launched (12 per cent of GDP over two years)[12] and, above all, there was a spectacular expansion of bank credit, a strategy that strengthened state banks in the financial sector to the detriment of institutions both private and foreign. From the middle of 2009, growth started to rise again. In 2010, China became the second largest economy in the world, overtaking Japan. Overall, growth in the period 2003–12 was particularly strong, at 10.4 per cent per year. Yet many observers believed it was a wasted decade when it came to economic reform. Admittedly, the leaders had tackled the issue of the rural communities, but little progress had been made in building the institutional framework on which future prosperity depended. One explanation often given, including in China, to explain the stagnation of the reform movement lay in referring to 'vested interests', those of monopoly companies, the most powerful families and corrupt officials.

The economic policy of Xi Jinping and Li Keqiang

Xi Jinping and Li Keqiang inherited an economic situation that was the opposite of the one which Jiang Zemin and Zhu Rongji had left to their successors: there were many urgent problems to be solved. They made important initiatives in at least three areas. Efforts were made to restructure the debts of local governments – mainly debts contracted since the global crisis. A new system of property was developed with the objective of protecting the peasants and at the same time allowing them to rent or mortgage agricultural land. In November 2014, a three-level ownership system was proposed that distinguished between the collective ownership of land, the long-term contractual right of rural households (which gave rise to land distribution) and a transferable right of use or management. A rural household could therefore rent agricultural land without losing the contractual right of ownership of it. The central idea was to create transferable property rights at a time when the issue was particularly sensitive and hotly debated. For economists most in favour of the market economy, the property rights of peasants did indeed have to be strengthened in order to create incentives for the restructuring of the agricultural sector. For others, further to the left, any form of private property raised fears that poor peasants would lose any agricultural property, which for them represented the ultimate safety net. The proposal was a compromise. The reality was that most young people had left the land and most rural income did not come from the land. Finally, in the third initiative, the new leadership relaunched efforts to liberalize trade between China and its partners: bilateral agreements were signed (with Korea and Australia in 2014), and free trade zones were created in several large Chinese cities in order to gradually open up certain service industries to international competition. All these reforms initiated under Xi Jinping's tenure were decided at the highest levels of the state and were part of an authoritarian practice of power, with the objective of strengthening the current system: there was no long-term vision. This was very far from the modalities of reform in the 1970s and 1980s when experiments were carried out at the local level before being generalized.

Both abroad and in China, there was heated debate over the current development model that most observers did not consider sustainable. Since the start of the 2000s, leaders had proclaimed that domestic demand must be the new pillar of growth and yet the share of investment continued to be particularly high; almost half of GDP was reinvested at the start of the 2010s and household consumption remained at only around a third. Another sign of the model's exhaustion was the increase in wages. In the 1990s and 2000s, employers recruited at will a migrant workforce whose wages increased very little. Since the beginning of the

2010s, they have grown by more than 10 per cent per year. For some observers, even as the working-age population has plateaued, this means the end of cheap labour.

An assessment of the structural transformations

Four decades after the launch of the reforms, the transformations of the Chinese economy have been spectacular. Agriculture came to represent less than 10 per cent of GDP, industry 40 per cent, and services passed the 50 per cent mark for the first time in 2015. Manufacturing industry has been the engine of growth: production has grown on average by nearly 12 per cent since the 1990s; in 2014, it represented a third of GDP. Exports have been a powerful engine of development; China's share in the global manufacturing industry rose from 5 per cent to 16 per cent between 1995 and 2011.[13] These structural transformations can also be seen in the evolution of the structure of employment. The share of the population employed in agriculture declined: it was 71 per cent in 1978 and dropped below 50 per cent in 2003 to 28 per cent in 2015. In the 1980s, this development was made possible by the development of enterprises in townships and districts; in the following decade, it was thanks to migrations to the cities. In absolute terms, the peak was reached in 1991 with 391 million workers engaged in agriculture. China is therefore no longer a predominantly agricultural economy. The share of industry in employment increased from 17 per cent in 1978 to 29 per cent in 2015, while services increased from 12 per cent to 42 per cent.[14]

China, like the former countries of Eastern Europe, has gone from an administered economy to a market economy: prices have been liberalized, forms of property have diversified, the state has seen its control over resources decrease. However, this was not the original goal. At the end of the 1970s, the Chinese leaders did not seek to administer a violent shock to their economy. A big bang strategy would have been accompanied by high adjustment costs – rising prices and unemployment – while the aim was to contain inflation and the level of unemployment. They acted as if they wanted to reduce these short-term costs even if this meant lengthening the adjustment process. In the 1980s, the reforms were of an experimental nature; the aim was to boost productivity and improve the existing system. They were the subject of particularist negotiations; the reforms did not take the form of a promulgation of new rules universally applicable throughout Chinese territory, but were the result of negotiations and haggling between central authorities and local actors seeking to maximize their particular interests. Reforms were also carried out gradually in order to maximize political support and minimize opposition. They were accompanied by a devolution of power from the centre to the provincial authorities (and not to the market) so as to gain support from the latter. Over the 1990s, however, systemic reforms were initiated. Almost all goods markets were liberalized, while state control over the price of factors of production was maintained. Since the mid-2000s, the state has once again taken the lead in steering the Chinese economy. After three decades of reforms, it retains many features that distinguish it from capitalist market economies.

The Chinese market economy

More than four decades of reforms have radically transformed the Chinese economic landscape. The actors have diversified, the state has seen its role modified, and international trade is now a driving force.

Diversification of economic actors

Within the framework of the planned economy, businesses were under the supervision of either central administrations (the state sector) or local governments (the collective sector). In the first decade of reforms, the 1980s, there was no privatization of this public sector. The structure of the economy changed with the arrival of new players: township and village enterprises, individual entrepreneurs and foreign companies.

Until the mid-1990s, the organization at the heart of China's economic dynamism was the collective enterprise, a unit owned by local governments, which were actually the primary beneficiaries of the reforms. These took the form not of a privatization of the economy but of a decentralization and devolution of powers to provincial, municipal and village authorities. Under these conditions, the private sector appeared weakened by the hesitations of economic policy and hampered by untimely levies by bureaucracies. Today, several elements point to the growing role of the private sector in the Chinese economy, a private sector whose shape I will here try to define.

The township and village enterprises were the engine of growth in the 1980s. They played a key role in the transition from an administered economy to a market economy because they entered into competition with state-owned enterprises and induced a generalized shift to the market. They allowed an increase in rural incomes, absorbed the under-employed agricultural labour force and contributed to a reduction in the income gap between urban and rural people. Initially, they were often the collective property of local governments; then they were privatized in the mid-1990s, and most often taken over by their employees or managers.

Township and village enterprises stemmed from the artisanal activity encouraged on two occasions in Maoist China during the Great Leap Forward when municipalities were encouraged to create industrial establishments and in 1970 when Mao Zedong launched a new Great Leap Forward encouraging the municipalities to set up so-called 'commune and brigade' businesses. After 1979, urban enterprises were encouraged to subcontract part of the production to these rural establishments, while local governments saw their development as a way out of poverty. Between 1978 and the mid-1990s, they formed the most dynamic part of the Chinese economy. They employed 28 million workers in 1978 and 135 million in 1996, representing an annual growth of 9 per cent. They represented 6 per cent of GDP in 1978 and 26 per cent in 1996. Their rapid development can be explained by several factors. Unlike state-owned enterprises, they were labour-intensive, mobilized little capital, and wages were much lower than in the former. While state-owned enterprises provided not only employment but also housing and care for their employees, township and district enterprises paid only for work. These companies were taxed at low rates and benefited from the institutional support of local governments, which helped them obtain bank loans. Very soon, they represented a very significant proportion of production in the sectors of building materials, textile articles, furniture and food products.

Several models coexisted and developed in the gaps of the command economy. In the vicinity of the Shanghai metropolis, in the south of Jiangsu, a traditionally rich and prosperous region and among the most advanced in China, these companies, owned by local governments, were the subcontractors of major Shanghai companies nearby. In Zhejiang province, and particularly in Wenzhou, their development was based on private initiative (in fact, family-based) much more than on local governments. Rural households filled gaps in the planned economy by producing a wide variety of very simple, low-tech, but labour-intensive items: buttons, ribbons, everyday items. In the Pearl River Delta in the southern province of Guangdong, these companies were partly controlled by Hong Kong investors, and their production was exported.

After 1996, township and village enterprises mostly became private businesses. They were no longer controlled by local governments and were bought up by their managers. In some provinces (Zhejiang, Fujian and Guangdong), specialized rural clusters emerged, bringing together a large number of companies in the production of the same item. This mode of industrialization was often accompanied by massive expenditure by local governments to promote local development, in particular through the financing of marketing structures – construction and management of specialized markets that were often both input markets for producers and markets for manufactured products.

Another actor that emerged at the start of the reforms was private enterprise (in Chinese *geti gongshang hu* 个体工商户, the literal translation of which is 'individual industrial or commercial household', or *getihu* 个体户).[15] With the launch of the opening-up policy, private businesses first developed as individual enterprises that appeared in the countryside. These activities could develop more easily since decollectivization was accompanied by a withdrawal of the state, so the vacuum needed to be filled. These companies emerged in the absence of a regulatory and legal framework. It was not until July 1981 that the State Council published a text legally defining these economic activities. This text specified that companies could only have a maximum of seven employees and that their activities could only be 'complementary' (*buchong* 补充) to those of state-owned and collective enterprises. The first form assumed by the private economy was therefore contained within strict limits, and in fact mainly concerned the countryside; individual enterprises were first and foremost the result of the restructuring of the rural economy. In the 1980s, several inspection and rectification campaigns took place and hampered initiatives. Although regulated, starting such a business remained risky. It was often the only solution for individuals without qualifications and without employment, and therefore without resources. The emergence of private enterprise in the form of economic activities initiated by individuals with a very low level of education also contributed for a long time to the socially negative image of the small private entrepreneur. In 1999, 60 per cent of small businesses were still located in rural areas.

The first time that the expression *siying qiye* (私营企业) – which literally means 'privately managed enterprises' – appeared in a Party document was in January 1987 in a paper from the Central Committee detailing 'decisions relating to the extending of reforms in the countryside'. In October 1987, the report to the Thirteenth Congress recognized the need to encourage the development of the 'privately managed economy' (*siying jingji* 私营经济). This political will was quickly translated into legislative terms. In April 1988, the National People's Congress amended article 11 of the Constitution, which now stated that 'the private economy is allowed to exist and develop within the framework of legal provisions. The private economy complements the economic system of the public ownership of socialism. The state guarantees the rights and interests of the private economy in accordance with the law.' In June 1988, the State Council adopted three new regulations relating to what were now referred to as private enterprises. These 'provisional regulations on private enterprises' constituted the body of the legislation according to which private enterprises were in fact managed, and specified their rights and duties. This document defined a private company as 'an organization that makes a profit, is owned by individuals, and employs at least eight people'. Three types of private enterprises are distinguished: private individual enterprises, private multi-owner partnerships and limited liability enterprises.

As always in the reform process in China, reality obviously preceded the adoption of the legislation. Hitherto, private companies, described as *gugong dahu* (雇工大户large households with employees) or *gugong qiye* (雇工企业 companies with employees) were officially registered with administrations either as individual companies (of the *getihu* 个体户 type), or as collective enterprises (*jiti qiye* 集体企业), the only two possible legal forms. In the first case, they were officially small businesses authorized to employ more than seven employees. In the second case, the private entrepreneur paid a rent fixed in advance to a collective unit and ran the business as if he owned it, and often accumulated considerable resources under this system. Firms of this second type were said to be 'wearing a red hat' under a system of 'dependence and attachment'.

Deng Xiaoping's visit to the south of the country in January 1992 revived the reform process. The Fourteenth Party Congress enshrined the expression 'socialist market economy', which was now the objective of the reform. In fact, it was in the wake of Deng's tour of the south that most Chinese private companies were set up. The law on companies, passed by the National People's Congress in December 1993, defined the rights and obligations of two types of companies – limited liability companies and joint-stock companies – regardless of the mode of ownership of the company, whether public, private, collective or foreign.

This chronology of the emergence of the private sector in China calls for two comments. First, private entrepreneurship first emerged on the fringes of mainstream economic activities in the countryside and is now mainly an urban phenomenon. The majority of small businesses are still located in rural areas; but during the decade 1989–99, rural private enterprises fell from 60 per cent to 40 per cent of the total. In 1999, 16.5 per cent of private companies were located in large or medium-sized towns, 55.2 per cent in townships, 28.2 per cent in rural villages. Second, as in other reform processes, reality preceded the development of the legal framework. The private sector emerged in experimental forms, even on the fringes of the law but tolerated locally – hence the necessary collusion between private companies and local governments. However, gradually, as elements of the rule of law emerge, a legislative and regulatory framework was defined.

During the first decade of the reforms, businesses in villages and districts were the engines of industrialization; in the 1990s, the torch was taken up by the national and foreign private sector. In 2009, the state sector accounted for 27 per cent of production and 20 per cent of the workforce, Chinese private enterprises 30 per cent and 34 per cent, and foreign companies 28 per cent of production, and the same proportion of the workforce.[16] In industry and commerce, most sectors were dominated by private companies. Very significant was the decrease in the share of state-owned enterprises in exports: their share fell from 56.5 per cent in 1997 to only 15 per cent in 2010, while that of foreign enterprises rose from 41 per cent to 55 per cent.[17] It was therefore a predominantly market economy that was created. The fact remains that the financial sector is still controlled by state banks; in heavy industry, energy, the exploitation of natural resources, the production of public goods, defence and telecommunications, state-owned enterprises continue to occupy a dominant position. A second restriction to this observation is the persistent difficulty in drawing clear boundaries between state-owned enterprises, collective enterprises and private enterprises. The largest state-owned companies – starting with the oil companies Petrochina and Sinopec – are joint stock companies with part of their capital listed on the stock exchange. Likewise, the real nature of the ownership of Chinese companies that are aggressively endeavouring to win a share of the international market – such as Huawei, ZTE and Haier – is difficult to establish.

Transformation of the economic role of the state

During the three decades of reform, the economic role of the state changed dramatically. While nonstate actors take on an increasingly important role, some observers have pointed out that the state can act sometimes as a facilitator, sometimes as a predator. Others have insisted on the direct involvement of public actors in the market economy. Beyond the diversity of interpretations, it is a transformation rather than a weakening of the state's role that we are witnessing.

It was initially within the rural economy, the first to be affected by the reforms, that the state was transformed. According to Jean Oi, the take-off of rural industry is partly to the credit of local governments and their involvement in business.[18] Borrowing from Chalmers Johnson the notion of state corporatism that the latter developed in connection with the action of the Ministry of International Trade and Industry in Japan, she has applied it to rural governments and forged the notion of a local corporate state. She says that, in the villages, local cadres have become the most ardent promoters of industrial growth for two reasons. The first is the property rights system and the fact that local governments often own small businesses. The second relates to the tax system; the new shape it has assumed allows governments to keep part of the taxes levied on local businesses and therefore encourages them to facilitate their development. The interest of this analysis lies in the way it underlines how industrial development in the Chinese countryside does not need to be the responsibility of companies that are the property of individuals or private companies, but that it can fall to local governments, provided they own these companies. In other words, institutions inherited from the Maoist era can, in another context, play a role that is very favourable to growth. Reform can be successful in a Leninist-type political system, provided the bureaucracy plays its part and is encouraged to do so.

Other studies have reached similar conclusions and show how political mechanisms inherited from the previous period have contributed to the dynamism of the rural economy. This is true of a study conducted by Sun Liping and Ma Mingjie in a village in Shandong province.[19] In the early 1990s, cereals and cotton made up the bulk of production when a new local Party Secretary, Mr Su, 'forced the people to get richer' by transforming the land he administered into a vast melon-producing company. Su used methods similar to those of collective farming in the 1960s to encourage farmers to invest personally, on a private basis, in the facilities necessary for this cultivation. He took groups of peasants to visit neighbouring districts where melon-growing had started; the government took care of the transport of these visitors, after which training seminars were organized and public assemblies convened. While the farm remained a private family business, the district government financed the direct sale of melons by opening sales offices in more than thirty towns; it also bought newspaper advertising space and commercials on one of the major national television channels. In this case, it was the categories and methods of mobilization specific to the socialist cycle that were used by local officials as the basis for their action.

In the case of one village studied by Anita Chan and Jonathan Unger in the southern province of Guangdong,[20] the local state is seen as 'developmentalist': without being directly involved in the management of businesses, it helps finance local projects and undertakes infrastructure works. Public action promotes the emergence of an entrepreneurial bourgeoisie and creates the conditions for its enrichment. This framework of analysis is particularly relevant in the case of rural communities where private activities dominate, in Zhejiang province for example, and particularly in the city of Wenzhou. Another example is the case of Xinji (Hebei), where the local government played an active role in the promotion and development of private enterprises in the leather and fur sector during the 1990s.[21] It invested in the construction of an industrial park and the running of a dedicated shopping centre. It played a role in planning economic development, calling on numerous experts, sometimes foreigners. So it was asking the authorities for the necessary financing and authorizations, and buying agricultural land from farmers that it then transformed into land for industrial use. All kinds of incentives were taken to attract businesses in the sector locally: banking favours, low rents, easier access to local schools for the children of entrepreneurs who came here to settle, etc. But one is obliged to note that, although the local authorities play this role, it is not really because members of the government are directly involved in production, but rather because they receive profits in the political and bureaucratic field. Indeed, presiding over the rapid development of the local economy increases their room for manoeuvre in the negotiations they conduct with the upper echelons of the administration. It also helps to accelerate their personal careers. Political and bureaucratic actors therefore have a specific interest in promoting growth. Local governments are all the more inclined to promote economic development as this helps them to maximize their own interests within the bureaucratic space.

In urban China too, the new context was leading public actors to renew their mode of action. This was the subject of the investigation conducted by Jane Duckett in Tianjin City in 1992–93.[22] In her view, the state itself became an entrepreneur to the extent that its agents, or certain offices, engaged directly in business in the quest for profit. The administrations in charge of real estate and commerce created subsidiary companies that first absorbed part of the overstaffed employees in the original administrations, and also generated profits that were partly redistributed to the original bureaucracies, increasing the administration's financial resources and thus helping to increase and improve the services provided by the latter to the community. Duckett draws on the model of the 'entrepreneurial state' which spread widely with the tacit agreement of central government to most local administrations in the early 1990s. She insists that bureaucracy is far from being homogeneous and that, in a municipal administration like that of Tianjin, each office takes different initiatives in the creation of subsidiary companies. Offices also compete with each other by creating companies operating in the same markets. The transitional bureaucracy benefits from the reforms by participating directly in the market economy, setting up subsidiary companies by itself. This analysis is particularly relevant for under-standing the conditions under which major Chinese cities were rebuilt. Indeed, during the 1990s, decision-making power over land use was ceded by municipal governments to the lower echelons of the districts, which made a great deal of money by selling building rights. They also reaped the rewards from the emergence of a private real-estate market by setting up companies present throughout the value chain, from building to sale, including the eviction of residents.

According to David L. Wank, the transitional bureaucracy has also benefited from the reforms through the development of corruption.[23] He chose as his field of investigation in the late 1980s the city of Xiamen, the capital of Fujian province, a hub for the development of private enter-prise and with a highly diversified economy – manufacturing production, and interregional and international trade. Here, the resurgence of private enterprise did not lead to a weakening of clientelist relationships, but to their commercialization. The local bureaucracy, as power broker, now offered its services for a fee. In a context where directives from the centre were changing rapidly and where their implementation was negotiated locally in a particularist way, clientelist relationships reduced uncertainty. In building up one's networks, backing them up with relationships of trust, the goal is always to lower transaction costs. The exchange between public and private spheres also has many advantages for the public partner: paying interest on its loans, paying salaries, generating income that does not go to the tax authorities, and even hiring other cadres. The detailed description of the codes used to designate a large number of economic practices that link the private to the public is enlightening: 'to create an opportunity' is to make decisions that will lead to profit; 'to provide information' is to specify the supply and demand of state-owned enterprises.

Across a country with continental dimensions, these different models (clientelist, predatory, entrepreneurial and developmentist) coexist. Local governments can be clientelist in one context and entrepreneurial in another, sometimes developmentalist and sometimes predatory. Locally, these different roles can be played by separate administrations. The challenge is to create conditions in which the relations between economic elites and bureaucracy will allow growth and development, and configu-rations favourable to the pursuit and realization of the general interest.

Restructuring the administration of the economy

The construction of a market economy requires a transformation in the way the state acts. Thus, a whole series of initiatives was made, from the 1990s onwards, to improve the efficiency of the bureaucratic apparatus. The objective was the professionalization and specialization of state agencies. So the ministries in charge of industrial sectors – textiles and mining – disappeared and sectoral professional associations took over. In 2003, the National Development and Reform Commission (*guojia fazhan he gaige weiyuanhui* 国家发展与改革委员会) replaced the State Planning Commission (*guojia jihua weiyuanhui* 国家计划委员会), in charge of planning since 1952. As an agent of macroeconomic management under the authority of the State Council, it defined national economic strategy, formulated macroeconomic policies, organized restructuring, supervised major building projects and was in charge of specific files such as the development of the west of the country and the supervision of the energy sector. The second major initiative was the creation, that same year, of SASAC. It had ministerial rank, and exercised control over the management of the largest public firms in the natural resources sector, electricity production and telecommunications. In order to distinguish between the state as owner and the state as manager, its mission was to rationalize the state sector, in particular by merging and slimming down companies, in order to bring about the emergence of large companies (monopolies or oligopolies); in some cases, their capital was listed on the Shenzhen or Shanghai stock exchange.

The modernization of the state's economic action also involved the creation of regulatory agencies, often on the model of equivalent institutions in mature capitalist economies: the commission for the regulation of stock market operations (1992), the commission for the regulation of the insurance sector (1998), the administration in charge of product quality control (2001), the civil aviation administration (2002), the commission for the regulation of electricity production (2003), the commission for the regulation of the banking sector (2003), the food and drugs administration (2003), and the occupational safety administration (2005). The state's aim was to provide itself with the means to organize equal competition for all in the best interests of consumers. This effort involved the publication in 2007 of an antimonopoly law, after more than ten years of preparation; inspired by the European Union model, it prohibited anti-competitive practices and controlled mergers.

These initiatives may suggest that, having been a producer at the planning stage, the state now essentially became a regulator of economic activity within the framework of the market. In this sense, Chinese policy reforms are akin to initiatives taken in the United States in the late nineteenth and early twentieth centuries. Faced with the excesses of capitalism and the growth of corruption, American progressives aimed at a better regulation of economic activity in the service of greater social justice and a more honest government: child labour was limited and the first antitrust law was passed. China is different – it is an authoritarian, not a democratic, regime in which the regulatory state is being built. In addition, the institutionalization of regulatory action remains problematic.

State weaknesses

State action in economic matters is still hampered by several factors. First, there is the multiplicity of administrations with sometimes divergent interests and their low levels of cooperation. This factor explains, for example, the difficulties in setting up an effective control system for the food-processing industry.[24] In the case of the contaminated milk scandal that broke out in the province of Anhui in 2004 and attracted the attention of the international media, many public agencies were concerned, including the Ministry of Health, the Ministry of Agriculture, the Administration for Industry and Commerce, the Administration for Food Processing and Medicine, etc. Although they all sought to preserve their own prerogatives, the various norms and standards were inconsistent and information did not circulate properly, the absence of any clear delimitation of the responsibilities of each agency made it de facto possible for them to evade regulation.

Another limitation is the frequent collusion between local authorities and companies under their jurisdiction. If a company in violation of a particular regulation is the source of many jobs or significant tax resources, local authorities prefer to impose a fine rather than sanction it by closing it down. In the case of the fight against occupational diseases, and in particular pneumoconiosis, local authorities are often complicit with employers. They are actively involved when local cadres are financially engaged in operating private mines that do not comply with occupational safety legislation: in such cases, they are therefore both judge and jury. Without even being personally interested in the results of businesses located in their constituency, public servants are often passively complicit because their careers depend on their ability to foster local economic development. As provinces and municipalities compete relentlessly for investors, local officials are encouraged to favour the interests of entrepreneurs at all costs and neglect those of workers or the environment.

Finally, the state is weakened by insufficient resources. In terms of occupational health, one of the main obstacles to improving the situation is the lack of professionals. When the law exists, it is often not enforced due to the lack of an independent and efficient judiciary. Labour legislation exists and indeed conforms to the standards defined by the International Labour Organization. For example, the maximum authorized working time is forty hours per week and, beyond that, payment of overtime is compulsory; minimum wages are defined locally; workers are entitled to a weekly day off. But these rights are widely flouted, especially by small and medium-sized enterprises, because there is no effective mechanism for correcting violations.

To this day, the question of the state's economic role is subject to debate. Some people, inspired by neoliberalism, believe that it has not yet withdrawn sufficiently from the economic sphere (and it is indeed still a significant producer), so that market forces should play a bigger role. Faced with the rise of various problems – social inequalities, pollution, crises in the health system and the education system – both political leaders and academics, among others, are calling for a pause, or even more public action.

Internationalization of the economy

Prior to 1979, China was one of the most closed economies in the world; the share of international trade in GDP never exceeded 10 per cent and even slumped to 5 per cent in the early 1970s. After 1979, China's integration into the world economy was a major component of the reforms, as indicated by an expression that links 'reform and opening-up' (*gaige yu kaifang* 改革与开放). Rather than the country going into debt with the international financial system, it was international investors who financed the modernization of the Chinese industrial apparatus, bringing in technologies and markets. The policy of opening-up therefore aimed to modernize industry by facilitating the importation of equipment and technology from abroad. Thirty years later, China had become a major player in international trade, with a degree of opening-up rare for a continental-sized economy.

Before 1978, China was not cut off from the rest of the world. In the 1950s, trade was mainly with the Communist world: China exported textile products and imported machinery and industrial inputs such as steel or petroleum. In the early 1970s, the share of trade in GDP (at 5 per cent) bottomed out. Several factors isolated China from the rest of the world economy. First, there was the monopoly of twelve state-owned companies on international trade; there was also the existence, alongside the national currency (the *renminbi* 人民币), of a nonconvertible currency with an administered exchange rate reserved for international trade, which isolated national prices from world prices. Opening-up, initially limited to certain territories, was gradual and selective. In the 1990s, the number of companies authorized to carry out import and export operations increased. In July 2004, a law definitively ended the monopolies of state agencies on international trade. Now all companies could buy and sell on the international market. As for the dual currency system, it was abolished in January 1994; China then had only one exchange rate. Since 2005, China has had an administered floating exchange rate. The central bank intervenes in the market to contain the rise in the exchange rate caused by net capital inflows due to the trade surplus, foreign investment inflows and speculative flows. The yuan appreciated in real terms (+ 30 per cent between 2005 and 2012) and its exchange rate approached its purchasing power parity. Its degree of undervaluation, however, is debatable. As regards customs tariffs, liberalization was gradual; they were 39 per cent on average in 1992 and fell to 15 per cent on average in 2001, the year of accession to the WTO.[25]

The adoption of a legal framework – a law on joint enterprises, bilateral investment protection and non-double-taxation treaties, etc. – and preferential measures caused massive inflows of capital. In 2020, the stock of foreign investment in China amounted to $1,918 billion, or

13 per cent of GDP (UNCTAD figures); that is four times more than India, but almost six times less than the United States. In 2014, China, with $128 billion in new foreign investments, became the world's leading destination for foreign investment in terms of flow.

Opening up to foreign investment was geographically gradual and selective. It was initially confined to Special Economic Zones. The first four zones were created in 1980 in the southern provinces of Guangdong (Shenzhen, Zhuhai and Shantou) and Fujian (Xiamen). In these territories, isolated from the rest of the production system, foreign companies were allowed to import without paying customs duties on condition of re-exporting their production. This was a classic strategy of creating export processing zones, implemented during the 1960s in many countries of East Asia, notably in Taiwan. These were laboratory zones in which reforms were tested and then extended to the rest of the country. In 1980, fourteen coastal cities, including Shanghai, were authorized to open economic and technological development zones offering advantages similar to SEZs. Each province then tried to obtain comparable advantages. In 1988, the entire island of Hainan became a SEZ. Then the entire Pearl River Delta, and the Yangtze River Delta, were open to investment. In the early 1990s, the Pudong SEZ in Shanghai was created. Ultimately, all the coastal provinces and then the whole country were open to foreign investment.

After 1992, that is to say after the relaunching of the reform process by Deng, foreign investments arrived en masse in China; they were concentrated in the manufacturing industry. The policy of opening up and welcoming foreign investment coincided with the offshoring and outsourcing strategies of companies. During the 1990s, China became the second host country for foreign direct investment after the United States. Between 1992 and 1998, the country benefited from $250 billion in new investments, or 30 per cent of all foreign direct investment in developing countries. This represented about 15 per cent of the total investment, and its stock at the end of 1998 was equivalent to 25 per cent of GDP. These investments were intended primarily for the secondary sector, especially in the absence of any opening-up in the services sector; this reinforced the industrial specialization of China as a workshop of the world. In line with its priorities, the government established lists of sectors where foreign investors were encouraged, permitted or prohibited. Entry into the WTO in 2001 reduced the government's discretionary leeway, and most industrial sectors were now open to foreign capital, with varying limits. In services such as telecommunications or banking, restrictions were more severe. Nowadays, investment in industry is dropping due to rising labour costs and it is mainly the service sector that benefits from the influx of foreign capital, in distribution, finance and transport.

These investments come primarily from Asia. In 2007, two-thirds of the stock of foreign investment came from China's regional neighbours. Hong Kong's share was huge at 39 per cent, ahead of Japan (7.8 per cent), Taiwan (5.8 per cent) and South Korea (4.9 per cent). Until that date, companies with foreign capital had benefited from a privileged tax regime, which explains why Chinese capital left China, mainly via Hong Kong, only to re-enter it, benefiting from the preferential treatment reserved for foreign investments.

Since the early 2000s, the government has encouraged Chinese companies to invest abroad, as part of its 'go global' policy (*zouchuqu zhanlüe* 走出去战略), a policy first formulated in 2000 by Premier Zhu Rongji. China, now an exporter of capital, created a sovereign wealth fund in May 2007. This usually involves securing raw material supplies and accessing technologies. In terms of stocks, Chinese investments abroad amounted to $2,351 billion in 2020, or 16 per cent of GDP (UNCTAD figures). One of the consequences of foreign direct investment in China is its rise in international trade.

International trade

After three decades of opening-up, China became the world's leading exporting power in 2015. It was responsible for 14 per cent of world exports, ahead of the United States (9 per cent). In 2016, for merchandise alone, China was the world's largest exporter (13.2 per cent) and the second largest importer (9.8 per cent) (WTO data). This performance reflected its integration into international production chains and was due in large part to its status as a workshop economy. Imports and exports are linked; more than half of exports come from international subcontracting operations in which China assembles imported components.[26] This specialization in the final stages of product manufacturing is natural in view of its comparative advantages, but also problematic because a relatively small fraction of the total added value of exported products is generated within its borders.

Until the mid-1990s, export growth was largely based on products with low added value and high labour content, where the Chinese advantage lay in price competitiveness and mass production, in particular of textiles and clothing. Today, textile products account for just 16 per cent of exports, far behind electrical goods (household appliances) and electronic goods (computers, mobile phones) which now constitute more than 40 per cent of exports.[27] During the 2000s, medium-tech products gradually replaced low-tech products as the main component of exports. However, in the information and communication technology industries, a large proportion of production and exports is created with imported components; assembly operations account for 8 per cent of Chinese exports and local content is in the order of 40 per cent.[28]

Since the crisis of the end of the 2000s, the growth of the country's foreign trade has continued to be faster than that of international trade, but its sources are now different. The role played by the Chinese economy in global production chains through assembly activities is no longer the main driver of business performance. For foreign companies, China is less and less of an assembly and export platform, and increasingly a domestic market to be captured. Firms with foreign capital have lost the dominant role they had in the country's foreign trade due to their strong positioning in assembly activities, which are now in decline. These firms were responsible for 59 per cent of Chinese trade in 2006; this share had fallen to 48 per cent by 2014.[29] The new engine of commerce is ordinary trade emanating from a supply based mainly on local inputs and domestic demand. China's role as 'workshop of the world' is slowing down and the country is shifting to a less extroverted mode of growth. These changes are the result of the new international environment, where global demand is refocusing on developing countries, but also of domestic transformations in China and the evolution of its development model. The increase in wage costs since the mid-2000s is a lasting trend linked to demographic change and government policy in favour of growth focused on increasing domestic demand.

China's main trading partners have long been its Asian regional neighbours and mature economies, but it is increasingly developing its trade with countries in Latin America and Africa. In recent decades, it has driven growth in Asia through its demand for manufactured goods and in Latin America and Africa through its demand for primary products.

Ultimately, the Chinese economy became internationalized at a particularly early stage in its development and this internationalization has been a source of growth. It has been made possible by the interplay of internal factors such as the policy of opening-up, and external factors such as the liberalization of trade in goods and capital, the flow of foreign investment from developed countries to emerging countries and development aid. Foreign companies have thus played a key role in the modernization of the Chinese industrial apparatus. However, China's ability to move from a production economy primarily based on a comparative advantage in terms of low-skilled labour to an information and knowledge economy is still controversial. Admittedly, large Chinese companies such as Huawei and Lenovo are emerging as major players in the international market, but in the 1960s, just two decades after the end of the Second World War, Japan was conquering international market shares not on the basis of its prices, but through the quality of its products.

Conclusion

Once the revolution had run its course and power had been conquered, the Communist Party, which had no experience of managing industry, looked to the only country ready to help in its modernization project. China thus organized its economy according to the Soviet model of central planning and administrative allocation of resources. In 1957, dissatisfied with the results, Mao Zedong accelerated the movement and radicalized the project. The result was catastrophic. Only with Mao's death was the debate between political mobilization and recourse to material incentives finally settled. In 1978, a major turning point was taken: to improve the system's operation, a number of market forces were introduced. Fourteen years later, in 1992, the Chinese leadership firmly committed the country to the path of building a market economy, a process that has not yet been completed. Forty-five years after the start of reforms, China had still not completely liberalized its interest and exchange rates; property rights are sometimes still unclear.

There are two competing views as to why the reforms succeeded. For some commentators, who support the idea of convergence, it was the adoption of the institutions of a market economy that ensured growth. For others, the Chinese path has been essentially experimental; the progressive and pragmatic nature of the reforms has led to the establishment of specific mechanisms. The former[30] attribute the performance of the Chinese economy since 1978 to the same factors that have enabled rapid economic growth in East and Southeast Asia: liberalization, internationalization, privatization. China owes its success to the convergence of its institutions with those of all the capitalist market economies. For these authors, the gradualism is mainly due to the lack of political consensus at the start of the reforms, which forced compromises within the leadership team. China's noncapitalist institutions should therefore be attributed exclusively to political circumstances. The three decades of reforms are not the result of decisions taken by a strong, efficient and pragmatic state, but the fruit of internal struggles within the Chinese leadership. Economic growth has taken place despite the gradualism of the reforms. And noncapitalist institutions have turned out to be failures and in need of reform.

The latter,[31] however, insist on the experimental dimension of Chinese reforms. China's economic growth is said to be due to the emergence of growth-friendly institutions that are not homologous to those of capitalist economies. The coherence of the reforms is a retrospective interpretation, and does not depend on a prior, planned strategy. Contrary to the big bang strategy implemented in the former Soviet Eastern Europe, gradualism has induced ambiguities that are found in the many successive semantic avatars of the official model assigned to the economy: 'a planned economy supplemented by market mechanisms', 'a planned economy of goods', 'regulation of the market by the state and of businesses by the market', 'organic combination of plan and market', 'a socialist market economy'. The pace of reforms has been held up, influenced by sometimes enigmatic political balances. The result is the uniqueness of Chinese institutions – the role of rural enterprises and state-owned enterprises.

One thing that is certain is that several institutional forms coexist today within the Chinese economy, including an indigenous capitalism (private companies, mostly small and medium-sized), state capitalism (the largest companies), and foreign capitalism (large multinationals from Japan, the United States or Europe, and small and medium-sized enterprises from Hong Kong and Taiwan). All of them lie at the heart of the challenges facing the country. It is up to companies to create jobs for the millions of new entrants who arrive every year on the labour market. It is up to them to create the wealth that will, via taxes, finance the modernization of the state. Their development is also at the root of some of the worst ills affecting the country: poor working conditions for employees, air and water pollution, and growing income inequalities. Because the concept of the rule of law is not firmly established, and despite the existence of a legislative and regulatory apparatus, the Chinese state does not yet have the necessary capacities to regulate the actions of companies. While legislation governing business practices exists, it is, in fact, not respected.

While China has become the world's second-largest economy and third-largest exporting power, this does not mean that it is a rich country. True, the average income almost tripled in China between 2000 and 2011, but there are great differences between the regions. While the standard of living in Shanghai is close to that of southern European countries, Guizhou is akin to a developing country in Africa. Relative prosperity in one part of the country contrasts with the extreme poverty elsewhere.

The main challenge facing the Chinese economy is that of transforming its growth mechanisms. So far, growth has been based on investment (which reached 43 per cent of nominal GDP in 2020) and industry; in the future, it must be based on consumption and services. Growth can no longer be based on the ever more extensive use of resources, and it needs to be less greedy for energy. Air and water have reached a hardly sustainable level of pollution. Degradation of air quality could be the major culprit in the increase in lung cancer; and nearly 40 per cent of surface water (rivers and lakes) is polluted.[32] Tensions are also emerging in the labour market for demographic reasons. Since 2012, the working-age population, which includes people aged 15 to 59, has started to decline; according to a World Bank report published in December 2015, the number of workers is likely to decline by 10 per cent by 2040 – a drop of 90 million people. Moreover, labour shortages have already appeared in the coastal regions. Industrial companies will therefore have to adapt to rising labour costs and improve the range of their production.

China will need to focus its long-term growth on expanding its domestic market and in so doing stimulate household consumption that has hitherto been sacrificed to investment. Consumption could be stimulated by increasing social spending – on pensions, health and education – to unleash purchasing power and reduce the propensity of households to save.

Four decades ago, the Chinese economy embarked on two unfinished transitions: from a socialist bureaucratic system to a market economy, and the ongoing transition from a rural to an urban society. Unlike what has happened in so many other transitional economies, what is most spectacular here is that these developments have taken place so rapidly, without social trauma or large-scale conflict.

SEVEN

Society on the Move:
Mobility and Inequality

In the first half of the twentieth century, many factors contributed to the geographic and social mobility of the Chinese population. Industrialization, urbanization and the development of services in open ports provided multiple opportunities. The working class was developing. Urban middle classes emerged, made up of doctors, teachers, lawyers and journalists. A small minority of capitalists, industrialists and traders accumulated considerable fortunes. The consequences of the structural transformations of the Chinese economy came with the geographical displacements resulting from the absence of a stable government capable of ensuring civil peace, whether during the period of the Warlords or the Sino-Japanese war, and also the famines that resulted in widespread displacement. Chinese society in the first part of the twentieth century therefore experienced large-scale population movements. After 1949, the first years of the Communist regime also offered many opportunities for mobility. But these circulations would gradually come to a halt. In 1960, placed under the close control of the Communist Party, society was immobilized.

This chapter looks at forms of mobility and inequality. It is devoted to the positions occupied by individuals and households in Chinese geographic and social space. In the Maoist period, inequalities were kept under control by the macroeconomic choices that were made. Most of the wealth produced was not distributed to households but reinvested in productive activities. The entire population suffered from a scarcity of useful goods. While, as in any Communist regime, a *nomenklatura* with privileged living conditions was established, the differences between different social tranches remained limited. More important still was the creation, in the 1950s, of mechanisms that froze people in their positions. It was now hardly possible over the course of a lifetime, or from one generation to the next, to move about in social space: positions assigned in the 1950s were reproduced; children occupied the same places as their parents. The rare cases of mobility were the result of political decisions over which social actors had little control.

At the end of the 1970s, Deng Xiaoping and his supporters decided to tolerate inequality. One of the slogans of the reform movement was to 'let a few get rich first' (*yibufen ren xian fuqilai* 一部分人先富起来). The wager was that the regional inequalities or inequalities between individuals that would arise could be tolerated because, by a ripple effect, everyone's incomes would be gradually raised. This assumption was consistent with economic theory according to which take-off phases are accompanied by rapid growth in inequalities that then diminish. In fact, after two decades of immobilization what happened was that industrialization, urbanization and the commodification of work and housing, along with the possibility for rural people to work in cities, gave new mobility to society. China was no longer a society of 'peasants and workers' as described in article 1 of successive constitutional texts, but an increasingly diverse society. However, new inequalities were appearing.

Maoist China: from movement to immobilization (1949–78)

The victory of the Communist Party marked the coming to power of the countryside over the cities. To consolidate its power, a great many cadres and military personnel were transferred from distant provinces to urban centres, and in particular to the country's three largest cities, the capital Beijing and also Shanghai and Tianjin, which, for many decades, had attracted migrant populations. Between 1950 and 1954, these three municipalities absorbed 20 per cent of all interprovincial migration. The revolutionary armies, composed mainly of peasants, left their original rural bases to settle there. Party cadres took charge of administrations and businesses. After the political victory, economic choices became factors of migration. The establishment of the first Five-Year Plan in 1953 was accompanied by the creation of new industrial sites for which new workers had to be recruited from the countryside. However, during the 1950s, the regime put an end to these population movements. Several factors made geographic and social mobility almost impossible: the population registration system (the *hukou* 户口) on the one hand, and the distribution of class labels on the other. Instead of abolishing social classes based on production relations, the Maoist regime created new ones through institutional arrangements. China was a long way from achieving the equality that had been promised by socialism.

Establishment of the hukou system

The first years of the regime were a period of relatively free movement for the population. The 1954 Constitution even guaranteed citizens of the People's Republic the 'right to free choice of place of residence and movement' – a right that would not be mentioned in subsequent constitutional texts. However, as arrivals of rural populations from the countryside increased, they threatened to become an excessive burden and the central government tried several measures to stop what it called 'blind flows' (*mangmu liuru* 盲目流入) of rural workers.[1]

On 3 August 1952, a first official decision aiming in particular to 'dissuade peasants from blindly entering the cities' was passed. The main reason for this policy was to preserve social stability. The concern was that the influx of rural people would exceed the demand for new labour arising from reconstruction sites and the resumption of industrial activity and might become an excessive burden on municipal governments. The harmful consequences of the unfettered arrival of an excessive population of rural origin were listed in the press and in political statements: they could threaten urban social order, have a harmful influence on neglected agricultural production, and place an excessive pressure on urban infrastructure. In the context of the launch of the first Five-Year Plan (1953–57), the authorities' concern was now to strictly control these migrations in order to limit them to needs.

Several regulations were gradually passed and in January 1958 led to a new law brought in by the National People's Congress, which systematized and institutionalized all the previous regulations on a national scale. This law established the *hukou* system still in force today. It divides the population into four categories: agricultural and non-agricultural according to the type of employment, urban and rural according to the place of administrative residence. Most citizens with an urban *hukou* are in non-agricultural employment but, due to the administrative definition of urban areas that include agricultural areas, some urban populations have an agricultural *hukou*. In towns and cities, public security forces keep a register for each family; in the countryside, the production brigade is responsible for this task. Although Chinese society is patrilineal, the child inherits from its mother's *hukou*.[2]

Ironically, just as these measures took effect, the radical Great Leap Forward campaign was launched. The government's priority was therefore to accelerate the growth of industrial production. The legislation was put aside during the years 1958–59, which were characterized by high levels of migration from the countryside to the cities. Paradoxically, the period experienced the greatest wave of urbanization in the first three decades of the People's Republic. Urban businesses were hiring, and millions of rural people migrated to cities to work in construction or industry. These population movements contributed to the neglect of agricultural tasks and therefore to starvation. From 1960 onwards, the state implemented the *hukou* restrictions on a large scale in order to win back control of the economy and society.

The *hukou* system, fully implemented from 1960, was the central institution of the system that henceforth structured Chinese society. Freedom of residence was formally abolished and migration to cities was subject to an elaborate procedure for obtaining certificates, making it almost impossible. Prohibiting any geographic mobility, separating rural and urban people, and conferring on the latter privileges denied to the former, this system froze and perpetuated the dual character of Chinese society, while segmenting it into an infinite number of statuses. Its effectiveness was due to the fact that it is integrated with other control mechanisms. The state exercised a monopoly on most resources that were not available in markets where individuals or households could freely obtain them. It was the administration that distributed jobs in the cities and it was therefore almost impossible to get an urban job outside the official channels. Employers were the ones who distributed housing. Finally, the surveillance systems made it almost impossible to live in the city without having the necessary registration documents: daily life was tightly controlled by the 'work units' (the *danwei* 单位), the police and residents' committees. It was therefore impossible to break the rules without being spotted. Admittedly, the system was not completely water-tight and there were unregistered migrants in the cities, even during the period of the Cultural Revolution. But overall, the *hukou*, supported by other control mechanisms, effectively managed to make migration from the countryside to the cities after 1960 almost impossible.

Labelling of the population

The registration booklet (*hukouben* 户口本) that follows every citizen throughout his or her life serves to prove his or her identity and status and plays a vital role in all aspects of life. This document gives details of the holder's date and place of birth, the place of registration of residence (urban or rural), the agricultural or non-agricultural nature of the *hukou*, the level of education, marital status, profession and work unit. Up until 1979, the holder's class origin was also included. Indeed, a second administrative measure helped to fix individuals and households in social space: the distribution by political power, throughout the 1950s, of class labels. This was the main mechanism by which social status was transmitted from one generation to the next.

The process of labelling the Chinese population began in the countryside, during the agrarian reforms. It concerned areas under the control of the Communist Party even before the seizure of power, and spread nationwide in the spring of 1950. In theory, the objective was to describe the economic and social condition of rural families. Each peasant was then assigned a status. This distinguished between agricultural workers, poor peasants, middle-ranking peasants, rich peasants and landowners. This classification made it possible to separate those who received land from those who were expropriated. Holding a status therefore conferred differential rights. In the cities, the labelling was carried out during the Three-anti and Five-anti Campaigns. In 1952, the entire Chinese population was labelled, and this classification then included sixty-two categories. Every citizen knew to which category he or she belonged and this detail appeared on many papers and documents.

One's status was defined by many overlapping criteria: the old social classes characteristic of the so-called 'feudal' society before 1949, the new classes created by socialism, one's real or supposed political attitude, and one's birth. The population was divided into three groups. The majority belonged to the 'red' (*hong* 红) categories, which brought together the classes 'exploited' before the revolution: landless peasants, poor peasants, industrial workers and the urban poor, together with the revolutionary households in which the father of the family was a Party member or had joined the PLA before 1949. Anyone belonging to these categories was considered as a representative of the people and therefore could be the main beneficiary of the achievements of socialism. According to one estimate, these categories represented 82.3 per cent of the urban population.[3]

In addition, there were the 'black' (*hei* 黑) or reactionary categories. From the economic point of view, these were the exploiting classes, defined by their ownership of the means of production – the capitalists, the landowners, the rich peasants – plus categories defined by their political position, former members of the Guomindang or its armies. These were the enemies of the regime. They represented 3.4 per cent of the urban population. Between the two groups, there was an intermediate population neither loyal to the Party nor reactionary. These were the urban and rural middle classes: white-collar workers, liberal professions, small traders, middle-ranking peasants. In pre-revolutionary society they had quite a high level of income, wealth and education, and owned property, but were not directly involved in the exploitation of other social classes. They represented 14.3 per cent of the urban population.

This system, analysed by Jean-François Billeter,[4] had several character-istics. First of all, it was sustainable – even if, in the countryside, once collectivization had been achieved, all peasants were de facto employees of the people's communes; one justification would be that subjective conditions change less rapidly than objective conditions. In fact, in September 1962, worried that China would follow the 'revisionist' path of the USSR, Mao mentioned the need to relaunch the class struggle in the countryside. This system was hereditary, transmitted from the father to his children, something that had not originally been envisaged and was the result of practice. It was also heterogeneous; while some categories had a socioeconomic definition, others were more political. The statuses were also supplemented with new expressions. The term 'rightist' (*youpai* 右派) appeared with the repression of the Hundred Flowers Campaign in 1957. Finally, this system was very largely arbitrary. During the land reform, the expropriation of landowners and rich peasants alone did not provide enough land to redistribute to the poorest, hence the temptation for Party officials to expropriate the middle-ranking peasants as well. It was also difficult to draw a clear line of demarcation between the different classes when Chinese rural society was characterized by a continuum, and not by the existence of antagonistic groups. An individual could also belong successively to two categories. A rich peasant may have become a worker. The intellectual son of a martyr of the revolution could be accused of rightist deviationism. It was then up to the Party to decide, and many negotiations and personal settlements were possible. Most often, the political dimension won out over the economic and social dimension. A landowner, rich peasant or capitalist who had joined the Communist Party or the PLA was classified as revolutionary while a poor peasant member of the Guomindang was classified as reactionary.

The main function of the system was to provide principles of distribution of rights, prestige and scarce goods. It played a role in professional careers, which was also the subject of debate. Party officials were in favour of it because it made their jobs easier: they had a criterion for handing out jobs and promotions. The intellectuals and children of the middle classes opposed it, demanding that their professional competence be recognized at least as much as their revolutionary virtue. The system also played an important role in matrimonial alliances, making it impossible for members of antagonistic categories to marry. These statuses were passed on to children regardless of their own political behaviour and had consequences for entry into schools, type of job obtained, professional career and membership of the Party. This generalized labelling of the population was the first mechanism for transmitting status and gave rise to a system of social categories with unequal rights. It structured a new system of inequalities.

A *nomenklatura*: a privileged caste

In the Maoist period, all efforts were turned towards productive investment, and the population therefore had access to few material goods. However, as in other Communist systems, state and Party leaders enjoyed privileges and formed a *nomenklatura*. The seizure of power by the Communist Party offered opportunities for social advancement to a population of peasant origin. In China, even more than in the USSR, the new bureaucratic class was largely of working-class origin. In 1949, 80 per cent of members of the Communist Party were peasants; most of them had been recruited during the previous decade from revolutionary bases in the north of the country. However, this proportion would continue to decrease. There were only 66 per cent of them in 1961, while the proportion of intellectuals tripled from 5 per cent to 15 per cent. As for the workers, very few in number in 1949, they also represented 15 per cent of CCP members in 1961.[5] The Party was urbanizing and had more and more cadres. Despite the language it used, the Party remained elitist.

At the top of this bureaucratic class stood the country's political elite, which has been the subject of an investigation by Jean-Luc Domenach.[6] The population under consideration, from the 1950s to the 1970s, were the 700 people who made up the ruling nucleus of the Party and state. It was associated with positions reserved for them. These men and women, their children and the staff they employed mostly lived in the Zhongnanhai residential complex, on the western edge of the former Imperial Palace in Beijing; they had at their disposal an 'archipelago of residences' dedicated to work and leisure. In Beijing, they were located in the Fragrant Hills, Jade Spring Mountain; later, in the early 1960s, the Diaoyutai residential complex was added. They also lived in tourist and seaside resorts (in Dalian, Qingdao and especially in Beidaihe), in the mountains (in Lushan, in Jiangxi province), in the regions of the lakes and canals of the Shanghai hinterland (in Hangzhou and Suzhou), and in Guangdong. It became customary to take a winter vacation in Guangzhou, especially on the small hot-spring island of Conghua, where villas were built. Every summer, from 1954 onwards, all the members of the Central Committee were invited with their families, servants and guests to the seaside resort of Beidaihe, near which many other organs of the Party and the provincial governments had their own holiday centres built. The working meetings of these leaders were also hosted by the largest and most luxurious hotels in the country, notably the Jinjiang in Shanghai and the Donghu in Wuhan. These places were where members of the elite could fraternize.

These families also had exclusive health services. In Beijing, these were the Xiehe hospital under the Ministry of Health, and Hospital 301 under the army. Children's education took place in specific establishments. In the 1950s, at the end of their secondary studies, the children of leaders were sent to study in the USSR, mainly to follow science courses, if possible those that would be useful for defence. A whole generation of future leaders was educated in this way, which explains why in 1988 the government headed by Li Peng included fourteen out of forty-one ministers who had spent time in the Soviet Union. Jean-Luc Domenach suggests that these 'residents of the red walls' gradually changed into a caste, that is to say into a social group seeking above all to guarantee the reproduction of its privileges. In addition, Chinese leaders lost the habit of going out into public places. Separated from the rest of society, they 'do not know their own people'.[7]

However, unlike in the Kremlin, Zhongnanhai was open to campaigns launched by the Party. During the Cultural Revolution, Mao settled outside Zhongnanhai, spending a significant portion of his time travelling the country on his special train. While these spaces were undoubtedly separated from the rest of society, they were permeable to the outside. During the Cultural Revolution, they were open to political disputes, then to campaigns of repression. After the Cultural Revolution, this nascent caste was partly destroyed; its children were sent to the countryside. This was the case with Xi Jinping, the current Secretary General of the Communist Party, born in 1953. Until his father's disgrace, he spent the first years of his life in Zhongnanhai in privileged conditions: the family had access to a cook, a housekeeper and a driver. In 1969, he was sent to Liangjiahe village, in Shaanxi province, where he lived for nearly seven years. After Mao's death, this political elite, which had just been targeted, joined forces against the radicals and supported the policy of the four modernizations. They were anxious to rebuild the red walls and hang on to its privileges. Thus, unlike the Stalinist purges, the Cultural Revolution did not physically eliminate those who were designated as a new bourgeoisie and enemies of the regime; after 1976, this caste endeavoured to win back its privileges.

Political mobility

In this context, the opportunities for geographic or social mobility were few. Travel was dependent on political decisions from above. For example, in the late 1950s and early 1960s, in the wake of the Sino-Soviet split, a systematic effort was made to populate the northern border provinces – Xinjiang, Inner Mongolia and Heilongjiang. Migration to Xinjiang, for example, increased and peaked during the years 1960–64, and declined only in the early 1970s.

The demographically most important case of these circulations decided by the authorities was the Down to the Countryside Movement (*xiaxiang* 下乡) which lasted from 1968 to 1980.[8] The sending of young urban graduates to the countryside in the wake of the Cultural Revolution was one of the most radical mass movements undertaken by the regime. Between 1968 and 1980, 17 million young city-dwellers, aged 15 and over, were forced to go from the towns to the countryside to be 're-educated by the poor and lower-middle peasants', according to the instructions given by Mao Zedong; that was half of the young people of this generation.[9] These 'educated young people' or *zhiqing* (知青) – short for *zhishi qingnian* (知识青年), literally 'young people with knowledge', those who had in fact just reached the end of their first or second cycle of secondary education – were meant to turn themselves into 'peasants of a new type'. At the end of the 1960s, this policy was not actually new: the sending of young people who had finished their primary or secondary education, and sometimes their higher education, down to the countryside had begun as early as 1955, but departures were then on a smaller scale and on a voluntary basis. At the end of 1968, it was a mass movement – one that came to a halt in the late 1970s, shortly after Mao's death, with the start of the reforms. On average, their stay in the countryside lasted six years.

In his study, Michel Bonnin seeks the causes of this episode. He rules out economic and demographic explanations. According to the former, educated young people were sent to develop the countryside and the border regions, but this is not the case: they were not given jobs they knew how to do (for example, keeping accounts or teaching), but quite simply given agricultural tasks. Some have argued that Mao wanted to relieve the cities of entrants into the labour market, but this explanation does not hold either – these educated young people were superfluous in the countryside, where excess labour was the rule. Michel Bonnin maintains that ideological and political motivations presided over the launch and continuation of the movement. In the short term, it was a matter of ridding the towns of the Red Guards whom Mao had manipulated from 1966 to 1968 (they constituted half of the displaced population). In the longer term, the imperative was to train revolutionaries, to subject these young people to perpetual movement in the name of relaunching the class struggle.

In reality, the educated young people often lived apart from the villagers thanks to the help of parcels received from their families, but they did experience peasant poverty, lack of hygiene, discomfort and a lack of proper food among the rural population, especially as they were arriving in villages that had barely recovered from the terrible famine following the failure of the Great Leap Forward. They did not really have jobs either, and learned how to be idle. They often refused to participate in the life of the peasants because they were obsessed with returning to the city as quickly as possible. Losing an urban *hukou* for a rural *hukou*, as did young women who were forced to marry a peasant when they became pregnant, was a social degradation.

Moreover, the movement did not affect all young urban people equally – proof that a social hierarchy persisted in the Communist system. The sons or daughters of senior cadres were more likely to be exempt from being forced into the countryside; they were often also those who managed to get back to the cities to enter university, or to be hired in factories, more quickly than young people of working-class or peasant origin. The former had more frequent opportunities to 'go through the back door' (*zou houmen* 走后门), in other words to circumvent the directive and the official regulations. On the other hand, young people of 'bad' origins (children of landowners, rich peasants, counter-revolutionaries, former capitalists, parents with foreign ties, and intellectuals) were discriminated against. They had no chance of escaping being sent to the countryside and were often accused of everything that went wrong there.

The results of these years of hardship were clearly negative. Far from reducing the inequalities between city and countryside, Mao's policy worsened them: while the differential between the expenses of a city-dweller and those of a peasant was 2.33 to 1 in 1964, it dropped to 3.15 to 1 in 1978.[10] The practice of *xiaxiang* (sending down to the countryside) resulted in the formation of a generation that lost its illusions, its hopes, and for the most part the possibility of an education. This was also a generation whose ordeals had made it more lucid about the reality of the exercise of political power, and one that would play a key role in the dismantling of the Maoist system.

At the end of the 1970s, the *zhiqing* had the greatest difficulty in finding their place in the city; unemployed, sometimes homeless, for several years they constituted a veritable urban underclass. The costs paid by the members of this sacrificed generation were very high: the compulsory cessation of their studies, the abandonment of their projects, a break with their family and their future, emotional, moral and physical suffering, and a feeling of rejection, of being displaced, with no true home.

When Mao Zedong took power, he promised to remedy the evils plaguing China in the early twentieth century, to erase the excesses of capitalism in the city and to remedy the misery of the greatest number in the countryside. All in all, through the *hukou* system and even more through the distribution of statuses to all members of the population, he created a society characterized by new inequalities that were transmitted from one generation to another, inequalities against which individuals and households could do nothing. After the 1950s, Chinese society was immobilized; the only possible circulation in geographical and social space was that enforced by the authorities.

The Communist Party had thus done little to contribute to building the new society that it had called for in 1949. An analysis carried out using survey data in urban China shows that certain privileged social groups of the previous period had, despite all the proclamations, managed to defend their interests.[11] Although the labelling of the population had raised barriers to prevent the pre-revolutionary elites from entering the new socialist elites, some of them managed to maintain their positions in social space. Admittedly, they were excluded from administrative and political careers, but, on the basis of the skills at their disposal, other upward trajectories remained possible in administrative and technical professions for members of the middle classes who did not belong to the black categories.

Society on the move again (after 1979)

In early 1979, the Party leadership announced the rehabilitation of all landowners, rich peasants, counter-revolutionaries, bad elements and rightists. There was rehabilitation for all those who had been given these labels in the first years of the regime, and all those who had inherited them. Class status information was no longer mentioned on official papers such as job application forms. The system lost its distributive function. Since then, several decades of reforms have got Chinese society back on the move. The transformation of the structure of the economy, the new jobs created (and the old ones that were destroyed) and the loosening of the *hukou* system all created opportunities for mobility both geographically (surplus labour power from the countryside could finally go to work in the cities) and social.

The winners

Huge progress was made in reducing absolute poverty. Between 1981 and 2001, the proportion of the total population living below the poverty line fell from 53 per cent to 8 per cent.[12] Half of this decline took place in the first half of the 1980s. The situation of the poor deteriorated again at the end of that decade and at the start of the next, only to improve again in the mid-1990s. At the end of the 1990s, new pockets of poverty emerged. Progress was mainly due to the transformation of the rural economy in the years immediately following decollectivization and the return to family farming. Progress was all the faster and easier as the Great Leap Forward and the Cultural Revolution had left some of the countryside in dire poverty.

Private entrepreneurs, nonexistent during the era of socialism, were a major example – one widely celebrated in China itself – of those who had gained from the way society was now on the move again.[13] Different generations of entrepreneurs with evolving strategies, mobilized resources and types of activity emerged during the three decades of reforms. The first generation dated from the early 1980s; it was that of individual enterprises authorized to register in 1981. Economic and political conditions were difficult. Entrepreneurs started out with a few hundred or thousand yuan. They were active in the services; they were restaurateurs or clothing merchants. Their activity filled a gap; either it responded to a demand left unsatisfied by the public sector, or it played on the lack of integration in Chinese space and on the differences in development between the different fractions of the territory (they bought products in the cities furthest along the path of reform – Shenzhen or Canton – and resold them to Beijing or Shanghai, for example). The individuals who founded these companies were young, around 30 years old, and did not have college degrees. If they started their own businesses, this was because there were no opportunities for them in the state system. They were often people on the fringes of urban society; at the start of the 1980s, they were unemployed young people (especially educated young people who had been sent down to the countryside ten years earlier). They set up on their own both on their own initiative and because they were forced to do so. They were entrepreneurs by default. Their objective was to become 'a household of 10,000 yuan' (*wanyuan hu* 万元户), an expression that designated the first generation of the nouveaux riches. Their activities remained small in scale and were subject to arbitrary interference from government officials. Poorly educated, sometimes getting rich quickly on the basis of imperfectly institutionalized activities, this first generation tarnished the image of private entrepreneurs in the population (and in the press) for a long time: they were perceived as thieves, profiteers and speculators.

The second generation emerged after Deng Xiaoping's trip to the south, which relaunched the reform process in January 1992. These entrepreneurs had a background in government bodies, in major state-owned enterprises, in universities or research institutes. After Deng's trip, which confirmed the direction of the reforms, they went into business voluntarily. Unlike the previous generation, they already had professional experience, sometimes a managerial background; they had social networks and access to funding sources. These are the people who were said to have quit their jobs (although some continued to carry out these jobs) to 'jump into the sea' (*xiahai* 下海). They were defectors from the state economy for whom the private sector was not a palliative for unemployment, but a means of enriching themselves. These entrepreneurs used the networks of which they were part (and which they inherited from the days of the planned economy) and created new ones to further their own activities. Some of them took advantage of their proximity to state or Party apparatuses to live as rentiers. This was particularly the case with those who found themselves at the intersection of the Chinese market and the international market, and whose rentier situations were linked to the gradual, selective nature of the opening-up. As the state had set up a whole series of regulatory constraints allowing its representatives to control flows to and from abroad, this system of partial regulation opened up opportunities for influence and enrichment to those in strategic positions.[14] One way to make one's fortune was to be the sole representative on Chinese soil, with the approval of the relevant administrations, of a particular product made abroad.

A third generation of highly qualified young people emerged at the end of the 1990s. On leaving university, with a master's degree or doctorate, they chose to set up their own business rather than take a job in the public sector; the reward for taking risks was a potentially higher income. Some of them worked for a few years for a public company or a foreign company before starting up by themselves. Others were students who went abroad and returned to China, in particular thanks to measures put in place by the authorities at the end of the 1990s, to develop the high-tech sectors (they benefited from financing facilities with the creation of venture capital funds, and access to specific land resources through the establishment of technology parks). Another group of business creators were the managers of foreign companies who left their employers, taking clients, technology and management experience with them. What all these individuals had in common was a high level of education, and technological and managerial skills. These graduate entrepreneurs developed their activities on the basis of the existence of a real market in their sector of activity, and, unlike the previous generation, did not occupy rentier positions. This was a time when the private economy was becoming widespread and competition was fierce.

Another generation was that of the unemployed, who became individual entrepreneurs at the turn of the twenty-first century when the authorities started to see the private sector as a solution to unemployment.[15] Former employees of the state sector, who were losing jobs on a massive scale, were encouraged to create their own businesses to support their needs, as the authorities would no longer provide work for all. For this generation too, active in what were generally modest service activities, shops or restaurants, competition was fierce, and the chances of rapid enrichment rare.

The identification of these successive generations shows the diversity of the starting conditions, and of the success or failure, of entrepreneurs. While they represented the vanguard of a changing society, it is difficult to see them as a single social group. Individual entrepreneurs (*getihu* 个体户) headed microenterprises, most often services, and their income brought them closer to the middle or even lower sections of society. Entrepreneurs (*qiyejia* 企业家), even those whose businesses were partially or totally family-owned, were close to the ruling elites of the country in their level of income, education and social networks. Some of them not only maintained links with the political and bureaucratic apparatus, but derived their fortune from this proximity.

The old working class and new urban poverty

The main losers in the changes in society since 1978 were employees in the state industrial sector. In urban China, in the days of the planned economy, the right to work was guaranteed by a system of administered job allocation, and the exercise of employment ensured the enjoyment of social rights. During the 1980s, plant closures were strictly controlled; but in the 1990s, the introduction of a bankruptcy law was followed by an increase in job losses. The introduction of a new labour law in January 1995 marked the end of lifelong employment with the 'iron rice bowl' (*tie fanwan* 铁饭碗), which was replaced by employment contracts (*laodong hetong* 劳动合同).[16] Where the economy was not very diversified, laid-off workers could not find work and entire regions were affected, such as the northeast of the country.[17]

Between 1992 and 2002, the salaried workforce in the state sector dropped from nearly 101 million to 71.6 million people, or, in percentage terms, from 73 per cent to 29 per cent of the urban workforce.[18] Thus, in a single decade, the state sector saw its workforce decrease by 30 million; of course, not all of them lost their jobs, because, in some cases, companies simply changed their legal status by becoming joint stock companies and therefore moved into a different statistical category. The growth in unemployment was mainly due to the stoppage of production in unprofitable state-owned enterprises, which particularly affected the northeast of the country where such businesses represented almost half of urban employment. At the end of the 1990s, unemployment became the first economic and social challenge facing the authorities. In 2002, the official figure for urban unemployment was 4 per cent.[19] Observers then agreed that it was actually at least twice as much; and it continued to increase. One estimate based on survey data in five cities concludes that the unemployment rate rose from 6.1 per cent in January 1996 to 11.1 per cent in September 2002.[20]

Administratively speaking, the dismissed employees of state-owned enterprises were not considered to be 'unemployed' (*shiye* 失业), but described as *xiagang* (下岗), literally 'having stepped down from their jobs'. De facto without work, they continued to be on the books of their original companies. In theory, they received a minimum income paid by their company, the amount of which – from one to several hundred yuan per month – was set locally by each municipality. In fact, the latter did not always have the means to do this. Moreover, they usually kept their housing and a whole series of material advantages related to their links with the state sector, including access to health and education services. They were thus employees who no longer occupied a productive position but who retained an organic link with their former employer who provided them with a basic allowance intended to cover their essential needs and access to social benefits. This system was designed to be provisional, pending the establishment of a proper system of unemployment and health insurance. In the mid-2000s, this system gradually disappeared, with the management of the *xiagang* being transferred from their former work unit to the unemployment offices.

On the ground, there could be widely differing situations. Dorothy Solinger has drawn on surveys conducted in Wuhan, Hubei Province, in 2001 to distinguish between seven distinct categories of the unemployed population: the *xiagang* who still enjoyed all the benefits (housing, access to healthcare) of former state employees; the *xiagang* who did not enjoy all those rights and whose companies could not pay them all the allowances due; workers who were not *xiagang* but who benefited from allowances as early retirees; unemployed people registered as such whose companies had gone bankrupt – if their companies has contributed, they could enjoy certain benefits; former employees of bankrupt collective enterprises; the urban poor; poor migrant workers.[21]

The consequence of these transformations of the labour market was the emergence of a new urban poverty for which organizations that had controlled society in the days of socialism – trade unions, the Women's Federation, neighbourhood committees – were now responsible. As the state withdrew from productive activity, it redeployed itself to deal with new social issues.[22] Its action was not due to the survival of a Communist social conscience but stemmed from the fear of popular protest movements when, for example, thousands of workers could, from one day to another, in the same locality, find themselves unemployed. It was at the local level that this fight against poverty was carried out; municipalities set up a minimum income (*jiben shenghuofei* 基本生活费 or basic subsistence income), created work and workshops, particularly for unemployed women, and tried to promote re-employment – training courses, employment agencies and incentives to become self-employed and to create one's own business.

The loss of a job in a state-owned enterprise was a strong psychological shock, a leap in the dark. For the individuals concerned, the whole world fell apart. A generation of workers who, in the days of socialism, were members of the elite of society, suddenly found themselves pushed down the social ladder. Their fall in status was all the more severe as, on the labour market, they found themselves in competition with the migrant population from the countryside, ready to work in the most difficult conditions for very low wages. Faced with the need to generate new sources of income, resourcefulness was at a prime. For women, it was still possible to provide home services for the rising middle classes: housework, childcare or looking after the elderly. Men could improvise artisanal skills and provide all kinds of repair services.

The *xiagang* showed great inventiveness in setting up small estab-lishments for production or trade.[23] One possible way was to create a self-employed activity within the walls of one's own home. The decisive factor here seems to have been that it cost nothing to initiate such an activity since the *xiagang* owned the walls in which they lived. Several picturesque expressions designated this type of economic activity. 'The economy of the doorstep' referred to those who opened a business estab-lishment, most often taking advantage of the location of their housing on a busy thoroughfare, for example near a hospital or a school. The 'balcony economy' referred to those who engaged in productive activity within their residential spaces. Some started to contract out production: an individual would record buyers' orders and distribute the tasks to the *xiagang* who worked on machines in their homes; the raw materials were supplied by the client and the *xiagang* were paid by the piece.

When a state-owned company ceased production, it would sometimes transfer to its workers, free of charge or for a fee, their old working tools, machines or premises. In a small town in Hunan Province, an area of more than five hectares was investigated, involving three state factories and apartment buildings where workers were housed.[24] In the 1970s, this area was one of the city's most prosperous. Fifteen years later, the state textile industry was decimated, businesses had been shut down, workers laid off, and both residential and industrial buildings were in a state of disrepair. After successive bankruptcies, *xiagang* workers found themselves without any income because no unemployment benefit was paid to them. In a few years, the site of one of the three factories had evolved into a market for independent shops/workshops created by the *xiagang*, while the other two factories hosted private companies within their walls. In 1998, there were around thirty shops/workshops. In the autumn of 2002, there were nearly three hundred of them within the perimeter of the three former state-owned enterprises. Most of them sold knitwear. This specialized market provided jobs for 2,000 people, most of them former employees of the three state-owned enterprises who had become *xiagang*. In addition to the shops/workshops which employed a maximum of ten people, around thirty private companies with several dozen employees had been set up, most of them on the initiative of former state-owned enterprise managers. Nearly 1,000 people were employed by these private companies. So a total of 3,000 people worked at the site in the autumn of 2002, and it can therefore be estimated that most of the former workers of the three state-owned enterprises had found employment. But this was not always the case. In order to survive, the laid-off workers had to rely on welfare or financial support from their children.

The new working class: migrant workers

As part of the old working class was being sacrificed on the altar of the commodification of labour, one major new social figure emerged: that of the migrant worker. These 'peasant workers' (*nongmin gong* 农民工) numbered 10 million in 1982; this figure doubled in 1989, and rose to 70 million in 1996. In 2020, official statistics estimated this population at 285 million people. In certain urban agglomerations, a third, even half – or more – of the resident population belonged to this administrative category: a population registered in its village of origin which had only a temporary permit to reside in the city.

The first generation, born before 1980, and unable to find employment in the countryside, left the poor and densely populated provinces of the interior, such as Hunan or Sichuan, to escape poverty and support their parents or send a younger brother to school. The income from factory work was so disproportionate to what they could expect in the villages that they were easily satisfied. The first generation of migrants was ready to accept the worst working conditions for minimum wages – they were hired en masse on construction sites, and built Chinese cities. Others moved to the dormitories of factories in the Pearl River Delta in Guangdong or the lower Yangtze Valley working for the domestic market and often for export. In this regard, Chinese industry invented a new labour regime. Unlike what capitalism in its paternalistic forms had produced in nineteenth- and twentieth-century Europe, employers in China were indifferent to the question of the reproduction of labour power. Migrant workers housed in dormitories on the production site itself were single people accommodated for short periods. This system, which combined workplace and accommodation on the same site, did not aim to offer decent living conditions to families, but to increase control over the daily life of workers in order to maximize their exploitation.[25]

The second generation of migrants, born after 1980, accounted for almost half of the migrant population in 2013; it had very different characteristics. Coming from much smaller families than their parents because of the single child policy, they enjoyed the attention of the whole family during their childhood. They were much better educated than their elders: 60 per cent of them were college graduates, 20 per cent had graduated from high school, 13 per cent had a higher education qualification. Most of them (70 per cent) were not yet married. Familiar with modernity – they were at home with the Internet and cell phones – they had no experience of working the land as they had gone straight from school to the factory. They did not intend to return to their villages but wished to become urban-dwellers – which explains why the expression 'peasant workers' (*nongmin gong* 农民工) has now replaced that of 'populations from outside' (*wailai renkou* 外来人口). Unlike their parents, they hoped to rise up the social hierarchy and were not satisfied with the difficult working conditions and wages that had been their lot. Their demands explain the turnover of the workforce experienced by large-scale Chinese industries, with some companies having to renew a third or half of their employees each year. Dissatisfied with the conditions provided by one employer, they did not hesitate to seek another.

Shi Lu conducted a survey among several hundred migrant workers,[26] several results of which should be highlighted. First, the nonlinearity of migration routes. These routes were complex, especially from the geographic point of view. Thus, over the course of two decades, one couple from Jiangsu province first went to work in the northeastern province of Jilin, then returned to Jiangsu, and left for the neighbouring provinces of Jiangxi and Anhui before returning to Jiangsu to finally settle in Shanghai in 2003. This was one household making several trips back and forth. This complexity was not only geographic, but also professional. While some people gradually accumulated skills in a specific professional sector, others moved from one job to another without any clear and coherent logic. One of the migrants interviewed had left the army to become a security guard in a supermarket, then became involved in mafia activities before becoming a factory worker. The lack of linearity suggests the fragility of positioning in both geographic and social space.

The pivotal moments in which individuals largely reoriented their activity often coincided with the stages of personal life – leaving the school system, marriage, birth, divorce, accident or illness; they were sometimes also linked to the experience of hardship. Experiences are sometimes painful, especially when the individual or household is the victim of deception on the part of a business associate, friend or even relative. Years of effort to accumulate capital or fulfil a plan involving geographic and social mobility can be wiped out in a few days or weeks by a bad meeting or a confidence trick played by a familiar acquaintance. This produces a general distrust of other people.

Finally, migration was a family project not in the sense that all members of the family are necessarily found in the same place but in the sense that it involved the spouse, children or parents. This was the case, for example, of those married women and mothers who, for the most part, left their children in the care of their own parents in their village. For others, the project of settling in the city with their children was mainly motivated by the prospect of their children's success in school. They wanted to provide the best possible environment for children to pursue their studies. Working hard only makes sense because of the hope that the next generation will escape their present condition. Migration can have another intergenerational dimension, as when migrants are the children of people sent into the countryside in the 1970s and who then returned to settle in their parents' city of origin. Finding one's place in urban society is experienced as a process of redressing an injustice committed several decades previously. So the migratory experience has to be understood in the light of a family history that encompasses several generations. The family, more or less extended, ultimately plays an ambiguous role. Social and knowledge networks certainly provide support and a framework that can be mobilized, but they also sometimes create hazards and obstacles and they are also a source of conflict.

In urban China at the time of the planned economy, the work scene was dominated by the figure of the employee in state-owned enterprise, and employees in the collective sector (benefiting from less favourable material conditions of life and employment). Today, not only have the statuses diversified – alongside employees in the state and collective sectors, there are also employees of foreign companies, private companies, and self-employed individuals, as well as unemployed jobseekers – but opportunities to move from one status to another have increased. Society is more mobile.

The debate about inequality

In Maoist society, the social position of an individual depends on innate or given factors. Those born into a family of peasants remained peasants. Those born into the family of a worker or a cadre remained workers or cadres. Upward or downward mobility was a function of political decisions, with the administration holding a monopoly on all resources. Since 1978, changes in the structure of the economy and the professions have led to the emergence of new categories, including, for example, private entrepreneurs or migrant workers, and changed the positions held in social space. Analysis of the new social stratification has become one of the most studied and debated subjects for both sociologists and the media. Some observers emphasize the diversification of society from a consensual perspective, while others stress the divisions and the social and political risks that they entail.

A diverse social space

The first comprehensive analysis of social stratification was conducted by a research group at the Chinese Academy of Social Sciences in Beijing, the CASS, and led to the formulation of a ten-layered representation of Chinese society.[27] Based on household surveys, this pioneering work set out a comprehensive nomenclature that represented the whole of society. At the heart of the analysis was the hypothesis of a diversification or pluralization of social space. For the authors of this nomenclature, occupations played a growing role in explaining social stratification thanks to two factors: there was a growing gap in terms of income between workers who used their physical strength and those who carried out intellectual work, and there was also an increasing difference between those who had managerial responsibilities and those who did not. This evolution was the consequence of the technological development of industrial society and the increasing sophistication of its organizations. In addition, two main factors lay behind the evolution of the structure of different professions: industrialization, urbanization and the development of service activities on the one hand, and the transition to a market economy which ensured the rapid development of the non-state economy on the other. China was moving from an agricultural society to an industrial society, resulting in the growth of the non-farming population and the decline in agricultural employment. In addition, this promoted the quantitative development of occupations in the highest strata. The transition to a market economy explains the emergence of two categories, such as private entrepreneurs and owners of individual businesses.

Individuals belonged to a stratum because of the profession they occupied and the resources on which they could draw. The proposed social structure was thus based on the greater or lesser possession by each profession of three types of capital: organizational capital (i.e., relations with the government and the Party), economic capital (the possession of resources needed to produce) and cultural or technological capital. Organizational resources were the most decisive because, the authors argued in 2002, it was still government and Party agencies that controlled the most important resources in society. However, since the 1980s, economic resources had risen in importance. Finally, cultural and technological resources had grown over the previous decade, as the levels of education and technical skill were increasingly crucial.

These ten strata therefore ranged from the category of the population that had the most capital to that which had the least. This was indeed a hierarchical representation of society, which is why this report came under attack from some conservative elements in the Communist Party. They criticized the authors for seeing bureaucrats and Party officials as forming an independent stratum situated at the top of the social ladder, while the peasants and workers languished at the very bottom.

This representation placed senior government officials at the top and the unemployed at the bottom of the social ladder. The first stratum was that of 'the leaders of the state apparatus and of society'. These were senior cadres, whether they worked in central government or provincial or municipal governments, or in nongovernmental organizations. This was the ruling stratum of society – the people who had done the most to promote reform over the previous two decades and also the ones who had benefited the most from it. According to the authors, in 2002, these occupations represented 2.1 per cent of the working population.

The second layer was that of 'managers'. These were managers with high levels of responsibility in large or medium-sized businesses, whether state-owned, collective, private or foreign. The line between this category and the two neighbouring categories (cadres and private entrepreneurs) was not clearly established. It was a category that emerged with economic reform and the spread of a market economy, of which people in this category were strong supporters. They controlled significant economic resources, enjoyed a high level of education and occupied a dominant position in political space. In the report, they represented 1.5 per cent of the working population.

The third stratum was that of 'private entrepreneurs', running companies with more than eight employees (it therefore excluded 'individual entrepreneurs' who constituted a separate category). This category also appeared with the reforms; it grew rapidly and represented 0.6 per cent of the population in 1999. In the 1980s, many of the people in this category were of rural origin, but after 1992 their level of education and technical competence rose markedly. Their position in the political space bore no resemblance to their position in the economic space.

The fourth stratum was that of 'specialized technicians' who worked either in state or Party institutions, or in collective units or businesses in the nonstate economy. They represented 5.1 per cent of the population. The fifth category was that of employees. These were mid- and low-level employees in Party and state organizations, but also in businesses, regardless of their ownership; they performed administrative tasks.

This was a rapidly growing intermediate category and represented 4.8 per cent of the working population. The sixth category was that of individual managers in commerce and industry. This category grew with the reforms; in the 1980s it included rural or urban unemployed people going into business and, in the 1990s, urban people who had lost their jobs due to restructuring of the state sector. It represented 4.2 per cent of the working population. The seventh category was that of employees in commerce and services. These were employees without any specialized skills. This category was growing with the development of service activities and urbanization, and represented 12 per cent of the working population.

Industrial workers formed the eighth category. This was a declining category within which situations varied greatly; after the launch of the reforms, this group saw its social position deteriorate. At the time of the reforms, a certain number of its members acquired new skills which allowed them to rise to a higher category. They represented 22 per cent of the working population. Workers in the agricultural sector formed the largest (ninth) category, representing almost half of the Chinese population. But, under the effect of industrialization and urbanization, the importance of this category declined – from 84 per cent of the population in 1952 to 44 per cent in 1999. They were at the bottom of the social ladder.

The last category was that of the unemployed, whether permanently or occasionally unemployed, whether or not they had lost a previous job, and whether they lived in town or in the countryside. This category included rural migrants seeking work in urban areas who had not found stable employment; it was the category most affected by poverty. In 2002, it represented 3.1 per cent of the working population.

A political project: construction of the middle classes

The authors of the two volumes mentioned set a goal to be achieved through economic development: the emergence of a social structure dominated by the middle classes, the only guarantee of social and political stability. According to them, history shows that a pyramid-shaped structure, with a minority at the top and a large majority at the bottom, foments social movements, even revolution or civil war. The existence of middle strata should allow harmonious development, as they ensure a stable and orderly social structure. In support of their argument, the authors resort to comparisons and cite the example of Western countries where, in the 1950s, civil servants and managers formed what was then called the 'new middle class' and represented about a third of the workforce, and Japan where in 1975 the new middle class represented 34 per cent of the workforce. Just as, in the advanced capitalist countries, observers were speaking of the disappearance of the middle classes, in China, the government was working hard to build up a middle class.

The literature differs widely on the quantitative importance of the Chinese middle classes, estimated at between 10 and 20 per cent of the population. Most often these include Party and state officials, private entrepreneurs, managers of large Chinese or foreign companies, members of the liberal professions (lawyers, accountants, architects) and employees in high-tech sectors. All of them share high levels of education and high incomes. They have college educations and engage in intellectual professions; in addition, they have a degree of authority in the exercise of their professional activity. Their income allows them to own their place of residence and a car. Another attribute of the middle class is travelling widely for their holidays. The Chinese middle class is often defined not so much by the relative position of its members in relation to the world of production – the class includes both employers and employees – but by its lifestyle and consumption, especially its residential consumption (members of the middle class are homeowners and live in the new urban neighbourhoods). If this is close to what is found from a sociological study of the middle classes in developed countries, some authors do not hesitate to underline the specificity of China: if part of the Chinese middle class has been enriched on the basis of skills valued on the labour market, another fraction has seen its material situation improve thanks to its relations with the government – and thus to unequal rules of competition and the appropriation of public goods.

These middle classes that the regime hopes to promote are defined not so much by their position in the productive space (whether or not they own the means of production) but by their level of income and their ability to consume (owning a home and a car; travel, contributing to charities, etc.). It is recognized that the income structure is wrong and poses a threat to stability: the distribution of income resembles a pyramid with a wide base and a narrow top. What the authorities are calling for is an 'olive-shaped' distribution where most of the population is said to have incomes that are neither too high nor too low. This project is not new, and we can recognize strategies that may have been pursued elsewhere, in Europe for example, in the post-Second World War era when the aim was to rebuild stable societies. Above all, this is another example of the long history of social engineering on the part of the Communist Party, which, in the past, relied successively on the peasants and the workers. The Communist Party is now working to build a large, grateful urban middle class.

At the heart of this strategy is the active promotion of consumers. Of course, China is now the workshop of the world and people remain for the most part bodily mobilized in mass production. The continued expansion – to the detriment of agriculture – of industrial zones covered with factories populated by migrants from the countryside attests to this. The irony, then, is that while China makes manufactured goods for consumers across the world, and its factory workers have never been so numerous, the official discourse obliterates this reality to promote the fantasy of a middle-class society, apparently reconciled in consumption.

Social divide hypothesis

Other observers have a less harmonious and peaceful view of the structure of Chinese society. Sociologist Sun Liping is one of them.[28] Instead of a plural or diverse society, he sees a fractured society. To the dreams of a middle-class society, he contrasts the reality of a 'total elite', and develops a theory of elites and their power. So he highlights the formation, in the second half of the 1990s, of an alliance of interests between the political and economic elites. According to him, this alliance is based on the search for political stability and constitutes a major obstacle to the formation of the middle strata. Only the political and economic elites now count in the decisions of the state; the disadvantaged sections of the population have no possibility of expression or any way of legally repre-senting their interests. This is all the more true as intellectuals, far from being critical of power, are allies of the elites; they are confined to being mere technical intellectuals in the service of the state's plans for economic and social transformation. Sun Liping, inspired in particular by the work of Pierre Bourdieu and Alain Touraine, here stands apart from the state and reveals the phenomena of domination and social reproduction in it.

For Sun, economic growth has changed in nature over the past three or four decades. In the 1980s, it led to a general improvement in the material living conditions of all members of society. Different social groups all faced the same economic problems: the low standard of living, the absence or lack of everyday consumer goods, the poor supply of public services; rapid growth solved these problems because it benefited everyone equally. But, in the 1990s, the nature of growth changed. Sun looks at the example of unemployment. In 1997, GNP grew by 8.8 per cent and the employed workforce increased by 1.1 per cent. In 1998, growth was 7.8 per cent and the workforce that was actually employed increased by 0.5 per cent. In 1999, the rates were 7.1 per cent and 0.89 per cent. In 2000, they were 8 per cent and 0.79 per cent. Thus, although there was sustained growth, it created fewer and fewer jobs and no longer contributed as much as before to solving social problems.

According to Sun, this transformation in the nature of economic growth was due to the concentration of power in the hands of a few. Until the 1980s, most national wealth was in the hands of the state. Then it started to be distributed according to each person's position in the social space. The poorest saw their standard of living improving. In the countryside, the contractualization of business, which ensured that companies in townships and districts had a growth rate higher than the national average, and the increase in the prices paid by the state to purchase grain from producers, fostered a rapid increase in peasants' income. Likewise, urban workers and employees saw their incomes increase. Some of the unemployed became individual entrepreneurs. During this first decade, the entire population benefited from the reforms, and individuals at the bottom of the social ladder were offered the chance of upward mobility. Society as a whole became more prosperous. Of course, those close to the Party or the administration also got richer, but their number remained limited, and they did not influence the distribution of income throughout society.

In the early 1990s, the phenomena associated with enrichment diversified under the impact of several factors. Corruption, the privatization of public goods, and the spread of the market system all contributed to the concentration of income and wealth in the hands of a few.

At the same time as a group of wealthy people was formed, urban unemployment became a mass phenomenon. At the margins of society, social groups entered into crisis. For example, in some rural areas entire villages were deserted by young people seeking work in urban centres. Roads and water supply systems were no longer repaired. Agriculture became a sector of activity with no future. While growth continued to be strong, the peasants' income stopped growing. In addition, the recentralization of tax revenues weakened local governments. In some districts, the government could no longer afford to pay the salaries of civil servants and teachers.

Two major transformations had taken place. On the one hand, from a time when the urgent need was to meet the basic needs of the population – fundamental necessities such as clothing, food, and shelter – China shifted to a consumer society. On the other hand, from a time when resources were evenly distributed across society, they had become concentrated in the hands of a few. From that moment on, a significant set of people leading precarious lives appeared in Chinese society, known collectively as 'weak groups' (*ruoshi qunti* 弱势群体). Admittedly, in the 1980s, this population already existed, mainly composed of the sick and the elderly or disabled. The phenomenon, until then concentrated in the countryside, grew hugely in the cities, under the effect of the widening differences in wealth. The number of people affected has been increasing, and includes rural migrants, the urban poor, people made redundant from state-owned enterprises and the unemployed. A growing population is thus excluded from society: excluded from the world of work, but also from all forms of insurance and welfare. To those who argue that the unemployment issue can be solved through the jobs that growth creates, Sun replies that these new jobs cannot be filled by older workers (at least between 35 and 40 years old), poorly educated (they have at best a primary education) and poorly qualified. Since new job opportunities demand young and skilled workers, it is unrealistic to assume that economic growth alone will solve the unemployment problem.

Sun Liping adds that China's joining the World Trade Organization has only deepened the disconnect between the upper fractions of society and the rest of Chinese society. Of course, foreign firms are moving to China and paying increasing wages to their skilled workers. Those who work in the high-tech sector, or who have high-level management responsibilities, are seeing their incomes approaching the wages paid in rich countries. But this is not the case for unskilled employees because foreign firms are actually just taking advantage of the differentials in labour costs. For Sun, the social divide is characterized by the coexistence, in a given historical period, of several eras. He takes issue with analyses that emphasize the diversification or pluralization of society. The idea of social diversity has its origins in the 1960s in the United States; it corresponds to a situation where different social groups may indeed have different interests within the same social structure, but where political forces and organizations such as parties or unions represent divergent interests. Such a society is also characterized by diversity in terms of values and culture. For Sun Liping, it is not social diversity that is found in China, but a social divide. When there is social diversity, the different social groups, within the same structure, influence each other; all the groups belong to the same period. Where there is a social divide, different groups belong to different eras. Borrowing from Alvin Toffler the notions of 'agricultural', 'industrial' and 'technological' civilizations that have followed one another chronologically in Western history, Sun Liping believes that these three civilizations coexist simultaneously in contemporary China. In his view, this is particularly the case on the cultural level, characterized by a lack of understanding between the cities and the countryside, between an urban younger generation that aspires to the consumer society, and a rural population which seeks first of all to feed and clothe itself. According to Sun, only the government can remedy this situation, but the state has turned itself into a business and is losing interest in activities that are not financially profitable. As a result, the future is bleak: Chinese society could be characterized by long-term polarization between an elite that holds a monopoly on all resources and the rest of the population.

Latin Americanization as a possible scenario

Other authors have formulated an equally pessimistic diagnosis of future developments. This is the case with journalist He Qinglian;[29] in her view, the future is not an averaging out of society but increasing polarization. At the start of the reforms, she says, it seemed very likely that China was heading towards a middle-class society, one that would guarantee social stability, with the middle classes playing the role of intermediary space between the upper and lower classes. These middle classes would be a place for the expression of moderate, even conservative, points of view, hostile to all radicalism; they would be the engine of the development of a consumer society, itself a guarantee of economic stability. The development of private businesses, the redistribution of state ownership and the introduction of corporate ownership were all elements that raised hopes for such a development. But, for He Qinglian, China has failed in this path and is now taking the opposite route. The structure of Chinese society is increasingly pyramidal and resembles that of the Philippines in Southeast Asia, or the Latin American countries.

According to He, the experience of modernization as experienced by developed economies demonstrates that the education system is the main instrument of production for the middle classes, notably through the dissemination of common standards. But in China, only a small fraction of the population has the opportunity to pursue higher education. Social polarization can also be seen in the new forms of Chinese cities, she notes – for example in the proliferation of gated residential spaces, or the growing differentiation of commercial spaces.

What He Qinglian denounces is also the growing porosity of the state to certain interests. Increasingly, economic policies are decided without taking into account the general interest, but aim to satisfy specific social groups. She notes, for example, the production of passenger cars, real-estate construction – which favours luxury housing to the detriment of simpler housing – and the operation of the Shanghai and Shenzhen stock exchanges. Between the interests of the majority of the population and those of the elites, the government of the People's Republic seem to have chosen the latter. And this choice stems, in part, from the nature of the social base of the Communist Party, which is in thrall to the elites. The author recognizes, of course, that here have been developments. Previously, the country's elite was selected on a political basis; now, it is recruited on the basis of wealth and merit. But these new elites are building their own interest groups, social organizations and means of exerting pressure and lobbying, while the peasants and the working class are marginalized. Before the reforms, the country was highly centralized and the value system was largely unified; the same individuals at the top of the power structure controlled all political, economic and ideological spaces. There were no resources that were not controlled by the government, just as there were no independent or intermediary organizations. It was impossible to form social groups with any independent objectives. The reforms led to a gradual redistribution of resources once controlled by the state. These have been partly legally privatized and have passed into the hands of those who control the apparatus of power. So, members of the elite did not make their fortunes because of their technological skills or their entrepreneurial spirit, but because they were able to occupy monopoly positions which enabled them to acquire immense wealth. Thus, He is led to an analysis of corruption, the nature of which she believes has changed. If, in the 1980s and 1990s, embezzlement was essentially an individual matter, from the mid-1990s onwards corruption became organized. It is now institutionalized and systematic.

According to He, Chinese society is breaking down into a small elite, a larger middle tier, and a rapidly growing marginal group. The elites themselves fall into several categories, depending on whether they control political, economic or intellectual resources. The political and economic elites include 1 per cent of the working population.[30] The political elite includes the most senior officials, at the central level as well as at local, provincial and municipal levels. This elite shows considerable continuity. The economic elites are the directors of state banks and large and medium-sized state-owned enterprises, as well as the owners of the largest private companies (often the latter have family members who belong to the political elite). He Qinglian breaks down large private business owners into three groups: those who, coming from families of civil servants, have by this means conquered rentier positions; those who, without family connections, have bought these same positions from officials; and those who have made their fortunes solely on the basis of their skills and the opportunities offered by the market (mainly in the high-tech sector). Only the third group corresponds to the model of social mobility as developed by the team of researchers at the CASS. In addition, private entrepreneurs are gradually organizing themselves into pressure groups in order to better assert their interests. Even if the lifestyles of the political and economic elites diverge, they share common characteristics: a fast lifestyle, intense schedules, high purchasing power and the same types of leisure activities. The existence of gated residential communities in urban centres should foster the emergence of class consciousness. The intellectual elite, for its part, is made up of a minority that constitutes an interest group that forges links with the political and economic elites, and a majority that has not benefited much from the reforms.

According to He, the middle classes are insufficiently developed. At the top are intellectual workers, managers of medium-sized companies in the state sector, owners of medium and small private companies, white-collar workers employed by foreign companies, and employees of state monopolies, namely, 4 per cent of the working population. Other members of the middle classes include specialized technicians, scientists, lawyers, teachers and middle-ranking civil servants, or 12 per cent of the working population – a well-educated group that corresponds to its equivalent in Western countries. But it constitutes a small part of the population as a whole.

The working population is seeing its situation deteriorate. With the exception of those employed in foreign companies, China's working-class population is in decline. The reforms have radicalized the working situation of this population; it was in control of its tasks before the reforms, but has since fallen into a state of exploitation reminiscent of the industrial revolution in Europe. Together with rural migrants living in the cities and the peasantry, this fraction of the Chinese population comprises 480 million workers, or 69 per cent of the working population. Finally, at the very bottom of the social scale, there is a marginalized and impoverished rural population estimated at 100 million people. This population represents 14 per cent of the working population.

This is a far cry from a perspective that emphasized the fluidity of society and the opportunities offered by the transition. It acts as a critique of the ability of the elites from the Maoist period to adapt to the new environment and to hoover up the resources redistributed by the state, so that a coalition of the dominant social forces has robbed most of society of what belongs to it.

Measuring inequalities

One of the possible indicators for measuring inequalities in the distribution of resources is the Gini coefficient.[31] At the beginning of the

1980s, this coefficient was close to 0.3. In 2005, it rose to 0.483 and placed China between the United States (0.4) and Brazil (0.591). In 2012, several separate evaluations gave a Gini coefficient of between 0.530 as a minimum and 0.539 as a maximum.[32] One Chinese research institute even came up with an estimate of 0.611 for the year 2011. So there has been a continuous increase in this coefficient since the end of the 1970s. Economic theory generally maintains that the link between inequalities and economic development is an inverted U-curve: if inequalities initially increase with development, they end up decreasing in a second phase. What an international comparison shows is that, even though there are countries of comparable socioeconomic development that have a higher coefficient, China is well above the average in its category. The level reached by inequalities in China is therefore historically high, both nationally and internationally.

The size of the inequalities in China rests on two structural causes. On the one hand, there are the regional inequalities that contrast the eastern provinces of the seaboard with those of the interior and the west. For example, as of 1 May 2013, the highest monthly minimum wage was in Shanghai (1,620 yuan), closely followed by Shenzhen (1,600 yuan), while the lowest minimum wage was in the central province of Anhui (1,010 yuan). From a comparative perspective, China's situation is also similar to that of other large developing countries or countries with middle-income levels, such as Brazil, India or Indonesia, which also experience large regional differences in income.

The other major inequality is that between the cities and the countryside. While the Gini coefficient is lower in China than in some Latin American countries, the gap between urban and rural income might be the largest in the world. In 1978, the average urban income was 1.6 times the rural income. The first decade of reforms saw both urban and rural incomes grow rapidly. But, since the 1990s, the growth of the former has been much faster than that of the latter. The ratio of urban income to rural income rose from 1.8 in the mid-1980s to 2.8 in 1995, then to 3.4 in 2010, dropping to 2.97 in 2014 – figures that do not take into account non-monetary income (which would only worsen the difference). The main reason is to be found in the evolution of agricultural commodity prices. Periods of narrowing income gaps correspond to periods of rising agricultural prices (and vice versa). To increase their income, rural households have also resorted to off-farm labour. But if economic development is inadequate locally, and geographic mobility is reduced, then they have no possibility of earning off-farm income. The ratio of 1 to 3 between rural income and urban income underestimates reality because it does not take into account many free goods to which urbanites have access: health, education, pensions, unemployment benefit and housing subsidies. Some estimates suggest a ratio of 1 to 4. Inequalities between cities and countryside are not unique to contemporary China, from the point of view of international or historical comparison. China before the reforms was already marked by significant gaps. In 1980, the Gini coefficient for urban incomes alone was 0.16 when it was 0.3 nationally – higher than in other socialist economies of the time.

Income inequalities have therefore grown rapidly over the past four decades and this increase is in part to be attributed to public policies that favour coastal regions and urban residents over interior provinces and rural residents. One of the possible options would therefore be to modify these public policies.

Conclusion

The official ideology is that the revolution swept away a feudal social order and tackled the inequalities characteristic of China in the first half of the twentieth century. In 1949, Mao Zedong aimed to redistribute a wealth that had been appropriated by landowners in the countryside and capitalists in the cities, allied with foreign imperialist forces and the Guomindang. In the early 1960s, worried about the reappearance of all-too-obvious social differences, Mao relaunched the class struggle and tried to create a more egalitarian society with the Cultural Revolution. In the last years of Maoism, China appeared to be a particularly egalitarian society. In cities, men and women differed little in terms of their clothes, the quality of their housing and the few material goods they owned. However, this image ignored the existence of a privileged caste of high Party and state officials, and especially the divide between the countryside and the cities, a divide that was the main source of inequality. By preventing any movement from the former to the latter, the Communist Party was institutionalizing a two-speed society. Having stalled in 1960, Chinese society started to move again after 1978. Deng and his supporters said goodbye to any egalitarian utopia, and justified, at least temporarily, the appearance of inequalities. The wealth produced made it possible to reduce absolute poverty and a rapid rise in living standards. Four decades later, society is more diverse and complex. But the legacies of the Maoist period still weigh heavily; Chinese society remains divided and the first of these inequalities is that between the towns and the countryside.

EIGHT

The Towns versus the Countryside

In 1949, 11 per cent of the Chinese population lived in towns or cities. Four main phases of urbanization followed. Until 1960, this was driven by the industrialization of the country and the Great Leap Forward; it reached nearly 20 per cent in 1960. From 1961 to 1976, China experienced a phase of de-urbanization, an exceptional event in the history of mankind. The reasons were the slowness of economic development – and in particular the absence of a tertiary sector within the framework of the planned economy – the population registration system that prohibited surplus populations in the countryside from settling in the cities, famine, and the *xiaxiang* movement (sending people from the towns to the countryside). In the late 1970s, with 20 per cent of the population living in cities, China was one of the least urbanized developing countries. This rate then increased continuously under the effect of rapid economic development. In 2011, for the first time, the majority of the population was now urban (51 per cent). In 2020, 64 per cent of the Chinese population lived in urban areas. The last three decades of reforms have therefore led to massive and rapid urbanization. If cities and urbanization have been the engines of economic growth, this is the result of a deliberate political decision. As the country opened up to foreigners, the cities were structured by the flow of capital, information and skills from around the world.

The previous chapter was devoted to circulation in geographic and social space. This chapter will look at the main inequality that characterizes Chinese society: the opposition between the world of cities and that of the countryside. Maoist society was a dual society with rural people in a subordinate position and urbanites in a privileged position. Despite the great social upheavals of the reform period, this duality has not been reduced. For Martin K. Whyte, while reforms brought about the equivalent of the emancipation of the serfs, urbanization has produced new forms of inequality.[1] While rural people can now migrate to cities, they do not have the same rights there. In the absence of universal citizenship, Chinese society today has in fact three factions: urban residents, rural dwellers and migrants.

The broken promises of the peasant revolution

Maoism sacrifices the peasants

While the peasants made it possible for the Communist Party to conquer power – a pragmatic decision, based on the Party's observation that the Chinese population was predominantly peasant – from the first decades of the regime onwards they were largely marginalized, politically, economically and socially. From before October 1949, as the Party extended its control over the territory, it carried out land reform. The main obstacle it faced was the 'low level of class consciousness' of rural populations. In some rural areas, the richest landowners had long since left their villages to live in the cities and employed local intermediaries to collect their rents; they could thus be regarded as parasites and intensely hated. But often, the most prosperous people in a rural community were not all that wealthy; they resided on site and maintained family ties with their farmers or demonstrated a protective and caring attitude towards them; in return, the latter showed them loyalty and respect. It was therefore up to the Party cadres coming from outside to forge the revolutionary spirit in the villages. Its teams determined who belonged to which class of the peasantry; in this process of classification, the mistakes made, deliberate or not, would be the source of resentment and of personal and political conflicts for decades to come. Once this task had been carried out, the worst was yet to come for landowners, described as 'despots' and 'counter-revolutionaries'; dragged in front of mass assemblies led by Communist cadres they were publicly denounced and sometimes physically molested – even killed. The main result of the land reforms was political: the old elites were brought down and Party representatives were now the new unchallenged authority. In economic terms, land belonging to landowners, including territory owned by traditional lineage or religious organizations, was redistributed. Each rural family now owned a small piece of land.

271

The next stage was that of collectivization, first meant to be voluntary and then imposed by the authorities during the winter of 1956–57. The tragedy was, however, less brutal and more discreet than in the USSR, even if it was sometimes accompanied by coercion. Rich peasants could be members of cooperatives, if not lead them, and they were neither imprisoned nor sent to develop the desert lands of Central Asia or the Mongolian steppes. In addition, by enlisting poor peasants into the Party, land reform had made them amenable to collectivization. The catastrophe arrived with the Great Leap Forward and the creation of immense working-class communes that brought together 15,000–25,000 people and severed all ties with the natural village. The turn to the left in the summer of 1959 together with bad weather conditions led to economic disaster and famine. As the authorities continued to supply the towns, grain became scarce in some rural areas; there, the peasants had to go looking for herbs, bark and wild animals to eat. Children and the elderly were the main victims.

At the beginning of the 1960s, the 'sixty articles' kept the people's communes in place but transformed the way they operated. They were small in size and above all limited their activity to the coordination of agricultural production, the management of schools, hospitals and workshops for repair or industrial production. The brigades consisted of some 200 families, i.e. one large or several small villages; they organized public security, and were in charge of political propaganda, primary schools and irrigation systems. Productive activity was managed on a daily basis at the level of the production team – around twenty families (some hundred or so people), usually neighbours or relatives. Peasants no longer had to take orders from anyone outside the community. Each team decided how to use the land and organize each member's work.

The great novelty introduced by Maoism was the closure of social space in the countryside. With the effective implementation of the *hukou* registration system, life became more cellular in rural areas than it had been for generations.[2] Hitherto, villages had been open and integrated into the rest of society through multiple links. Products and people circulated within multiple networks of exchange. Villagers regularly went to local markets to exchange their produce, whether agricultural or artisanal, with other rural communities. However, while free markets were briefly authorized in the early 1960s, they were then abolished in the middle of the decade in the name of the necessary realization of socialism. Girls married outside the village and wives were recruited from elsewhere. This practice continued, but in a mitigated way because the authorities denounced as a feudal superstition the traditional taboo that existed on marrying within rural communities. Sometimes men left their places of birth to migrate to the city, or entire families moved to other provinces where the land for cultivation would be more fertile. It was now almost impossible for a peasant to settle in the city, and more and more difficult to move freely in the countryside itself. Since 1949, the state had spared no efforts to use propaganda to forge a sense of national belonging, but one of the unintended consequences of the rural policy of the last two decades of Maoism was ultimately a withdrawal of the rural communities into themselves. After 1960, these circulations ceased and rural people's horizon was henceforth limited to the production team. The only possible way of moving was to join the People's Liberation Army.

In his famous *Report on the Peasant Movement in Hunan* published in 1927, Mao identified four forms of authority at the origin of the 'feudal and patriarchal' system characteristic of the Chinese countryside: the power of the state, the power of lineages, the power of religious deities, and the power of men over women. If the aim of the Communist Party was to sever these forms of bondage, its promises were largely broken.[3] Admittedly, lineage associations, whose power was also economic and rested on the ownership of buildings and land, were dissolved. Similarly, religious worship was prohibited and temples destroyed. The struggle for their eradication culminated in the campaign against the 'Four Olds' during the Cultural Revolution. The Red Guards went out from the towns into the countryside and forced peasants to destroy their most sacred objects: the tablets on which were engraved the names of their ancestors, as well as images of divinities, and religious books. Neither lineages nor temples could any longer constitute the basis of local, moral or economic solidarities, able to put up political resistance to the central power. But the old political order was replaced by new, no less powerful institutions. The Party, through its representatives, was as close to rural society as it could possibly be.

After the tragedy of the Great Leap Forward, the excesses of the Cultural Revolution and the campaigns of the early 1970s against Lin

Biao and Confucius, peasants retreated into their private space, far from the collective impetus required by the construction of socialism. Moreover, family institutions had not weakened. Despite the adoption of a new marriage law in 1950 that abolished the 'feudal system of marriage' and proclaimed equality between men and women, peasants continued to marry and bring up their children according to the customs that had hitherto prevailed. Even if the views of newlyweds were taken more into account, marriage remained primarily a matter negotiated between two families and not between two individuals. It remained patrilocal; the wife joined her husband's family, was responsible for the upkeep of her parent-in-laws and was subject to their authority. Moreover, while the wife now worked in the fields, her income was not paid to her personally, but to the household. In addition, the majority of rural cadres were made up of men; in general, the only female manager in a production brigade was the one in charge of her colleagues' work. Another example of the failure to change was that inheritance procedures did not respect the new legal code that established equal rights for boys and girls, but continued to follow customs: preference always went to sons. This patriarchal system was due to the fact that sons – and their wives – had to ensure the well-being of their parents in their old age. Most often, elderly parents lived with one of their married sons, usually the eldest, while the other sons lived nearby in their own homes. And this is also why sons were always preferred over daughters.

In the end, Maoism built an insurmountable barrier between the towns and the countryside, two social worlds opposed to one another. Urban-dwellers perceived rural-dwellers as rustic, dangerous and inferior, a view that the peasants themselves accepted. Admittedly, many rural communities saw their material conditions improve with the construction of roads, the arrival of electricity, better hygiene and access to healthcare. But despite the intense propaganda from the authorities to justify their political decisions and give everyone the feeling of participating in politics, the peasants were sceptical and kept their distance, focused on family life and village activities. The economic transformations of socialism did not fundamentally alter rural society.

The main failure of the people's commune system was still economic: it was unable to increase agricultural production at a rate greater than that of population growth, and therefore to enable a rise in the standard of living. One of the main causes was the lack of any link between productivity at work and the remuneration received. According to some authors, the peasants themselves, and particularly the poorest among them, tried to overcome these rigid arrangements after Mao's death. In Sichuan and Anhui provinces, land was allocated to families or groups of families; rural cadres were persuaded to turn a blind eye by bribes. Thus, the peasants found new solutions to the problems of agricultural production and social organization by restoring the central role of family farming. Yang Dali even argues that there was a strong correlation between the efforts of some provincial leaders to comply with Mao Zedong's slogans during the Great Leap Forward, the severity of the famine and the subsequent ability of the peasants to take the initiative for reforms at the end of the 1970s.[4] In fact, the provinces that experienced the highest death rates during the famine – Anhui, Sichuan, Henan and Guizhou – were the first to call for a decentralized organization of production at the start of the 1980s. The gains were so rapid that it was impossible not to extend this new system; at the end of 1983, most of the people's communes had disappeared. Ironically, therefore, decollectivization was the indirect product of Mao's most tragic mistake.

Building a working class

Just as the Communist Party transformed the Chinese peasants into revolutionary soldiers in the 1930s and 1940s, once power had been conquered it endeavoured to give birth to a working class that had hardly existed in 1949. At the time of the planned economy, the dominant figure on the social scene was therefore that of the worker in a state enterprise, someone who benefited from the best wages, working conditions and even accommodation. The Party, concerned about observing Marxist orthodoxy, attempted to make the worker its main point of support. Workers constituted the privileged class of the regime, the heroes of socialism. They produced the steel, built the bridges and assembled the locomotives and machines that would make China a modern nation at last. Not only were they the best paid, housed and cared for, but they represented a large proportion of Party members. They constituted the class that was economically, socially and politically privileged.

275

The central institution of urban China was the work unit (the *danwei* 单位).[5] Every urban resident belonged to a work unit, whether this was an educational establishment, an administration, a state-owned enterprise or a collective business – the difference lay in the administrative level of the supervisory authority, which was the central state in the first case and the local government (provincial or municipal) in the second. The employment system was centrally managed, and upon leaving school or university, every young adult was given a job. The *danwei* was, first and foremost, the place and the body that organized productive labour. But it also ensured other economic, social and political functions: the distribution of housing and of ration coupons giving access to both basic and scarce commodities (watches, radios and sewing machine, to mention those that were most desired), access to healthcare, the management of schools, the registration of households and marriages, the implementation of public policies such as improved hygiene (and later birth control), and the mobilization of the masses during political campaigns. Physically, the work units of the biggest companies appeared as closed spaces, delimited by walls and wire fences, inside which could be found everything that made up the daily life of an urban resident: production workshops, places of residence, nurseries, schools, leisure centres (usually cinemas), cooperative businesses and Party offices – and all this was for the exclusive use of the members of the unit concerned. The *danwei* were social communities closed in on themselves by jobs for life and exclusive access to social services; they presented themselves as so many mini-societies, which when added together constituted urban society.

The functioning of these urban villages was a far cry from the Weberian bureaucratic ideal characterized by impersonal rules applying uniformly to all; Andrew Walder[6] has shown that, on the contrary, it was dominated by clientelism and the ethics of reciprocity. It was complex, personal and in some ways premodern social relationships that bound management to workers within the company – hence Walder's use of the term 'neotraditionalism'. In his view, what characterized state-owned enterprises of the 1970s were the relationships of dependency that developed within them. The discretionary power of shop managers in the distribution of basic goods and services placed employees in a situation of 'organized dependency'. There were two types of vertical relations in companies:

on the one hand, clientelist relations with a minority of activists, and, on the other, instrumental and more ad hoc relations with the rest of the employees. Company officials sought to establish patronage relationships with a handful of activists in order to control the workforce and ensure political stability. These clientelist relationships were publicly and regularly marked by a more favourable treatment of this minority; they made it possible to stir up antagonisms between the employees at ground level and a small number of loyal customers, so as to prevent the formation of solidarity between workers in the same workshop or the same company. Unit members thus competed with each other for access to scarce resources controlled by their superiors (moving to larger housing was the main concern for urban households, or getting their hands on the ration tickets that would buy a bike or an air fan); so the former competed for the favours of the latter. The support given by the greatest number to political slogans was the main currency of exchange for accessing resources distributed unequally and sparingly. This clientelism involved only a minority of workers and employees, but it formed the fabric of a 'subculture of exchange and mutual support' between the latter and their superiors. The patronage that Andrew Walder describes was therefore based on the extent of the social and economic functions of the state production units, and on the fact that these were relatively closed; employees remained attached to their businesses throughout their lives, and since there was no access to basic social services outside the company, they had no way of reaching out to other interlocutors.

Between 1950 and the end of the 1970s, cities were thus conceived as an aggregate of those self-sufficient cells known as work units. However, the condition of workers and employees was far from homogeneous. Situations varied from unit to unit, from institution to institution, from province to province. These differences hampered the emergence of a single Chinese working class.

The non-development of cities

In 1949, Chinese cities performed a variety of functions; some were administrative centres, others townships, while yet others were at the heart of transport, river or rail networks. The Party's strategy on urbanization was twofold. It continued to rely primarily on the largest cities, which assumed the main economic and political functions and where the most modern industrial infrastructure was located. These were, in particular, the provincial capitals. The most advanced of them, open to foreigners for more than a century, were located on the coastal fringe. In the case of Shanghai, the city most compromised by its links with the nationalist regime, some local resources – a number of its factories, but also of its engineers – were transferred to the provinces of the interior. This was the second policy pursued: to conduct a rebalancing in favour of the northeast, central and western regions that would experience much faster urbanization. In the 1950s, there were massive investments in Harbin, Changchun and Shenyang. In the following decade, the objective became a strategic one, as the country was militarily threatened both on its northern border by the Soviet Union and on its maritime and southern borders by the United States: this was the policy of the Third Front, which primarily concerned the military industry.

In terms of urban development, the watchword was the transformation of the cities, as places of consumption, into places of production. While there was heavy investment in industry, investments in urban infrastructure, housing and transport were considered nonproductive and therefore reduced to a minimum. The new regime, which came from rural China, was wary of cities and opted for industrialization without urbanization. During the first Five-Year Plan, investment in construction represented 9.1 per cent of total investment, a rate that fell to 4 per cent during the Cultural Revolution and rose to between 5 and 7 per cent in the following years.[7] In 1949, part of the urban population was already living in difficult conditions, in the self-built neighbourhoods of quasi-slums. In Beijing, 61 per cent of dwellings were considered dangerous. As the private housing market disappeared in the mid-1950s, it was up to work units to build new, functional but austere neighbourhoods. For the majority, kitchens and toilets were shared. In the old districts, in ancient housing, people continued to cook outside, on the doorsteps. It was not uncommon for a family to have only one room that housed several generations. The status of the position held by the head of the family and clientelist strategies often determined housing conditions. Despite collectivist and egalitarian principles, there were inequalities between cadres who enjoyed privileges and employees and workers at ground level. Due to insufficient investment, overcrowding and lack of comfort characterized the housing stock and were the source of many informal transactions. In the late 1970s, in fact, Chinese cities largely resembled what they had been in 1949, with the exception of new neighbourhoods and the iconic buildings of socialism.

In the end, Maoist society juxtaposed cells isolated from each other, leading a life of their own, within which individuals were closely integrated: people's communes in the countryside, work units in the cities. Partitioning and self-sufficiency characterized this 'cellular, segmental society, where each segment was a microcosm of society as a whole'.[8] Paradoxically, the differences between urban and rural China were never greater than during the Maoist period.

The urban miracle: urbanization without revolution

The launch of economic reforms at the end of the 1970s marked a turning point in relations between towns and countryside. As part of a policy that legitimized territorial inequalities, coastal areas were the privileged place for public and private, Chinese and international investments, which ensured a rapid and spectacular transformation of the landscapes. Cities were catching up with their counterparts in richer countries. The countryside was not to be outdone; it was covered with semi-industrial production workshops. Material modernity – factories, highways, high-speed railways, airports, high-rise buildings – was now visible everywhere.

Urban growth: a political choice

In 1979, the authorities experimented with new methods of economic organization in the four Special Economic Zones: Shantou, Shenzhen and Zhuhai in Guangdong province, and Xiamen in Fujian. These cities were requested to welcome investments from Chinese people overseas, from Hong Kong, Macao and Taiwan. However, in the 1980s, most of the urbanization took place from below, through the industrialization of the countryside; the Chinese countryside, in particular in the southern coastal regions, now resembled that of Japan or Taiwan: residential constructions, industrial buildings and agricultural areas coexisted in an apparent jumble. Not until the early 1990s were huge investments made in urban areas. In 1984, fourteen coastal towns were opened to foreign investment, including Dalian and Tianjin in the north. In 1991, the Pudong development zone was created in Shanghai, on the west bank of the Huangpu river; the aim of the municipality was to turn the city into the country's financial centre.[9] At the end of the 1990s, all the cities created development zones and competed with each other to attract Chinese and foreign investors.

Inscriptions 'To be destroyed' multiply in Shanghai, 2002.
Source: Marc Riboud / Fonds Marc Riboud au MNAAG / Magnum Photos

The city of Shanghai, and particularly the new districts of Pudong, constituted the symbol of this urban renewal. At the end of the Maoist period, the city was in disrepair. Having been the country's economic capital since the end of the eighteenth century, and the first port open to trade, its wealth was tapped to contribute to the development of the whole of China. Between 1990 and 2000, Shanghai found the means to achieve its ambitions, thanks to two key politicians, Jiang Zemin, Mayor from 1985 to 1987 then President of the Republic, and Zhu Rongji, who succeeded him until 1991, before continuing his career in central government. As a result of the political will of national and local authorities, within a few years the city had become a world-class metropolis, endowed with essential infrastructures: a dense network of highways around and within the city, bridges and tunnels that facilitate travel from one bank of the river to the other, one of the most extensive metro networks in the world, a world-class airport, a new railway station, and a deep-water port. Factories moved far away from the historic centre, and the Pudong market gardening districts gave way to high-rise office buildings and residential areas. The art deco-style façades of the buildings along the Bund in Puxi, on the west bank of the river, were the pride of the city in the first half of the twentieth century. Later, the towers of the Lujiazui financial district facing came to symbolize the city's renewed pride. All the major international, Japanese, American, English and European banks set up headquarters of their Chinese activities here. Thanks to this urban expansion and reconfiguration, the condition of city residents rapidly improved; the average area per capita increased from 4 square metres in 1989 to 12 square metres in 2000 and 20 square metres today. The polluting factories have been transferred out of the urbanized space. New areas for consumption and leisure have appeared.

Growing urbanization in China has been due to the increase in the number of large cities but also the increase of medium and small towns. In 2010, the five largest cities were Shanghai (15 million inhabitants), Beijing (11 million), Canton (9 million), Shenzhen (8 million) and Tianjin (7 million). The country now has five major metropolitan areas: from north to south, they are Shenyang-Anshan-Dalian, Beijing-Tianjin, Qingdao-Jinan, Nanjing-Suzhou-Shanghai-Hangzhou, and Canton-Shenzhen-Hong Kong. In 2011, for the first time, the urban population represented more than 50 per cent of the Chinese population.

Improving housing conditions

One of the main aspects of the urban revolution of recent decades has been the improvement of the material living conditions of city-dwellers, and particularly their housing. In the 1980s, the reforms allowed companies to keep a part of their profits, which were used to satisfy one of their employees' longstanding demands: to improve housing conditions. Companies immediately invested in the construction of residential buildings. In the following decade, a twofold path was followed as more of the residential stock came on the market, enabling urban-dwellers to become owners. On the one hand, work units built new homes for their employees or sold existing homes to their occupants at heavily subsidized prices. On the other hand, real-estate companies – most often state-owned enterprises linked to municipal authorities, often emerging from the former Housing Offices – started to build and sell at market prices. These new market conditions were made possible by the establishment of bank loans and compulsory employee savings plans – from 1994, employees and employers contributed to a fund that could be used for purchase or maintenance expenses. For the wisest and best placed households, maximizing their interests now involved simultaneously buying the two types of goods at subsidized and market prices, provided that one member of the couple was employed by a work unit and the other was an employee under contract and receiving a wage that was high enough for them to pay cash or incur a debt. In 1998, work units were no longer allowed to provide, build or finance housing for their employees. The market became the only way in which households could find housing.

The privatization of the housing stock was part of the plan to turn the construction industry into a pillar of growth. Landownership remained collective; it was user rights – for seventy years – that were sold. The sale of user rights was the responsibility of urban districts (*qu* 区) and became a major source of income for local authorities. The result was a high rate of homeowners in major cities. According to figures from the Ministry of Housing, in 2010, 72.8 per cent of Chinese urban families – with a residence permit – owned real estate, and the average living space per capita increased from 6.7 square metres in 1978 to 30 square metres in 2008. This transformation in living conditions, financed

Shenzhen, 1993.
Source: Marc Riboud / Fonds Marc Riboud au MNAAG / Magnum Photos

by households, was accompanied by a rapid increase in prices. In the so-called first-tier cities – Beijing, Shanghai, Shenzhen and Hangzhou – they doubled or tripled, or even more, during the 2000s. All kinds of initiatives were taken to try to control real-estate inflation – reducing access to bank credit, increasing the production of housing, introducing a tax on landownership, etc. – but were largely ineffectual, while municipal governments derived a great part of their income from land resources. In 2010, a new social or low-cost housing policy was finally launched for households with the lowest incomes, unable to afford market prices.

Another consequence of housing entering the market has been the emergence of spatial segregation based on income. In Maoist China, cadres might have had better equipped housing than basic workers, but they all lived within the same perimeter, even the same building, near their place of work, administration or company. Now, families had to find housing in market conditions where prices varied considerably. The quality of the building, the provision of comfort and services, and the lifestyles now differ according to socioeconomic conditions. Unsanitary housing where impoverished populations used to live was destroyed and replaced in the city centres by luxurious, high-security residences for the economic and political elites. These residential complexes bear names – Manhattan, Versailles or Fontainebleau – that evoke a luxurious lifestyle. An alternative choice is to live in huge villas (*bieshu* 别墅) built on the outskirts, in wooded and landscaped areas where the roads are privatized, on the model of American gated residential communities. These constructions are often inspired by foreign models and, as in the urban China of the first half of the twentieth century, one can choose a house in the Spanish, Canadian or sometimes even Chinese style. To ensure a maximum degree of comfort, residents employ domestic staff; they send their children to the best schools, near or far, but preferably international so as to prepare them for life abroad, and they have access to exclusive spaces where they can socialize at ease, such as sports facilities and private clubs. The highly variegated middle classes now have access to housing that is spacious, well equipped, close to catchment areas, and produced in large quantities. The residential spaces intended for them house up to tens of thousands of households, and they have made the fortunes of real-estate developers. They organize them as so many closed worlds, where the inhabitants can obtain a maximum of goods and services but also enjoy leisure activities or practise their favourite sports; it's a lifestyle, much more than just a home, that is sold to them. The least well-off populations are sent to the outskirts of cities, far from schools, hospitals and public transport networks, where they live in new urbanized spaces that encroach on the countryside, and where the housing is of poor quality.[10]

Many other urban forms have appeared. For example, during the 2000s, it was decided to create from scratch university hubs on the outskirts of cities to house tens of thousands of new residents. Most often, this was done to respond to a twofold need: first, the increase in the number of students and teachers within the framework of the massification of higher education that made inner-city campuses obsolete; and second, the development of land resources formerly dedicated to industry and converted to new uses. On the edge of these university hubs, developers built residential blocks for the middle classes.

Another novelty were the spaces dedicated to commerce. Between 1950 and 1976, the cities offered largely grey, uniform landscapes. In the early 1990s, cities began to grow around nodes specializing in commerce, finance and business, embodied by high-rise towers and huge shopping malls. This was the case in Shanghai, which reclaimed its status as China's consumer capital. Moving on from the time when it was the home of a manufacturing industry developed at the end of the nineteenth century by Chinese and foreign capitalists, and of the heavy industry on which Communism relied, Shanghai became an international capital of the postindustrial era, and the provision of businesses lay at the heart of this strategy. In less than twenty years, at the cost of a change in the commercial landscape, Shanghai returned to the vocation it had followed in the first half of the twentieth century.[11] The city was reconstituted around commercial spaces intended to accommodate both residents and the transient population. As the country's commercial capital, it contained as many distinct commercial spaces as groups of different clienteles. The Bund was a showcase for the metropolis, with luxury shops for an international clientele; the old Chinese city became a tourist area for visitors from the interior provinces; the shopping malls of the city centre were intended for local and national high-spending customers while, on the outskirts, catchment areas were established for the middle classes. In the mid-1990s, at the national level Shanghai pioneered another new form of distribution: shopping malls. The first of them opened in 1993. By the end of 2005, there were nearly forty. Most were linked to major urban planning or redevelopment operations in the city centre, including on Nanjing and Huaihai roads. They are built in traditional shopping districts served by metro lines. It is only more recently that they have appeared on the outskirts of cities; customers reach them by private car or dedicated bus routes.

The demolitions also raised the issue of heritage protection. The decision was taken to protect individual buildings, though this did not prevent massive destruction. The arguments put forward to justify renovation, eviction and destruction were overcrowding, unsanitary conditions, and lack of hygiene and amenities. So it was a health-based, modernizing discourse that presided over the destruction and reconstruction of urban centres. Faced with this destruction, architects, town planners, historians and journalists all mobilized and gave birth to several organizations. One solution often adopted consisted in museumifying certain isolated zones with a view to tourist development. The first project for combining urban renewal and heritage protection was that of the *Xintiandi* district (新天地, literally 'the new heaven and earth' or 'the new world') in Shanghai. This was a quadrangle that included a set of *shikumen* (石库门), two-storey houses emblematic of early twentieth-century architecture and intended to house the working classes. In 1997, the municipality signed an agreement with a Hong Kong real-estate developer: in exchange for the right to build luxury office buildings and residential spaces, he undertook to preserve the architectural heritage. The resident population was evicted (not without difficulties), and the *shikumen* were restored and refurbished to accommodate restaurants and shops. As a residential area for the working classes, Xintiandi is now home to businesses intended for consumers with high purchasing power. And as a flagship urban project, copied by many other cities, Xintiandi is founded on the exclusion of its original inhabitants.

Anxious to give physical form to urban renewal, municipalities are calling on architects from all over the world to develop flagship projects. In Beijing, the Frenchman Paul Andreu built the national theatre, Herzog and de Meuron from Switzerland built the Olympic swimming pool, and the Dutchman Rem Koolhass designed the central television tower. In Shanghai, the French Arte Charpentier designed the Opera on the iconic site of the People's Square and the American agency Skidmore, Owings & Merill built the Jinmao tower in Pudong.[12] This is all a sign of the aspiration to join the largest metropolises in the world, where modernity is embodied in emblematic buildings. It also indicates the significant role played by the central state and local authorities. They produce policies, draw up plans, call on international architects and engage in partnerships with the private sector.

New urban governance

Housing reform is not just economic reform. Privatization has major effects on the organization of society and on the ways in which power is exercised. Previously, the work unit was the preferred mechanism for the supervision, control and political mobilization of urban populations. Once these units had disappeared, the place of residence took over, via the reactivation of a former institution, the residents' committee. In both sociological and administrative terms, urban-dwellers, until then 'men [and women members] of work units' (*danwei ren* 单位人) become 'men [and women members] of neighbourhoods' (*shequ ren* 社区人).

Residents' committees (*jumin weiyuanhui* 居民委员会) were established in 1954 to supervise individuals who did not report to a work unit. Having been marginal during the Maoist period, this institution now played an important role in the local management of the new urban society. It was close to city-dwellers, and acted as the last mediating link for public action. Its functions included the implementation of public policies (census, family planning), the preservation of security (the fight against theft and fires), hygiene and the environment, the distribution of welfare to the most vulnerable populations (the elderly, the sick, the disabled, the unemployed) and running events in the neighbourhood, or even providing mediation during neighbourhood conflicts. Committee members were responsible for residents' problems. While their functions diversified, committees became more professional: formerly composed mainly of elderly people concerned with getting a full pension, their employees are now younger, more numerous (between five and nine members per committee, by law), and better qualified – often being graduates of university courses in social work.

Urban renewal has thus led to a transformation in the methods of governing populations. These actually vary with the types of neighbourhoods.[13] The old, privatized *danwei* housing quarters – easily recognizable four-storey concrete buildings – are inhabited by residents who often share the same professional history as former employees of the same factory or administration. Sometimes the first owners have risen up the social ladder and left the premises. Either they have sold, or they rent out to people from outside. The neighbourhood committee plays an important role in the control of the poorest city-dwellers, who might threaten social stability. It distributes basic social essentials and helps in finding employment; it is both an adviser and a protector. In middle-class residences, people enjoy greater autonomy from the state. Being much more mobile, they are harder to control. In addition, some of the functions are de facto privatized, as they have been delegated to the co-owners' unions. In luxury residences, the action of the committees is even more distant.

The residents' committee is also in charge of preventing discontent, now that the city had become a space of struggles. In this regard, the aim of President Hu Jintao's talk of social harmony (*shehui hexie* 社会和谐) referred not so much to the elimination of social conflicts as to their containment. Urban development has provoked resistance everywhere; it is sometimes violent, whether individual or collective. The reasons for protest movements are varied. Residents, often members of the impoverished classes, are less opposed to their expropriation as they are to the conditions in which it takes place: they dispute the amount of compensation received (calculated either on the basis of square metres, or depending on the number of inhabitants registered in the housing) or the place to which they are relocated (most often remote suburbs). Subsidiaries of real-estate developers and local governments are specialized in the management of evictions and rehousing, and they can come down hard on the most recalcitrant residents: there are water and electricity cuts, non-collection of household waste, arson, physical threats by hired thugs. The middle classes, having become owners, are also mobilizing to defend their rights. They sometimes come into conflict with developers or local authorities when the latter replace the promised green open space under their windows with a rubbish incinerator, an industrial plant, a railway line or a highway; the struggles are then conducted in the name of the defence of their threatened property or the right to live in a decent environment, where the air is breathable and noise pollution is limited. Another source of anxiety is the decline in the value of an asset in which a lifetime's savings are invested; in the case of a couple where each partner is an only child, it is not only two people who have raised funds, but sometimes four (the couple and the parents of the father) or even six (the couple, the parents and the in-laws). Another recurring reason for protest is dissatisfaction with property management companies, accused of defending their own interests and not those of the co-owners. When action becomes collective, it involves the creation of associations – often in competition with those set up by these companies – and the use of social networks to disseminate testimonials and slogans. Locally, the younger generations of white-collar workers have also come together to oppose the soaring prices that make home-ownership in the city centre inaccessible even to a couple of two employees. However, the expression of discontent against local officials and management associations is not necessarily a challenge to the state. Conducting their actions in the name of legality or morality, the owners of the reconstructed cities are also intent on fighting against corruption, prevarication and the incompetence of local officials and private actors.

In the context of the new urban society, city-dwellers are more autonomous than before. However, it is difficult to conclude that the state has withdrawn. It has merely transformed its modes of governance. It has also emerged strengthened because it is the primary financial and political beneficiary of the process. Much of the wealth created by land development has fallen into the hands of local governments through the sale of building rights or public or parastatal real estate companies. The modernization of cities covered with highways, skyscrapers, gleaming – even if sometimes empty – shopping malls, where bright lights decorate the proud skylines at night, is also an immense source of legitimacy for the government.[14] Chinese tourists and tourists from all over the world come to admire this urban miracle. The destruction and reconstruction of cities has taken place without any revolution; however, one major problem remains to be resolved: that of the integration of populations from the countryside.

New rural issues

The countryside, especially near large coastal towns, has benefited greatly from the first decade of reform. In the context of farms that are once more family-owned, the shift from cereal crops to cash crops (vegetables, fruit trees, peanuts, beets, oil crops, etc.) ensures outlets in urban markets and a rapid increase in income. The other major transformation is the rapid development of a rural industry which employs surplus labour. Between 1978 and 1984, rural income increased at an exceptionally high rate (+14.2 per cent per year). It is in the countryside that the first 'nouveaux riches' made an appearance, indulging in lavish – and unproductive – spending at weddings or funerals, attracting criticism from the authorities. However, by the middle of the following decade, the gap widened between peasant income and urban income. In 1978, on the cusp of reforms, the gap was 1 to 2.5; it was reduced to 1 to 1.7 in 1984, but in 2007 it was 1 to 3.3. The average annual urban income was therefore about three times higher than the average annual rural income. In addition, this ratio was far from the reality if we take into account the greater social benefits granted in cities, and also regional variations. The situation varies with the nature and productivity of agricultural activities, the presence or absence of rural industry and the proximity or lack of it to large industrial and urban centres.

Indeed, while in 1985 these non-agricultural incomes constituted a third of rural incomes, after decollectivization, they have since the early 2000s amounted to more than half. Almost all Chinese farms now have non-agricultural sources of income that are essential to them: the husband works in the small factory in the township, the son has gone to town to work in the construction industry, the daughter to a textile factory in Guangdong or elsewhere, while the wife does outsourced work on a machine installed in the house. Agriculture helps people to subsist, but not to escape from poverty.

The 'three nong'

In the mid-2000s, a debate began on rural issues. In 2004, for the sixth time since 1982, and the first since 1987, the first political document published at the beginning of each year by the Party was devoted to rural issues. Entitled 'the point of view of the central government and the Communist Party on a policy likely to increase the peasants' incomes', it directly addressed the problem of the insufficiency of the incomes that rural people derived from agricultural activity, while mentioning growing inequalities, sources of tension and the necessary continuation of political reforms. This was the first time that the rural question had been mentioned in its three dimensions: economic (*nongye* 农业, agriculture), social (*nongmin* 农民, the peasants) and political (*nongcun* 农村, the villages). The challenge lay in simultaneously increasing the incomes of the peasants, ensuring the stability of society and improving their participation in political life.

For a long time, the Chinese state took more from farmers than it gave them. A large part of these levies took the form of the obligation for peasants to deliver quotas of grains (mainly wheat and rice) paid at low administrative prices. After decollectivization and the establishment in 1985 of a 'double rail' (administered prices for quotas and market prices for non-quotas), this indirect levy continued until 1996, the prices of quotas being lower than the market price. Market liberalization was completed with the total abolition of quotas in 2004. But the 'peasant burden' (*nongmin fudan* 农民负担) was then largely fiscal. While city-dwellers paid taxes only on incomes above a certain level (state resources came mainly from businesses), benefited from almost free education up to secondary school and enjoyed adequate social coverage, peasants were overwhelmed by the levies that represented more than 10 per cent of their net income.[15] In addition to the tax on agricultural production, there were taxes paid directly to the district and township, fuelling the bloated bureaucracy. It was also the peasants who paid primary and secondary school teachers. In the early 2000s, schooling cost 150 yuan per semester per pupil in primary school, and up to 450 yuan in middle school, from a very low monetary peasant income. Finally, there were the deductions intended for villages, with the money often going into the pockets of cadres. Collecting these levies was a difficult task, sometimes accompanied by the use of force, with peasants being physically abused and even beaten to death.

In the early 2000s, the debate on rural issues spread beyond the circles of politicians and experts through several publications aimed at the general public, including *I Will Tell the Premier the Truth* by Li Changping[16] and *China Along the Yellow River* by Cao Jinqing.[17] Following these, the *Report on Chinese Peasants*, by the writer Chen Guidi and his wife Chun Tao,[18] sold hundreds of thousands of copies, and had a big impact. The two authors investigated the countryside of the poor province of Anhui, where they were born. They denounced the wretched condition of the peasants, not so much in its economic aspects – poverty – as in its social and political dimension: how the peasants are victims of the exactions of the local representatives of power. In four cases, a detailed description was given of the exploitation to which the peasants were subjected by local officials, heads of villages or districts. The authors related how the peasants lodged complaints with higher administrative bodies, in vain. In some cases, the police were mobilized to crack down on complainants, sometimes physically molesting them or throwing them in jail. The authors refer to the case of a peasant who went to Beijing where his complaint was duly filed and registered; back in his village, he was beaten by the police, locked up and tortured to death. The authors also relate violent clashes within villages, for example when a village head mobilized all his relatives to physically suppress villagers protesting against his decisions. One of these clashes resulted in several deaths within just a few minutes.

The main reason for the peasants' complaints was the countless deductions made from their income. The heads of villages demanded that peasants pay one tax one month, and yet another a few months later. If the peasants refused, the taxes were increased. According to the central government, moreover, ninety-three separate levies were made on the peasants to finance the construction of roads, schools, family planning, radio broadcasts, the financing of a local cinema or the activities of the Communist Party.

The book was not just negative, also reporting cases of reformist cadres duly noting problems, writing letters to the provincial and central government, and making positive proposals for reform. The Central Complaints Office in Beijing was given a positive report. The main obstacle to improving the situation of the peasants seemed to lie with the provincial authorities, which were tempted to conceal the realities on the ground from the central government. The mode of government was criticized – the 'symbolic and superficial measures' which, for example, obliged each village to equip itself with a school at the expense of the peasants without taking into consideration the reality of their needs.

The question was basically one of understanding why, after fifty years of a socialist system, the peasants were still living in a state of great poverty and why their status was still so unfavourable compared to the urban population. These publications helped to make urbanites aware of the reality of the peasant condition.

Collective action in the countryside

Faced with these abuses, rural people protested, sometimes mobilizing tens of thousands of people.[19] The publication by the Chinese authorities of figures relating to class actions has suggested that, over recent decades, they have become both more numerous and more regular. Not only are such episodes becoming more frequent, but they involve a growing number of people. In some cases, several hundred people, or even several thousand, are mobilized. In 2000, for example, in the province of Jiangxi, 20,000 peasants mobilized against the imposition of a new tax and ransacked the seat of a local government. These actions took a variety of forms: collective petitions filed with the Bureau of Letters and Visits, demonstrations on the public highway, sieges of local government headquarters, attacks on administrative buildings, the destruction of police vehicles, and the closure of roads, railway lines and bridges. Peasants very frequently referred to the rhetoric of the authorities and used the very words of the regime, mentioning the defence of their 'legal rights and interests' (*hefa quanyi* 合法权益).

Using the typology established by historian Charles Tilly, observers distinguish between 'competitive' claims, which consist in demanding resources available to others in society, 'reactive' claims, which consist in defending rights or privileges (most often against state agents), and 'proactive' claims, which consist in demanding new rights that they do not as yet possess. Competitive claims were very common in the Chinese countryside before 1949. Villages fought each other over access to a hydraulic resource – a river, a lake – over land to be worked or over control of a market. In contrast to social conflict, this was a private war between communities of a similar and heterogeneous social structure. This type of conflict re-emerged between people's communes or between brigades within the framework of people's communes, and continued with the return to family-based working of the land; peasants argued over the borders of their property, or over hydraulic or forest resources.

At the root of most conflicts lay reactive demands – actions against irregular taxes levied by officials, the arbitrary exercise of power, or corruption, as well as struggles against land requisitions without compensation (common in the neighbourhood of cities). The protests were not directed at the central government, but at the level immediately above that of the village, which was called upon to right the wrongs of local officials.

This was the case during the mobilization of the inhabitants of Taishi in 2005. For six months, the action of the inhabitants of this village of 2,000 inhabitants, located forty-five minutes south of Canton, in the rich province of Guangdong, symbolized the demands made by Chinese peasants. The episode began just after the re-election of the village head – who was also Party Secretary – retrospectively accused of irregularities, mismanagement and embezzlement of community funds. Villagers repeatedly confronted police as they attempted to stop the illegal construction of factories on farmland. On 29 July 2005, after discussions and consultations with Chinese activists and intellectuals specializing in the protection of the rights of rural populations, the inhabitants of Taishi launched a campaign aimed at removing Chen by popular vote, as permitted by law. They demanded that the local authorities implement the procedure for the dismissal of the village head following a petition signed by more than 500 inhabitants.

During one demonstration, several villagers were arrested, triggering a hunger strike by some of them outside a government office to demand the release and the removal of the village head. At the same time, the villagers set up an uninterrupted guard of the offices where the accounts of the village were kept in order to prevent the theft or the disappearance of evidence that would prove the official's guilt. The villagers organized a rotation of strikers, with several dozen protestors going in daily to continue the strike despite the police's attempts to control them. After twelve days of sit-ins, the local authorities decided to follow up on the petition and, as provided by law, to elect a committee of seven people empowered to rule on the dismissal of the village head.

When the villagers seemed on the verge of winning their case, in the middle of September, more than 1,000 police officers with riot gear entered the village, seized accounts and arrested dozens of protesters. There were then multiple acts of violence against Chinese and foreign activists and journalists who had come to cover the event at the request of the protest leaders. Access to the village became almost impossible, with local authorities calling in groups of thugs to physically attack those who sought to make contact with the villagers and threaten the residents who were seeking to continue the fight or communicate with journalists. On 28 September, the villagers of Taishi officially abandoned their request for the removal of the village head in a letter signed by more than 1,000 people. At the same time and for the same reasons, the seven elected members of the dismissal committee resigned and were replaced by the seven members previously proposed by the authorities. Unsurprisingly, local authorities stated on 30 September that no evidence of embezzlement or misappropriation could be found against the village head. This revolt, like others, demonstrates how the Chinese countryside had become politicized and shows how local authorities could react: with radical repression and the sidelining of observers. One of the risks was indeed that such an episode might be repeated elsewhere; if the people of Taishi had won their case, many villages in the province would have been encouraged to do the same.

Not many analysts argue that protests of the proactive type occur in rural China. In the best of cases, in the most prosperous villages, where industrialization is very advanced, villagers require elected officials to be truly accountable to the community, demand the rule of law and the opportunity to make their voices heard in such a way that they can manage their own affairs. The authorities tolerate such movements as long as they attack only the local authorities and do not question the regime. For Lucien Bianco, the rise in protests is explained in large part by the lower effectiveness of social control compared to what it was in Mao Zedong's time, and by less severe repression – but it is still the regime 'that essentially determines the forms and the intensity of the protest'.[20]

New rural policies

Faced with the growing number of peasant protests, the authorities recognized the emergence of the 'three rural problems' and initiated a new rural development policy. In 2004, an ambitious tax reform was launched. It was announced that the tax on agricultural activity, which was a function of both the area cultivated and the amount of the harvest in value, should decrease. In 2006, this 5 per cent tax was finally abolished. In the spring of the same year, the National People's Congress formally approved the policy of building 'new socialist countrysides' (*shehui zhuyi xin nongcun* 社会主义新农村). This aimed not only to increase rural incomes but also to improve access to education, to extend the new rural cooperative medical system launched in 2003, and to set up a minimum allowance system for the unemployed rural workforce. The goal was also to reshape the countryside by moving populations from the most remote and poorest villages to new villages built in district capitals, along new road transport infrastructures. Between 2007 and 2012, central government spending on agriculture, welfare of peasants and development of rural areas increased by 23.5 per cent per year.[21]

However, the basic problem lay in the differences in the state's treatment of rural and urban areas. The *hukou* system had become much more flexible: peasants could go into the cities and find work there. But their agricultural status did not allow them to send their children to urban schools, while they generally had little or no access to the social services available to urbanites. So far, the authorities' announcements on possible reforms to the population registration system do not seem to have been followed up. Admittedly, locally, in small towns, migrants can officially settle permanently and change *hukou*, but at least in the interior provinces, the chance of any major new employment is small. In some large cities, special programmes, co-organized by the provinces from which the migrants come, facilitate their integration, but these are limited and there is still no question of giving all rural-dwellers access to the full range of urban services.

Despite the greater flexibility, the authorities have still not taken the step of suppressing the *hukou*. Admittedly, more and more reforming voices have risen in recent years to demand a more rational movement of individuals. In March 2010, for example, more than a dozen media outlets simultaneously published the same editorial: they underlined the contradiction between the constitutional text of the People's Republic, which proclaims the equality of all citizens, and the discrepancy in mobility rights available to rural- and urban-dwellers. According to the most radical reformers, territorial inequalities make the reform of the residence permit system urgent. The transfer of surplus peasant labour from the countryside to the cities would boost the rural economy, allowing new concentrations of land while providing additional labour for urban development. For these supporters of reform, it is now essential that obtaining privileges reserved only for city-dwellers should no longer be subject to residence conditions. This point of view, however, continues to clash with that of the conservatives: for the latter, a massive influx of rural population into urban areas would widen the already significant gap between a developed eastern region and the disadvantaged central and western regions; above all, it would also lead to the emergence of an urban proletariat which, having sold its agricultural land, could no longer return to its villages in the event of a crisis. For conservatives, the *hukou* system remains an essential tool allowing the state to regulate the size of the urban population whose middle classes, the main beneficiaries of the reforms, constitute the regime's main support.

Lifting administrative restrictions and integrating migrant families into cities would require providing funds for the education, health and housing of newcomers, while most urban-dwellers are unwilling to share their privileges. So it is still the peasants who have to bear the brunt of the social costs of maintaining the immigrant labour force working in the cities. And the possibility for migrants to return to their village of origin and to own arable land there constitutes their main social insurance in the event of an economic slowdown in the cities. If the wages of migrant workers have been kept so low for so long – until the 2010 workers' mobilizations – this is because it is not intended to allow the reproduction of the labour force, the cost of which is borne by rural villages. It is the rural communities that are supposed, even when they cannot afford it, to deliver the services that urban areas do not provide to migrants: housing, education, health. As Pun Ngai puts it, production is carried out in urban areas and reproduction in the countryside.[22] How else can one explain the differences in income between migrant workers and urban workers? A survey shows that, in 2011, migrant workers born after 1980 earned an average monthly salary 40 per cent lower than that of workers with permanent resident permits. Under these conditions, if we are to use Marxist vocabulary, it is the society and the rural economy of the interior provinces that can be said to ensure the reproduction of the cheap migrant labour exploited by the capitalist coastal areas. While this situation has long benefited the growth of the economy as a whole, it is not sustainable over time. Indeed, growth cannot do without an internal market whose rural component is essential. The city/countryside divide, and the unenviable fate of both migrants and peasants who have remained in the countryside, are the source of social tensions threatening the very stability of the regime.

Conclusion

Urbanization is one of the main priorities of the Chinese authorities. The goal is to achieve an urbanization rate of 70 per cent by 2025, which will correspond to 900 million people. The spontaneous or controlled transfer of millions of rural people to cities is therefore a major challenge. The constitutional text of the People's Republic proclaims the equality of all before the law. However, in practice, the Maoist regime had established a society of statuses. Unlike national and universal citizenship, citizenship under Mao was 'local, layered, and functional'.[23] With the reforms, the two-speed society characteristic of the previous period now comprises three groups: rural, urban and migrant. The latter number 285 million and often constitute one-third or more of the population of the largest cities. Their integration into the city is only partial because they remain second-class citizens whose condition is inferior in terms of access to employment, housing and education for the simple reason that they were born in a town. They are the modern variant of the reserve army of workers identified by Marx.

Thus, the reforms have not called into question this conception of citizenship. However, they have brought about the emergence of a society where relationships between individuals and with institutions are regulated by contracts that recognize the rights of individuals. Citizens seize on this fact, and mobilize. We are thus witnessing the beginnings of a politicization of the countryside, though the resistance movements do not question the regime as such. An alliance with the urban movements also seems improbable, because the townspeople despise the country folk. The construction of a society where citizenship is universal risks remaining a piece of wishful thinking as long as migrants and their families cannot settle permanently and integrate into cities.

NINE

Populations: The Modernization of Society

One of the ambitions of all reformers since the beginning of the twentieth century has been the modernization of society. Indeed, China's backwardness vis-à-vis the imperialist powers and its weakness in the face of their economic and territorial demands have often been blamed on social structures that slow down transformation; too much respect for elders, inequality between men and women, and the low degree of autonomy of individuals within families are all evils that have been denounced. The 1919 May Fourth movement was a moment of crystallization in the aspiration for modernity embodied in Western science and democracy, and in the denunciation of tradition. 'Down with the Confucian store!' is one of the slogans of those who hold Confucianism responsible for the country's backwardness.

From this point of view, once it had come to power, the socialist regime fitted in with the hopes nursed by many intellectuals for half a century. The forms of family and conjugal life had already evolved considerably in the most advanced Chinese metropolises during the first half of the twentieth century. The measures taken by the Communist government after 1949 aimed to spread these developments throughout the country. Later, in the 1970s, the government initiated a policy of birth control unparalleled in modern history. In doing so, it intruded into the most intimate sphere of citizens' lives. However, the capacity of the regime in its totalitarian Maoist version to transform society is debatable. An alternative hypothesis is to consider that Chinese society resisted the injunctions of political power. Since 1978, by loosening its control, leaving more autonomy to individuals and families, and under the effect of a generalized process of opening up to market forces, the authorities have enabled major transformations to take place.

This chapter examines these changes, whether they have been the result of utopian Maoist ambitions to build a new kind of human being and a new society or stem from more spontaneous dynamics, driven from below. I look first at demographic issues – the size of the population and its development, given the birth control measures in force. I then discuss the construction of social policies which aim to protect populations against illness, unemployment and retirement. I end with an analysis of family forms and the rise of individualism.

Counting the population, controlling the demographics

With a population of 1.411 billion in 2020, or nearly 20 per cent of the world's population, China is the most populous country in the world. If the mass of the population looked like an asset during the Maoist era, it has been seen for the past four decades as a constraint. Efforts to rapidly reduce the birth rate have significantly slowed down the rate of population growth, but have entailed alarming consequences: the imbalance between men and women, the ageing of the population.

Demographic transition

The rapid growth of the population is evidenced by successive censuses (1953, 1964, 1982, 1990, 2000 and 2010); China had 583 million inhabitants in 1953, 649 million in 1957, 830 million in 1970, 1.008 billion in 1982, 1.133 billion in 1990, 1.265 billion in 2000 and 1.411 billion in 2020. The Chinese population is expected to peak in about 2050, at around 1.450 billion, when it will be overtaken by the Indian population.

The birth rate remained very high in the 1950s and 1960s (more than 35 per thousand), with a major drop in the early 1960s. There was then a sharp decline in the 1970s (from 33 in 1970 to 18 in 1980). Since the early 2000s, it has been around 12 per thousand. The mortality rate fell rapidly in the 1950s (20 per thousand in 1949, 10.1 per thousand in 1957) but there was an exceptional peak in mortality between 1958 and 1961 (25 per thousand in 1960). Then there was a resumption of the downward curve which stabilized at a low level (7 per thousand) in the 1970s and has remained at this level until today. These declines in birth rates and mortality correspond to a classic pattern of demographic transition with Chinese specificities. The demographic drop in 1958–61 was temporary and corresponded to the crisis caused by the famine following the Great Leap Forward: it resulted in a peak in mortality interrupting the regular decline in the previous decade, and a strong deficit in births. Once the country had caught up, marked by a vigorous birth rate in 1963–64, the authorities stepped up family planning efforts – promoting families with two children, raising the legal age of marriage – resulting in a slowdown in population growth. Fertility, very high in the 1950s and 1960s – six children per woman, except during the famine crisis – fell rapidly in the 1970s and dropped below the reproduction threshold (2.1 children per woman) at the start of the 1990s. From 1995 until today, it has been close to 1.5 or 1.6, at a lower level than that of France (two children per woman in 2015). China seems to have come close to the final stage of the demographic transition; we are witnessing, especially in the big cities, patterns of behaviour mirroring those in Europe and Japan. The speed of this demographic transition varies from region to region. By 1975, Shanghai and Beijing had fallen below the generation renewal threshold, a level that was not reached by China as a whole until 2000. The decline in fertility happened earlier in prosperous coastal urban areas and later spread to poor rural areas in the west of the country.[1]

The pragmatism of Maoist population policies

In 1949, the demographic situation did not alarm the authorities. Marxist orthodoxy rejected any idea of Malthusian politics; Malthusianism was an 'anti-proletarian bourgeois ideology', and poverty was bound to disappear with the defects of the existing social order. The priority was to fight against mortality, which was declining sharply thanks to a variety of initiatives: the dissemination of preventive medicine, systematic vaccination campaigns (against typhoid, smallpox, measles and tuberculosis), the fight against rats and the plague they carried, and sanitary measures to control parasitic diseases (cholera, malaria). This decline in mortality was nevertheless coupled with a high birth rate, which led to a rapid increase in the population, estimated at 2 per cent per year in the 1953 census. This established the population at 583 million – alerting the authorities to the demographic issue.

In the first Five-Year Plan, a birth control research committee headed by demographer Ma Yinchu, rector of Peking University, was established. In 1955, the government launched a campaign for birth control. 'With the exception of areas inhabited by national minorities', declared Mao

Zedong in January 1956, 'there is a need to publicize and popularize fertility control and promote birth control in all densely populated areas.' Sterilization and voluntary termination of pregnancy then become available to women. In 1957, a major anti-birth campaign – with mass meetings and the distribution of contraceptive material – was organized. But this came to a halt in 1958 with the launch of the Great Leap Forward. The argument now was that China was lacking manpower. Ma Yinchu was dismissed from his post and then placed under house arrest. The consequences were dire. Excess mortality has been estimated at between 20 and 50 million people – more, in the view of some authors. Births were declining, and then caught up in 1963–64.

In the period that followed, the authorities did not formulate an openly anti-birth policy, but several initiatives were taken in this direction. In 1964, the State Council established the Commission for Family Planning (*jihua shengyu weiyuanhui* 计划生育委员会). The manufacture of contraceptive pills and the dissemination of propaganda to encourage their use also began. The legal age of marriage was raised to 20, and propaganda urged people to wait longer, with the aim of reducing the number of fertile years. The Cultural Revolution constituted an exceptional moment of sexual freedom, in a morally prudent society where social control was strong; the result was an increase in births.

The real turning point came in the 1970s when the objective was clearly to restrict births. For the first time, quantified objectives were formulated. In 1971, there was talk of reducing demographic growth from 2.5 per cent in 1970 to 1 per cent in the towns and 1.5 per cent in the countryside; in 1975, the objectives were reduced to 0.6 per cent and 1 per cent. In terms of procreation, the norm was now summed up by the slogan: *wan, xi, shao* (晚、稀、少 late, spaced, few). New efforts were made to raise the age at marriage: 25 for women and 27 for men in towns, 23 and 25 in the countryside. An interval of four years was required between two births. Finally, the number of children was limited to two in cities and three in rural areas, with penalties for those who violated this injunction. A veritable birth control bureaucracy was thereupon set up; its staff was in charge of monitoring women in each people's commune, village, work unit or urban district. These family planning officials recorded information about each woman: births, contraceptive use and her menstrual cycle. Birth quotas were allocated and only a couple who had received permission could embark on conceiving a child. For births outside the quota, families were threatened with not being able to register their child – depriving them of access to education or ration tickets. The authorities also resorted massively to surgical interventions: between 1971 and 1973, the number of female sterilizations increased by 70 per cent, to 2.95 million women, and abortions rose by 30 per cent, to 5.11 million.

As a result of this drastic policy, in the 1970s China experienced the fastest decline in the fertility rate in human history. This slumped from 5.9 children per woman in 1970 to 2.7 in 1979; simultaneously, the birth rate fell from 33 to 18 per thousand.

The one-child policy

On coming to power in 1978, Deng Xiaoping launched his reforms. A year later, the 'family planning policy' (*jihua shengyu zhengce* 计划生育政策) became the one-child policy (*dusheng zinü zhengce* 独生子女政策). Its rationale is clearly economic: if population growth was not contained by vigorous measures, the country's future was in jeopardy. The new policy aimed to accelerate development. As the population approached 1 billion, the goal was to not exceed 1.2 billion by the year 2000.

The theorist of the one-child policy was a military engineer, Song Jian, influenced by the theme of degrowth popularized by the Club of Rome. According to the official version, the decision was taken by the highest political leaders, and scientists played only a secondary role. Studying the genealogy of this public policy, Susan Greenhalgh has shown the conditions in which the position of military engineers prevailed over that of social scientists – who could nevertheless see other means of achieving the quantitative objective set.[2] The former viewed the size of the population to be an essentially biological issue, urgent enough to be resolved by coercive measures; they belonged to the country's elite and were listened to by politicians. Social scientists, demographers included, were politically more fragile, less frequently listened to, and had been weakened by repressive policies against intellectuals over the previous two decades.

The new measures set the target of one child per couple, with the exception of national minorities. To promote single-child families, bonuses were granted and sanctions imposed. Couples who respected the imperative benefited from a whole series of advantages: priority access to housing, supplementary food rations, reductions in public transport and bonuses. Couples who agreed to sterilization received a premium. The birth of a second child led to the elimination of these benefits and from the third child onwards – the second in some provinces – sanctions were imposed: reductions in wages and in the number of coupons for rationed foodstuffs. The use of coercion was reinforced, in particular in 1983, a year in which there were more than 14 million abortions and more than 20 million sterilizations.

However, the situations varied between different provinces and municipalities, as it was up to the local authorities to implement this policy. Before long, due to people's reluctance to accept it, the programme was relaxed. In 1984, rural families were allowed to have a second child if the first was a girl, while controls were tightened in the larger towns. In 2002, the first law on population and family planning replaced all local regulations and specified which categories of population were allowed to have two, or even three, children – the case of regions with national minorities or employees in dangerous sectors. In the 2000s, the policy concerned only big cities, that is to say one-third of the population. The list of exceptions was so great that it was now difficult to speak of a national policy. From the start, in 1979, couples where each partner was an only child were allowed to have two children. At the end of 2013, this possibility was extended to couples where only one of the two partners was an only child. Since 2016, any couple has been allowed to have two children.

The result of this draconian policy was a rapid decline in fertility and family size. According to the official version, there was a shortfall of 400 million births. The fertility rate fell from 2.29 children per woman in 1980 to 1.6 in 2015, well below the replacement rate of 2.1. The situations were in fact contrasted. In towns and cities, the penalties for exceeding the limit were very dissuasive and the results were satisfactory. In Shanghai, the birth rate fell to 13 per thousand in 1990, and 4 per thousand in 2001. The fertility rate there was 0.7 in 2016, among the lowest in the world; the overwhelming majority of children were only children. In the countryside, success was much more mixed because it was usual to have two children, as the return to family farming of agricultural land had encouraged peasants to promote births, as more children meant a bigger labour force in the fields. This draconian policy was also at the origin of two major problems: the demographic imbalance between men and women on the one hand, and the accelerated ageing of the population on the other.

Harmful consequences of the one-child policy

The issue of the imbalance between male and female births – the normal biological rate is 103–107 boys for every 100 girls – was neither new nor unique to China. We find the same imbalance before 1949, or today in Taiwan, India and Korea, albeit in lesser proportions. In 1980, the rate was already over 108 boys for every 100 girls. In 1990, this ratio rose to 113 in 1990, then nearly 120 in 2000. The maximum rate was reached in 2008, with 123 boys; it has been just above 110 for several years – a result of the one-child policy, the use of technologies to identify the sex of the child during pregnancy, and the selection of the child's sex by infanticide.

The reason for this is the preference of families for male births, the tradition requiring that they have at least one son. Indeed, in the absence of a national pension or social security system for the elderly in rural areas, it is the son who economically supports his elderly parents. For families whose only child is a girl, the one-child policy means the risk of impoverishment in their old age.

To deal with this situation, initiatives have been taken. In 1986, abortion based on the desire to select the child's sex was banned; this ban was repeated in 2002, in the Population and Family Planning Act. Propaganda campaigns were carried out. Cadres in villages where the imbalance in births had not been resolved were punished. The key issue, however, is not the one-child policy per se, but the economic, social and political conditions that make having a girl as an only child unacceptable.

As a result of the sex ratio imbalance, there are not enough women in rural areas for men in search of a marriage partner, which should encourage an exodus to the cities. As of now, we are seeing long-distance marital migration, trafficking of young girls, and the development of migration channels of girls from Vietnam to fill the gap.

The other negative consequence of the one-child policy is the rapid ageing of the population. In 1980, China was a country dominated by a young population; only 5 per cent of the population was over 65. In 2010, this proportion rose to 8 per cent and it was higher than 10 per cent in 2016. It might rise to 20 per cent by 2030 and to more than 30 per cent in 2050. The phenomenon is not unique – Japan, Germany, Italy are experiencing it too – but China is going to be old before it gets rich. The problem is twofold. On the one hand, China does not have the pension system and social insurance programmes that would support these populations, and the country is therefore not ready for this influx of elderly people. In the countryside, the elderly have to count on family solidarity; however, changes in society have under-mined traditional support for the elderly by their families. Migration to the developed coasts drives sons away from their parents, while women's entry into the labour market limits their availability to care for the elderly. On the other hand, this ageing could also upset the model of economic development. In the 2030s and 2040s, China will lack the manpower to meet the needs of the many elderly people and finance their retirement.

As a consequence of this worrying situation for the future, the one-child policy ended on 1 January 2016. Since that date, all married couples have been allowed to have a second child, while restrictions on additional births remain. This decision, sometimes presented as a gesture of political power relaxing its control over the privacy of citizens, is in fact an economic and social imperative. Between the 1980s and the end of the 2000s, the country enjoyed an extremely favourable demographic structure: the proportion of the working population – those aged between 15 and 59 – was exceptionally high. It has since reached 70 per cent of the total population. But this proportion is starting to decrease and the number of old people will increase; and because in the lower birth rate, the adult population will decrease. All observers believe that the permission granted to all couples to have two children should not lead to a rise in fertility because of the considerable burden that this represents, due to the absence of collective care in early childhood, the high tuition fees from kindergarten to University, and even the costs of access to care.

In the end, it is important to stress that, contrary to popular belief, Mao Zedong did not always oppose the control of population growth and that the decrease in births is not the consequence of the one-child policy. It was the result of an earlier strategy carried out in the 1970s which consisted of raising the age of marriage and spacing out births. The most significant decline in fertility dates from the 1970s, during which massive sterilization campaigns were deployed. In the following decades, the transformation of economic and social conditions also clearly contributed greatly to the decrease in births, as happened spontaneously in Japan, Korea and Taiwan earlier. These elements obviously call into question the need for a social engineering project that has been found rarely in the history of mankind and which has had disastrous consequences.[3]

Still, the success achieved by a stabilization of the birth rate and an increase in wealth per capita justified the Party's policies for most people. In the majority of cases, the state has succeeded in gaining acceptance for a policy closely related to individual choice without resorting to violence or physical coercion. In the cities at least, this policy, although radical, has been accepted as a solution to the problems of population growth and underdevelopment. Moreover, in the 1980s, the regime's ability to control the population became one of the pillars of its legitimacy. In the cities, the choice to limit births gradually became largely voluntary. For Susan Greenhalgh, the state has thus been able to abandon the micro-management of population issues in order to institutionalize a framework within which it is the individuals themselves who decide to limit the number of their offspring. The evolution of the one-child policy thus becomes the most striking example of the shift from Leninist management to a neoliberal management of population issues.[4]

Protecting the population: social policies

The People's Republic was founded on the promise of a better future for its citizens. The construction of socialism therefore logically requires the establishment of social policies that protect populations against the risks of illness, accidents and even retirement. In this area, an almost complete system of protection was developed during the Maoist period. The reforms involved its dismantling and the transition to a market logic. While a large part of the population was no longer covered, the state relaunched the project of generalized care at the turn of the twenty-first century.

The Maoist period: protection for those who work

In socialist China, the construction of a welfare system is the result neither of social struggles nor of corporate traditions; it was initiated by the Party-State within the framework of the realization of socialism. Its benefits are linked to work. Priority is given to aid and subsidies in kind to ensure the well-being of the urban population (10 per cent of the total population) and the rural population (90 per cent).

Although not part of welfare strictly speaking, price subsidies on certain commodities and food aid constitute a central mechanism of redistribution. They represent an important proportion of household income both in the countryside and in the city. In cities, the work unit distributes ration tickets (*bupiao* 补票) to its employees, allowing them to buy basic necessities such as oil, flour, eggs, sugar and, sometimes, meat and vegetables at low prices, as well as obtaining grain rations or fabric for making clothes. Luxury goods (watches, bicycles, sewing machines) also require purchase coupons. In the countryside, state subsidies take the form of distribution of fertilizers and guaranteed grain. A minimum level, which varies according to regions and periods, is irregularly distributed; it is most often regions that have suffered from natural disasters that benefit.

Urban people benefit from the 'iron rice bowl': a job for life, a salary that increases with seniority and that is not linked to skills or results, in-kind subsidies and access to the social services of the work unit. The socio-professional insurance introduced in 1951 by the labour law covers the risks of sickness, retirement, invalidity, work accidents and maternity. Only urban workers belonging to a state-owned enterprise or a large collective business (with more than 100 employees), as well as civil servants and the military, are eligible. People who do not belong to any *danwei* are covered by welfare. Not all risks are uniformly covered and situations vary by region and period. Urban workers benefit from a state-funded pension. The retirement age is set at 60 for men and 50 for women, but it differs according to the sector of activity, depending on the difficulty and risks involved.

In rural areas, in the 1960s and 1970s, one of Maoism's main contributions to the protection of populations was the establishment of a health system. Care was provided by paramedical staff, the so-called 'barefoot doctors' (*chijiao yisheng* 赤脚医生). Chosen from among the peasants, they were given basic medical training and then placed in charge of preventive activities and delivering essential care. The medical course that they followed lasted a few months – much shorter than the normal medical training – and focused on preventive acts and rudimentary care; it was then followed by an internship, which consisted of working with an experienced doctor in the countryside, as a locum in a hospital, or following courses in a university hospital. Often applicants had already received training in traditional Chinese medicine in a family setting, or from older doctors. After their training in local medical schools or hospitals, they returned to work in their villages. Strictly speaking, they were not doctors but personnel trained to identify and treat a number of diseases. They continued to participate in productive work, and their income was increased by 10 per cent compared to other members of the production brigades. This system guaranteed the rural population access to cheap medical care. In 1975, there were 1.5 million practising barefoot doctors, present in 90 per cent of the villages.

Thanks to them, the health of the Chinese people improved significantly. Together with the improvement of hygiene, water sanitation and the promotion of vaccination, they have played a major role in reducing epidemics, extending life expectancy at birth (35 years in 1949, 44 years in 1960 and 67 years in 1980) and lowering the death rate (25 per 1,000 in 1960 and 6 per thousand in 1980). Much of the progress in public health was de facto made during this period. Since then, the death rate has remained around 6 to 7 per thousand and life expectancy has continued to increase, but at a slower rate (70 years in 1995, 76 years in 2015).

The state's withdrawal after 1978

After 1978, the dismantling of the people's communes and then the questioning of the social functions of work units led to the collapse of the welfare system. The state withdrew massively from health financing. The share of public expenditure in total health expenditure sank to a minimum in 2001 (35 per cent) before rising steadily thereafter (55 per cent in 2014, according to the World Bank). As a result, health establishments need paying patients in order to compensate for the decline in their public resources. A logic of profit has been established, leading to a sharp increase in the price of care. In the course of a few years, there was a shift from a centralized and planned health system to a market-oriented system.

In rural China, 95 per cent of the population was covered by the health insurance system in the late 1970s; this rate was less than 5 per cent by the end of the 1980s. Users now face a health system that is costly and beyond the reach of the poorest; the quality of care it provides has deteriorated sharply. Barefoot doctors are disappearing – the title was officially abolished in 1985. Some doctors moved into private practice, others gave up the practice of medicine. The many collective clinics are either being privatized or disappearing altogether. Village doctors (*xiangcun yisheng* 乡村医生) have become private entrepreneurs, billing according to the care provided. They have moved from prevention and public health work to treatment-oriented work, from basic and inexpensive medical practice to more adequate and expensive medical aid, frequently prescribing intravenous infusions and injections, and sometimes also overprescribing.

This has indeed become one of the major problems of the public health system. By the 1990s, public funding represented only 10 per cent of the total income of hospitals.[5] While the prices of basic medical services remained strictly controlled, permission was given to increase the pricing of more sophisticated examinations (CT or MRI scans) and of certain drugs. To ensure their financial survival, many facilities therefore placed income-generation at the top of their goals and there was strong pressure on physicians to increase hospital incomes by overprescribing tests and medications.

In cities, with the launch of the reforms, companies no longer had to pay for social security. A public social security system was gradually being built, financed by contributions from employers and employees. The hospitals of the largest companies were transformed into public establishments administered by health units. Launched in the mid-1980s, the reform of old-age insurance saw the creation of common funds aimed at unifying the management of pensions for employees of state and collective businesses; this amounted to establishing basic universal coverage for workers in public and private sectors whose funding was shared between the state, companies and employees.

Reconstruction of a welfare system

In the early 2000s, the impossibility of access to healthcare for the most fragile populations – most rural people on the one hand, and urban-dwellers without duly declared paid employment on the other – was becoming a major problem. Inequalities in access to welfare were so glaring that the government resolved to rebuild the public insurance system. Today, the basic social security scheme is defined by the law on social insurance. It came into force on 1 July 2011, and is based on five pillars: old age insurance, unemployment insurance, health insurance, insurance against accidents at work, and maternity insurance. Unemployment insurance, work-related accident insurance and maternity insurance apply only to urban workers and coverage rates are below 50 per cent. Old age insurance and health insurance are intended, in the long term, to cover the entire urban and rural population. In fact, public social spending has risen sharply. All the resources allocated by the public authorities to the pension, social assistance and health sectors reached 9 per cent of GDP by 2012 as against 6 per cent in 2007 – a level that is still well below the average for OECD countries (22 per cent of GDP in 2013).[6] The relatively low level of public social spending explains why households show a strong propensity to save – around a third of the disposable income of urban households, a quarter for rural people.

In terms of health, this urgency is also due to the new threats facing populations: the return of certain infectious diseases; new epidemiological threats such as HIV, SARS and Covid-10; and ageing. In 2003, a new cooperative health system for rural populations was launched. Unlike the old system, mainly financed by rural communities, this one was tripartite, financed by central government, local governments and farmers. It aimed to rationalize the supply of care by transferring demand from higher-level, overburdened hospitals to health structures at the village and county level. Even though membership was voluntary, the system met with rapid and strong support from households. While only 20 per cent of rural people were covered at the end of the 1990s, almost all are now protected. But the system remains rudimentary; programme participants still have to cover 50–60 per cent of their medical costs. In 2009, a new rural pension scheme offered basic insurance to rural residents.

In cities, a growing proportion of workers are now covered against work accidents and maternity, but coverage rates remain low. And the share of urban workers with unemployment insurance stagnated at around 40 per cent in 2012. This is due to the fact that part of the salaried workforce is not declared, so as to avoid having to pay contributions that are deemed too high.

All in all, despite the initiatives taken in the early 2000s to make the welfare system more inclusive, it remains inadequate. Geographically fragmented and disparate, it provides uneven protection to urban- and rural-dwellers. Old age insurance, for example, has four separate schemes, for civil servants, urbanites, the urban unemployed and rural people. Health insurance distinguishes between urban workers and urban and rural residents, and an assistance programme covers the poorest. Levels of contributions and benefits vary greatly between groups. Civil servants receive a pension calculated according to their number of years of service, which can reach 90 per cent of the last salary for employees of public institutions, as against a maximum of 59 per cent for company employees (in 2012), which explains the great variability in retirement pensions. Health insurance covers variable care depending on the programme: all types of care for urban workers, and hospitalization for rural people and urban non-salaried workers.

Health spending is a heavy burden on household budgets and many families fall into poverty or have to borrow from loved ones to meet health costs. The situation of rural retirees is especially difficult. Particularly vulnerable when faced with high health costs, they are very dependent on help from their families. Child support plays a major role and was even the subject of a law in 1996, revised in 2012, which allows parents over 60 to sue their children in the absence of intergenerational support. Migrant workers, because of their precarious status, remain largely excluded from the welfare system.

Geographical inequalities remain. Beijing, a provincial municipality, has five times more hospitals per capita than Guangxi province. In 2011, there were 6.24 beds per 1,000 inhabitants in urban areas and 0.98 in rural areas.[7] Moreover, rights are difficult to transfer. The 2011 social insurance law established such transfer, but many administrative and technical obstacles stand in the way. The same is true of the minimum living allowance established in 1993; there is no national standard but a variable level from city to city, and between urban and rural areas.

The ageing of the population ultimately raises the question of the sustainability of old age and health insurance. One solution would be to delay the current retirement age for employees. The healthcare system must be reorganized in order to take care of patients in long-term care or in a situation of dependency. While the state appeals to private charity through the rapid development of a third sector, households have no other option but to rely on family solidarity. Faced with the inadequate services provided by social insurance programmes, intergenerational assistance continues to play a preponderant role.

The private and intimate sphere

The family, the basic unit of society, is the focus of the Communist government's full attention in its modernizing project. Urbanization and massive migration have, since the 1980s, been accelerating the transformation of the family, as state control loosens. But other imperatives linked to the construction of a capitalist market economy impose themselves on individuals and suggest that the hypothesis of liberalization needs to be questioned.

The family

From the very start, the new regime manifested its intention to modernize the family institution. It did so by passing a new law on marriage on 1 May 1950. It abolished feudal forms of union and enshrined the free choice of the contracting parties, established the principle of equality between men and women, prohibited polygamy, the keeping of concubines, the ban on widows remarrying, and the requirement for gifts when contracting a marriage. Marriage arranged through intermediaries or under pressure from parents became illegal. A new right to divorce was recognized for both partners, as well as a right to alimony. The Party enforced the law by relying on mass campaigns between 1950 and 1953 in which 'despotic' spouses were sentenced in public courts and 'feudal' marriages dissolved. By promoting freedom of choice in these propaganda campaigns, the new law presented itself as a thorough break with Confucianist and patriarchal practices.

However, in doing so, rather than being particularly revolutionary, the Communist Party was continuing debates that had animated the country since the beginning of the twentieth century. All reformers had agreed, especially since the 1919 May Fourth movement, to link the salvation of the Chinese nation to the development of small families, composed of a couple and their children, based on freedom of marriage and the greater economic independence of its members. According to Susan L. Glosser,[8] the primary objective of the marriage law was not actually to raise the status of women. Though Chinese women were legally freed from the yoke of their husbands, this was in order to put them at the service of the socialist project. The law was not intended to strengthen the institution of the family so much as to increase state control over individuals. Integrated into the great revolutionary cause, marriage became a tool for the politicization of bodies, which needed to serve the interests of society as a whole.

In fact, while the power of the head of the family waned, it was replaced by that of the Party, which intervened more and more in personal and family affairs, setting class-based criteria for the choice of spouses and imposing its mediation in the event of marital disagreement. In the 1960s, romantic relationships were subject to strict political supervision. Any marriage was preceded by an investigation into the political backgrounds of the engaged couple in order to make misalliances impossible. A feudal patriarchy had given way to a socialist patriarchy.

Numerous studies have shown that the law did not have a significant effect in rural China where family structures were not fundamentally disrupted. Neil J. Diamant argues, however, that it did transform marital and family relationships during the Maoist period, with sometimes unexpected effects.[9] He relates cases of men and women using the law to justify having multiple sexual partners, obtaining gifts when they got engaged, or divorcing many times. Those best positioned to take advantage of the more liberal dimensions of the law were not the educated urban elites – these were already modernized – but the illiterate rural women who had never heard of gender equality.

The law was amended several times. In 1980, a clause was introduced authorizing divorce on grounds of incompatibility of temperament.

While the legal framework allowed divorce only in cases of extreme abuse or for political reasons, couples were now allowed to divorce without going to court if both parties agreed. This was a clear sign of the decline in the state's hold over the daily lives of its citizens. In 2003, the Ministry of Civil Affairs lifted the requirement for two people wishing to marry or divorce to obtain the consent of their village head or employer. The new regulations simplified both marriage and divorce procedures if there were no property disputes. As a result, the divorce rate grew rapidly. In 1980, the country had fewer than 350,000 divorces; their number increased to 1 million in 1990 and to more than 3.6 million at the start of 2014.

However, marriage remains the social norm. Staying single is not encouraged and living together is usually only a prerequisite for marital union. This is due in part to the fact that the law prohibits births out of wedlock, which exposes offenders to penalties. The nuclear family – parents and their children – therefore remains the basic unit of society. Social norms are nonetheless probably bound to change because of the surplus of men – the number of men reaching marrying age was significantly more numerous than women in the same situation – and a consequent increase in the number of men forced to stay single.

While the nuclear family remains the norm, it has nevertheless undergone notable developments in recent decades. The lack of siblings has meant that attention focuses on the only child – nicknamed the 'little emperor' (*xiao huangdi* 小皇帝) – in urban families.[10] He is the object of the greatest solicitude from his two parents and four grandparents, often being the only small child in the family – hence the nickname '4-2-1' for such families. This explains the importance of the budget devoted to meeting the child's needs – an urban household spends almost half of its income on him: private lessons in addition to his normal schooling, better-quality food, games, travel, etc. It is also a source of psychological pressure and tension for the children themselves. Surrounded by six adults – their two active parents and four retired grandparents – they have little interaction with other children of their age and are under constant adult supervision. Later, they must meet the aspirations of six people when it comes to academic success, professional careers, marital choice and income level.

Another example of the changes concerns forms of filial piety. In the case of a village in Hubei, anthropologist Guo Yuhua studied the conflicts between elderly parents and sons and daughters-in-law.[11] Care of the elderly takes various forms. When the elderly person lives alone, their situation varies depending on the care provided by the son(s). Sometimes, the elderly person moves between the homes of the different married sons. In a third case, the elderly person cohabits with one of his or her married sons, his or her daughter-in-law and his or her grandchildren – especially in the case of an only son. Old people living alone are the most common category. While the moral principle of filial piety would require sons to take care of their elderly parents, Guo Yuhua notes that this support is now conditional. It depends on the behaviour adopted by parents towards their children, and a breach of certain social norms may justify a refusal of support. This is also quantifiable. Members of younger generations place more value on the material aspects of the exchange – that is, they help their parents in proportion to what they received, besides life and education. These transformations do not date from the economic reforms, but go back earlier. After 1949, the penetration of the state into society brought about the collapse of ideological principles as well as of the system of social control represented by kinship groups (as prohibited clan organizations disappeared), and social models formerly in force were modified. Economic reforms merely amplified the changes observed in the first decades of the Communist regime.

Forms of sexuality: a liberation?

Forms of sexuality constitute another space of intimacy that has undergone significant changes. In the Maoist period, only sexuality within the framework of marriage was legitimate. In the first months of the new regime, prostitutes were thrown into jail. A vigorous moral control was gradually established, which was not be relaxed until the exceptional years of the Cultural Revolution. In the early 1970s, the establishment of a family planning policy was accompanied by increased control over bodies.

According to some writers, such as Pan Suiming,[12] since the 1980s China has experienced an unprecedented transformation in sexual morality. Under the impact of Western influences, a restricted sexuality within the limited framework of reproduction gave way to a sexuality freed from this imperative. Conceived until then as primarily utilitarian, sexuality is now primarily motivated by pleasure or love, although the official discourse remains very prudish. This modernization took the form of the adoption of imported standards. Indeed, issues relating to nonmarital forms of sexuality began to gain popularity in print, radio and television broadcasts in the 1990s. Extramarital relations were now a favourite subject of works of fiction – both novels and cinematographic or television works. The advent of the Internet then accelerated the evolution of attitudes and behaviours and there is no doubt that the environment is now more favourable to alternative sexual behaviours. In certain circles, to maintain 'a second wife' (*ernai* 二奶) is essential for a man who seeks to preserve his social status.

The transformation of the economy has been accompanied by a commodification of sexuality. The first sex shops appeared under the guise of selling items officially considered beneficial to the health of their customers. Then, the state relaxed its control over manufacturers and sellers, though only to the extent that they complied with health and economic regulations and the law on pornography. Prostitution has become widespread and places where sexual relations are consumed – discotheques, karaoke bars, massage parlours – are ubiquitous, aimed at a variety of clienteles, whether the migrant working population or businessmen.

However, the hypothesis of a sexual revolution (*xing geming* 性革命) – as if repression had yielded to liberation – is questionable. For Jean-Baptiste Pettier, the current situation does not appear 'as a "liberation" from the state repression of sexuality but as a re-sexualization of the social world, in the context of the liberal economic opening-up and the competition for individual success that it has brought about'.[13] According to Pettier, today we are witnessing an 'opening-up without liberation': there is a greater tolerance with regard to individual practices, but this opening-up in fact remains subject to the framework of generalized capitalist competition, and does not allow an emancipation of individuals or sexes, or a relaxation of the normative framework of gender categories.

Homosexuality is now tolerated

Although widely tolerated in classical China, homosexuality became a criminal act with the advent of the People's Republic in 1949. During the Cultural Revolution, homosexuals were among the 'bad elements', along with landowners, rich peasants, counter-revolutionaries and rightists. Any deviant sexuality, being nonreproductive and different from the monogamous, heterosexual and patriarchal family model promoted by the state as the basis of society, was repressed. In the 1980s and 1990s, homosexuals were still often prosecuted by the police. In 1997, homosexuality was finally legalized and sodomy decriminalized; in 2001, the Chinese Psychiatric Association removed homosexuality from its list of mental illnesses, thus complying with the recommendations of the World Health Organization. In the 2000s, homosexuality became a subject of scholarly studies that were taken up by authors such as Pan Suiming and Li Yinhe. In the context of the spread of the AIDS epidemic, most of this work was inspired by public health issues. However, despite legal changes and increased openness, Chinese homosexuals continued to feel misunderstood and discriminated against. Occasionally, the police continued to harass homosexuals in public gardens, close down bars and saunas or ban demonstrations.

During the 1990s, the Internet and the lesbian, gay, bi and trans (LGBT) movement emerged as key factors that enabled individuals to assert their desires. Despite censorship, it now became possible for online media, discussion networks – QQ, WeChat and Weibo – and blogs where everyone could share their personal experiences to become 'privileged spaces for the representation and discussion of homosexuality'.[14] They were places of information as well as sociability, as the Internet made it possible to put into words and images experiences and discourses on desire that, until then, could not find expression. In addition, due in particular to the role of such bodies in the prevention of AIDS, the state authorized the development of an LGBT movement.

In the big cities – Beijing, Shanghai and Canton – homosexuals from the middle and upper classes acquired new ways of living out their desires and identities that resembled the models invented in Western countries. Their organizations often benefited from the support of their North American counterparts. This population appropriated the identity category of 'homosexual' (*tongxinglian* 同性恋); spaces for socializing, bars and other places of entertainment made gays and lesbians visible in the public spaces of metropolitan areas.

However, only a fraction of China became involved in this globalization of practices and standards. In a survey conducted in Hefei, the capital of the poor province of Anhui, Pierre Miège showed that young homosexuals could not favour an identity based on their sexuality over others based on other social roles.[15] The norms of marriage and kinship – providing one's parents with grandchildren – continued to be the accepted way forward. Of course, there were spaces where these men existed in all their difference – the Internet, sporting and cultural events organized by homosexual associations – but these moments remained fragmentary 'like moving archipelagos, separated by walls from the rest of their lives'. In Hefei, there was no 'homosexual identity' or 'homosexual community'. Social life was lived in different and compartmentalized spaces, and above all there were no stable, structured, protected spaces that were organized or even institutionalized. For these young men, it was not so much sexual orientation that posed a social problem as the fact of not getting married and not having children. This is something you cannot tell your parents.

In another survey, Lucas Monteil focuses on the sexual and emotional relations that develop between old working-class men and young migrant workers, locally designated by the term of 'old-young love' or 'old-young sexuality' (*laoshaolian* 老少恋).[16] In the context of openly negotiated paid-for sex, temporary or long-term relationships, economic exchanges take place between old and young: the former invite the latter to go out, they provide accommodation and help in finding a job, and lend or give them money. Alongside the globalized forms specific to the middle and upper classes, there thus coexist other practices and representations of homosexuality, which are not the expression of a supposedly traditional Chinese culture, but are part of the contemporary transformations of urban society.

Persistent gender inequalities

The changing situation of women in Chinese society invites the same nuanced assessment. In the 1950s, there was a movement to promote equality of spouses within the family. Thanks to the Constitution of 1954, then that of 1982, women enjoyed equal rights with men. However, during the Maoist period, they were not so much freed from the yoke of their fathers and husbands as placed at the service of the Party and the socialist project. In cities, nurseries, kindergartens, nursery and primary schools were built to enable women to participate in the productive effort. However, efforts to collectivize the care of younger children had limited impact, and most children were still in the care of their parents, while women continued to do domestic chores. In the countryside, women – in addition to their full-time employment in the fields – maintained their activity within the household. Due to the insufficiency of available consumer goods – the fabric ration tickets distributed to rural families did not cover their needs – women were not freed from their weaving and spinning tasks.

It seemed as if women were entering productive life on an equal footing; socialist propaganda celebrated model workers, students and scientists. But this participation oscillated with economic cycles. In times of labour shortage, especially during the Great Leap Forward, women were mobilized in large numbers to join the salaried labour force, most of the time in order to free up men for more highly skilled tasks. In times of economic downturn, such as the mid-1950s or early 1960s, state exhortations praised the important role of women as wives and mothers who were confined to home life.

Tang Xiaojing has shown how, in the name of female empowerment, the state actually constructed a subordinate labour market.[17] From 1956, under the system of lifelong employment, women with diplomas or other qualifications obtained statutory or managerial positions. But women without diplomas or technical skills were administratively considered as 'housewives', a category that made it possible for them not to be counted as job-seekers. During the Great Leap Forward, they were mobilized with contractual or temporary statuses. The most onerous tasks were reserved for them and their temporary contracts did not provide them with any protection in the event of illness, pregnancy or maternity. In the 1960s, many women were hired as 'subcontract workers' (*waibao gong* 外包工); their employer was the neighbourhood committee that provided labour to factories that needed it. Behind an egalitarian discourse stigmatizing individual interest and encouraging self-sacrifice for the country, the state – while supposedly promoting equality – actually established a category of precarious female jobs, a veritable under-proletariat.

The Fourth World Conference on Women in Beijing in 1995 marked a milestone in the promotion of women's status. The Chinese authorities set up a first Programme for the Development of Women (1995–2000) with the objectives of promoting equality between spouses; fighting against domestic violence, trafficking in women and prostitution; and increasing women's political participation and their representation in government bodies. A second programme extended this initiative in the decade 2000–10. Chinese women now have, in theory, the same rights as men in all areas of life, political, economic, cultural and social. Yet, despite these initiatives, the goal of gender equality has not been met. Gender inequalities remain, particularly in access to education, employment and health, but also in terms of inheritance, wages, political representation and decision-making within the family.

In terms of employment, the participation rate of women in China is one of the highest in the world. Nearly three out of four women work – compared to one out of three in India, and fewer than one out of two in Japan. But this rate is declining, as women were particularly affected by the dismantling of work units in the 1990s and have more difficulty in finding a job. The percentage of urban women in paid employment thus fell from 76 per cent in 1990 to 61 per cent in 2010. During the process of restructuring, women, being less qualified, were more exposed to precarious employment conditions. In addition, the highly competitive labour market has confined them to occupations that are extensions of the domestic sphere: catering, commerce, housework and other caring professions. Isabelle Attané[18] even suggests that 'traditional gender roles are now being reinforced, due in particular to the growing insecurity of women in the labour market, including among the most highly educated'. In the end, and despite the economic reforms and the social transformations that have resulted from them, Chinese society remains fundamentally anchored in highly gendered social and family roles, which prioritize the masculine.

The individualization of society

The great change in Chinese society since the 1980s has been its individualization. The idea of developing individualities is far from new and took hold in reformist and revolutionary circles at the beginning of the twentieth century. Under the influence of the American philosopher John Dewey, Lu Xun, Hu Shi and the founder of the Communist Party Chen Duxiu all considered this to be a crucial precondition for modernization.

In the Maoist period, entirely collective values were promoted. Those who had been supposedly freed from the yoke of capitalist exploitation in the cities or feudal exploitation in the countryside had to devote themselves to building the new China. The promotion of devotion to the nation and selflessness reached its climax during the 1960s. In 1962, the character of Lei Feng was invented. He was the son of poor peasants, and born in Hunan in 1940; his father starved to death and his mother committed suicide after being raped by a landowner. The child became a beggar, and was taken in by the Communist authorities in 1949. At the age of 16, Lei Feng joined the People's Liberation Army, where he became a cook and a truck driver, and legend presents him as a man devoted to others and to his work, whatever the difficulty, until his accidental death in 1961. His journal was then published, and his motto, 'To live is to serve the people, to make others happy', became one of the slogans of the Cultural Revolution. Thus, the whole of China was instructed to learn from this hero in the service of others.

After three decades of prioritizing collective values, it was the government's reforms that revived the historical process of individualization. The disappearance of work units and people's communes freed individuals from state controls in town and country; they were now ordered to rely only on their own strength. One consequence of the withdrawal of the state, which reduced or eliminated the institutional support it had provided, and given the new geographical and social mobility, was a loosening of ties with families and traditional communities. This individualization can be read in the changing conditions for choosing a spouse, in the new interest in self-development, and in the vitality of the religious domain.

The choice of spouse: a freely chosen alliance between two families

In the 1950s, marriage was a matter between two families. The feelings of the young people concerned were irrelevant. The ideal spouse should be of good character, be ready to work hard, and respect older people. Class membership was taken into account in order to avoid misalliances as well as the physical strength that conditioned the amount of work performed each day and therefore the level of remuneration in work points. It was a matter of two families with similar economic and social statuses coming together. Today, the focus is more on the harmony between the personalities of the newlyweds and their individual traits. While the ability to earn a good living matters, the selection criteria relate to physical appearance and the ability to speak well. It is therefore necessary to have language skills because, compared to their elders, young people now have at their disposal a broader vocabulary to express their love; they are therefore more able to express their emotions. Mutual compatibility and affection are crucial for young men and women. A young man is now expected to be sensitive and able to earn money, a young woman should be beautiful and sweet-natured. These were the results of a survey conducted by the anthropologist Yan Yunxiang in the 1990s, in a rural village in the northern province of Heilongjiang.[18] From among nearly 500 marriages studied, the researcher noted a regular drop in the proportion of marriages where the choice of parents predominated: it was 87 per cent in the decade 1949–59, 38 per cent between 1960 and 1989, 28 per cent between 1970 and 1979, 25 per cent between 1980 and 1989, and 24 per cent in the 1990s.

One novelty is the possibility for young people to get to know each other better after their engagement and before their marriage, a period that can last several months. In the 1950s and 1960s, young people became acquainted by visiting each other a few times – visits that did not last longer than a day and that generally involved sharing a meal. In the early 1970s, the future couple travelled to the neighbouring town to choose wedding gifts and clothes for the ceremony, and to put together a photo album in a professional studio. It was not uncommon for them to spend a night or two together in a hotel or at the home of a relative in town. So there was now a period in which the young couple could develop real marital feelings, and consider their future life. In the 1980s and 1990s, the bride and groom could live together for several days, or even weeks, with their parents, which made it possible to develop true intimacy. While premarital sex was impossible – there was neither space nor time to escape the gaze of others, and the bride's virginity was also an imperative – attitudes have now changed. Among the most recently married couples, a quarter have had premarital sex.

There are now different places to meet up, too. In the first decades of socialism, collective activities – theatre groups, cinema screenings, sporting activities – were the main opportunities. In the 1980s, many young people left the land to find work in the city, which had consequences on their aspirations. They also experienced discrimination in the city. They socialized and integrated with other migrants. Of the freely chosen marriages in the 1990s, a third were with spouses met outside the village. Those who had remained in the village had new aspirations, fostered by watching television and seeing images from urban China or from abroad. The widespread dissemination of media and popular culture (songs) allowed villagers to use a new vocabulary to express their feelings. Henceforth, the social imagination of the younger generation was no longer confined to the physical limits of the village.

In fact, the search for autonomy and privacy predated the start of the reforms and was the consequence of the policy of family planning. Sara L. Friedman notes that the state injunction to postpone the date of marriage in the early 1970s had the effect of encouraging couples to take the time to get to know each other, even to live together and to have premarital sex, although discussions about sexual activity and pleasure were often socially unwelcome.[19]

China is therefore seeing the triumph of a marriage system where each partner chooses his or her spouse – a development in line with what has been observed elsewhere under the impact of urbanization, migration and access to better education. Since the early 1980s, the engaged couple has found new ways of expressing their emotions, developing feelings for each other and also having premarital sex, which promotes the emergence and development of individualities among rural youth. The ability to woo one's future husband or wife goes hand in hand with the right to have times and spaces where young people are not subject to scrutiny or intrusion by parental authority. The possibility of developing intimate relationships has direct consequences on marital and family relationships. Now, Yan Yunxiang notes, it is not uncommon to see young couples walking side by side – and no longer the woman behind her husband. Newlyweds defend their intimacy and their privacy from their parents. These new individual rights go hand in hand with obligations to family and community. The amounts requested in dowries (which the families of the two married couples must invest) have thus increased significantly. Migration has only reinforced this development; the geographical distance between the parents' home and the place where the future couple resides is part of a generational shift in the degree of autonomy enjoyed by young people. This contributes to the emergence of an ethos of personal development, emphasizing feelings, individual desires, family affection and the expression of personal opinions.

Self-interest

The individualization of society also takes the form of the increasing importance of the private sphere and an exploration of oneself.[20] One indicator is the growing public interest in psychology. This was first spread during the 1990s through numerous publications: books, notably with translations of European or American authors, and magazines and articles in many media. As in many Western countries, bookstores now have a section devoted to self-help books. Since the 2000s, there has been a quantitative explosion in psychological counselling services, whether they be telephone hotlines, or radio and television programs that confirm the growing public interest in emotions, personality and self-development.

Psychological counsellors are now ubiquitous, providing support and advice in large companies, in universities and on television.[21] Their number far exceeds that of psychiatrists and psychologists, and the majority of them work in the private sector. Internet counselling, through platforms bringing together professionals and clients, is the latest development in the discipline.

This craze for psychology stems primarily from the middle classes in urban centres. It is partly due to the consequences of social transformations. As a result of the opening up of the economy and society to the market, citizens, now responsible for themselves and forced to be self-reliant, have faced fierce competition to find work, housing or schools for their children. With the new organization of society came a great deal of pressure on individuals to succeed. Conjugal relations between spouses and intergenerational relations between parents and their child are marked by new tensions. The new environment and a better understanding of mental disorders by clinicians are leading to an increase in diagnoses of phobia, depression, anxiety and paranoia.

The interest in mental health is also part of a vast movement to improve the physical and moral quality of the population, largely led by the government. In 2006, the Central Committee of the Communist

Party issued a directive making 'psychological harmony' one of the keystones of a harmonious society. Thus, the state places mental health at the heart of its social policy and invites citizens to become personally involved in the search for psychological balance. The dissemination of psychology as a practice is therefore the combined result of requests from the population and official directives to improve the quality of life. According to anthropologist Li Zhang, China is thus experimenting with new neoliberal methods of managing its population, after resorting to the coercive methods of the Maoist era. In the same perspective, the professionalization of social work with the most disadvantaged, piloted in particular by neighbourhood committees, can be interpreted as a device to neutralize the anger of marginalized populations.[22] Psychology is a discipline of intimate life in the service of the interests of the state and of the new capitalist economic and social model.

The ongoing process of individualization is complex and does not exclude consideration of larger collectives. In the case of the choice of one's spouse, the family continues to be a resource; while young rural people can choose their partners, this choice also involves negotiations with relatives. Young women from rural areas who leave their homes to work in the city face the drastic experience of being uprooted. This is indeed a process of individualization. However, while their parents no longer decide their futures for them, their relatives – a group of people who can also include brothers and sisters, or grandparents – remain important interlocutors with whom individual choices are discussed and negotiated. These young women are both modern women and filial. They feel eminently responsible for their individual futures, and simultaneously think of the family as the only stable source of social, economic and emotional security.[23] While young people wish to be recognized as individuals, they simultaneously participate in new forms of collectives. This is, for example, the lesson that anthropologists have learned from a study of members of the Association of Young Volunteers of China (*Zhongguo qingnian zhiyuan xiehui* 中国青年志愿协会), an organization dependent on the Communist Party.[24] Volunteering in the service of vulnerable or disadvantaged populations is one of the new forms of citizen engagement; it was seen in particular in the aftermath of the Sichuan earthquake in the spring of 2008, which sparked a large number of donations across the country.

Reconfiguration of the religious domain

In recent decades, there has been a spectacular renaissance and reconfiguration of the sphere of religious activity. After the destruction and persecution of the Cultural Revolution, this can be explained first of all by the relative relaxation of state policy towards religions. Since the end of the 1970s, believers have enjoyed greater freedom to undertake the restoration of temples or monasteries, to organize rituals, or to work for the propagation of their belief. The discrediting of the grand narrative of Communist society that underlies the official value system is also leading more and more people to turn to religion in order to find a meaning for their lives in a society in upheaval. The Chinese religious scene is therefore in rapid evolution and constitutes a 'decentred universe … exploding centrifugally in all directions'.[25] All forms of religion, traditional and modern, indigenous and foreign, ancient and recently invented, are developing rapidly and constantly changing. The Party, meanwhile, has resigned itself to a policy of compromise with religious communities, even asking for their help with its social policy. Moreover, with the opening up of the country, Chinese religious communities are increasingly linked to international networks, effectively reducing the regime's control over information flows and developing spaces for transnational alliances.[26]

The revival of religion has first of all taken the form of the reconstruction of temples and monasteries in the countryside. During the 1980s and 1990s, as the state withdrew some of its control from villages, local temples, both Taoist and Buddhist, appeared as institutions for the collection and allocation of resources.[27] By providing public services – building roads or schools, for example – they have been recovering some of the social functions they had in imperial times and which they now perform in collaboration with state officials. Some of the funds raised to rebuild temples and monasteries come from Chinese people living overseas with the agreement of local governments, which played an active role in convincing diaspora businessmen to invest in their homeland. This model, which first appeared in the southern province of Guangdong, then spread throughout China.[28]

In most cities, the only contact between city-dwellers and religion came via the small number of officially authorized temples, churches and mosques. The former, whether Buddhist or Taoist, functioned mainly as tourist attractions. Despite the weakness of the institutional supply, religious renewal was very real in the city too. The first expression of urban religiosity lay in groups that provided training to improve physical well-being.[29] Initially a simple bodily technique, *qigong* (气功) took on a religious dimension as its masters referred more and more to Taoist and Buddhist texts in their teaching. The *qigong* movement represented the most important expression of popular religiosity in cities from the late 1970s until the suppression of Falungong in 1999. In this period, a fifth of the urban population is said to have been in direct contact with *qigong* in one form or another.

Protestantism has been one of the most striking examples of this religious revival.[30] It takes a variety of forms, involving small groups of people who come together in their homes, or their places of work or study, forming large congregations. Believers include poor peasants as well as urban intellectuals and members of the middle classes. They number between 25 and 50 million, and are mostly members of autonomous communities, while congregations belong to an official organization. Its success is due to the variety of beliefs on offer – an explanation for suffering, an ethic, a promise of salvation – in economic conditions much less costly than other religions that require regular offerings or participation in festivities. Protestantism is also widely involved with civil society, in particular through the Amity Foundation (*Aide jijinhui* 爱德基金会) created in 1985, providing assistance to the poorest peasants.

The revival of Confucianism[31] is a good example of the complex relationships in belief and religious practice between popular and official initiatives. It was neither initiated by intellectuals nor stemmed from a state-imposed ideology, and its resurgence did not mark the return of a trend antedating Communism. Indeed, the practices that gradually emerged during the 1990s and 2000s were quite new – including the reappropriation of classical Chinese texts, a culture of the body, and the creation of a neo-ritualism – in a variety of contexts and places. Educational professionals provide children with courses in reading and memorizing the classics, starting in elementary school. There are also business leaders who invite their employees to read these texts, and who themselves follow training courses where they find the resources for existential or spiritual fulfilment. Popular Confucianism is addressed as much to ordinary people as to representatives of the middle classes.

Alongside these initiatives within society, the state actively promotes the figure of Confucius. For example, ceremonies are now organized in his honour every year at the end of September in the city of Qufu (Shandong), as in all the temples across the country. But it would be more accurate to speak of a continuum between official initiatives and those that tend to become independent. Thus, Confucian activists are present within the educational system itself, which helps to alleviate any tensions with the institutional and political environment. In Confucianism, as in other religions, institutional and popular aspects are intertwined, and this configuration opens up possibilities for negotiations between autonomous activists and local authorities.

Often presented as a revival of tradition after 1978, the burgeoning Chinese religious scene is in fact a wave of reinventions and innovations that developed and adapted themselves to the contexts of the late twentieth and early twenty-first centuries. The modernization of society is not leading to the decline of religiosity, but to its expansion.

Conclusion

Since 1949, policies for managing the population have undergone several phases, all part of an overall modernization project. Today, Chinese society, especially urban society, is subject to forms of organization and is characterized by practices that are similar to those found in advanced capitalist societies. Under the effect of decisions taken by the government, but also of dynamics induced by urbanization, migration and market forces, individuals are now autonomous and responsible. The process of forming individuals in China, however, has followed a different path from what happened in Europe.[32] The European trajectory has been based on the conquest of civil, political and social rights; the social bond is ensured by political systems of a democratic nature. In Europe, the ending of paternalism, familialism and professional hierarchies was made possible because the state protected the individual from the excesses of the boss or the father of the family, and a public system of welfare replaced the old solidarities when it came to coping with the main risks of life. Institutions therefore enabled individuals to become autonomous. In addition, these rights were the result of struggles led by the most fragile factions. Society, by mobilizing its own resources, conquered these rights.

In the case of China, the state itself freed individuals so as to stimulate economic growth; individualization was encouraged by the government. The state and public policies have triggered the transformation of society. The individual therefore occupies a growing place in China, but without the institutional framework characteristic of the European trajectory. Neoliberal deregulation of the economy, the labour market and consumption was initiated before the advent of political and social rights. The Chinese trajectory has led to a limited individualization – one that is possible and even desired in order to ensure economic growth: but the process is constrained and remains restricted to the sphere of economic activities and private life.

From this point of view, Chinese society is experiencing multiple tensions. On the one hand, the Party-State encourages individual initiative by supporting development and personal economic success; on the other hand, it achieves an extreme form of control by maintaining a pervasive censorship system and limiting demands for political participation. The individual is called upon to be autonomous and responsible, but at the same time individualism as such is condemned: everyone must first and foremost serve the interests of their family and the Chinese nation.

TEN

Education and Culture

In 1949, in education and culture, the country experienced glaring inequalities. On the one hand, a large number of citizens, rural as well as urban, were illiterate. On the other hand, the elites, especially in large cities with foreign concessions, were trained in Chinese establishments or foreign establishments established in China, while a minority was able to go to Japan, the United States or elsewhere. The literary scene was rich, and the new cultural movement gave rise to progressive authors such as Lu Xun, Shen Congwen, Ba Jin, Mao Dun, Lao She and Eileen Chang. After the 1919 May Fourth movement, the future of the country was seen as involving a commitment to science, and intellectual links between China and, in particular, the United States were intense. Chinese artists were significant too, and some were involved with the avant-garde. Lin Fengmian (1900–91) arrived in France in 1920, and completed his studies there. Back in China, he directed the new fine arts school founded in Hangzhou in 1928 and developed an œuvre that borrowed both from Chinese folk art and from the masters of Western modernity. In Shanghai, the film industry enjoyed remarkable prosperity; a star system was born and foreign exchanges were frequent – Charlie Chaplin stayed there briefly in 1936.

Enriched by this heritage and its practice in Yan'an, the Communist Party very quickly began to follow the Soviet Union. In the context of the Cold War, exchanges with the West ceased. The only possible destination for academics, students and artists was Moscow. From 1957, the deterioration of relations with the Soviet Big Brother led to a period of withdrawal. While notable efforts were made in the field of education, the political sphere was fraught and the Cultural Revolution ended up ruining them. Only in 1979 did a major shift take place. A new educational policy was developed and bore fruit. Creators and intellectuals experimented and reconnected with their foreign counterparts.

Education and science

Priority given to the early years (1949–76)

When the Communist Party came to power, education had long been seen as one of the keys to modernizing the country. Faithful to the intellectual legacy of the 1919 May Fourth movement, and in line with the efforts of the nationalist government to build universal basic education for boys and girls, the People's Republic believed in the transformative virtue of education.[1] However, the existing modern schools not only were not sufficient to meet the needs, but also their distribution was uneven; they were concentrated in coastal regions and large cities. Moreover, much of education was in the hands of private institutions (40 per cent of higher education institutions). The first initiative of the new government was to gradually take control of these establishments, a process that was not completed until the mid-1950s, at the same time as the industrial and commercial establishments were being nationalized. The Communist Party also drew on the experience gained in the revolutionary bases. It relied on the younger generations to lead the revolution; education was now associated with the goal of national reconstruction (*jianguo* 建国). The priority was therefore political in nature; education needed to be at the service of the foundation of a new order. At the end of 1949, under the influence of the Stalinist Soviet Union, a link was made between public education and economic development. Guo Moruo, Chairman of the Education Commission stated that 'if, before 1949, only the Revolution could solve economic problems, since then this has been the mission of education'.[2]

In order to eradicate illiteracy, which affected 80 per cent of young people and adults between 12 and 40 years old, a massive effort was made to generalize primary education. The proportion of illiterates fell to 43 per cent in 1959 and to 30 per cent in 1979. Another goal was to improve the training of political and administrative cadres and workers. The repression of the Hundred Flowers Campaign and then the Great Leap Forward were also an opportunity to promote a new pedagogy: manual work was introduced in many schools beyond primary level. There were now three types of school: full-time, half-work/half-study, and outside working time. Until 1961, the education system experienced spectacular enrolment growth – in 1958 the growth was 34 per cent for primary, 42 per cent for secondary and 50 per cent for tertiary sectors in full-time educational institutions.[3] This led to disorganization in studies and the proliferation of establishments with insufficient resources. The launch of the Socialist Education Movement in 1962 again placed more emphasis on being 'red' than on being an 'expert'. In the autumn of 1965–66, the half-work/half-study system was introduced into the school system of full-time establishments.

The Cultural Revolution undermined the efforts of the previous decade and marked the culmination of a strategy that put education at the service of politics and combined it with productive work. Its initiation in 1966 led to the interruption of studies in practically all educational institutions. They did not resume until spring 1968 in primary schools, in autumn in secondary schools and in 1970 in higher education. In universities, a national recruitment competition based on knowledge skills was not reinstated until 1977; it was therefore on political criteria that students were recruited during the first half of the decade. Millions of students, teachers and researchers were sent down to the countryside.

Primary and lower secondary education underwent considerable development in the form of locally run rural schools. Between 1965 and 1976, primary school enrolment rose from 116 to 150 million children. Numbers in secondary schools grew from 14 to 59 million. The duration of studies was shortened: five years for primary, four years for secondary schools (divided into two cycles of two years). At the same time, a proportion of manual labour was introduced, often comprising more than 50 per cent, and political activities occupied at least 20 per cent of the time, alongside an extremely limited syllabus.[4] Education during the Cultural Revolution aimed to shape a new collective consciousness; however, it also disseminated technical knowledge at the middle and lower levels.

The massification, marketization and internationalization of higher education since 1979

In 1977, the new government restored science and technology to the rank of productive forces by giving them a central place. The pragmatic Deng Xiaoping emphasized the link between economic and social progress and the development of education, science and technology. He reaffirmed that the function of education was to spread science and technology, to train talents. The first measures concerned higher education. The duration of studies was extended to four, five or six years. The syllabuses were completely redesigned, based on Western and Japanese models. Students and researchers were sent abroad for further training and foreign specialists were invited to teach. A network of high-priority primary and secondary schools benefited from more funds and better-quality teachers; they were intended to train the elites. Technical and vocational secondary schools were rehabilitated. In the decades that followed, the education system underwent three major developments: massification, marketization and internationalization.

The 1986 Compulsory Education Act stipulated that all children had the right to nine years of compulsory education: six years of primary school starting at the age of 6, followed by three years of junior secondary education. The enrolment rate in primary school became close to 100 per cent of an age group, and about the same for junior secondary education. Children could then continue the second cycle of their secondary education, which lasted three years. Their result in the senior high school entrance exam, the *zhongkao* (中考), pointed them towards a general or a vocational education. The vast majority of children then progressed from primary to secondary schools – the continuation rate between primary and secondary school increased from only 40 per cent in 2005 to 95 per cent in 2014. In 2010, only 3.5 per cent of the Chinese population over the age of 20 had never been to school, 25 per cent had graduated from school, and 3.7 per cent from university.[5]

The second transformation since the 1980s has been that of funding modalities, bearing in mind that primary and secondary schools are the responsibility of local governments and higher education comes under provincial or central government. The state has offloaded part of the financial burden of education without relinquishing control, especially over the syllabus. Thus, at all levels – nursery schools, primary schools, middle schools, high schools and higher education – a private sector has emerged. Even within public establishments, the border with the private sector is difficult to ascertain. For example, secondary or higher institutions accept students who have not yet passed the entrance exam on condition that they can pay. While the funding of primary schools, especially in rural areas, obliged local governments to demand contributions from families, and undermined universality, the law has since 2007 stipulated that compulsory education is exempt from fees – a 2015 amendment specifies that textbooks can only be sold with a very small profit margin. In fact, public investment in education rose from 2.7 per cent of GDP in 2005 to over 4 per cent in 2014, which represents 80 per cent of expenditure – the rest being provided by private funding and by families. Spending on children's education is the second biggest financial burden on families today, after housing.

It is mainly higher education that has developed rapidly in recent decades. Students either follow three-year short courses (*dazhuan* 大专) or take general degrees (*benke* 本科) over four years. Beyond that, students can go on to a master's (two years) or a doctorate (three years), access being granted each time by competitive examination. The share of a generation enrolled in higher education rose from 3.4 per cent in 1990 to 21 per cent in 2006 and 39 per cent in 2014 (UNESCO figures), with student numbers rising from 17 million in 2006 to 27 million in 2016. To cope with this flow of new entrants, universities are building huge campuses to house tens of thousands of students on the outskirts of large cities. At the top of the hierarchy of institutions are the elite universities that report directly to the Ministry of Education, then, below these, universities under provincial or municipal governments, the public universities of a local government, and the private universities that are supervised at the provincial or municipal level but do not benefit from any public funding. To support the development of educational establishments, registration fees became widespread from 1996.

Higher education has not only massified, it has also become international. In 1978, Deng Xiaoping decided to send more than 2,000 students abroad each year. Their numbers would continue to grow. These departures took place either within the framework of numerous joint programmes between Chinese universities and their partners, or were funded by students and their families. The number of students leaving each year rose from fewer than 10,000 at the end of the 1980s to 100,000 in 2002, and more than 500,000 in 2015. Nearly 1 million students now reside outside the country; for some of them, it is a way of escaping the fiercely selective nature of Chinese establishments. China has thus become the main country sending students abroad, and is faced with the question of their return. In the 1980s and 1990s (especially after the events of 1989), the country faced a serious brain drain. In the 2000s, the situation changed as a result of several factors. A formal public policy was developed to encourage the return of scientists trained abroad. Programmes developed locally by municipal governments included bonuses, the assurance of benefiting from very high-quality working conditions, competitive with those in the United States or Europe, and favourable salaries and housing conditions. Facilities were granted to allow returnees to set up a business, in particular in the high-tech sector (in Beijing, Shanghai and Shenzhen); science parks were specially dedicated to them. The Education Ministry estimated that 70 per cent to 80 per cent of students who left were now returning.

Persistent problems: selectivity, inequality

Overall, illiteracy has been radically reduced, and compulsory education generally enforced; and higher education is now open to an ever greater proportion of younger generations. However, there is no shortage of problems. The system as a whole is characterized by its very high selectivity, with exams determining entrance to college, high school and university; at each stage, students are sorted, with the best performers being directed to the elite institutions. Funding favours senior secondary schools and higher education to the detriment of primary and junior secondary schools. The priority schools and university establishments under the supervision of the central government obtain significant funding, attract the best teachers and are ultimately institutions for reproducing the social order.

The cost of access to education is a serious obstacle for many families, who finance their children, sometimes going into debt, from primary school onwards, paying for private lessons so that exam results will ensure their children a place in the best establishments. In addition, public funding remains insufficient to compensate for the income gap between rich and poor regions, and between urban and rural families. The press has reported cases of peasants committing suicide because they were unable to fund their child's higher education, even if the latter has passed his or her exams.

The vast majority of children between the ages of 7 and 16 now attend school, including in the countryside. However, most rural children do not have access to preschool education, unlike their urban counterparts. Most urban children actually attend kindergartens from the age of 3 and have already acquired basic learning when they enter primary school. In the countryside, there is virtually no access to nursery education, in the absence of any public provision. And most of the children excluded from compulsory education are from national minorities, living in the poorest western provinces of the country.

Another major area of concern is access to education for children of migrants. For a long time, they were allowed to take the college entrance exam only in the locality where they had the *hukou*. So they had to return to their home provinces to continue their education. They could attend state schools only if they paid fees that sometimes amounted to tens of thousands of yuan. Private schools were an alternative: operated by migrant entrepreneurs and only open to these children, they often lacked qualified teachers and did not enjoy the infrastructure that was theoretically guaranteed to them by the education laws. In 2008, the State Council demanded that all local governments come into compliance with the Compulsory Education Act by providing free compulsory education to all children of migrants with the proper documentation. Since then, the presence of migrants in state schools in some cities has increased, although illegal fees persist. In Shanghai, in 2009, migrant children were allowed to continue their education in vocational schools, but only in certain specialties: hotel and restaurant work, hairdressing, and car repair, for example. Since 2014, local governments have allowed the children of migrants to continue their education in the locality where they reside with their parents. However, the children of migrants accommodated in state schools remain victims of discrimination and segregation. Teachers and administrative teams are often reluctant to welcome children from the countryside on the grounds of an alleged 'inferior quality' (*suzhi tai di* 素质太低); they are sometimes put in separate classes where they cannot study with urban children.

The professionalization and internationalization of scientific activity since 1979

As in education, the science policy pursued by the Communists during the seizure of power was marked by a twofold influence: the legacy of the nationalist government on the one hand and the Soviet model on the other. The highest scientific institution in the country, the Academy of Sciences (*Zhongguo kexue yuan* 中国科学院) emerged from the Academia Sinica created in 1928. Chaired by the writer Guo Moruo from 1949 to 1978, it was the counterpart of the Soviet Academy of Sciences. It was mobilized in the service of the development of strategic weapons but also to train scientists through the University of Science and Technology, founded in Beijing in 1958 and then transferred to Hefei, in Anhui, in 1969. In 1952, within the framework of the reorganization of the higher education system on the Soviet model, a certain number of disciplines, such as sociology, political science and law, now seen as bourgeois, disappeared. Emphasis was instead placed on the engineering sciences, with the creation of the Beijing Aeronautical and Astronautical University (*Beijing hangkong hangtian daxue* 北京航空航天大学). The transfer of technology from the Soviet Union to China had two objectives: industrial development and the modernization of the defence apparatus. The emphasis on military objectives allowed China to test its first atomic bomb in 1964.

It was not until the turning point marked by 1978 and the proclamation by Deng Xiaoping of China's ambition to catch up with the rest of the world that scientific development was placed again at the top of the agenda. In the early 1980s, in order to increase and diversify their sources of funding, scientists were encouraged to create companies. One example was Legend, founded in 1984 under the aegis of the Academy of Sciences and renamed Lenovo in 2003. The social sciences that had disappeared were restored. The most prestigious institution in this field was now the Chinese Academy of Social Sciences (*Zhongguo shehui kexue yuan* 中国社会科学院), founded in 1977 and reporting directly to the State Council. The aim was pragmatic and instrumental – a matter of helping the authorities to solve the social problems they faced, whether these were the consequences of the ten years of the Cultural Revolution (urban youth unemployment and underemployment in the countryside) or the new challenges accompanying reform (crime, urbanization and, later, migration).

Among the re-established disciplines, sociology was reborn as an applied science in the service of the modernization of the country. The actors of this reconstruction were former sociologists trained in the discipline before 1949. The most famous of them was Fei Xiaotong (1910–2005), who occupied a whole series of official functions: first, President of the Chinese Society of Sociology, then Director of the Institute of Sociology of the Academy of Social Sciences and of the Institute of Sociology of Peking University. Foreign researchers, mainly American but also European or from Hong Kong, played a major role in the importing of quantitative survey methods and the use of statistics. In the 1980s, research was dominated by the conducting of large social surveys by questionnaires, on subjects related to public policies. As Aurore Merle notes, these descriptive surveys, with their normative scope, 'aim[ed] to provide the Party-State with a snapshot of society or proposals for policy development … The rationality embodied by sociology was fully in line with the project of scientifically reforming Chinese society and the aspiration for modernity of some of the political and intellectual elites.'[6]

The events of 1989 marked a halt in the institutionalization of scientific disciplines, a movement that resumed only after the relaunch of reforms during Deng Xiaoping's trip to the south in January 1992. The decade that followed was one of rapid internationalization. It was first enabled by the massive translation of Western authors. In the social sciences, Anthony Giddens, Pierre Bourdieu and Michel Foucault, to name the best known, had their work published in full. Chinese researchers were also learning about the latest scientific developments by sending students abroad; on their return, the latter brought new methods and theoretical references with them. Thanks to the increased funding that allowed them to join international scientific associations and attend their Congresses, large numbers of Chinese professionals were now part of international communities. For example, in July 2003 the thirty-sixth congress of the International Institute of Sociology, an association founded in Paris in 1893, was held in Beijing. This was the first time that this body of sociologists from all over the world had met on Chinese soil. The two co-organizers were Immanuel Wallerstein, a professor at Yale University and President of the Institute, and Fei Xiaotong, a professor at Peking University. In their opening speeches, both welcomed both the integration of Chinese researchers into the international community and the latter's opening-up to China.

Recognized internationally, and engaged in dialogue with its counterparts around the world, Chinese science was also seeking to forge its own path. Sociologists, for example, relaunched the debate that began in the 1930s on the Sinization of the discipline. They were anxious to adapt it to the national context, and the key concept they used to describe the path taken since 1979 was no longer that of 'modernization' but that of 'transition'. This was an attempt to mark the uncertainty of the course being followed by China, which would not inevitably lead to the advent of a Western-type modernity. Chinese sociologists, like some of their colleagues elsewhere in the world, engaged in the construction of a complex and plural vision of modernity.

Four decades after the reforms began, China was, scientifically speaking, well on the way to catching up. In 2003, it was ranked sixth in the world for its scientific publications, with 30,000 articles. In 2011, it rose to second behind the United States with more than 150,000 publications. It now has scientific equipment that rivals the best in the world, for example in biology and quantum technologies. This catching-up was mainly the consequence of the intensification of budgetary efforts; China's share of research and development spending rose from 0.56 per cent of GDP in 1996 to 2.07 per cent in 2015. It was also made possible by opening-up and integrating into the international community. It also resulted from the policy of assessing researchers in a rigid and dogmatic way based on the number of articles they publish. This requirement is not without its problems, since fraud is a systemic problem.

In terms of the two figures mentioned in the 1919 May Fourth movement, there is no doubt that while 'Mr Democracy' (*de xiansheng* 德先生) has not yet been invited to settle in China, 'Mr Science' (*sai xiansheng* 赛先生) is firmly established there. Chinese researchers are mobile, endowed with significant resources, connected to industry and private funding, and ahead of their foreign colleagues in certain fields; they are now part of international communities. So, an authoritarian state has allowed the emergence of a scientific and technological power. We find this same apparent paradox in the field of the arts: here too, China is now fully integrated with the rest of the world.

Culture and creation

When the new regime was proclaimed, many artists, creators and intellectuals, who had not been close to the Party in the years of the conquest of power, were ready to contribute to the national renaissance and to place themselves at its service. For its part, the CCP, which had withdrawn for so many years to rural China, wooed urban cultural elites in order to gain their support. But from 1952 to 1953, the whole field was brought under control, although the line people were supposed to follow was not always clear. In the Cultural Revolution, many fell victim to persecution. It was not until the end of the 1970s that a real revival took place. The 1980s saw a proliferation of avant-garde attempts in all the arts. In the decades that followed, the conversion of culture to the market upset the balance.

Culture at the service of the political project (1949–79)

In a famous speech given in Yan'an in 1942, entitled 'Interventions to the talks on literature and the arts in Yan'an' (*Yan'an wenyi zuotanhui jianghua* 延安文艺座谈会讲话), Mao Zedong clarified the role that creators should play; they were placed 'at the service of the worker-peasants and the soldiers'. In each area of creative activity, the Party gradually put in place the institutions inspired by the Soviet model which allowed it to exercise its control; these included professional associations, university courses, publishing houses, film studios, distribution channels, etc. All of them assured the state that they were putting artistic expression at the service of its projects.

Membership in the Writers' Association provided one with status and an income; in return, its members had to create works, novels, short stories, poems or plays to the glory of the new regime and its achievements. The state also had a monopoly on publishing and distribution through the Xinhua bookstores. While a few writers like Lin Yutang, Hu Shi or Liang Shiqiu went to Taiwan or the United States, most of them rallied to the new regime. Some, already established under the Republic, placed themselves at its service. Ba Jin (1904–2005), for example, moved into writing reports reflecting the social reality of the time; he wrote about the Korean War and extolled the anti-imperialist struggle. Lao She (1899–1966), on the other hand, devoted himself mainly to theatre and essays. After 1949, Mao Dun (1897–1981) occupied high positions in government; he was Minister of Culture until 1965. Until 1966, most novels and short stories uncritically praised the regime's achievements.

Only a few writers, including Liu Binyan and Wang Meng, two writers labelled 'rightists' in 1957, attempted to enjoy a certain degree of freedom. However, artistic and literary life was punctuated by controversies: critique of the film *The Life of Wu Xun* in 1951; denunciation of the writer and philosopher Hu Shi, accused of liberalism, in 1952; attacks on Hu Feng, a former disciple of Lu Xun, who was arrested in 1955 then sentenced and imprisoned until 1978.

In the field of the visual arts, the Association of Chinese Artists was founded on 21 July 1949 and Xu Beihong was elected as its president. Born in 1895, he studied in Tokyo and Paris, and taught at the University of Nanjing. Xu was a recognized painter, keen to integrate Western techniques with Chinese tradition. The education system was overhauled; the Central Academy of Fine Arts in Beijing, also headed by Xu, was at the top of the institutional hierarchy. At the end of their university training, the artists selected to participate in official exhibitions – the only authorized exhibitions – joined national or local associations, which ensured them an income and a definite reputation.

In the case of cinema, the takeover of the industry by the Communist Party was gradual.[7] When the Civil War ended, much of Shanghai's industry fled to Taiwan and Hong Kong; however, several private studios continued to operate. Progressive filmmakers greeted the Communists enthusiastically. During the first two years of the new regime, they collaborated with the CCP, the central government even providing them with significant financial assistance. However, some films were also violently attacked by the press. In May 1951, in the *People's Daily*, Mao Zedong launched a critical campaign against *The Life of Wu Xun*, a film directed by the progressive director Sun Yu and produced by the Kunlun studio. The film enjoyed great success with audiences – but it depicted peaceful relations between rich and poor that went against the idea of class struggle through violence and the necessary revolt against the old regime. The attitude of the hero, a beggar who opens schools for the poor, was condemned by Mao. At the end of 1951, a nationwide campaign of overhaul and rectification was launched. All those who were categorized as intellectuals were obliged to participate and to engage in self-criticism. The affair of the attacks on *The Life of Wu Xun*, whose impact went beyond the film industry alone and formed a model for subsequent campaigns, weakened the liberal intelligentsia for a long time. In 1952, the last private studios were placed under state control.

In fact, in April 1949, the Central Cinema Bureau, chaired by Yuan Muzhi and answering to the Propaganda Department of the Central Committee, was created to administer the industry. Its cadres were drawn from the CCP and army propaganda bureaux. It controlled national studios in Beijing, Shanghai and Changchun. The state gradually became the sole employer of cinema workers and guaranteed them wages, housing, social security, etc. The central administration thus fully controlled the process of making films – including writing and directing and, after 1951, distribution too. Between 1949 and 1952, an increasing number of films focusing on workers, peasants, revolution and war were produced. Built on homogeneous narrative models and presenting stereotypical characters, they defined the new genres of cinema. At the same time, due to insufficient production, and to make up for the disappearance of Western films in the autumn of 1950, China imported Soviet and East European films.

The period of coexistence between public and private studios ended in 1953 when, simultaneously, the Film Bureau imposed socialist realism, a principle borrowed directly from the Stalinist Soviet Union. During the rectification of thought movement in 1952, Zhdanov's speeches and texts, which had already been cited in the 1940s, now defined the frameworks of artistic life. At the second National Conference of Workers in Literature and Art, inaugurated in September 1953, Xi Zhongxun, head of the Propaganda Department, said that 'when it comes to the method of creation in literature and art, we must unreservedly follow the Soviet Union's path of socialist realism'. Henceforth, artistic expression was entirely subordinate to ideology.

Director Zheng Junli was one example of the vicissitudes of the regime's cultural policies. Like other personalities in the world of culture, after 1949 he pursued a career begun during the Republican period, enthusiastically welcoming the prospect of working with the new Communist authorities.[8] In the early years of the transition, Zheng continued to work for the Kunlun private studio in Shanghai. His film *Husband and Wife* (*Women fufu zhi jian* 我们夫妇之间), distributed in 1951, although based on a propagandistic novel, was violently attacked by the press. The problem was not its content but the political context of

its release, during the first major campaign against counter-revolutionaries; to protect his interests, Zheng Junli wrote a self-criticism. He was
rehabilitated and sent as part of a delegation of filmmakers to meet Mao
on the occasion of his visit to Shanghai in 1957. The following year, he
was contacted to make a film on the occasion of the tenth anniversary
of the People's Republic, meant to be devoted to Lin Zexu, an imperial
official known for his hostility to the British opium trade in Canton.
Zheng's ambition was to make not just a Marxist, but indeed a Maoist
film, in order to prove his loyalty to Communism and to the supreme
leader. The film, openly anti-imperialist and nationalist, was released on 1
October 1959, and was very well received by critics, being presented as the
most important film made since 1949. But at the same time, the policy
of the Great Leap Forward was launched and the press abruptly changed
tone. In the Cultural Revolution, Zheng was denounced as a reactionary.
Arrested in 1967, he died in prison two years later at the age of 58.

The Cultural Revolution was the most dramatic episode in the artistic
history of the People's Republic. Writers were silenced. Several of them,
including Lao Shi, committed suicide or died of ill-treatment. Guo
Moruo, a renowned writer, and president of the Academy of Sciences,
supported the movement; he 'preferred to deny his writings and engaged
in resounding self-criticism rather than defending his peers'.[9] Film
production was completely stopped for three years and restarted very
slowly only in 1970, when it was restricted to films of hard-line revolutionary propaganda, ballets and operas that followed the model defined
by Jiang Qing, such as *The Red Detachment of Women* (*Hongse niangzijun*
红色娘子军) by Xie Jin in 1971 and *The White-Haired Girl* (*Baimao nü*
白毛女) by Sang Hu in 1972.

A decade of experiments (1979–89)

The end of the 1970s was a moment of rare freedom marked by attempts
at experimentation that involved all the arts. These were obviously in
reaction to the restrictions of the previous period. Artists also depicted
the trauma that the country had just gone through.

In the literary field, the democratic movement of 1978–79 saw
the emergence of a poetry denounced as 'obscure', written by young
authors such as Bei Dao, Shu Ting and Gu Cheng, who made names

for themselves through the magazine *Jintian* (今天 *Today*), published from 1978 to 1980, when it was banned. The 'literature of scars' (*shanghen wenxue* 伤痕文学), which examined the tragic dimensions of the Cultural Revolution for ordinary people, especially for educated younger people, was a great success. Many texts of so-called 'reportage' were published and dealt with social issues such as divorce, the one-child policy and the housing shortage. This literary form was governed by theoretical considerations: it had to consist of one-third real facts, one-third artistic form and one-third personal opinion. One of the most famous texts was *Between Men and Demons* (*Renyao zhi jian* 人妖之间) by Liu Binyan, published in September 1979; this denounced a case of corruption. Other writers engaged in a process of introspection to understand the catastrophe that had occurred and its social and political consequences: this was known as the literature of reflection (*fansi wenxue* 反思文学). In 1985, Zhang Xianliang, who had spent twenty years in a labour camp but who remained a Communist, published *Half of Man is Woman* (*Nanren de yiban shi nüren* 男人的一半是女人), a novel that denounced the failures of socialism and saw the Great Leap Forward and the Cultural Revolution as perversions of Marxist ideology. *Wings of Lead* (*Chenzhong de chibang* 沉重的翅膀) by Zhang Jie, published in 1981, which described the bureaucracy of the Ministry of Industry, was a critique of the conservative cadres that were holding back the reforms.

In the mid-1980s, a group of writers emerged who drew their inspiration from their enforced stay in the Chinese countryside in the late 1960s and the discovery of a world they did not know: this was the movement known as the 'literature of the root-seeking' (*xungen wenxue* 寻根文学). For these authors – Han Shaogong, A Cheng, Zheng Wanlong, Li Hangyu – who often drew inspiration from their native regions, literature had to be rooted in national culture. They revealed what they had witnessed first hand: a world of superstitions and folk beliefs. The content as well as the form of their work drew its novelty from 'relying as much on the processes of the most classical realism as on magical realism, the fantastic and poetic prose'.[10] Mo Yan, who published *The Land of Alcohol* (*Jiuguo* 酒国) in 1993, was part of this trend. He was of peasant origin, and educated entirely thanks to the army; his texts evoke his native province of Shandong in a hyperrealist, even surrealist, style.

The 1980s also saw greater access to literature from all over the world thanks to the relaxation of censorship and the activities of translators. The works of Gabriel García Márquez, Jorge Luis Borges and Alain Robbe-Grillet were published in Chinese. Readers discovered surrealism, psychoanalysis, existentialism, the French New Novel, etc. Writers such as Yu Hua and Gao Xingjian were influenced by these currents in their quest for formal innovation.

In the visual arts, the group of artists known as The Stars (*Xingxing* 星星), founded by Ma Desheng and Huang Rui, is the best-known example of the new avant-garde. Most of its members had not received any artistic training and were not affiliated with official institutions. In 1979, they defied the authorities by organizing an exhibition in a public park near the National Museum of Art in Beijing. Although this exhibition was quickly shut down, the group organized a historic demonstration that united all who demanded freedom of expression and the right to an individual practice of art far removed from socialist realism. They managed to get the exhibition reopened. In the 1980s, the members of the group would take divergent paths; several of them went abroad. The decade ended with the first national avant-garde retrospective, China/Avant-garde Art Exhibition (*Zhongguo/xiandai yishu zhan* 中国 / 现代艺术展) at the Beijing Fine Arts Palace, being opened on 5 February 1989. Described by Emmanuel Lincot as a 'successful aesthetic putsch',[11] the exhibition did not present any traditional Chinese painting or calligraphy, contrary to official state-sponsored art, but rather works of experimental fine art (*shiyan meishu* 实验美术). The event was marked by a performance by Tang Song and Xiao Lu: gunshots were fired on their installation at point blank range, while a telephone booth was ironically called 'dialogue'.

Another major current was called Political Pop Art (*zhengzhi bopu yishu* 政治波普艺术). It was founded by Wang Guangyi. Born in 1956 in Harbin, Heilongjiang, he graduated from the Zhejiang Academy of Fine Arts in Hangzhou. In his paintings from the *Great Criticism* series, which began in the 1990s, he hijacked Maoist propaganda by juxtaposing posters extolling the Cultural Revolution with symbols and commercial advertisements from the West. These works bore witness to rapid economic and social transformations, while at the same time interacting with the images of propaganda from the socialist era.

Cinema also experienced a renaissance. Several successful films referred to the traumas of the Cultural Revolution; they included *Hibiscus Town* (1986) by Xie Jin, an on-screen equivalent of the literature of scars. In 1982, the first class to emerge from the Beijing Film Institute, reopened in 1978, constituted 'the fifth generation' of Chinese filmmakers. The films of the generations before the Cultural Revolution were all made the same way, with stereotyped characters, low-angle shots for the heroes, and with the villains always lit from below. The fifth generation deviated from these methods with a freer and less commercial approach that resembled French *auteur* cinema. It favoured rural subjects. *Yellow Earth* (1984), directed by Chen Kaige with Zhang Yimou responsible for the cinematography, was the emblem of this revival. The film broke with melodramatic conventions by adapting a raw realism: the heroine was crushed by society, its traditions and its conventions. The film was innovative both in style and in the boldness of the subject; it suggested that peasants had nothing to expect from the Party. Almost ten years later, in 1993, Chen won the first Chinese Palme d'Or at the Cannes Film Festival with *Farewell My Concubine*. Zhang Yimou, another fifth-generation filmmaker, found success with films such as *Red Sorghum*, *Wives and Concubines*, *Qiuju*, *A Chinese Woman* and *Live!* These directors, with very diverse styles, shared their rejection of the cinematographic tradition of socialist realism.

Culture opens up to the market

The events of June 1989 put an end to this decade of experimentation and avant-garde productivity. A few years later, however, creativity found other spaces to express itself as culture opened up to the market, as a result of the influx of capital following the soaring stock market and the prosperity of the real-estate market; art became the object of Chinese and international speculative investment. Cinema also attracted capital, both in production and distribution.

The development of a market offered artists a chance to exist outside the public system (which also continued). For the plastic arts, a commercial space gradually took shape, with its own institutions: galleries, fairs, exhibition curators, auction houses, etc. The first art biennial was held in Canton in 1992, at the initiative of art critic Lu

Peng; it was financed by a private company. Other regular exhibitions of the same type followed in Shanghai and Chengdu: today, around ten art biennials or triennials are held nationwide. These events are organized according to international standards. They are chaired by an exhibition curator. They bring together the arts in a variety of formats, including installations and video and multimedia works. These events are also an opportunity to set Chinese artists alongside their foreign counterparts and therefore to make the latter better known to the public.

The career of Zhang Huan, an internationally renowned artist, is a good example of the transformations in the artistic field. Born to a family of peasants in 1965 in Anyang in the province of Henan, he graduated from Henan University in 1988 and then from the Central Academy of Fine Arts in Beijing in 1993. He began his career within a small artistic community on the outskirts of the capital, called Beijing East Village (*Beijing dongcun* 北京东村), whose name explicitly referred to its New York counterpart. Like other members of this group, he practised performance art – an avant-garde kind of creativity. His interventions involved his or another person's body, often naked, sometimes in a masochistic context, which aroused hostile reactions from the authorities. In 1994, he covered himself with honey and fish oil and offered himself to the flies in public latrines. In other works, he covered his body with calligraphic texts. Between 1998 and 2006, he lived and worked in New York where he acquired worldwide notoriety; he participated in the Venice Biennale in 1999 and entered the collections of prestigious American museums such as the Museum of Modern art and the Guggenheim. In 2006, he returned to China and radically renewed his types of intervention. As head of a workshop in Shanghai that employed nearly 100 people on several dozen hectares of land, he produced monumental sculptures. He is a Buddhist, and his favourite materials are the ashes of incense sticks collected from temples, which he turns into statues and paintings. Like other star artists on the international scene, he collaborates with major French luxury brands. His career, Chinese and then global, has led him from an austere avant-garde practice to works whose manufacturing costs and market values have been reaching new heights.

While cinema remains an industry controlled by the Cinema Bureau at all levels – production, distribution and exhibition – it is the subject of increasing investment from the private sector. The development of a commercial cinema focused on a few genres – historical film, martial arts film and comedies – is being achieved with ever-increasing budgets. The interest of investors rests on the rapid increase in the number of cinemas – often multiplexes located in shopping centres – supported by the rapid growth of the urban middle classes. In just a few years, China became the second biggest world market after the United States. The powerful real-estate group Wanda, the leading Chinese operator, became the world's leading cinema owner after its takeover of the American network AMC in 2012. Another spur to the transformation of the sector was the arrival on mainland China of actors and producers from Hong Kong and Taiwan, so that the Chinese film industry now largely involves all three territories. A popular mass culture is emerging, one that marginalizes creators.

In the field of literature, market forces have also opened up spaces for works that the official authorities denigrate. In 2000, there appeared two novels by young women; their publication caused a scandal before they were banned – which helped to increase their sales. Weihui and Mian Mian described their sex lives without taboos. The former, born in Zhejiang in 1973, graduated in Chinese from Fudan University in Shanghai; *Shanghai Baby* (*Shanghai baobei* 上海宝贝) tells the story of a young woman's affairs with Chinese and foreigner lovers. The latter was born in Shanghai in 1970, then moved to Shenzhen. *Chinese Candy* (*Tang* 糖) tells about her dissolute life as a drug-taking young woman who undergoes drug treatment. Both volumes depict full-on the lifestyles and individualism of one section of the urban younger generation. Their success also signalled the inability of censorship to prevent the publication of works that disturbed it.

In the 2000s, the Internet became a new space for literary experimentation that was partly outside the control of censorship. Han Han (born in 1982), who is also a popular singer and a rally driver, published his first novel at the age of 17 and has been blogging since 2006. Some of his columns, read online daily by millions of readers, are published on paper. Without taking a position on sensitive subjects, they mention the questions that preoccupy Internet users: democracy, quarrels between intellectuals, and more trivial subjects. This constitutes a space for discussion with which political power must come to terms.

There are also creators who choose not to compromise themselves with the demands of censorship and prefer to produce free work, even if this means being confined to semi-clandestine spaces. This is particularly the case with a certain number of 'sixth-generation' filmmakers who emerged after the events of Tiananmen. Banned from commercial circuits, their films have been shown at festivals, on university campuses, in film clubs. They shoot their films in town, quickly, at low cost, which gives their films the appearance of documentaries. These directors thus develop a style at odds with that of their predecessors, mixing fiction and realism. They film the changes in society that they see before their eyes: unemployment, the growing gap between the rich and the poor, prostitution and crime. They show in particular the daily lives of idealistic and impoverished urban young people, subject to Western influences, far from the lifestyles laid down by the canons of dominant Communist or Confucian morality. The most famous of these filmmakers are Wang Xiaoshuai (born in 1966) with *The Days* and *Beijing Bicycle*, Zhang Yuan (born in 1963) with *East Palace West Palace*, Lou Ye (born in 1965) with *Weekend Lover* and Jia Zhangke (born in 1970) with *Xiao Wu* (also known as *Pickpocket*). Jia Zhangke occupies a special position thanks to his success abroad. Once he had won multiple international awards, Chinese professional circles and media accepted him and it became impossible to censor him. After ten years working underground, *The World* (2004) was the first film he made with full official permission. All his work can now be seen in China – not on commercial channels, but on DVD: proof of the authorities' relative opening-up.

Cultural policies: the case of museums

It became possible to open culture up to the market because this process was encouraged by the authorities. In the case of museums, which rapidly increased in number, two moments can be distinguished. In the 1980s, history museums devoted to the twentieth century celebrated the nation and the Chinese revolution and its collective values, as if to respond to the rising individualism that was triumphing in urban China. Most of them were state-funded museums. At the end of the decade, undoubtedly in part as a reaction to the fall of the Communist countries in Eastern Europe, new establishments were created and old ones renovated. These museums and memorials aimed to restore dormant socialist values, and to cultivate patriotism and nationalism. They reminded the Chinese people of their previous humiliations and also of the heroism of their revolutionary past. A prime example is the construction of the Nanjing Massacre Memorial in the capital of Jiangsu Province. It was inaugurated on 15 August 1985, the anniversary of the victory over Japan. The museum is a place of remembrance where survivors and witnesses of the Nanjing massacre, cadres and senior leaders of the country, and personalities from the artistic and intellectual world, all came to reflect. The latter included the painter Liu Haisu (1896–1994), at the time honorary director of the Nanjing Institute of Fine Arts, and Yang Zhengning, the American Nobel Prize winner.[12]

Contemporary with these museums, other efforts were made to allow the population to reclaim its past. Also in the 1980s, the ancient and centuries-old tradition (the first dated back to the Song period in the tenth century) of publishing local monographs (*difangzhi* 地方志), a tradition that had been interrupted by the war and then the victory of the Communist Party, was resumed.[13] These works, which run to between 500 and 1,000 pages, have an encyclopaedic vocation and contain a large amount of information: geographical maps (the administrative borders of districts, urban and rural areas, the layout of roads, railways, and transport channels), a description of natural conditions (climate, geology, hydrology, flora and fauna) and demography, a (quantified) history of economic activities by sector (agriculture, industry, trade), a description of the infrastructure (roads, railways, electricity, number of telecommunications lines, etc.), financial information (taxes collected, public expenditure, loans, savings), political life (political organizations), military life, social life (the education system, care services, education, religious life) and cultural life (local customs, local dialects), a chronology of major events, biographies of important people (great revolutionaries in particular), and finally a large number of references and sources. The originality of the enterprise lay in its consideration of the most recent history – a central government document in 1985 stated that it was the history of the locality up to that date that needed to be written. But it was indeed an official history, subjected (in particular for the more delicate chapters, notably political history) to the scrutiny of the Communist Party.

The enterprise was presented as meeting objectives that were at once pragmatic, heritage-based and educational. Scientific information was gathered in order to allow local cadres to take the appropriate decisions (the volume was a working instrument for bureaucrats), to collect scattered data and to preserve them for the future, and finally to disseminate patriotic, Communist and revolutionary values. Of these three aims, the first was probably the most important, but it was undoubtedly also because the publication of these works was a tradition of the Chinese bureaucracy that the authorities revived a practice neglected during the first three decades of the Communist regime. These works also contributed to the deinstitutionalization of the memory of the past in the wake of a decade of unrest.

The main message conveyed by museums of revolutionary history and memorials centred around heroism in the revolutionary struggle against capitalists and imperialists. In the 1990s, the museum institution, a traditional propaganda tool in the service of the Party, had to face a new reality: the country was integrated into the world economy, people were now motivated solely by the pursuit of their own personal interests. How could one draw a link between the revolutionary past and the consumerist present? Museums adapted to the evolution of official ideology both in their form – an up-to-date museography and bold architecture that followed international standards – and in their content. Because the official ideology was changing, so were museums. China was now integrated with the rest of the world, and everything had become a commodity. If museums continued their mission of patriotic education, they must also generate support for reforms and the transition to a market economy. Museums now supplied representations of the past that legitimized the contemporary ideology of commerce and business.[14]

In the case of the Shanghai History Museum, partly housed in the Oriental Pearl Tower of the new Pudong business district,[15] the epic history of the nation as a whole was replaced by a nostalgic reconstruction of old Shanghai (*lao Shanghai* 老上海) – a representation of daily life in the metropolis in the first half of the twentieth century through slide shows, wax figures, miniature reproductions of the city's finest mansions (even though these had been built by the city's capitalists). The museum, in the heart of the new financial district of the country's economic capital, evokes the grandeur and prosperity of the turn of the century. This positive representation of republican capitalist China obviously serves the construction of a socialist market economy. In Yiwu, a medium-sized city in Zhejiang province (south of Shanghai), a museum was opened that celebrates the trading traditions of the locals. It is housed within the walls of a huge trade exhibition complex of several tens of thousands of square metres. The local authorities clearly sought to establish a link between a proactive strategy of economic development – the construction of wholesale markets for consumer products, open all year round to Chinese and foreign buyers – and local economic history, in this case a centuries-old tradition of peddling.[16]

Twenty years later, in the mid-2000s, the development of cultural industries was openly encouraged by the authorities, who saw it as a source of growth and jobs. In all the cities, the municipalities started setting up places specifically intended to accommodate businesses linked to culture. The big Chinese cities are now covered with sites meant for the 'cultural and creative industries' (wenhua chuanyi chanye 文化创意产业). Dashanzi (大山子) in Beijing is such a space. The story of its emergence shows how many initiatives taken by creators, associated with foreigners, end up being taken over by the authorities.[17] In the northeastern suburb of Beijing, around a former factory built by German engineers, the site comprises a set of industrial buildings which, in a few years, brought together artists then galleries and museums. In the 1990s, the reform of state-controlled businesses led to the dismissal of thousands of workers who worked there, and freed up vast spaces. Two personalities played an active role in its transformation: Robert Bernell and Huang Rui. The former was an American citizen who in 2002 opened a bookshop and gallery. The same year, the latter, a visual artist and former member of The Stars Art Group, moved there after fifteen years of exile in Japan. Several dozen artists, and then galleries both national and international, followed. In May 2004, a first international festival was held. A conflict arose with the owners of the site and representatives of the state who intended this place to be a breeding ground for high-tech companies. Artists threatened with being moved out protested, supported by foreign personalities. Finally, the local government took over the project and in 2006 the place officially became the 798 Art District (798 yishuqu

七九八艺术区), borrowing the name of the site's main factory. The state thus took over a project that had been set up by a few artist-entrepreneurs. Indeed, in the meantime, the central government had shifted its policy and aimed to stimulate the emergence of cultural and creative areas. Cultural industries were officially recognized as creators of wealth and sources of employment, and their development was now encouraged. Dashanzi became an asset for Beijing, which was aiming to become a global city just like Paris, London or New York. The set-up clearly illustrates the tensions within the Chinese art worlds, where there are many different actors – artists and authors, investors and merchants in search of profit, political actors and foreigners – whose relationships are complex. Artists can be both Chinese and global if they have lived abroad or are internationally recognized; they can also be astute businessmen/women; an exhibition curator can have his or her own artistic practice and own a gallery; all can be involved in dissent and at the same time maintain links with the political elite.

Municipalities compete with one another. In Shanghai, the ambition is to make the metropolis a global capital not only in economic and financial, but also cultural, terms. Numerous infrastructures dedicated to art and creativity have been set up. These include public museums, such as the Power Station of Art, the Shanghai Museum of Contemporary Art (*Shanghai dangdai yishu bowuguan* 上海当代艺术博物馆) set up in an old power station, and the China Art Palace (*zhonghua yishu gong* 中华艺术宫). Both were opened in 2012 on both sides of the Huangpu River, and were the result of urban redevelopments following the holding of the 2010 World Expo; the latter was installed in the Chinese national pavilion built for the occasion. Other establishments have been funded by private actors, including the Zengdai Museum of Modern Art (2005), the Minshen Art Museum (2010), the Rockbund Art Museum (2010), the 21st Century Minsheng Art Museum (2014), the Long Museum built on two sites (Pudong 2012 and Xuhui 2014) and the Yuz Museum (2014). The creation of several of them on the edge of Huangpu corresponds to a municipal programme that aims to create a 'cultural corridor' on the west bank of the river bringing together museums, art galleries, cultural and entertainment industries, and ancient as well as more recent heritage. In the case of the Long Museum West Bund and the Yuz Museum, the municipality also aimed to turn a formerly industrial zone into an upscale residential area. The ambition of large private collectors combined with the will of the local government to stimulate cultural development and enhance land resources. In addition, museum projects are also frequently real-estate projects.

In the end, culture in China now brings together art and commerce, the local and the global, the present and the past. In this regard, the figure of artist Ai Weiwei is emblematic. Born in 1958, he is the son of the famous poet Ai Qing, labelled a 'rightist' during the Hundred Flowers Campaign and sent for re-education to Inner Mongolia in 1957, then to Xinjiang. In 1979, after studying cinema, Ai Weiwei was a founding member of the Stars Art Group. He lived in the United States from 1981 to 1993; he studied at the Parsons School of Design in New York, and learned about European and Anglo-American art – notably Duchamp and Warhol – forging links with American and Chinese artists; he produced paintings and *détournements* (creative misappropriations) of objects. Back in China, he settled in Beijing. In a series of 1995 photographs, he dropped and smashed a Han Dynasty vase, a scathing allusion to the highly politicized way the nation's heritage was being restored across the country to celebrate the greatness of its history. At the 2000 Shanghai Biennale, he curated an exhibition including a series of photos in which he stuck up his middle finger in front of iconic monuments from around the world. On the eve of the 2008 Beijing Olympics, he joined forces with Swiss architects Herzog and de Meuron to design a building in the shape of a bird's nest, an achievement hailed by the official media. That same year, after the earthquake in Sichuan province, he took to the Internet to defend families who had lost children in the collapse of poorly constructed schools, and denounced the corruption that had caused it. Ai Weiwei had become outspoken in his opposition to the authorities; he was finally arrested in spring 2011 for tax evasion, then released less than three months later. He is less active than in the past on the Internet; much of his career has been spent abroad, where his exhibitions are hosted in the world's largest museums. Ai Wewei has become both a Chinese and very international artist who mixes genres – paintings, installation art and photos. He is also an exhibition curator, a collector, an agitator who has collaborated with the authorities and then moved away from them; someone who knows how to manipulate the media.

Conclusion

Thanks to the spread of compulsory education, China has achieved one undeniable success: the reduction of the illiteracy rate for adults aged between 15 and 50 from 80 per cent in 1949 to less than 5 per cent today (UNESCO figures). Through its investments in education and research, China has risen to the second rank in the world. In education, the challenge is to resolve the issue of inequalities in access; among the populations discriminated against are the children of national minorities in the poorest western provinces and those of migrants in the cities. In terms of creativity, the relationship between politics and art has not weakened; it has become more complex. The Propaganda Department still exercises its oversight over all productions, but at the same time the authorities recognize the need in both economic and geopolitical terms for an intense cultural life – one that creates jobs and wealth and has an impact on the international scene. At the same time, the diversification of modes of expression and the emergence of new spaces is fostering the activities of marginal creators. Some are skilfully managing to navigate an independent way through gaps in the structure. After more than four decades of opening-up, the cultural scene is now widely open to foreign influences, just as the whole world has become open to Chinese creations.

Epilogue

To ensure that China could enter modernity just as its Japanese neighbours had under the Meiji dynasty – such was the ambition of all reformers and revolutionaries of the twentieth century. The dying Manchu dynasty was too concerned with keeping power in its own hands. The Republic of 1911 was too weak to take any initiative. The authoritarian regime of Chiang Kai-shek was mainly preoccupied with the struggle against its Communist and then Japanese enemies. Mao Zedong conquered power by mobilizing and supervising the peasants, then amassing around him a large number of people, including non-Communists, who aspired to rebuild a country that had finally been reunified. Unfortunately, Mao persisted in favouring the objective of revolution over that of modernization. To his credit, he took on the fight against illiteracy and reducing mortality. But when he died in 1976, China was one of the poorest countries in the world. The population had suffered many hardships. Some had experienced famine. Children had been forced to denounce their parents. All were dragooned into movements whose direction and meaning varied with clashes in the upper political echelons. Society was exhausted and the government largely delegitimized.

The reforms initiated in 1979 carried out the programme that had been constantly postponed until then. More than decades later, China is prosperous; it has become the second largest economy in the world after the United States. Its power has been restored on the regional and international scene; it is respected and feared. Industrialization, urbanization, migration between the countryside and the cities, the rise in the level of education, and the completion of the demographic transition have transformed the country at a rate unparalleled in history. These changes have allowed the population to access the attributes of modernity: comfort and material well-being, mass culture and leisure, and the most advanced technologies. China has caught up with its neighbours both near and far; in many areas it has even taken the lead. This spectacular development continues to reshape the world. Compared to other authoritarian regimes, beginning with the Soviet Union, China's successes are undeniable.

In July 2021, on the occasion of the hundredth anniversary of the Chinese Communist Party, Xi Jinping paid tribute to the leaders who had preceded him – Mao, Deng and their successors – but he especially insisted on his own achievements since taking office in 2012. The eradication of poverty, economic prosperity and a growing military force illustrated, he claimed, 'the great rejuvenation of the Chinese nation'. A modern, powerful China was entering a new era in which, proud of its success, it aimed to exercise global power. In his anniversary speech, Xi Jinping stressed that the Party would not tolerate any foreign power obstructing China's rise. 'The Chinese people will never allow foreign forces to bully, oppress or enslave us', he declared. Moreover, the Covid-19 pandemic has only reinforced the conviction of Chinese political elites that Western liberal democracy is in a state of irremediable decline and that, as a result, China now has a strategic opportunity.

Xi Jinping, who is simultaneously Party General Secretary, President of the Republic and Chairman of the Central Military Commission, is also the most powerful Chinese leader for decades. In 2001, when China became a member of the World Trade Organization, many observers were convinced that the country would become a democracy. Against all odds, the reforms actually resulted in the construction of a 'socialism with Chinese characteristics'. At the end of the 1970s, Deng Xiaoping revived the legitimacy of the Party by turning his back on the errors of Maoism; fifty years later, Xi Jinping opted for a headlong rush forward to a more totalitarian system. With nearly 100 million members in all strata of society, from the economic elites to the smallest village, the Party aims to represent the entire people. In his 'hundredth anniversary' speech, Xi also issued a warning to anyone who attempted to split the Party from the Chinese people: 'Anyone who wants to divide the Chinese Communist Party from the Chinese people will never get their way', he stated. The Chinese Party and people must remain united behind their supreme leader.

However, the problems remain immense. There are glaring social inequalities. The degradation of natural resources is a source of daily dissatisfaction. Changing demographics pose challenges to families and government that no one else has ever had to solve on this scale. Corruption, denounced for more than twenty years, is widespread. The political system is no more transparent, and its stability remains questionable. Paradoxically, just as China was aiming to become a global power, the Covid-19 epidemic cut it off from the rest of the world. Moreover, its human rights abuses and military expansion mean that it is now seen as a threat by a majority of citizens in developed countries. For some, China is now not only an ideological and military adversary, but also a technological and economic one. Because time and space have shrunk, the solutions to these challenges in China concern all the citizens of the world.

Illustrations

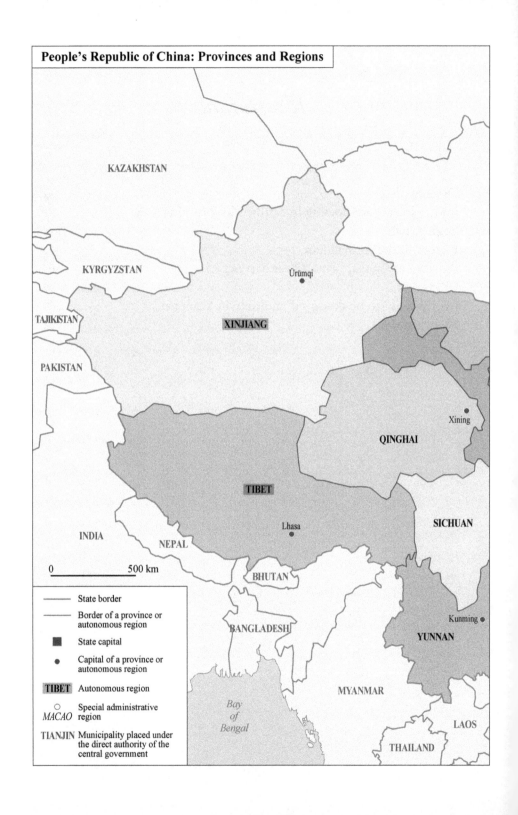

People's Republic of China: Provinces and Regions

KAZAKHSTAN

KYRGYZSTAN

TAJIKISTAN

PAKISTAN

Ürümqi

XINJIANG

QINGHAI

Xining

TIBET

Lhasa

SICHUAN

INDIA

NEPAL

BHUTAN

BANGLADESH

Kunming

YUNNAN

MYANMAR

Bay
of
Bengal

LAOS

THAILAND

	State border
	Border of a province or autonomous region
■	State capital
●	Capital of a province or autonomous region
TIBET	Autonomous region
○ MACAO	Special administrative region
TIANJIN	Municipality placed under the direct authority of the central government

0 ————— 500 km

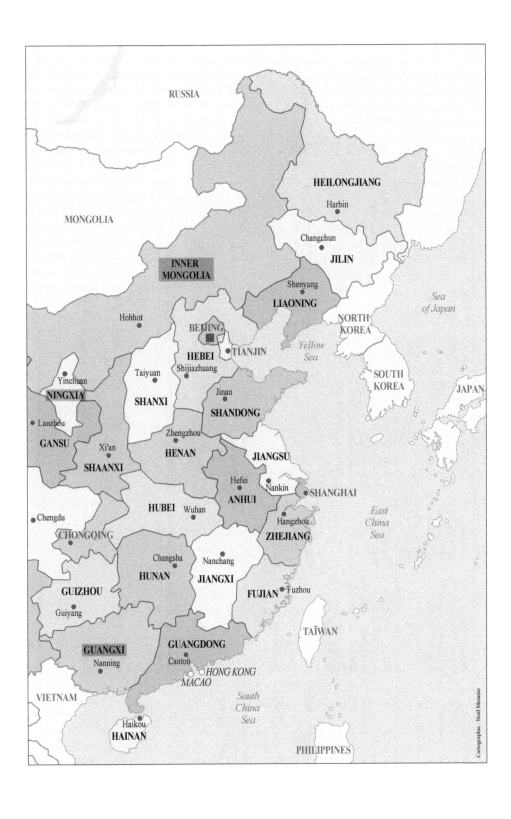

Title-holders of the Main Positions in the Government of the People's Republic of China (1949–2022)

Chairman of the Central Committee of the Communist Party of China 中国共产党中央委员会主席	Secretary General of the Central Committee of the Chinese Communist Party 中共中央总书记	Chairman of the Central Military Commission of the Communist Party of China 军事委员会主席	President of the People's Republic of China 中华人民共和国主席	Premier 中华人民共和国国务院总理	Chairman of the Standing Committee of the National People's Congress 全国人民代表大会	Chairman of the National Committee of the Chinese People's Political Consultative Conference (CPPCC) 政治协商会议主席
Mao Zedong 毛泽东 (1945–76) Position created in 1945 at the Seventh Congress	Mao de facto directs the Secretariat, established in 1943, but does not take the title Deng Xiaoping 邓小平 (1956–66)	Mao Zedong (1935–76)	Mao Zedong (1954–59) Liu Shaoqi 刘少奇 (1959–68) Institution suspended between 1969 and 1982	Zhou Enlai 周恩来 (1949–76)	Liu Shaoqi (1954–59) Zhu De 朱德 (1959–76)	Mao Zedong (1949–54) Zhou Enlai (1954–66) The CPPCC ceases all activity between 1966 and 1978
Hua Guofeng 华国锋 (1976–81)	Hua Guofeng (1976–81)	Hua Guofeng (1976–81)	Li Xiannian 李先念 (1983–88)	Hua Guofeng (1976–80)	Ye Jianying 叶剑英 (1978–83)	Deng Xiaoping (1978–83)
Hu Yaobang 胡耀邦 (1981–82)	Hu Yaobang (1980–87)	Deng Xiaoping (1981–89)	Yang Shangkun 杨尚昆 (1988–93)	Zhao Ziyang 赵紫阳 (1980–87)	Peng Zhen 彭真 (1983–88)	Deng Yingchao 邓颖超 (1983–88)
Position suppressed in September 1982 (Twelfth Congress)	Zhao Ziyang 赵紫阳 (1987–89)	Jiang Zemin (1989–2004)	Jiang Zemin (1993–2003)	Li Peng 李鹏 (1987–98)	Wan Li 万里 (1988–93)	Li Xiannian 李先念 (1988–93)
	Jiang Zemin 江泽民 (1989–2002)	Hu Jintao (2004–12)	Hu Jintao 胡锦涛 (2003–13)	Zhu Rongji 朱镕基 (1998–2003)	Qiao Shi 乔石 (1993–98) Li Peng 李鹏 (1998–2003)	Li Ruihuan 李瑞环 (1993–2003)
	Hu Jintao 胡锦涛 (2002–12)	Xi Jinping (2012–)	Xi Jinping 习近平 (2013–)	Wen Jiabao 温家宝 (2003–13)	Wu Bangguo 吴邦国 (2003–13)	Jia Qinglin 贾庆林 (2003–13)
	Xi Jinping 习近平 (2012–)			Li Keqiang 李克强 (2013–)	Zhang Dejiang 张德江 (2013–18) Li Zhanshu 栗战书 (2018–)	Yu Zhengsheng 俞正声 (2013–18) Wang Yang 汪洋 (2018–)

Chronology (1949–2022)

1 October 1949	Proclamation in Beijing of the People's Republic of China.
14 February 1950	Signing in Moscow of the Chinese–Soviet treaty of friendship, alliance and mutual assistance.
30 April 1950	Marriage law.
28 June 1950	Launching of the agrarian reform (*tudi gaige*).
25 October 1950	Beginning of the participation of Chinese 'volunteers' in the Korean War.
December 1951	Three-anti Campaign (*sanfan*).
April 1952	Five-anti Campaign (*wufan*).
20 September 1954	Adoption of the Constitution by the First National People's Congress.
October 1955	Acceleration of agricultural collectivization.
January 1956	Nationalization of industries and businesses in the cities.
2 May 1956	Mao Zedong launches the Hundred Flowers slogan.
15 September 1956	Eighth Party Congress.
27 February 1957	Mao Zedong's speech 'On the just solution to the contradictions within the people.'
12 March 1957	Launch of the Hundred Flowers Campaign (*baihua qifang*).
8 June 1957	Launch of the anti-rightist campaign.
May 1958	Launch of the Great Leap Forward (*da yuejin*).
August 1958	Spread of people's communes.
17–23 March 1959	Uprising in Lhasa (Tibet) and flight of the Dalai Lama to India.
April 1959	Election of Liu Shaoqi as Chairman of the Republic by the National People's Congress.
2–16 August 1959	Plenary Session of the Central Committee in Lushan. Mao attacks Peng Dehuai.

17 September 1959	Lin Biao succeeds Peng Dehuai at the Ministry of Defence.
16 July 1960	The USSR recalls its experts from China.
January 1961	Adoption of a policy of economic liberalization.
January 1962	Conference of 7,000 cadres.
September 1962	Launch of the Socialist Education Movement.
16 October 1964	First nuclear test.
10 November 1965	Publication of Yao Wenyuan's article attacking Wu Han's play, *Hai Rui Dismissed from Office*.
16 May 1966	Creation of the Cultural Revolution group and distribution of the 16 May Circular.
25 May 1966	Nie Yuanzi's *Dazibao* at Peking University.
8 August 1966	Adoption of the 'Sixteen Point Declaration', the charter of the Cultural Revolution.
5 February 1967	Proclamation of the Shanghai commune.
July 1967	Military rebellion in Wuhan.
3 August 1967	Invasion of the Foreign Ministry by the Red Guards.
March 1969	Military clashes with the USSR on the Ussuri River.
1–24 April 1969	Ninth Congress of the CCP.
12 September 1971	'Accidental' death of Lin Biao.
25 October 1971	The People's Republic succeeds the Republic of China (Taipei) as China's representative to the United Nations.
24–28 August 1973	Tenth Congress of the CCP.
13–17 January 1975	Fourth National People's Congress. It relaunches Zhou Enlai's Four Modernizations programme and adopts a new Constitution.
8 January 1976	Death of Zhou Enlai.
4–5 April 1976	Demonstrations in Tiananmen Square in tribute to Zhou Enlai.
7 April 1976	Appointment of Hua Guofeng as Premier and first Vice Chairman of the Party.
28 July 1976	Tangshan earthquake.
9 September 1976	Death of Mao Zedong.
6 October 1976	Arrest of the Gang of Four.

12–18 August 1976	Eleventh Party Congress.
February 1978	The Fifth People's Congress adopts a new Constitution.
December 1978	Democracy Wall in Beijing.
12–18 December 1978	Third Plenary Session of the Eleventh Central Committee. Deng Xiaoping beats Hua Guofeng. Launch of the rural liberalization policy.
30 March 1979	Deng Xiaoping formulates the four fundamental principles. Repression of the democracy movement.
July 1979	Creation of four Special Economic Zones (SEZ).
November 1980	Trial of the Gang of Four.
June 1981	Sixth plenary session of the Eleventh Central Committee. Hu Yaobang is elected Party Chairman.
1–12 September 1982	Twelfth Congress of the CCP. Hu Yaobang becomes Secretary General of the CCP.
4 December 1982	The Fifth National People's Congress adopts a new Constitution.
December 1986	Student demonstrations.
16 January 1987	Dismissal of Hu Yaobang.
25–31 October 1987	Thirteenth Congress of the CCP. Zhao Ziyang becomes Secretary General of the CCP.
4 November 1987	Li Peng is appointed Premier.
March 1989	Uprising in Lhasa. Proclamation of martial law.
15 April 1989	Death of Hu Yaobang.
25 April 1989	Demonstrations by Beijing students in memory of Hu Yaobang.
19 May 1989	Proclamation of martial law.
5 June 1989	Entry of People's Liberation Army troops in Beijing.
23–24 June 1989	Fourth plenary session of the Thirteenth Congress. Zhao Ziyang is replaced by Jiang Zemin as the Party's Secretary General.
January 15–February 21 1992	Deng Xiaoping tours the South.

12–18 October 1992	Fourteenth Congress of the CCP.
1 July 1997	Handover of Hong Kong back to China.
12–18 September 1997	Fifteenth Congress of the CCP.
25 April 1999	10,000 members of Falungong demonstrate in Beijing.
11 December 2001	China becomes a member of the World Trade Organization.
14 November 2002	Sixteenth Congress of the CCP. Hu Jintao becomes General Secretary.
October 2007	Seventeenth Congress of the CCP.
12 May 2008	Earthquake in Sichuan province.
8 August 2008	Opening of the Beijing Olympics.
1 May 2010	World Expo opens in Shanghai.
8 October 2010	Nobel Peace Prize awarded to Liu Xiaobo.
15 March 2012	Arrest of Bo Xilai.
2 September 2012	Bo Xilai sentenced to life imprisonment.
November 2012	Eighteenth Congress of the CCP. Election of Xi Jinping as General Secretary.
March 2013	Tenth National People's Congress. Xi Jinping is elected President of the Republic and Li Keqiang Premier. At the Congress, Xi calls for 'a great renaissance of the Chinese nation'.
7 September 2013	Xi Jinping formulates his project for a New Silk Road (*yidai yilu*, literally 'one belt one road').
13 July 2017	Liu Xiaobo dies in prison.
October 2017	The Nineteenth Party Congress re-elects Xi Jinping as Secretary General of the CCP.
March 2018	Eleventh National People's Congress elects Xi Jinping to a second term as President of the Republic.
23 January 2020	Wuhan (Hubei) under lockdown until April 8 to fight the outbreak of Covid-19.
20 June 2020	Standing Committee of the NPC adopts the Hong Kong National Security Law.
July 2021	100th anniversary of the CCP.
February 2022	Beijing Winter Olympics

April 2022	Shanghai under 2 months lockdown to fight against Covid-19 outbreak.
16–22 October 2022	20th Congress of the CCP; Xi Jinping re-elected for a third term.
November 2022	Protests against Covid-19 measures.
December 2022	Lifting of restrictions related to Covid-19.

Notes

Introduction

1 Lucien Bianco, 'Voyage en Chine', *Esprit*, March 1975, pp. 430–436.
2 Jean-Luc Domenach, 'Chine: Les balbutiements de l'histoire', *Critique internationale*, 24/4, 2004, pp. 81–103 (p. 102).
3 Jean-Luc Domenach and Xiahong Xiao-Planes, 'De nouvelles sources pour l'histoire politique de la "première Chine populaire" (1949–1976)', *Vingtième Siècle. Revue d'histoire*, 116/4, 2012, pp. 121–135.
4 See Gilles Guiheux, 'Les matériaux pour la monographie d'un territoire chinois. Le cas d'une ville marchande', *Terrains & Travaux*, 16, 2009, pp. 153–174.
5 Robert Ash, David Shambaugh and Seiichiro Takagi, *China Watching: Perspectives from Europe, Japan and the United States* (London: Routledge, 2007).

Chapter 1   Establishment of a New Regime (1949–1957)

1 Jian Chen, 'The Chinese Communist "liberation" of Tibet, 1949–1951', in Jeremy Brown and Paul G. Pickowicz (eds.), *Dilemmas of Victory. The Early Years of the People's Republic of China* (Cambridge, MA: Harvard University Press, 2007), pp. 130–159 (pp. 138–139).
2 Sherman Cochran and Andrew Hsieh, *The Lius of Shanghai* (Cambridge, MA: Harvard University Press, 2013).
3 Frederic Wakeman Jr, '"Cleanup": The new order in Shanghai', in Brown and Pickowicz (eds.), *Dilemmas of Victory*, pp. 21–58 (p. 38).
4 Julian Strauss, 'Morality, coercion and state building by campaign in the early PRC: Regime consolidation and after, 1949–1956', *The China Quarterly*, 188/1, 2006, pp. 891–912.
5 Ibid.
6 Isabelle Thireau and Linshan Hua, *Les Ruses de la démocratie. Protester en Chine* (Paris: Seuil, 2010), p. 57.
7 Strauss, 'Morality, coercion and state building'.
8 Nakajima Mineo, 'Foreign relations: From the Korean War to the Bandung Line', in Denis Twitchett and John K. Fairbank (eds.), *Cambridge History of China*, vol. 14-1 (Cambridge: Cambridge University Press, 1987), pp. 258–289.
9 Lucien Bianco, *La Récidive. Révolution russe, révolution chinoise* (Paris: Gallimard, 2014), ch. 4, pp. 121–180.
10 William C. Kirby, 'Continuity and change in modern China: Economic planning on the mainland and on Taiwan, 1943–1958', *The Australian Journal of Chinese Affairs*, 24, 1990, pp. 121–142.
11 Frederick C. Teiwes, *Politics at Mao's Court. Gao Gang and Party Factionalism in the Early 1950s* (Armonk, NY: M. E. Sharpe, 1990).
12 Frederick C. Teiwes, 'Establishment and consolidation of the new regime', in Denis

Twitchett and John K. Fairbank (eds.), *Cambridge History of China*, vol. 14-1 (Cambridge: Cambridge University Press, 1987), pp. 51–143.

13 Paul A. Cohen, 'Ambiguities of a watershed state: The 1949 divide in Chinese History', in Paul A. Cohen, *China Unbound: Evolving Perspectives on the Chinese Past* (London: Routledge, 2003), pp. 13–34.

Chapter 2   Maoism and Its Excesses (1958–1976)

1 Jean-Luc Domenach, *Aux origines du Grand Bond en avant. Le cas d'une province chinoise, 1956–1958* (Paris: Éditions de l'EHESS, 1982), p. 177.

2 Jisheng Yang, *Stèles. La grande famine en Chine, 1958–1961* (Paris: Seuil, 2012), pp. 138–139.

3 This new historiographical trend was inaugurated by Jasper Becker in *Hungry Ghosts: China's Secret Famine* (London: Murray, 1996). This was followed by Frank Dikötter, *Mao's Great Famine. The History of China's Most Devasting Catastrophe, 1958–1962* (London: Bloomsbury, 2010); Kimberley Ens Manning and Felix Wemheur (eds.), *Eating Bitterness: New Perspectives on China's Great Leap Forward and Famine* (Vancouver: UBC Press, 2011); Xun Zhou (ed.), *The Great Famine in China, 1958–1962: A Documentary History* (New Haven, CT: Yale University Press, 2012); and Yang, *Stèles*.

4 Xizhe Peng, 'Demographic consequences of the Great Leap Forward in China's provinces', *Population and Development Review*, 13/4, 1987, pp. 639–670 (p. 649).

5 Basil Ashton, Kenneth Hill, Alan Piazza and Robin Zeitz, 'Famine in China, 1958–1961', *Population and Development Review*, 10/4, 1984, pp. 613–645 (p. 614).

6 Becker, *Hungry Ghosts*, p. 272.

7 Yixin Chen, 'Under the same Maoist sky: Accounting for death rate discrepancies in Anhui and Jiangxi', in Kimberley Ens Manning and Felix Wemheur (eds.), *Eating Bitterness: New Perspectives on China's Great Leap Forward and Famine* (Vancouver: UBC Press, 2011), pp. 197–225.

8 Yang, *Stèles*.

9 William A. Joseph, 'A tragedy of good intentions: Post-Mao views of the Great Leap Forward', *Modern China*, 12/4, 1986, pp. 419–457.

10 Yang, *Stèles*, pp. 483–494.

11 Dali L. Yang, *Calamity and Reform in China: State, Rural Society, and Institutional Change Since the Great Leap Forward* (Stanford, CA: Stanford University Press, 1996).

12 Frederick C. Teiwes and Warren Sun, in *China's Road to Disaster: Mao, Central Politicians, and Provincial Leaders in the Unfolding of the Great Leap Forward* (Armonk, NY: M. E. Sharpe, 1999), draw on the work of Chinese historians to highlight the major role played by Mao.

13 Thomas P. Bernstein, 'Mao Zedong and the famine of 1959–1960: A study in wilfulness', *The China Quarterly*, 186, 2006, pp. 421–445.

14 F. Dikötter, *Mao's Great Famine*, pp. 58–59.

15 Felix Wemheur, 'Dealing with responsibility for the Great Leap Famine in the People's Republic of China', *The China Quarterly*, 201, 2010, pp. 176–194.

16 David Bachman, 'Aspects of an Institutionalizing Political System: China, 1958–1965', *The China Quarterly*, 188, 2006, pp. 933–958.

17 Roderick MacFarquhar and Michael Schoenhals, *Mao's Last Revolution* (Cambridge, MA: Harvard University Press, 2008).

18 Simon Leys (*alias* Pierre Ryckmans), *Les Habits neufs du président Mao* (Paris: Champ libre, 1971).

19 MacFarquhar and Schoenhals, *Mao's Last Revolution*.
20 Andrew G. Walder, 'Factional conflict at Peking University, 1966–1968', *The China Quarterly*, 188, 2006, pp. 1023–1047.
21 Ibid.
22 Michel Bonnin, *Génération perdue: Le mouvement d'envoi des jeunes instruits à la campagne en Chine, 1968–1980* (Paris: Éditions de l'EHESS, 2004). See also Thomas Bernstein, *Up to the Mountains and Down to the Villages. The Transfer of Youth from Urban to Rural China* (New Haven, CT: Yale University Press, 1977).
23 MacFarquhar and Schoenhals, *Mao's Last Revolution*.
24 Roderick MacFarquhar, 'The succession to Mao and the end of Maoism', in Roderick MacFarquhar and John Fairbank (eds.), *Cambridge History of China, The PRC, Revolutions within the Chinese Revolution, 1966–1982*, vol. 15 (Cambridge: Cambridge University Press, 1991), pp. 303–401 (p. 315).
25 Political divisions were now compounded by the geographical scattering of the elites. See Jean-Luc Domenach, *Mao, sa cour et ses complots. Derrière les murs rouges* (Paris: Fayard, 2012), pp. 425–426.
26 Lucien Bianco, 'Mao et son modèle', *Vingtième siècle. Revue d'histoire*, 101, 2009, pp. 81–93 (p. 83).

Chapter 3   Giving Priority to Economic Modernization (1976–1992)
1 Harry Harding, 'The Chinese state in crisis', in Roderick MacFarquhar and John Fairbank (eds.), *Cambridge History of China, The PRC, Revolutions within the Chinese Revolution, 1966–1982*, vol. 15 (Cambridge: Cambridge University Press, 1991), pp. 105–217 (p. 213).
2 Warren Sun and Frederick C. Teiwes, 'China's new economic policy under Hua Guofeng: Party consensus and party myths', *China Journal*, 66, 2011, pp. 1–23; Warren Sun and Frederick C. Teiwes, *Paradoxes of Post-Mao Rural Reform: Initial Steps Toward a New Chinese Countryside 1976–1981* (New York: Routledge, 2016).
3 Jianfu Chen, 'La révision de la Constitution en République populaire de Chine. De l'évolution du concept de "socialisme aux couleurs de la Chine"', *Perspectives chinoises*, 53, 1999, pp. 66–79 (p. 68).
4 Text cited from https://china.usc.edu/sites/default/files/article/attachments/peoples-republic-of-china-constitution-1978.pdf.
5 Kjeld Erik Brodsgaard, 'The democracy movement in China, 1978–1979: Opposition movements, wall poster campaigns, and underground journals', *Asian Survey*, 21/7, 1981, pp. 747–774.
6 Jingsheng Wei, *La Cinquième Modernisation et autres écrits du Printemps de Pékin* (Paris: Bourgois, 1997).
7 Brodsgaard, 'The democracy movement in China', pp. 762ff.
8 Ibid., pp. 768–769.
9 This is the figure given by Jean-Pierre Cabestan, *Le Système politique chinois. Un nouvel équilibre autoritaire* (Paris: Presses de Sciences Po, 2014), p. 167, n.1.
10 Benjamin Yang, 'The making of a pragmatic Communist: The early life of Deng Xiaoping, 1904–1949', *The China Quarterly*, 135, 1993, pp. 444–456.
11 Bernard Debord and Marie Holzman, *Wei Jingsheng, un Chinois inflexible* (Paris: Bleu de Chine, 2005).
12 Michel Bonnin, 'The threatened history and collective memory of the Cultural Revolution's lost generation', *China Perspectives*, 2007/4, pp. 52–64.

13 On the rehabilitation of the victims of unjust political sanctions and the withdrawing of the labels applied to class enemies since 1949, see Isabelle Thireau and Linshan Hua, *Les Ruses de la démocratie. Protester en Chine* (Paris: Seuil, 2010), chap. VI, 'Révision, réhabilitation, restitution', pp. 179–212.

14 Text cited from https://www.constituteproject.org/constitution/China_2004.pdf.

15 Text cited from http://www.bjreview.com/Special_Reports/2018/40th_Anniversary_of_Reform_and_Opening_up/Timeline/201806/t20180626_800133641.html.

16 Text cited from https://www.constituteproject.org/constitution/China_2004.pdf.

17 For a detailed account of the events and the reactions among senior Party officials, see Liang Zhang, *Les Archives de Tian'anmen* (Paris: Le Félin, 2004).

18 The elders were an informal and varied group that included some of the most senior figures in the Party (Deng Xiaoping, Chen Yun, Li Xiannian, Yang Shangkun), veterans close to Mao (Wang Zhen), other leaders who had disagreed with Mao Zedong but who had been proved right by history (Peng Zheng, Bo Yibo) and a single woman, Deng Yichao, the widow of Zhou Enlai.

Chapter 4 Building a New Model (after 1992)

1 'Les discours de Deng Xiaoping dans le Sud', *Perspectives chinoises*, 2, April 1992, pp. 10–14.

2 Michel Bonnin, 'Le XIVe Congrès: Le sacre de Deng Xiaoping', *Perspectives chinoises*, 8/9, 1992, pp. 9–16.

3 For Yves Chevrier, this was a major change; see his 'De la révolution à l'état par le Communisme', *Le Débat*, 117/5, 2001, pp. 92–113.

4 The preamble of the Constitution of 1982 specifies: 'Taiwan is part of the sacred territory of the People's Republic of China. It is the sacred duty of all the Chinese people, including our fellow Chinese in Taiwan, to achieve the great reunification of the motherland.' http://www.npc.gov.cn/englishnpc/constitution2019/201911/1f65146fb6104dd3a2793875d19b5b29.shtml, accessed 23 February 2022.

5 Cheng Li, and Lynn White, 'The Fifteenth Central Committee of the Chinese Communist Party: full-fledged technocratic leadership with partial control by Jiang Zemin', *Asian Survey*, 38/3, 1998, pp. 231–264.

6 Cheng Li, 'Jiang Zemin's Successors: the rise of the fourth generation of leaders in the PRC', *The China Quarterly*, 161, 2000, pp. 1–40.

7 See David A. Palmer, *Qigong Fever: Body, Science, and Utopia in China* (New York: Columbia University Press, 2007).

8 David A. Palmer, 'La doctrine de Li Hongzhi', *Perspectives chinoises*, 64, March–April 2001, pp. 14–24.

9 David Shambaugh, 'The dynamics of elite politics during the Jiang Era', *The China Journal*, 45, 2001, pp. 101–111.

10 Cheng Li, 'Jiang Zemin's Successors: the rise of the fourth generation of leaders in the PRC', *The China Quarterly*, 161, 2000, pp. 1–40.

11 In 2007, the Seventeenth Politburo included five representatives of the Party apparatus, five representatives of state organs, five representatives of regional governments and three representatives of the military and security apparatus.

12 Jianfu Chen, 'The revision of the Constitution in the PRC. A great leap forward or a symbolic gesture?', *China Perspectives*, 53, 2004. DOI: 10.4000/chinaperspectives.2922.

13 1999 amendment to article 11. See: http://www.npc.gov.cn/englishnpc/constitution2019/201911/1f65146fb6104dd3a2793875d19b5b29.shtml.

14 See the revised article 10 of the Constitution.
15 Sébastien Colin, 'La Chine et ses campagnes. "L'édification de nouvelles campagnes socialistes": Un remède contre le malaise rural chinois?', *Transcontinentales*, 3, 2006, pp. 47–66.
16 Figures quoted by Colin, 'La Chine et ses campagnes', p. 50.
17 Alice Miller, 'China's new party Leadership', *China Leadership Monitor*, 23, 2007.
18 See Michel Bonnin, 'Far from harmonious: The Chinese authorities' handling of the 2008 Tibet crisis', *China Perspectives*, 2009/3, pp. 66–72; Robert Barnett, 'The Tibet protests of spring 2008', *China Perspectives*, 2009/3, pp. 6–23; Andrew Martin Fischer, 'The political economy of boomerang aid in China's Tibet', *China Perspectives*, 2009/3, pp. 38–54.
19 Shawn Shieh and Guosheng Deng, 'Emerging civil society: The impact of the 2008 Sichuan earthquake on grass-roots associations in China', *The China Journal*, 65, 2011, pp. 181–194.
20 Anne-Marie Brady, 'The Beijing Olympics as a campaign of mass distraction', *The China Quarterly*, 197, 2009, pp. 1–24.
21 Geremie R. Barmé, 'China's flat earth: History and 8 August 2008', *The China Quarterly*, 197, 2009, pp. 64–86.
22 Cheng Li, 'A biographical and factional analysis of the post-2012 Politburo', *China Leadership Monitor*, 41, 2013. https://www.hoover.org/research/biographical-and-factional-analysis-post-2012-politburo.

Chapter 5 Forms of Government: From Arbitrary Rule to the Aborted Attempt at Institutionalization

1 David Shambaugh, *China's Communist Party. Atrophy and Adaptation* (Berkeley, CA: University of California Press, 2008).
2 I have taken this term from Andrew J. Nathan, 'Authoritarian resilience', *Journal of Democracy*, 14/1, 2003, pp. 6–17.
3 Jean-Pierre Cabestan, *Le Système politique chinois. Un nouvel équilibre autoritaire* (Paris: Presses de Sciences Po, 2014), p. 77.
4 Ibid., p. 81.
5 Ibid., p. 402.
6 This is the case argued by Heike Holobig in 'Remaking the CCP's Ideology: Determinants, progress, and limits under Hu Jintao', *Journal of Current Chinese Affairs*, 3, 2009, pp. 35–61.
7 Lucien Bianco, 'La Révolution fourvoyée', *Le Monde*, 10 September 1976.
8 See Alain Roux, *Le Singe et le tigre. Mao, un destin chinois* (Paris: Larousse, 2009).
9 Jean-Pierre Cabestan, 'Is China moving towards "enlightened" but plutocratic authoritarianism?', *China Perspectives*, 55, 2004. DOI: 10.4000/chinaperspectives.412.
10 Cheng Li, 'Jiang Zemin's successors: The rise of the fourth generation of leaders in the PRC', *The China Quarterly*, 161, 2000, pp. 1–40.
11 Cheng Li, 'A biographical and factional analysis of the post-2012 Politburo', *China Leadership Monitor*, 41, 2013. https://www.hoover.org/research/biographical-and-factional-analysis-post-2012-politburo.
12 Lucien W. Pye, 'Jiang Zemin's style of rule: Go for stability, monopolize power and settle for limited effectiveness', *The China Journal*, 45, 2001, pp. 45–51.
13 Deng Xiaoping (1904–1997), Chen Yun (1905–1995), Peng Zhen (1902–1997), Wang

Zhen (1908–1993), Bo Yibo (1908–2007), Yang Shangkun (1907–1998), Song Renqiong (1909–2005) and Li Xiannian (1909–1992). In 1980, they were all more than 80 years old.

14 I take this term from Jean-Pierre Cabestan, 'Chine: un état de lois sans état de droit', *Revue Tiers-Monde*, XXXVII/147, 1996, pp. 649–668.

15 See also Stéphanie Balme, *Chine. Les visages de la justice ordinaire. Entre faits et droit* (Paris: Presses de Sciences Po, 2016).

16 See note 14.

17 Cabestan, *Le Système politique chinois*, p. 377.

18 David Shambaugh, *Modernizing China's Military: Progress, Problems, and Prospects* (Berkeley, CA: University of California Press, 2004).

19 Jean-Luc Domenach, *L'Archipel oublié* (Paris: Fayard, 1992).

20 Ibid., p. 299.

21 This is the argument put forward by Jürgen Domes in 'La société politique', in Marie-Claude Bergère, Lucien Bianco and Jürgen Domes (eds.), *La Chine au XXe siècle, de 1949 à aujourd'hui* (Paris: Fayard, 1990), pp. 239–254. In his view, 'both the seizure of power by the totalitarian elite and the stability of the political systems dominated by these same elites depend on the creation and maintenance of social coalitions' (p. 246).

22 Sherman Cochran and Andrew Hsieh, *The Lius of Shanghai* (Cambridge, MA: Harvard University Press, 2013).

23 See Jean-Philippe Béja, *À la recherche d'une ombre chinoise* (Paris: Le Seuil, 2004), pp. 206–224.

24 This is sometimes known as the Bureau for Letters and Calls. [Translator's note.] See also Isabelle Thireau and Linshan Hua, *Les Ruses de la démocratie. Protester en Chine* (Paris: Seuil, 2010).

25 Séverine Arsène, *Internet et politique en Chine* (Paris: Karthala, 2011), p. 411.

26 Béja, *À la recherche d'une ombre chinoise*, p. 244.

27 Yves Chevrier, 'L'empire distendu: Esquisse du politique en Chine des Qing à Deng Xiaoping', in Jean–François Bayart (ed.), *La Greffe de l'état* (Paris: Karthala, 1996), pp. 263–395.

28 Yves Chevrier, 'La question de la société civile, la Chine et le chat du Cheshire', *Études chinoises*, XIV/2, 1995, pp. 153–248.

29 I take this expression from Li Zehou and Liu Zaifu, *Gaobie geming. Huiwang ershi shiqi* [*Farewell to the Revolution. Looking back at the twentieth century*] (Hong Kong: Tiandi tushu, 1995), quoted in Yves Chevrier, 'De la révolution à l'état par le Communisme', *Le Débat*, 117/5, 2001, pp. 92–113 (p. 107).

30 Jean-Louis Rocca, 'Is China becoming an ordinary state?', in Hibou, Béatrice, *Privatizing the State*, trans. Jonathan Derrick (New York: Columbia University Press, 2004), pp. 169–182.

31 Michel Bonnin, 'Les métamorphoses du totalitarisme', *Le Débat*, 117/5, 2001, pp. 114–135.

32 Jean-Pierre Béja, 'Crise sociale endémique et renforcement de la dictature en Chine populaire', *Esprit*, December 2001, pp. 126–145.

33 Béja, *À la recherche d'une ombre chinoise*, pp. 243–244.

34 Ibid., p. 243.

35 Cabestan, 'La Chine évoluerait-elle?', p. 21.

36 Yves Chevrier, 'De la révolution à l'état par le Communisme', *Le Débat*, 117/5, 2001, pp. 92–113. p. 109.

37 Jean-Pierre Cabestan, 'The 10th National People's Congress and after: Moving towards a

new authoritarianism – both elitist and consultative?', *China Perspectives*, 47, 2003. DOI: 10.4000/chinaperspectives.272.

38 Andrew Nathan, *China's Transition* (New York: Columbia University Press, 1998).

39 Shambaugh, *China's Communist Party.*

Chapter 6   The Creation of Wealth: From Planned Economy to the Market

1 Angus Maddison, *Chinese Economic Performance in the Long Run* (Paris: OECD Publishing, 1998).

2 William C. Kirby, 'Continuity and Change in Modern China: Economic planning on the mainland and on Taiwan, 1943–1958', *The Australian Journal of Chinese Affairs*, 24, 1990, pp. 121–142.

3 Barry Naughton, *The Chinese Economy. Transitions and Growth* (Cambridge, MA: MIT Press, 2007), p. 56.

4 Ibid., p. 67.

5 Lucien Bianco, *La Récidive. Révolution russe, révolution chinoise* (Paris: Gallimard, 2014), p. 90.

6 Claude Aubert, 'Économie et sociétés rurales', in Marie-Claire Bergère, Lucien Bianco and Jürgen Domes (eds.), *La Chine au XXe siècle* (Paris: Fayard, 1990), pp. 149–180 (p. 165).

7 Barry Naughton, *The Chinese Economy. Transitions and Growth* (Cambridge, MA: MIT Press, 2007), p. 80.

8 Ibid., pp. 80–81.

9 Ibid., p. 81.

10 Barry Naughton, *Growing Out of the Plan. Chinese Economic Reform, 1978–1993* (Cambridge: Cambridge University Press, 1996).

11 Barry Naughton, 'China's economic policy today: The new state activism', *Eurasian Geography and Economics*, 52/3, 2011, pp. 313–329.

12 Ibid., p. 321.

13 Françoise Lemoine, *L'Économie des BRIC* (Paris: La Découverte, 2013), p. 19.

14 *China Labour Statistical Yearbook.*

15 Gilles Guiheux, 'The incomplete crystallisation of the private sector', *China Perspectives*, 42, 2002, pp. 24–36.

16 Figures quoted by Naughton in 'China's economic policy today', p. 315, for businesses with a turnover of more than 5 million RMB.

17 Figures quoted by Naughton, ibid., p. 315.

18 Jean C. Oi, *Rural China Takes Off. Institutional Foundations of Economic Reform* (Berkeley, CA: University of California Press, 1999).

19 Liping Sun and Mingjie Ma, 'Forcer le peuple à s'enrichir!', *Études rurales*, 161/162, 2002, pp. 165–182.

20 Jonathan Unger and Anita Chan, 'Inheritors of the boom: Private enterprise and the role of government in a rural South China township', *The China Journal*, 42, 1999, pp. 45–74.

21 Marc Blecher and Vivienne Shue, 'Into leather: State-led development and the private sector in Xinji', *The China Quarterly*, 166, 2001, pp. 368–393.

22 Jane Duckett, *The Entrepreneurial State in China. Real Estate and Commerce Departments in Reform Era Tianjin* (London: Routledge, 1998).

23 David L. Wank, 1999, *Commodifying Communism: Business, Trust and Politics in a Chinese City* (Cambridge: Cambridge University Press, 1999).

24 Dali L. Yang and Waikeung Tam, 'Food safety and the development of regulatory institutions in China', *Asian Perspective*, 29/4, 2005, pp. 5–36.
25 Lemoine, *L'Économie des BRIC*, p. 56.
26 Ibid., p. 61.
27 Ibid., p. 61.
28 Ibid., p. 65.
29 Françoise Lemoine and Deniz Ünal, 'Mutations du commerce chinois', *La lettre du CEPII*, 352, March 2015.
30 Wing-thye Woo, Jeffrey Sachs, Fan Gang, Geng Xiao, Michael Bruno.
31 Thomas Rawski, Barry Naughton, Gary Jefferson, Peter Nolan.
32 Jean-François Huchet, *La Crise environnementale en Chine* (Paris: Presses de Sciences Po, 2016), pp. 35, 49.

Chapter 7 Society on the Move: Mobility and Inequality

1 Éric Florence, 'Debates and classification struggles regarding the representation of migrants workers', *China Perspectives*, 65, 2006. DOI: 10.4000/chinaperspectives.629.
2 Since 1998, a child has been able to inherit its *hukou* either from its mother, or from its father.
3 Andrew G. Walder and Songhua Hu, 'Revolution, Reform, and Status Inheritance: Urban China, 1949–1996', *American Journal of Sociology*, 114/5, 2009, pp. 1395–1427.
4 Jean-François Billeter, 'The System of "class status"', in Stuart R. Scharm (ed.), *The Scope of State Power in China*, London (London: SOAS, University of London, 1985), pp. 127–171.
5 Lucien Bianco, *La Récidive. Révolution russe, révolution chinoise* (Paris: Gallimard, 2014), p. 256.
6 Jean-Luc Domenach, *Mao, sa cour et ses complots. Derrière les murs rouges* (Paris: Fayard, 2012).
7 Ibid., p. 75.
8 Stanley Rosen, *The Role of the Sent-down Youth in the Chinese Cultural Revolution: The Case of Guangzhou* (Berkeley, CA: University of California Press, 1981); Michel Bonnin, *Génération perdue: Le mouvement d'envoi des jeunes instruits à la campagne en Chine, 1968–1980* (Paris: Éditions de l'EHESS, 2004).
9 Bonnin, *Génération perdue*, p. 425.
10 Ibid., p. 413.
11 Andrew G. Walder and Songhua Hu, 'Revolution, reform, and status inheritance: Urban China, 1949–1996', *American Journal of Sociology*, 114/5, 2009, pp. 1395–1427.
12 Martin Ravallion and Shaohua Chen, 'China's (uneven) progress against poverty', *Journal of Development Economics*, 82/1, 2007, pp. 1–42.
13 Gilles Guiheux, 'Chinese socialist heroes: From workers to entrepreneurs', in Éric Florence and Pierre Defraigne (eds.), *Towards a New Development Paradigm in Twenty-First Century China. Economy, Society and Politics* (London: Routledge, 2012), pp. 115–126.
14 David Zweig, *Internationalizing China. Domestic Interests and Global Linkages* (Ithaca, NY: Cornell University Press, 2002), pp. 42–43.
15 Gilles Guiheux, 'The promotion of a new calculating Chinese subject: The case of laid-off workers turning into entrepreneurs', *Journal of Contemporary China*, 16/50, February 2007, pp. 149–171.
16 The first employment contracts date back to 1987.

17 Antoine Kernen, *La Chine vers l'économie de marché. Privatisations à Shenyang* (Paris: Karthala, 2004).

18 *China Statistical Yearbook*, 1993 and 2003.

19 *China Statistical Yearbook*, 2003, p. 123.

20 John Giles, Albert Park and Juwei Zhang, 'What is China's true unemployment rate?', *China Economic Review*, 16, 2005, pp. 149–170.

21 Dorothy Solinger, 'Why we cannot count the "unemployed"', *The China Quarterly*, 167, 2001, pp. 671–688.

22 Antoine Kernen and Jean-Louis Rocca, 'La réforme des entreprises publiques en Chine et sa gestion sociale. Le cas de Shenyang et du Liaoning', *Études du Ceri*, 37, 1998; Antoine Kernen and Jean-Louis Rocca, 'Traitement social du chômage et nouvelle pauvreté urbaine. Le cas de Shenyang et du Liaoning', *Perspectives chinoises*, 56, 1999, pp. 35–51.

23 Gilles Guiheux, 'Le nouveau "retournement" des corps et des esprits: La mise à leur compte des travailleurs licenciés du secteur d'état en Chine', *L'Homme et la société*, 152–153, 2004, pp. 97–128.

24 Gilles Guiheux, 'The transformation of an urban economic area in Hunan province', *China Perspectives*, 49, 2003, pp. 4–16.

25 Ngai Pun and Chris Smith, 'Putting transnational labour process in its place: The dormitory labour regime in post-socialist China', *Work, Employment & Society*, 21/1, 2007, pp. 27–45.

26 Lu Shi, *Voix de migrants* (Toulouse: Presses Universitaires de Toulouse, 2014).

27 Two volumes based on national surveys on inequality carried out in 1988, 1995 and 2002 have been published: Xueyi Lu (ed.), *Dangdai zhongguo shehui jieceng yanjiu baogao [Research report on social stratification in contemporary China]* (Beijing: Shehui kexue wenxian chubanshe, 2002) and Xueyi Lu (ed.), *Dangdai zhongguo shehui liudong [Social mobility in contemporary China]* (Beijing: Shehui kexue wenxian chubanshe, 2004).

28 Sun Liping, *Duanlie [The break]* (Beijing: Shehui kexui wenxian chubanshe, 2003).

29 He Qinglian, *Zhongguo de xianjing [The traps of China]* (Hong Kong: Mingjing chubanshe, 1997); He Qinglian, 'China's Listing Social Structure', *New Left Review*, September–October 2000, pp. 69–99.

30 Jisheng Yang, 'An overall analysis of current social stratification in China', *Zhongguo shehui kexue qikan* [Chinese Social Sciences quarterly], 3, 1999.

31 A coefficient of 0 signifies maximal equality between all the members of the community under consideration and a coefficient of 1 signifies a maximal inequality, with one member taking all the resources.

32 Yu Xie and Xiang Zhou, 'Income inequality in today's China', *Proceedings of the National Academy of Sciences of the United States of America*, 111/19, 2014, pp. 6928–6933.

Chapter 8 The Towns versus the Countryside

1 Martin King Whyte, 'The paradoxes of rural–urban inequality in contemporary China', in Martin King Whyte (ed.), *One Country, Two Societies. Rural–Urban Inequality in Contemporary China* (Cambridge, MA: Harvard University Press, 2010), pp. 1–25.

2 Richard Madsen, 'The countryside under Communism', in Roderick MacFarquhar and John K. Fairbank (eds.), *Cambridge History of China: The PRC, Revolutions within the Chinese Revolution, 1966–1982*, vol. 15 (Cambridge: Cambridge University Press, 1991), pp. 617–681 (p. 650).

3 Ibid., pp. 619, 680.

4 Dali L. Yang, *Calamity and Reform in China: State, Rural Society, and Institutional Change Since the Great Leap Forward* (Stanford, CA: Stanford University Press, 1996). See also Kate Zhou Xiao, *How the Farmers Changed China: Power of the People* (London: Routledge, 1996). However, Jonathan Unger, in *The Transformation of Rural China* (Armonk, NY: M. E. Sharpe, 2002), argues that decollectivization was a plan devised on high and imposed on the rural population.

5 Xiaobo Lü and Elizabeth J. Perry (eds.), *Danwei: The Changing Chinese Workplace in Historical and Comparative Perspective* (Armonk, NY: M. E. Sharpe, 1997).

6 Andrew G. Walder, *Communist neo-Traditionalism* (Berkeley, CA: University of California Press, 1986).

7 Figures quoted in Judith Audin, 'Politiques du logement urbain en Chine, du Communisme à l'économie de marché: genèse d'une économie politique de l'assujettissement', *Le Banquet*, 31, 2012–2013, pp. 79–97 (p. 80).

8 Corinne Eyraud, *L'Entreprise d'État chinoise. De 'l'institution sociale totale' vers l'entité économique?* (Paris: L'Harmattan, 1999), p. 148.

9 Hélène Hovasse, 'Pudong. Le nouveau poumon de Shanghai', *Perspectives chinoises*, 16, 1993, pp. 26–36.

10 On the conditions in which migrants were integrated into housing, see Yeqin Zhao, *Construction des espaces urbains et rénovation d'un quartier de Shangai: la problématique de la migration et du changement social* (Shanghai: Sanlian Shudian, 2011).

11 See Gilles Guiheux, 'Shanghai, société de consommation', in Nicolas Idler (ed.), *Shanghai* (Paris: Robert Laffont, 2010), pp. 322–339.

12 On the role of Chinese and international architects in the designing of the new Shanghai cityscape, see Françoise Ged, *Shanghai. L'ordinaire et l'exceptionnel* (Paris: Buchet Chastel, 2014), pp. 110–122.

13 Luigi Tomba, 'Making neighbourhoods', China Perspectives, 2008/4, pp. 48–61.

14 Yingfang Chen, 'Légitimité, rationalité et compétences politiques. Comment le "miracle urbain chinois" a-t-il été possible?', *Terrains & travaux*, 16, 2009, pp. 97–136.

15 Claude Aubert, 'Le devenir de l'économie paysanne en Chine', *Revue Tiers-Monde*, XLVI/183, 2005, pp. 491–515.

16 Changping Li, *Wo xiang Zongli shuo shihua* (Beijing: Guangming ribao chubanshe, 2001).

17 Jinqing Cao, *Huanghe bian de Zhongguo* (Shanghai: Shanghai wenyi chubanshe, 2002).

18 Guidi Chen and Chun Tao, *Zhongguo nongmin diaocha* (Beijing: Renmin wenxue chubanshe, 2004).

19 Lucien Bianco, *Jacqueries et revolution dans la Chine du XXe siècle* (Paris: La Martinière, 2005); Kevin O'Brien and Lianjiang Li, *Rightful Resistance in Rural China* (Cambridge: Cambridge University Press, 2006).

20 Bianco, *Jacqueries*, p. 493.

21 Sébastien Colin, 'Le défi rural du "rêve chinois"', *Hérodote*, 150/3, 2013, pp. 9–26 (p. 15).

22 Ngai Pun, *Migrant Labor in China: Post-Socialist Transformations* (Cambridge: Polity, 2016), p. 81.

23 Chloé Froissart, *La Chine et ses migrants. La conquête d'une citoyenneté* (Rennes: PUR, 2013), p. 16.

Chapter 9 Populations: The Modernization of Society

1 Yves Boquet, 'La démographie chinoise en mutation', *Espace populations sociétés*, 2009/3, pp. 551–568.

2 Susan Greenhalgh, *Just One Child: Science and Policy in Deng's China* (Berkeley, CA: University of California Press, 2008).

3 Martin King Whyte, Feng Wang and Cai Yong, 'Challenging Myths about China's One-Child Policy', *The China Journal*, 74, 2015, pp. 144–159.

4 Susan Greenhalgh and Edwin A. Winckler, *Governing China's Population: From Leninist to Neoliberal Biopolitics* (Stanford, CA: Stanford University Press, 2005); Susan Greenhalgh, *Cultivating Global Citizens: Population in the Rise of China* (Cambridge, MA: Harvard University Press, 2010).

5 Longwen Fu and Cheris Shun-Ching Chan, 'The Hippocratic dilemmas. Guanxi and professional work in hospital care in China', *China Perspectives*, 2016/4, pp. 19–27.

6 Marie Urban, 'L'état de la protection sociale en Chine', *Revue française d'administration publique*, 150/2, 2014, pp. 467–479.

7 Figures quoted in Carine Milcent, 'Evolution of the health system: Inefficiency, violence, and digital healthcare', *China Perspectives*, 2016/4, pp. 39–50 (p. 43).

8 Susan L. Glosser, *Chinese Visions of Family and State, 1915–1953* (Berkeley, CA., University of California Press, 2003).

9 Neil J. Diamant, *Revolutionizing the Family, Politics, Love, and Divorce in Urban and Rural China, 1949–1968* (Berkeley, CA: University of California Press, 2000).

10 Gladys Chicharro, *Le Fardeau des petits empereurs. Une génération d'enfants uniques en Chine* (Nanterre: Société d'ethnologie, 2010).

11 Yuhua Guo, 'D'une forme de réciprocité à l'autre. Une analyse de la prise en charge des personnes âgées dans les villages du Hubei', in Isabelle Thireau and Hansheng Wang, *Disputes au village chinois. Formes du juste et recompositions locales des espaces normatifs* (Paris: Maison des sciences de l'homme, 2001), pp. 13–37.

12 Suiming Pan, *Dangdai Zhongguo ren de xingwei weiyu xing guanxi* (Beijing: Shehui kexue wenxian chubanshe, 2004).

13 Jean-Baptiste Pettier, 'Politiques de l'amour et du sexe dans la Chine de la "révolution sexuelle"', *Genre, sexualité & société*, 3, 2010.

14 Tao Hong and Lucas Monteil, 'LGBT, chinois.e.s et connecté.e.s', *La Vie des idées*, 20 June 2017. http://www.laviedesidees.fr/LGBT-chinois-e-set-connecte-e-s.html.

15 Pierre Miège, 'In my opinion, most *Tongzhi* are dutiful sons!', *China Perspectives*, 2009/1, pp. 40–53.

16 Lucas Monteil, 'De "l'Amour vieux-jeune". Âge, classe et homosexualité masculine en Chine post-maoïste', *Clio. Femmes, Genre, Histoire*, 42, 2015, pp. 147–163.

17 Xiaojing Tang, 'Les femmes du Grand bond en avant', *Travail, genre et sociétés*, 23, 2010, pp. 61–78.

18 Yunxiang Yan, 'Courtship, love and premarital sex in a north China village', *The China Journal*, 48, 2002, pp. 29–53.

19 Sara L. Friedman, 'The intimacy of state power: Marriage, liberation and socialist subjects in Southeastern China', *American Ethnologist*, 32/2, 2005, pp. 312–327; see also William L. Parish and Martin K. Whyte, *Village and Family in Contemporary China* (Chicago, IL: Chicago University Press, 1978).

20 Yunxiang Yan, *The Individualization of Chinese Society* (Oxford: Berg, 2009); Arthur Kleinman, Yunxiang Yan and Jun Jing (eds.), *Deep China: The Moral Life of the Person* (Berkeley, CA: University of California Press, 2011).

21 Marc Bodet, 'Le *counselling* sur Internet en Chine. La psychothérapie au service de la biopolitique', Master's dissertation, Université Paris Diderot, 2017.

22 Yang Jie, 'The politics and regulation of anger in urban China', *Culture, Medicine, and Psychiatry*, 40/1, 2016, pp. 100–123.

23 Mette Halskov Hansen and Cuiming Pang, 'Me and my family: Perceptions of individual and collective among young rural Chinese', *European Journal of East Asian Studies*, 7/1, 2008, pp. 75–99.

24 Unn Malfrid H. Rolandsen, 'A collective of their own: Young volunteers at the fringes of the party realm', in Mette Halskov Hansen and Rune Svarverud (eds.), *iChina. The Rise of the Individual in Modern Chinese Society* (Copenhagen: Nias, 2010), pp. 132–163.

25 Vincent Goossaert and David A. Palmer, *La Question religieuse en Chine* (Paris: CNRS éditions, 2012), p. 13.

26 Ibid., p. 423.

27 Ibid., p. 271.

28 See Khun Eng Kuah-Pearce, *Rebuilding the Ancestral Village: Singaporeans in China* (London: Ashgate, 2000), on the role of Singaporeans in the revitalization of religious activities in the villages of their ancestors in southern China.

29 Vincent Goossaert and David A. Palmer, *La Question religieuse en Chine* (Paris: CNRS éditions, 2012), pp. 301–307.

30 Daniel H. Bays, 'Chinese Protestant Christianity today', *China Quarterly*, 174, 2003, pp. 488–504.

31 Sébastien Billioud and Joël Thoraval, *Le Sage et le peuple. Le renouveau confucéen en Chine* (Paris: CNRS éditions, 2014).

32 Ulrich Beck and Elisabeth Beck-Gernsheim, 'Foreword: Varieties of individualization', in Mete Halskov Hansen and Rune Svarverud (eds.), *iChina. The Rise of the Individual in Modern Chinese Society* (Copenhagen: Nias, 2010), pp. xii–xx.

Chapter 10   Education and Culture

1 Marianne Bastid, 'À la recherche d'une stratégie de l'éducation: École et développement économique depuis 1949', *Revue Tiers-Monde*, XXII/86, 1981, pp. 317–329 (p. 317).

2 Ibid., p. 319.

3 Ibid., p. 323.

4 Ibid., p. 327.

5 Census figures quoted in Donald J. Treiman, 'Trends in educational attainment in China', *Chinese Sociological Review*, 45/3, 2013, pp. 3–25 (p. 6).

6 Aurore Merle, 'De la reconstruction de la discipline à l'interrogation sur la transition: La sociologie chinoise à l'épreuve du temps', *Cahiers internationaux de sociologie*, 122/1, 2007, pp. 31–52 (pp. 36, 38).

7 Kai Yin, 'De l'étatisation à la propagande: La mise en place du système du cinéma Communiste chinois (1938–1952)', *Mise au point*. http://journals. openedition.org/map /1844.

8 Paul G. Pickowicz, 'Zheng Junli, complicity and the cultural history of socialist China, 1949–1976', *The China Quarterly*, 188, 2006, pp. 1048–1069.

9 Noël Dutrait, *Petit précis à l'usage de l'amateur de littérature chinoise contemporaine (1976–2006)* (Arles: Picquier, 2006), p. 13.

10 Ibid., p. 53.

11 Emmanuel Lincot, 'Contemporary Chinese art under Deng Xiaoping', *China Perspectives*, 53, 2004. DOI: 10.4000/chinaperspectives.2952 (p. 2).

12 Françoise Kreissler, 'Le Mémorial de Nankin, lectures et relectures de l'histoire', *Matériaux pour l'histoire de notre temps*, 88/4, 2007, pp. 8–12.

13 Stig Thøgersen and Søren Clausen, 'New reflections in the mirror: Local Chinese gazetteers [*difangzhi*)] in the 1980s', *The Australian Journal of Chinese Affairs*, 27, 1992, pp. 161–184.

14 Kirk A. Denton, 'Museums, memorial sites and exhibitionary culture in the People's Republic of China', *The China Quarterly*, 183, 2005, pp. 565–586 (p. 567).

15 Ibid., pp. 581–582.

16 Gilles Guiheux, 'Les matériaux pour la monographie d'un territoire chinois. Le cas d'une ville marchande', *Terrains & Travaux*, 16, 2009, pp. 153–174.

17 Marc Abélès, *Pékin 798* (Paris: Stock, 2011).

Bibliography

Abélès, Marc, *Pékin 798* (Paris: Stock, 2011).

Arsène, Séverine, *Internet et politique en Chine* (Paris: Karthala, 2011).

Ash, Robert, David Shambaugh and Seiichiro Takagi, *China Watching: Perspectives from Europe, Japan and the United States* (London: Routledge, 2007).

Ashton, Basil, Kenneth Hill, Alan Piazza and Robin Zeitz, 'Famine in China, 1958–1961', *Population and Development Review*, 10/4, 1984, pp. 613–645.

Attané, Isabelle, 'Being a woman in China today: A demography of gender', *China Perspectives*, 2012/4, pp. 5–15.

Aubert, Claude, 'Économie et sociétés rurales', in Marie-Claire Bergère, Lucien Bianco and Jürgen Domes (eds.), *La Chine au XXe siècle* (Paris: Fayard, 1990), pp. 149–180.

Aubert, Claude, 'Le devenir de l'économie paysanne en Chine', *Revue Tiers-Monde*, XLVI/183, 2005, pp. 491–515.

Audin, Judith, 'Politiques du logement urbain en Chine, du Communisme à l'économie de marché: Genèse d'une économie politique de l'assujettissement', *Le Banquet*, 31/3, 2012, pp. 79–97.

Bachman, David, 'Aspects of an institutionalizing political system: China, 1958–1965', *The China Quarterly*, 188, 2006, pp. 933–958.

Balme, Stéphanie, *Chine. Les visages de la justice ordinaire. Entre faits et droit* (Paris: Presses de Sciences Po, 2016).

Barmé, Geremie R., 'China's flat earth: History and 8 August 2008', *The China Quarterly*, 197, 2009, pp. 64–86.

Barnett, Robert, 'The Tibet protests of spring 2008', *China Perspectives*, 2009/3, pp. 6–23.

Bastid, Marianne, 'À la recherche d'une stratégie de l'éducation: École et développement économique depuis 1949', *Revue Tiers-Monde*, XXII/86, 1981, pp. 317–329.

Bays, Daniel H., 'Chinese Protestant Christianity today', *The China Quarterly*, 174, 2003, pp. 488–504.

Beck, Ulrich and Elisabeth Beck-Gernsheim, 'Foreword: Varieties of individualization', in Mete Halskov Hansen and Rune Svarverud (eds.), *iChina. The Rise of the Individual in Modern Chinese Society* (Copenhagen: Nias, 2010), pp. xii–xx.

Becker, Jasper, *Hungry Ghosts: China's Secret Famine* (London: Murray, 1996).

Béja, Jean-Philippe, 'Crise sociale endémique et renforcement de la dictature en Chine populaire', *Esprit*, December 2001, pp. 126–145.

Béja, Jean-Philippe, *À la Recherche d'une ombre chinoise* (Paris: Le Seuil, 2004).

Bernstein, Thomas P., *Up to the Mountains and Down to the Villages. The Transfer of Youth from Urban to Rural China* (New Haven, CT: Yale University Press, 1977).

Bianco, Lucien, 'Voyage en Chine', *Esprit*, March 1975, pp. 430–436.

Bianco, Lucien, 'La Révolution fourvoyée', *Le Monde*, 10 September 1976.

Bianco, Lucien, *Jacqueries et Révolution dans la Chine du XXe siècle* (Paris: La Martinière, 2005).

Bernstein, Thomas P., 'Mao Zedong and the famine of 1959–1960: A study in wilfulness', *The China Quarterly*, 186, 2006, pp. 421–445.

Bianco, Lucien, 'Mao et son modèle', *Vingtième siècle. Revue d'histoire*, 101, 2009, pp. 81–93.

Bianco, Lucien, *La Récidive. Révolution russe, révolution chinoise* (Paris: Gallimard, 2014).

Billeter, Jean-François, 'The system of "class status"', in Stuart R. Scharm (ed.), *The Scope of State Power in China* (London: SOAS, University of London, 1985), pp. 127–171.

Billioud, Sébastien and Joël Thoraval, *Le Sage et le peuple. Le renouveau confucéen en Chine* (Paris: CNRS éditions, 2014).

Blecher, Marc and Vivienne Shue, 'Into leather: State-led development and the private sector in Xinjin', *The China Quarterly*, 166, 2001, pp. 368–393.

Bodet, Marc, 'Le *counselling* sur internet en Chine. La psychothérapie au service de la biopolitique', Master's dissertation, Université Paris Diderot, 2017.

Bonnin, Michel, 'Le XIVe Congrès: Le sacre de Deng Xiaoping', *Perspectives chinoises*, 8/9, 1992, pp. 9–16.

Bonnin, Michel, 'Les métamorphoses du totalitarisme', *Le Débat*, 117/5, 2001, pp. 114–135.

Bonnin, Michel, *Génération perdue: Le mouvement d'envoi des jeunes instruits à la campagne en Chine, 1968–1980* (Paris: Éditions de l'EHESS, 2004).

Bonnin, Michel, 'The threatened history and collective memory of the Cultural Revolution's lost generation', *China Perspectives*, 2007/4, pp. 52–64.

Bonnin, Michel, 'Far from harmonious: The Chinese authorities' handling of the 2008 Tibet crisis', *China Perspectives*, 2009/3, pp. 66–72.

Boquet, Yves, 'La démographie chinoise en mutation', *Espace populations sociétés*, 2009/3, pp. 551–568.

Brady, Anne-Marie, 'The Beijing Olympics as a campaign of mass distraction', *The China Quarterly*, 197, 2009, pp. 1–24.

Brodsgaard, Kjeld Erik, 'The democracy movement in China, 1978–1979: Opposition movements, wall poster campaigns, and underground journals', *Asian Survey*, 21/7, 1981, pp. 747–774.

Cabestan, Jean-Pierre, *Le Système politique de la Chine populaire* (Paris: PUF, 1994).

Cabestan, Jean-Pierre, 'Chine: Un état de lois sans état de droit', *Revue Tiers-Monde*, XXXVII/147, 1996, pp. 649–668.

Cabestan, Jean-Pierre, 'The 10th National People's Congress and after: Moving towards a new authoritarianism – both elitist and consultative?', *China Perspectives*, 47, 2003. DOI: 10.4000/chinaperspectives.272.

Cabestan, Jean-Pierre, 'Is China moving towards "enlightened" but plutocratic authoritarianism?', *China Perspectives*, 55, 2004. DOI: 10.4000/chinaperspectives.412.

Cabestan, Jean-Pierre, *Le Système politique chinois. Un nouvel équilibre autoritaire* (Paris: Presses de Sciences Po, 2014).

Cao, Jinqing, *Huanghe bian de Zhongguo* (Shanghai: Shanghai wenyi chubanshe, 2002).

Chen, Guidi and Chun Tao, *Zhongguo nongmin diaocha* (Beijing: Renmin wenxue chubanshe, 2004).

Chen, Jian, 'The Chinese Communist "liberation" of Tibet, 1949–1951', in Jeremy Brown and Paul G. Pickowicz (eds.), *Dilemmas of Victory. The Early Years of the People's Republic of China* (Cambridge, MA: Harvard University Press, 2007), pp. 130–159.

Chen, Jianfu, 'La révision de la Constitution en République populaire de Chine. De l'évolution du concept de "socialisme aux couleurs de la Chine"', *Perspectives chinoises*, 53, 1999, pp. 66–79.

Chen, Jianfu, 'The revision of the Constitution in the PRC. A great leap forward or a symbolic gesture?', *China Perspectives*, 53, 2004, DOI: 10.4000/chinaperspectives.2922.

Chen, Yingfang, 'Légitimité, rationalité et compétences politiques. Comment le "miracle urbain chinois" a-t-il été possible?', *Terrains & travaux*, 16, 2009, pp. 97–136.

Chen, Yixin, 'Under the same Maoist sky: Accounting for death rate discrepancies in Anhui and Jiangxi', in Kimberley Ens Manning and Felix Wemheur (eds.), *Eating Bitterness: New Perspectives on China's Great Leap Forward and Famine* (Vancouver: UBC Press, 2011), pp. 197–225.

Chevrier, Yves, 'La question de la société civile, la Chine et le chat du Cheshire', *Études chinoises*, XIV/2, 1995, pp. 153–248.

Chevrier, Yves, 'L'empire distendu: Esquisse du politique en Chine des Qing à Deng Xiaoping', in Jean-François Bayart (ed.), *La Greffe de l'État* (Paris: Karthala, 1996), pp. 263–395.

Chevrier, Yves, 'De la révolution à l'état par le Communisme', *Le Débat*, 117/5, 2001, pp. 92–113.

Chicharro, Gladys, *Le Fardeau des petits empereurs. Une génération d'enfants uniques en Chine* (Nanterre: Société d'ethnologie, 2010).

China Statistical Yearbook (Beijing: China Statistics Press).

Cochran, Sherman and Andrew Hsieh, *The Lius of Shanghai* (Cambridge, MA: Harvard University Press, 2013).

Cohen, Paul A., 'Ambiguities of a watershed state: The 1949 divide in Chinese history', in Paul A. Cohen, *China Unbound: Evolving Perspectives on the Chinese Past* (London: Routledge, 2003), pp. 27–36.

Colin, Sébastien, 'La Chine et ses campagnes. "L'édification de nouvelles campagnes social-istes": Un remède contre le malaise rural chinois? *Transcontinentales*, 3, 2006, pp. 47–66.

Colin, Sébastien, 'Le défi rural du "rêve chinois"', *Hérodote*, 150/3, 2013, pp. 9–26.

Debord, Bernard and Marie Holzman, *Wei Jingsheng, un Chinois inflexible* (Paris: Bleu de Chine, 2005).

Denton, Kirk A., 'Museums, memorial sites and exhibitionary culture in the People's Republic of China', *The China Quarterly*, 183, 2005, pp. 565–586.

Diamant, Neil J., *Revolutionizing the Family: Politics, Love, and Divorce in Urban and Rural China, 1949–1968* (Berkeley, CA: University of California Press, 2000).

Dikötter, Frank, 'Les discours de Deng Xiaoping dans le Sud', *Perspectives chinoises*, 2, April 1992, pp. 10–14.

Dikötter, Frank, *Mao's Great Famine: The History of China's Most Devasting Catastrophe, 1958–1962* (London: Bloomsbury, 2010).

Domenach, Jean-Luc, *Aux origines du Grand Bond en avant. Le cas d'une province chinoise, 1956–1958* (Paris: Éditions de l'EHESS, 1982).

Domenach, Jean-Luc, *L'Archipel oublié* (Paris: Fayard, 1992).

Domenach, Jean-Luc, 'Chine: Les balbutiements de l'histoire', *Critique internationale*, 24/4, 2004, pp. 81–103.

Domenach, Jean-Luc, *Mao, sa cour et ses complots. Derrière les murs rouges* (Paris: Fayard, 2012).

Domenach, Jean-Luc and Xiahong Xiao-Planes, 'De nouvelles sources pour l'histoire politique de la "première Chine populaire" (1949–1976)', *Vingtième Siècle. Revue d'histoire*, 116/4, 2012, pp. 121–135.

Domes, Jürgen, 'La société politique', in Marie-Claire Bergère, Lucien Bianco and Jürgen

Domes (eds.), *La Chine au XXe siècle, de 1949 à aujourd'hui* (Paris: Fayard, 1990), pp. 239–254.

Duckett, Jane, *The Entrepreneurial State in China: Real Estate and Commerce Departments in Reform Era in Tianjin* (London: Routledge, 1998).

Dutrait, Noël, *Petit precis à l'usage de l'amateur de littérature chinoise contemporaine (1976–2006)* (Arles: Picquier, 2006).

Eyraud, Corinne, *L'Entreprise d'état chinoise. De 'l'institution sociale totale' vers l'entité économique?* (Paris: L'Harmattan, 1999).

Fischer, Andrew Martin, 'The political economy of boomerang aid in China's Tibet', *China Perspectives*, 2009/3, pp. 38–54.

Florence, Éric, 'Debates and classification struggles regarding the representation of migrant workers', *China Perspectives*, 65, 2006. DOI: 10.4000/chinaperspectives.629.

Friedman, Sara L., 'The intimacy of state power: Marriage, liberation and socialist subjects in Southeastern China', *American Ethnologist*, 32/2, 2005, pp. 312–327.

Froissart, Chloé, *La Chine et ses migrants. La conquête d'une citoyenneté* (Rennes: PUR, 2013).

Fu, Longwen and Cheris Shun-Ching Chan, 'The Hippocratic dilemmas: Guanxi and professional work in hospital care in China', *China Perspectives*, 2016/4, pp. 19–27.

Ged, Françoise, *Shanghai. L'ordinaire et l'exceptionnel* (Paris: Buchet Chastel, 2014).

Giles, John, Albert Park and Juwei Zhang, 'What is China's true unemployment rate?', *China Economic Review*, 16, 2005, pp. 149–170.

Glosser, Susan L., *Chinese Visions of Family and State, 1915–1953* (Berkeley, CA: University of California Press, 2003).

Goossaert, Vincent and David A. Palmer, *La Question religieuse en Chine* (Paris: CNRS éditions, 2012).

Greenhalgh, Susan, *Just One Child: Science and Policy in Deng's China* (Berkeley, CA: University of California Press, 2008).

Greenhalgh, Susan, *Cultivating Global Citizens: Population in the Rise of China* (Cambridge, MA: Harvard University Press, 2010).

Greenhalgh, Susan and Edwin A. Winckler, *Governing China's Population: From Leninist to Neoliberal Biopolitics* (Stanford, CA: Stanford University Press, 2005).

Guiheux, Gilles, 'The incomplete crystallisation of the private sector', *China Perspectives*, 42, 2002, pp. 24–36.

Guiheux, Gilles, 'The transformation of an urban economic area in Hunan province', *China Perspectives*, 49, 2003, pp. 4–16.

Guiheux, Gilles, 'Le nouveau "retournement" des corps et des esprits. La mise à leur compte des travailleurs licenciés du secteur d'état en Chine', *L'Homme et la société*, 152–153, 2004, pp. 97–128.

Guiheux, Gilles, 'The promotion of a new calculating Chinese subject: The case of laid-off workers turning into entrepreneurs', *Journal of Contemporary China*, 16/50, February 2007, pp. 149–171.

Guiheux, Gilles, 'Les matériaux pour la monographie d'un territoire chinois. Le cas d'une ville marchande', *Terrains & Travaux*, 16, 2009, pp. 153–174.

Guiheux, Gilles, 'Shanghai, société de consommation', in Nicolas Idler (ed.), *Shanghai* (Paris: Robert Laffont, 2010), pp. 322–339.

Guiheux, Gilles, 'Chinese socialist heroes: From workers to entrepreneurs', in Éric Florence and Pierre Defraigne (eds.), *Towards a New Development Paradigm in Twenty-First Century China. Economy, Society and Politics* (London: Routledge, 2012), pp. 115–126.

Guo, Yuhua, 'D'une forme de réciprocité à l'autre. Une analyse de la prise en charge des personnes âgées dans les villages du Hubei', in Isabelle Thireau and Hansheng Wang, *Disputes au village chinois. Formes du juste et recompositions locales des espaces normatifs* (Paris: Maison des sciences de l'homme, 2001), pp. 13–37.

Hansen, Mette Halskov and Cuiming Pang, 'Me and my family: Perceptions of individual and collective among young rural Chinese', *European Journal of East Asian Studies*, 7/1, 2008, pp. 75–99.

Harding, Harry, 'The Chinese state in crisis', in Roderick MacFarquhar and John Fairbank (eds.), *Cambridge History of China, The PRC, Revolutions within the Chinese Revolution, 1966–1982*, vol. 15 (Cambridge: Cambridge University Press, 1991), pp. 105–217.

He, Qinglian, *Zhongguo de xianjing [The traps of China]* (Hong Kong: Mingjing chubanshe, 1997).

He, Qinglian, 'China's listing social structure', *New Left Review*, September–October 2000, pp. 69–99.

Holbig, Heike, 'Remaking the CCP's ideology: Determinants, progress, and limits under Hu Jintao', *Journal of Current Chinese Affairs*, 3, 2009, pp. 35–61.

Hong, Tao and Lucas Monteil, 'LGBT, chinois.e.s et connecté.e.s', *La Vie des idées*, 20 June 2017. http://www.laviedesidees.fr/LGBT-chinois-e-set-connecte-e-s.html.

Hovasse, Hélène, 'Pudong. Le nouveau poumon de Shanghai', *Perspectives chinoises*, 16, 1993, pp. 26–36.

Huchet, Jean-François, *La crise environnementale en Chine* (Paris: Presses de Sciences Po, 2016).

Jie, Yang, 'The politics and regulation of anger in urban China', *Culture, Medicine, and Psychiatry*, 40/1, 2016, pp. 100–123.

Joseph, William A., 'A tragedy of good intentions: Post-Mao views of the Great Leap Forward', *Modern China*, 12/4, 1986, pp. 419–457.

Kuah-Pearce, Khun Eng, *Rebuilding the Ancestral Village: Singaporeans in China* (London: Ashgate, 2000).

Kernen, Antoine, *La Chine vers l'économie de marché. Privatisations à Shenyang* (Paris: Karthala, 2004).

Kernan, Antoine and Jean-Louis Rocca, 'La réforme des entreprises publiques en Chine et sa gestion sociale. Le cas de Shenyang et du Liaoning', *Études du Ceri*, 37, 1998.

Kernan, Antoine and Jean-Louis Rocca, 'Traitement social du chômage et nouvelle pauvreté urbaine. Le cas de Shenyang et du Liaoning', *Perspectives chinoises*, 56, 1999, pp. 35–51.

Kirby, William C., 'Continuity and change in modern China: Economic planning on the mainland and on Taiwan, 1943–1958', *The Australian Journal of Chinese Affairs*, 24, 1990, pp. 121–142.

Kleinman, Arthur, Yunxiang Yan and Jun Jing (eds.), *Deep China: The Moral Life of the Person* (Berkeley, CA: University of California Press, 2011).

Kreissler, Françoise, 'Le Mémorial de Nankin, lectures et relectures de l'histoire', *Matériaux pour l'histoire de notre temps*, 88/4, 2007, pp. 8–12.

Lemoine, Françoise, *L'Économie des BRIC* (Paris: La Découverte, 2013).

Lemoine, Françoise and Deniz Ünal, 'Mutations du commerce chinois', *La Lettre du CEPII*, 352, March 2015.

Leys, Simon (*alias* Pierre Ryckmans), *Les Habits neufs du président Mao* (Paris: Champ libre, 1971).

Li, Changping, *Wo xiang Zongli shuo shihua* (Beijing: Guangming ribao chubanshe, 2001).

Li, Cheng, 'Jiang Zemin's successors: The rise of the fourth generation of leaders in the PRC', *The China Quarterly*, 161, 2000, pp. 1–40.

Li, Cheng, 'A biographical and factional analysis of the post-2012 Politburo', *China Leadership Monitor*, 41, 2013. https://www.hoover.org/research/biographical-and-factional-analysis-post-2012-politburo.

Li, Cheng and Lynn White, 'The Fifteenth Central Committee of the Chinese Communist Party: Full-fledged technocratic leadership with partial control by Jiang Zemin', *Asian Survey*, 38/3, 1998, pp. 231–264.

Lincot, Emmanuel, 'Contemporary Chinese art under Deng Xiaoping', *China Perspectives*, 53, 2004. DOI: 10.4000/chinaperspectives.2952.

Lü, Xiaobo and Elizabeth J. Perry (eds.), *Danwei: The Changing Chinese Workplace in Historical and Comparative Perspective* (Armonk, NY: M. E. Sharpe, 1997).

Lu, Xueyi (ed.), *Dangdai zhongguo shehui jieceng yanjiu baogao* [*Research Report on Social Stratification in Contemporary China*] (Beijing: Shehui kexue wenxian chubanshe, 2002).

Lu, Xueyi (ed.), *Dangdai zhongguo shehui liudong* [*Social Mobility in Contemporary China*] (Beijing: Shehui kexue wenxian chubanshe, 2004).

MacFarquhar, Roderick, 'The succession to Mao and the end of Maoism', in Roderick MacFarquhar and John Fairbank (eds.), *Cambridge History of China: The PRC, Revolutions within the Chinese Revolution, 1966–1982*, vol. 15 (Cambridge: Cambridge University Press, 1991), pp. 303–401.

MacFarquhar, Roderick and Michael Schoenhals, *Mao's Last Revolution* (Cambridge, MA: Harvard University Press, 2008).

Maddison, Angus, *Chinese Economic Performance in the Long Run* (Paris: OECD Publishing, 1998).

Madsen, Richard, 'The Countryside under Communism', in Roderick MacFarquhar and John Fairbank (eds.), *Cambridge History of China: The PRC, Revolutions within the Chinese Revolution, 1966–1982*, vol. 15 (Cambridge: Cambridge University Press, 1991), pp. 617–681.

Merle, Aurore, 'De la reconstruction de la discipline à l'interrogation sur la transition: la sociologie chinoise à l'épreuve du temps', *Cahiers internationaux de sociologie*, 122/1, 2007, pp. 31–52.

Miège, Pierre, 'In my opinion, most Tongzhi are dutiful sons!', *China Perspectives*, 2009/1, pp. 40–53.

Milcent, Carine, 'Evolution of the health system: Inefficiency, violence, and digital healthcare', *China Perspectives*, 2016/4, pp. 39–50.

Miller, Alice, 'China's new party leadership', *China Leadership Monitor*, 23, 2007.

Mineo, Nakajima, 'Foreign relations: From the Korean War to the Bandung Line', in Denis Twitchett and John K. Fairbank (eds.), *Cambridge History of China*, vol. 14/1 (Cambridge: Cambridge University Press, 1987), pp. 258–289.

Minzner, Carl, *End of an Era* (New York: Oxford University Press, 2018).

Monteil, Lucas, 'De "l'Amour vieux-jeune". Âge, classe et homosexualité masculine en Chine post-maoïste', *Clio. Femmes, Genre, Histoire*, 42, 2015, pp. 147–163.

Nathan, Andrew J., *China's Transition* (New York: Columbia University Press, 1998).

Nathan, Andrew J., 'Authoritarian Resilience', *Journal of Democracy*, 14/1, 2003, pp. 6–17.

Naughton, Barry, *Growing Out of the Plan. Chinese Economic Reform, 1978–1993* (Cambridge: Cambridge University Press, 1996).

Naughton, Barry, *The Chinese Economy. Transitions and Growth* (Cambridge, MA: MIT Press, 2007).

Naughton, Barry, 'China's economic policy today: the new state activism', *Eurasian Geography and Economics*, 52/3, 2011, pp. 313–329.

O'Brien, Kevin and Lianjiang Li, *Rightful Resistance in Rural China* (Cambridge: Cambridge University Press, 2006).

Oi, Jean C., *Rural China Takes Off: Institutional Foundations of Economic Reform* (Berkeley, CA: University of California Press, 1999).

Palmer, David A., 'La doctrine de Li Hongzhi', *Perspectives chinoises*, 64, March–April 2001, pp. 14–24.

Palmer, David A., *Qigong Fever: Body, Science, and Utopia in China* (New York: Columbia University Press, 2007).

Pan, Suiming, *Dangdai Zhongguo ren de xingwei weiyu xing guanxi* (Beijing: Shehui kexue wenxian chubanshe, 2004).

Parish, William L. and Martin K. Whyte, *Village and Family in Contemporary China* (Chicago, IL: Chicago University Press, 1978).

Peng, Xizhe, 'Demographic consequences of the Great Leap Forward in China's provinces', *Population and Development Review*, 13/4, 1987, pp. 639–670.

Pettier, Jean-Baptiste, 'Politiques de l'amour et du sexe dans la Chine de la "révolution sexuelle"', *Genre, sexualité & société*, 3, 2010.

Pickowicz, Paul G., 'Zheng Junli, complicity and the cultural history of socialist China, 1949–1976', *The China Quarterly*, 188, 2006, pp. 1048–1069.

Pun, Ngai, *Migrant Labor in China: Post-Socialist Transformations* (Cambridge: Polity, 2016).

Pun, Ngai and Chris Smith, 'Putting transnational labour process in its place: The dormitory labour regime in post-socialist China', *Work, Employment & Society*, 21/1, 2007, pp. 27–45.

Pye, Lucian W., 'Jiang Zemin's Style of Rule: Go for stability, monopolize power and settle for limited effectiveness', *The China Journal*, 45, 2001, pp. 45–51.

Ravallion, Martin, Shaohua Chen, 'China's (uneven) progress against poverty', *Journal of Development Economics*, 82/1, 2007, pp. 1–42.

Rocca, Jean-Louis, 'Is China becoming an ordinary state?', in Béatrice Hibou (ed.), *Privatizing the State*, trans. Jonathan Derrick (New York: Columbia University Press, 2004), pp. 169–182.

Rolandsen, Unn Målfrid H., 'A collective of their own: Young volunteers at the fringes of the party realm', in Mette Halskov Hansen and Rune Svarverud (eds.), *iChina. The Rise of the Individual in Modern Chinese Society* (Copenhagen: Nias, 2010), pp. 132–163.

Rosen, Stanley, *The Role of the Sent-down Youth in the Chinese Cultural Revolution: The Case of Guangzhou* (Berkeley, CA: University of California Press, 1981).

Roux, Alain, *Le Singe et le tigre. Mao, un destin chinois* (Paris: Larousse, 2009).

Shambaugh, David, 'The dynamics of elite politics during the Jiang Era', *The China Journal*, 45, 2001, pp. 101–111.

Shambaugh, David, *Modernizing China's Military: Progress, Problems, and Prospects* (Berkeley, CA: University of California Press, 2004).

Shambaugh, David, *China's Communist Party: Atrophy and Adaptation* (Berkeley, CA: University of California Press, 2008).

Shi, Lu, *Voix de migrants* (Toulouse: Presses Universitaires de Toulouse, 2014).

Shieh, Shawn and Guosheng Deng, 'Emerging civil society: The impact of the 2008 Sichuan earthquake on grass-roots associations in China', *The China Journal*, 65, 2011, pp. 181–194.

Solinger, Dorothy, 'Why we cannot count the "unemployed"', *The China Quarterly*, 167, 2001, pp. 671–688.

Strauss, Julian, 'Morality, coercion and state building by campaign in the early PRC: Regime consolidation and after, 1949–1956', *The China Quarterly*, 188/1, 2006, pp. 891–912.

Sun, Liping, *Duanlie* [*The break*] (Beijing: Shehui kexui wenxian chubanshe, 2003).

Sun, Liping and Mingjie Ma, 'Forcer le peuple à s'enrichir!', *Études rurales*, 161/162, 2002, pp. 165–182.

Tang, Xiaojing, 'Les femmes du Grand bond en avant', *Travail, genre et sociétés*, 23, 2010, pp. 61–78.

Teiwes, Frederick C., 'Establishment and consolidation of the new regime', in Denis Twitchett and John K. Fairbank (eds.), *Cambridge History of China*, vol. 14/1 (Cambridge: Cambridge University Press, 1987), pp. 51–143.

Teiwes, Frederick C., *Politics at Mao's Court. Gao Gang and Party Factionalism in the Early 1950s* (Armonk, NY: M. E. Sharpe, 1990).

Teiwes, Frederick C. and Warren Sun, *China's Road to Disaster: Mao, Central Politicians, and Provincial Leaders in the Unfolding of the Great Leap Forward* (Armonk, NY: M. E. Sharpe, 1999).

Thireau, Isabelle and Linshan Hua, *Les Ruses de la démocratie. Protester en Chine* (Paris: Seuil, 2010).

Thogersen, Stig and Soren Clausen, 'New reflections in the mirror: Local Chinese gazetteers [*difangzhi*] in the 1980s', *The Australian Journal of Chinese Affairs*, 27, 1992, pp. 161–184.

Tomba, Luigi, 'Making Neighbourhoods', *China Perspectives*, 2008/4, pp. 48–61.

Treiman, Donald J., 'Trends in educational attainment in China', *Chinese Sociological Review*, 45/3, 2013, pp. 3–25.

Unger, Jonathan and Anita Chan, 'Inheritors of the boom: Private enterprise and the role of government in a rural South China township', *The China Journal*, 42, 1999, pp. 45–74.

Unger, Jonathan and Anita Chan, *The Transformation of Rural China* (Armonk, NY: M. E. Sharpe, 2002).

Urban, Marie, 'L'état de la protection sociale en Chine', *Revue française d'administration publique*, 150/2, 2014, pp. 467–479.

Wakeman Jr, Frederic, '"Cleanup": The new order in Shanghai', in Jeremy Brown and Paul G. Pickowicz (eds.), *Dilemmas of Victory. The Early Years of the People's Republic of China* (Cambridge, MA: Harvard University Press, 2007), pp. 21–58.

Walder, Andrew G., *Communist Neo-Traditionalism* (Berkeley, CA: University of California Press, 1986).

Walder, Andrew G., 'Factional Conflict at Peking University, 1966–1968', *The China Quarterly*, 188, 2006, pp. 1023–1047.

Walder, Andrew G. and Songhua Hu, 'Revolution, reform, and status inheritance: Urban China, 1949–1996', *American Journal of Sociology*, 114/5, 2009, pp. 1395–1427.

Wank, David L., *Commodifying Communism: Business, Trust and Politics in a Chinese City* (Cambridge: Cambridge University Press, 1999).

Wei, Jingsheng, *La Cinquième Modernisation et autres écrits du Printemps de Pékin* (Paris: Bourgois, 1997).

Wemheuer, Felix, 'Dealing with responsibility for the Great Leap Famine in the People's Republic of China', *The China Quarterly*, 201, 2010, p. 176–194.

Whyte, Martin King, 'The paradoxes of rural–urban inequality in contemporary China', in Martin King Whyte (ed.), *One Country, Two Societies. Rural–Urban Inequality in Contemporary China* (Cambridge, MA: Harvard University Press, 2010), pp. 1–25.

Whyte, Martin King, Feng Wang and Cai Yong, 'Challenging myths about China's one-child policy', *The China Journal*, 74, 2015, pp. 144–159.

Xiao, Kate Zhou, *How the Farmers Changed China: Power of the People* (London: Routledge, 1996).

Xie, Yu and Xiang Zhou, 'Income inequality in today's China', *Proceedings of the National Academy of Sciences of the United States of America*, 111/19, 2014, pp. 6928–6933.

Yan, Yunxiang, 'Courtship, love and premarital sex in a north China village', *The China Journal*, 48, 2002, pp. 29–53.

Yan, Yunxiang, *Private Life Under Socialism* (Stanford, CA: Stanford University Press, 2003).

Yan, Yunxiang, *The Individualization of Chinese Society* (Oxford: Berg, 2009).

Yang, Benjamin, 'The making of a pragmatic Communist: The early life of Deng Xiaoping, 1904–1949', *The China Quarterly*, 135, 1993, pp. 444–456.

Yang, Dali L., *Calamity and Reform in China: State, Rural Society, and Institutional Change since the Great Leap Forward* (Stanford, CA: Stanford University Press, 1996).

Yang, Dali L. and Waikeung Tam, 'Food safety and the development of regulatory institutions in China', *Asian Perspective*, 29/4, 2005, pp. 5–36.

Yang, Jisheng, 'An overall analysis of current social stratification in China', *Zhongguo shehui kexue qikan* [Chinese Social Sciences quarterly], 3, 1999.

Yang, Jisheng, *Stèles. La grande famine en Chine, 1958–1961* (Paris: Seuil, 2012).

Yin, Kai, 'De l'étatisation à la propagande: La mise en place du système du cinéma Communiste chinois (1938–1952)', *Mise au point.* http://journals. openedition.org/map /1844.

Zhang, Liang, *Les Archives de Tiananmen* (Paris: Le Félin, 2004).

Zhao, Yeqin, *Construction des espaces urbains et rénovation d'un quartier de Shangai: La problématique de la migration et du changement social* (Shanghai: Sanlian Shudian, 2011).

Zhou, Xun (ed.), *The Great Famine in China, 1958–1962: A Documentary History* (New Haven, CT: Yale University Press, 2012).

Zweig, David, *Internationalizing China. Domestic Interests and Global Linkages* (Ithaca, NY: Cornell University Press, 2002).

Index